1, 2, 4, 17
14, 15, 16

The Authors

NEIL W. CHAMBERLAIN received his Ph.D. from The Ohio State University. From 1947-54 he taught in the Department of Economics at Yale University and was active in the Labor and Management Center, serving first as Research Director and then as Assistant Director. He was Professor of Economics at Columbia University's Graduate School of Business from 1954-57, and from 1957-60 served as Director of the Ford Foundation's Program in Economic Development and Administration. In 1960 he returned to Yale University as Professor of Economics.

Professor Chamberlain is on the Board of Advisors for *Management International* and is a member of the Board, Salzburg Seminar in American Studies. He has served on the Executive Committee of the Industrial Relations Research Association and on the Board of Editors for the *American Economic Review*. He is the author of numerous monographs and books including THE LABOR SECTOR (a recently published revision of LABOR), SOURCEBOOK ON LABOR, and THE FIRM: MICRO-ECONOMIC PLANNING AND ACTION.

JAMES W. KUHN received his Ph.D. from Yale University and was a Fulbright Scholar at the University of Sydney, Australia, in 1951. He taught at Pomona College and the University of Oregon. In 1955 he joined the faculty of Columbia University and is presently Associate Professor of Industrial Relations in the Graduate School of Business. In 1961-62 he was awarded a Ford Fellowship for Research on white collar unions.

Articles by Professor Kuhn have appeared in numerous journals including *Review of Economics and Statistics, Industrial and Labor Relations Review, Political Science Quarterly, California Management Review, Challenge, Columbia Forum,* and *Labor Law Journal.* He is the author of BARGAINING IN GRIEVANCE SETTLEMENT and is currently at work on two other books: a monograph on the manpower aspects of nuclear power development and a study of white collar workers and their efforts to organize.

COLLECTIVE BARGAINING

Collective Bargaining

NEIL W. CHAMBERLAIN

Professor of Economics
Yale University

JAMES W. KUHN

Associate Professor of Industrial Relations
Columbia University

2d edition

McGraw-Hill BOOK COMPANY

New York   *St. Louis*   *San Francisco*   *Toronto*   *London*   *Sydney*

Preface

This book originally appeared in 1951 as a response to a teaching need for a single volume on collective bargaining. It was a study of the history, nature, problems, and potential of collective bargaining, examining it as an institution in its own right and not merely as one activity of unions or as a procedure for determining wages and conditions of work. New research and new developments in the years since then have left the first edition dated. At the urging of friends, and at the particularly insistent prodding of Frank DeVyver, of Duke University, a revision has been undertaken, this time by two authors rather than one.

The basic approach of the first edition remains substantially unchanged. Great stress is placed on the evolutionary nature of the bargaining process, the continuing changes in its procedures, and even its conception. This emphasis seems even more appropriate today, when so much dissatisfaction is being expressed with the anachronisms and purported failures of present collective bargaining institutions. A "crisis" in union-management relations is frequently forecast in professional as well as journalistic writings.

Arthur Goldberg, now Associate Justice of the United States Supreme Court and then general counsel of the United Steelworkers and special counsel of the AFL-CIO, stimulated serious consideration of new approaches to old needs when he called for high-level discussions between representatives of organized labor and business on issues with which existing bargaining procedures could not adequately deal. The climate of experimentalism which he helped encourage may have been at least partially responsible for some of the more recent developments in the steel, meat-packing, and automobile industries. This second edition pays somewhat less attention than the first to the rationale and practice of union-management cooperation programs (at least the variety which are so labeled) while recognizing the importance of some of the still unfolding programs in these industries. They are directly in the evolutionary tradition, which is examined at some length in Chapters 1 and 2.

Policy with respect to the appropriate role of government in labor relations is also undergoing change. Attitudes toward public authority and responsibility on the strike and wage fronts have been subjected to critical review. If there is a large measure of inconclusiveness in the results, this too reflects a continued questioning of whether old problems, now rising in changed contexts, do not present the need for fresh solutions—yet to be devised.

We have thus attempted to incorporate more the attitude of quest than conclusion in these pages, and more the need for analysis as a basis for modifying policies that inevitably become obsolete than analysis to explain exisiting practices.

Finally, we wish to acknowledge our intellectual debt to the innumerable scholars and researchers who have created many of the materials out of which these pages have been spun. Many lively minds have reflected on the issues of collective bargaining, to our benefit. We have enjoyed and profited from discussions and exchanges with our colleagues, not only in our home universities, but in the profession at large.

In acknowledgment of this debt, rather than as an assertion of accomplishment, this book can properly be said to be a collaboration of many more than two people. But we should like particularly to pay our respect to one whom we have known as teacher, colleague, and friend for a good many years, whose insights have been enormously stimulating to our thinking, and whose continued encouragement to "pursue the quest" has been a resource we have often drawn on, Prof. E. Wight Bakke.

Neil W. Chamberlain

James W. Kuhn

Contents

3 THE NEGOTIATION PROCESS   51

4 THE SUBJECT MATTER OF COLLECTIVE BARGAINING   82

5 THE NATURE OF COLLECTIVE BARGAINING   108

A Historical Introduction to Collective Bargaining in the United States, 1800 to 1850

chapter 1

Collective bargaining is both old and new. It is of recent development, and yet it was carried on as long as 150 years ago in a fashion reminiscent of that used today. The term itself belongs to our own century. Though it originated in 1891 in the writings of Beatrice Webb,[1] its use spread slowly. The Industrial Commission, created by act of Congress in 1898, wrote in its final report four years later: "This term, collective bargaining, is not often employed in common speech in the United States, but is gradually coming into use among employers and employees in Great Britain. It evidently describes quite accurately the practice by which employers and em-

---

[1] Beatrice Potter (Mrs. Sidney Webb), *The Cooperative Movement in Great Britain*, London: Gorge Allen & Unwin, Ltd., 1891, p. 217. However, Terence Powderly, who served as General Master Wordman in the Knights of Labor, says in his autobiography that Andrew Roy, a student of, and participant in, coal miners' organizations, wrote as early as 1874 of the "right of the miners to bargain collectively." Terence V. Powderly, *The Path I Trod*, Harry J. Carman, Henry David, and Paul N. Guthrie (eds.), New York: Columbia University Press, 1940, p. 310.

1

ployees in conference, from time to time, agree upon the terms under which labor shall be performed." [2]

What are the reasons for this bifocal view of a process that today is invoked in virtually every industrial community in this country—a process so new that its name was received little more than sixty years ago, but so old that it had been followed 100 years before its christening? The reasons are several: discontinuity in the use of the bargaining method, variation in its practice from place to place, and changes in the structure of unionism and business enterprise.

The discontinuous resort to collective bargaining stems from the fact that it is inseparable from unionism, which throughout much of the nineteenth century was unstable in organization. Prior to the Civil War there were spasms of union activity, generally coinciding with the prosperity phase of business cycles. These were followed by periods of disorganization, usually in times of depression, that were sometimes so complete that the labor movement virtually ceased to exist. Ever since then, unionism has lived through periods of both intense activity and deep quiescence, and there have been frequent births and deaths of individual unions within the union movement as a whole. This discontinuity and the uncertain strength of labor organizations themselves have had their natural impact upon the collective bargaining process. An early development of bargaining techniques might be killed before it could take root and spread. Neither workers nor employers could learn to use effectively a system that depended for existence upon unions which themselves had uncertain existence. Before collective bargaining could develop as a well-defined process, unions had to become continuing organizations capable of weathering the ups and downs of economic activity and of withstanding employer opposition.

Another partial explanation for the simultaneous newness and oldness of collective bargaining, besides the discontinuity in its use, is that practice varied in different localities and different unions. Unionism and its concomitant organized relations with management sprang up first along the Atlantic seaboard. They were by-products of urbanization. Occupations or trades had to be represented by numbers of workers before they could be "organized." It is thus in the oldest and largest cities—Boston, New York, and Philadelphia, in particular—that we find the first traces of unionism and collective negotiations. Likewise, organization appears earlier in some trades than in others—the printers and shoemakers (or cordwainers, as they were known) were among the first to form into unions. Consequently, as interior communities grew into industrial centers and as new trades and industries developed and became organized, new ventures into collective

---

[2] *Final Report of the Industrial Commission,* Reports of the Industrial Commission, vol. 19 (1902), p. 834.

bargaining were undertaken at a time when the general process had already been followed in older communities and trades for some time. In some cases the new efforts were throwbacks to earlier methods; in some cases they benefited from the experiences of others; and in some cases they resulted in original patterns. Thus variation in the rise and development of unions in different industries and localities, as well as the discontinuous and uncertain growth of the union movement as a whole, helps to explain why collective bargaining appears with the marks of both youth and old age.

The presence of a particularly forceful union leader or of an employer who dominated his fellows in a particular community; the response to public appeal, favorable to the organized employees under certain circumstances and unfavorable under others; the attitude of the judiciary or of the press; the bid by municipal politicians for labor support or their defiance of its antagonism—all these and other local influences, acting with varying effect over time and among localities and trades, also help to explain why collective bargaining "arrived" earlier in some places and industries than in others, even if only to wither or die out at a later day under less propitious circumstances.

Further, collective bargaining has been modified by changes in the unions' organizational structures, which in turn have been influenced in large part by changes in the character of business enterprise. Bargaining by simple craft unions may differ considerably from bargaining by industrial unions in mass-production enterprises. Bargaining in a local shop is likely to be different from bargaining for an agreement covering the widely scattered plants of a giant corporation. It is largely the expansion of industrial unionism in the 1930s and its penetration into mass-production industries that are responsible for the belief that collective bargaining is an innovation of recent years.

The collective bargaining of which we are here speaking concerns the agreement by employers and union on the general terms under which employees will consent to work. In the early days of the last century, such terms were usually confined to little more than a scale of wage rates, but by 1900 the agreement had become considerably more elaborated in a number of industries. Also by 1900 the distinction was being made between negotiations to settle the terms of employment and negotiations to settle disputes arising over the application of those terms—disputes, for example, over whether employees were being paid the rates agreed on. The latter came to be known as "grievances." This distinction led to the devising of different processes to handle the two types of negotiations. Whereas in former days all disputes, of whatever origin, were usually given similar treatment, now specially organized grievance procedures for handling day-to-day disputes became part of the newer collective bargaining systems.

In this study we shall not be concerned with the labor movement or unionism as a whole, but only with its negotiatory relationships with employers. Labor's political activities and programs, reform movements, and organizational efforts will be given at most passing reference. The long succession of famous strikes all looking toward eventual recognition of the union will be ignored. The names of famous labor leaders will seldom appear in these pages. For this is in no sense a history of unionism in the United States nor a survey of worker organization in all its aspects. Although we shall draw upon history, it will be only to clarify our understanding of the collective bargaining process.

A distinction is therefore to be made for our purposes between the historical motivation for the organization of unions, which will not be developed in this study,[3] and the rationale of collective bargaining, as one instrument of unions, which we shall examine in some detail at a later stage, after we have explored the evolution of the process and described its current practices. Let us then, without further delay, trace briefly the collective bargaining movement as it has arisen in this country. In wrestling with some of the momentous issues that have been introduced by the unions in their collective bargaining relationships, we shall discover the value of such a historical perspective.

It should be understood that the "periods" that have been marked off represent only rough boundaries, defined for the sake of convenience. They are not intended as precise delimitations of epochs.

Beginnings

The efforts at unionization prior to 1825 were sporadic. Indeed, we have virtually no records of organized activity by employees until the 1800s. Prior to that time there had been short-lived and uncoordinated attempts that resulted in journeymen societies of such craftsmen as printers, shoemakers, coopers, carpenters, and masons. The latter two groups evoked a public protest by their success in securing a wage increase in 1795 in New York City,[4] but it was not until the so-called "conspiracy trials," beginning

[3] But very brief summaries of the leading theories will be found in Chapter 13.

[4] The *New York Daily Advertiser* on March 30, 1795, carried the following notice:

> The carpenters and masons of this city, having combined and raised their wages two shillings a day beyond the price of last season, it behooves the citizens in general but particularly those who intend to build the present year, to oppose designs as unjust as they are impolitic. An acquiescence on the part of the citizens on this occasion will in all probability not only excite similar attempts among all other descriptions of persons who live by manual labor, but induce reiterated efforts to increase their wages at

in Philadelphia in 1806, that opposition to unions was focused. It is largely from records of these early trials that we have a picture of how unions operated at that time. From them, we can piece together the story of the germinal phase of the process that we now know as "collective bargaining."

The unions of that period were not even known as "unions." What we would call a union was then known among its members as a "society" or as "the body," and sometimes employers referred to them opprobriously as "combinations." A society, body, or combination seldom had continuity of actual organization. It existed rather as a quiescent state of trade unity and was raised to life for particular occasions. On such occasions the members would hold meetings at one another's homes, elect temporary officers, and decide on programs of action. The cordwainers and a few others made more serious but nevertheless vain attempts to build permanent organizations, even to the extent of making attendance compulsory, under pain of fine and ultimate expulsion from the body.

The method of seeking wage change seems to have been simple and direct. The members of the trade society would gather, agree among themselves on the "price list" or piece rates that were to be sought, and take an oath that none would work for less or work alongside any journeyman who worked for less. At times, they would observe the solemn formality of inserting the revised wage list between the pages of a Bible, the assembled workers placing their hands upon it and swearing not to work for less. Committees from among their number would then be appointed to visit the shops of the masters to inform them of the action taken and to advise them that their employees would not report for work until the demand had been met. The practice of the employers appears to have been to delay answering the visiting unionist, not wishing to be the first or the last to grant the wage increase. As one master shoemaker recounted:

> There was a turn-out of the journeymen of October last, and Hepburn, Snyder and Barnes, with three or four others called on me, but

---

seasons when they find their services most wanted. That a trifling addition to their former wages may by some be deemed proper will not be disputed, but when a combination is formed to extort an unreasonable advance every man will deem it an imposition and set his face against the measure. Those who conceive themselves affected by the present combination are requested to meet at Batten's Tavern near the theater, on Wednesday evening at 7 o'clock, to consider the means that ought to be adopted on this occasion.

Reproduced from George A. Stevens, *New York Typographical Union No. 6,* New York State Department of Labor, Annual Report of the Bureau of Labor Statistics (1911), part I, pp. 36–37. The infrequency of such organized action is suggested by the fear of the writer of this notice that the carpenters and masons might set a precedent.

not being acquainted with them, I did not take much notice of them: they came with the list of the advance of wages from the body, as they called it, and enquired to know whether I would give the prices or not; they had a list in their hands. I looked at the list, and found half a dollar was charged additional on the shortest size bootees; What, said I, half a dollar for these? Yes, said Barnes, and I'll be damned if we do not have half a dollar more next fall. . . .

And from another employer:

In the present turn-out, Harket, Pullis, and others, in all nine or ten came to my shop, as a committee from the body, to demand higher wages. Harket and one or two others were then in my employ. They asked me if I was willing to give the new rise: I told them I did not know what it was; they read the paper, and I thought the rise exorbitant; one was three quarters of a dollar, another of half a dollar, and so on. I had thought formerly a rise of three-pence, or six-pence, was a smart rise, but now they think little of a dollar. I told them I supposed I must give it, and asked if any one had agreed to give it . . . they mentioned Mr. Ryan gave it. I then said, if he gave it I must of course. I took it for granted that Mr. Ryan had agreed, but found he had only said, if the other masters would give it, he would also give it.[5]

The general strategy of such a unilateral campaign was to call a strike ("turning out" or "standing out," in the language of the day) without delay against those employers who refused to accept the revised "bill of wages." Since all employers seldom conceded to the union on the initial notice, a strike almost inevitably accompanied union wage action. In fact, when the body was considering making a wage demand upon its employers, the question before them was often whether the members should stand out against the employers, the underlying assumption being that the strike was a necessary and integral part of the process of increasing wages.

The demands that the body drew up were demands that they expected to have met in full. They were not bargaining proposals, set two or three times higher than the settlement price, but specific bills of wages, sometimes printed and ready to be posted in the shops immediately upon acceptance. Compromise was therefore not intended. The union members had previously sworn among themselves not to work for less than the wages stated in their demands, and they were serious in that oath.

This was not, therefore, a process of negotiation. It was a procedure for a trial of economic strength to determine whose wage decisions would prevail—the union's or the employer's. The spirit of no compromise was

[5] Reprinted by permission of the publishers from John R. Commons et al. (eds.), *Documentary History of American Industrial Society*, Glendale, Calif.: The Arthur H. Clark Company, 1910–1911, vol. 3, pp. 97, 101, 102.

further encouraged because certain of the employers, disorganized as they were, frequently conceded to the union at the start of the campaign. This broke the possibility of bringing all the employers into a solid front and also made it difficult for the unions to negotiate for a settlement on any less favorable terms than those already won. As these contests of strength between organized employees and disorganized employers became more frequent and the pattern became better understood, the employers began to acquire the habit of consulting one another before committing themselves individually to the union. The aim was to establish a common understanding which would lead to group action, involving either acceptance or rejection of the union's terms. These efforts at employer organization were sometimes defeated, however, by mavericks who refused to unite with their competitors but insisted on adopting individualistic policies. Against such holdouts the employers occasionally undertook punitive action, usually blacklisting.

In general, the effort of such informal employers' associations was to put down the strike, not by any process of reaching an agreement, but simply by wearing down the strikers. The attitude on the part of both organized workers and associated employers at the start was, thus, win or lose and no compromise. This was true regardless of whether initiative rested with the workers to secure wage increases or with the employers to secure wage reductions. The fight, once started, continued with each side holding to its original position, until one or the other was worn out and surrendered or until its organization began to fall apart, with members giving in on a piecemeal basis. Concerning the strike of the Philadelphia cordwainers in 1805, one of the workers subsequently related: "There was a division in the body, and they were forced to go to work at the old price. . . . They did not gain the cause; they stood it out six or seven weeks, but then they found it impossible to get their wages advanced, and they went back to work again." [6]

Although this was the customary method of union-management dealings, once both employees and employers had acquired the habit of organizing when confronted by organization, it is not surprising that occasions would arise when both groups would find advantage in conferring instead of continuing simple attritional economic warfare. Particularly on those occasions when each felt the strength of the other party equal to its own did common sense dictate negotiation rather than prolongation of a doubtful contest. There is evidence of a rather casual sort of offer and counteroffer in the Philadelphia shoemakers' strike of 1799. [7]

[6] Reprinted by permission of the publishers from the same, p. 87.

[7] Similarly, during the course of the 1806 conspiracy trial it was asserted:

When the full-dress-fancy-top-back-strap-boots, were introduced into New York, the employers there, at first, objected to making any extra allow-

Negotiations and Unilateral Action

The bargaining relationship between union and employers of the type with which we are familiar today was rare indeed, but it was not altogether unknown. We have an account of negotiations between journeymen and master printers in New York City in 1809 that reads surprisingly like a description of some of today's procedures. It is worth reproducing for its very novelty, when we recall that the events recounted occurred more than a century and a half ago and at a time when unionization was in its infancy. We have here evidence of a rather highly developed negotiation procedure coexisting with the exceedingly primitive methods of extracting economic concessions already described.

> In less than two months after the formation of the [New York Typographical] society the wage question came to the fore and caused considerable debate. From the minutes of the Board of Directors it is gleaned that on August 26, 1809, "Mr. Thompson, seconded by Mr. Hyer, moved that a committee of seven should be appointed to draw up a list of prices." . . . A scale of prices was prepared by the committee and submitted on September 16th. It regulated rates for composition and presswork. The report was twice read and after a few amendments had been made all articles but one were adopted. On September 20th the schedule was completed, and on the 27th instant a committee was appointed to draft a communication to accompany it. The directors convened on September 30th, when the following circular, addressed "to the master printers of the City of New York," was presented and unanimously approved:
>
> "GENTLEMEN:-Between employers and the employed there are mutual interests dependent; mutual duties to be performed. To the end that these may result in harmony certain rules and regulations should be adopted.
>
> "Therefore, we, the journeymen printers of the City of New York, have duly and deliberately taken into consideration the present irregular state of the prices in many of the printing offices, and conceiving that they are inadequate to a comfortable subsistence have united ourselves into an association for the purpose of regulating and establishing the same. The annexed list, formed with a due deference to justice and equability, is presented with a view that it may meet your approbation."

---

ance to the journeymen, for the difference of labour, and loss of time; but afterwards, actuated by a better spirit of liberality, they held a meeting with the workmen; and after entering into a full explanation of the case, the employers were convinced, of the justice of the workmen's demand, and resolved, to comply with it.

Reprinted by permission of the publishers from the same, p. 111.

Minor changes were again made in the new bill of prices on October 7th, and finally on the fourteenth of that month it was adopted as a whole and forwarded to the employers.

Meeting on October 21st the directors again discussed the scale, and resolved "that the secretary be authorized to transmit a copy of the list of prices to each of the typographical societies in the United States and inform them of our intention of standing out for the wages mentioned therein, in order that their members might not be deceived by advertisements for journeymen." This action was put into effect on October 23d, on which date Secretary Reins sent the following to unions in other places:

"GENTLEMEN:-Inclosed is a list of prices of the New York Typographical Society, by which they intend to be governed after the 29th inst. As some of the employers may be unwilling to conform to the regulations of the society, in hopes of procuring journeymen from other parts, I am directed to make this communication to you, in order that the members of your society might not be deceived by advertisements for journeymen in this city."

Upon receipt of the notification from the journeymen's society the master printers convened on October 25th to consider the claims of the workmen. The meeting adopted a counter proposal, and appointed a committee consisting of J. Swords, J. Crooks and G. Bruce to submit it to the union. On the following day the employers' representatives sent their scale to the men's organization, prefacing it with the statement that "the master printers of the City of New York, having convened on the 25th inst., by public notice, to deliberate upon certain propositions, which have been made to them by the journeymen for an increase of wages, unanimously (except in two or three trifling instances) adopted the subsequent resolutions. In presenting them to the consideration of the Typographical Society they think it proper to remark that, although no circumstances have come to their knowledge which would justify on the part of the journeymen a demand for more than the customary wages, yet, desirous of meeting them in the spirit of conciliation and harmony, and to remove every obstacle that might have a tendency to interrupt a mutual good understanding, the master printers have made considerable advances on the prices hitherto given, and to as great an extent as the present state of the printing business would admit. The scale which is now offered may, therefore, be considered as a *maximum,* beyond which it would be highly injurious, if not ruinous, to the interests of the trade to venture." . . .

The Typographical Society met in general session on October 28th and received a report from the Scale Committee, the members of which informed the association "that they had delivered a printed list of the prices to each master printer, agreeable to instructions; that the master printers themselves made a list of prices, which they presented for the consideration of the society, and that they had received a note directed to the committee of journeymen printers in which they requested that a committee of the society might be appointed to confer with their committee in order, if possible, to effect an accommodation." The reading of the communication from the master printers elicited an observation by one of the members of the society, as described in the minutes, "that though he disliked the stile of the note, which savored much of despotism, yet he thought it consistent that we should comply with their request; he therefore moved that a committee of three from our body be appointed to confer with the committee of master printers." This was carried. Then it was "moved that the list of prices be read by articles and the voice of the meeting taken on each, in order that the committee might be instructed wherein to adhere to the list, and in what article they would be willing to relax; which, after some opposition, being carried, the list was read and considered by articles. The committee were then instructed to adhere strictly to the original list, excepting the third article of composition and the fifth, eighth and tenth of presswork, which articles the society were of the opinion might be modified."

A special meeting was held by the society on October 30th. The committeemen, through Mr. Gleason, their chairman, "reported that they had waited on the committee of master printers," says the minutes, "who met them with a frankness which was highly creditable to themselves and pleasing to the committee. They had made many concessions, and the committee, desirous of putting a speedy termination to our differences, has also consented to advocate some trifling concessions on our part of points which they conceived to be in some measure unjust and which, in the present state of our affairs, were not worth contending for. Some points, however, insisted on by them, in the opinion of the committee, were not proper to be conceded, and hope that the meeting will be of the same opinion; but respectfully submitted the whole to the consideration of the meeting. Mr. Gleason then proceeded to read the articles of the list and explain the objections of the master printers and likewise their concessions in a stile and manner which did him much honor. After some observations from Mr. Eaton respecting the infancy of our society, our want of funds, and the inability of some of the members to stand out a great length of time, he moved that the meeting adopt the whole list of prices so far as the two committees had agreed. This motion was strenuously opposed; not being seconded, another motion was made to have it considered by articles, which was carried. It would be impossible to follow the members in their arguments in the course of the debate that ensued, in which was displayed a spirit worthy of the cause in which we are engaged, and an eloquence that would have graced a senate house. It is only necessary to observe that in many points they were willing to conform to the propositions of the master printers; but in the principal items set forth in our original list they determined to adhere to at all hazards. It was also moved that the list of prices as settled this evening be returned to the committee, by them to be again presented to the committee of master printers for their deliberation, and that this be considered the ultimatum of our deliberations on the subject."

Further conferences with the employers resulted in a satisfactory adjustment of the points at issue, although some members of the society had "turned out" to enforce the scale and received strike pay during the term of their idleness for sustaining the principles of the union, while a few others were disciplined for working for less than the prescribed rates. The wage schedule as finally established by the association and accepted by the master printers in 1809 consisted of piece rates and a minimum for time work, whereas the employers' tentative scale provided that the compensation named by them for work performed by the week should be the maximum, albeit their figure was $1 less than that advocated by the journeymen. Additional prices were specified for different kinds of extra work, although in a few exceptional instances the question of payment for extras was left to the judgment of the journeymen and the employer for settlement.[8]

In the conspiracy trial of the Philadelphia Journeymen Tailors in 1827, we have another though less elaborate account of a bargaining relationship:

In September, 1825, a bill of prices was agreed on by the journeymen tailors of this city, intended as a standard by which their wages were to be regulated, and the terms on which they were to work were to be settled. It was submitted to several of the master tailors, admitted by them, among others expressly by Messrs. Robb & Winebrener, and . . . continued so to regulate the prices, without the least objection on their part or difficulty on the part of their workmen, from that time to the present. . . . Previously to the adoption of this bill of prices, difficulties had occurred on points in all respects analogous to the one in which this dispute originated. Distinctions of various kinds had been attempted between thick and thin clothing, which in most instances had been resolutely resisted by the journeymen, and rarely insisted on by the employers. In some articles of dress, the men were willing to admit a distinction, in others they were not, and to put an end for ever to such altercations, always unpleasant and never profitable, a specification of prices was determined on, and such a printed document prepared as would effectually preclude any further ambiguity. Such was this bill of prices, being really a compromise between two conflicting interests, by which each party surrendered something and received a satisfactory equivalent. All the distinctions which the journeymen admitted were specified; where, as in the case of coats

[8] Stevens, *New York Typographical Union No. 6*, pp. 51–57.

and coatees, they were to receive less for summer than winter clothes, it was so set forth. . . .[9]

The organizations of employees and employers were still informal. No established relationship between them existed. A relationship was initiated when the occasion demanded and then was allowed to lapse. Consequently, a year after the adoption of this standard "bill of prices," when a dispute broke out between "Messrs. Robb & Winebrener" and their employees, there was not even a continuing formal relationship between union and employers to handle it. The dispute was of a kind that today would be labeled a "grievance," involving an application of the agreed-upon wage scales. Now, it would be handled through specially devised grievance procedures, but at that time no such procedures for settlement existed. Here is how the journeymen's lawyer told the result in the trial before the Mayor's Court in 1827:

> We come now to the origin of this difficulty, and the occurrences in the shop of Messrs. Robb & Winebrener. Early in late August, these gentlemen received an order to make a pongee riding habit; the notice being short, it was put in the hands of six of the men. . . . It was finished and delivered. On pay night, when these men went to receive their wages, they were surprised at an offer made by Mr. Winebrener of six dollars for what their bill of prices secured them at least seven dollars. They however distinctly declined receiving the six dollars, as not being the compensation they were entitled to, and their employers as distinctly refused to give them more. Both parties immediately instituted inquiries as to the practice in other establishments, and each, it appears, returned equally satisfied with the propriety of their original determination. Messrs. Robb & Winebrener at last yielded, paid the seven dollars, and as a punishment for asserting their undoubted rights, dismissed the six men from their service.
>
> On the dismission of these workmen, the others, fourteen in number, without premeditation or preconcert, influenced by no other motive than indignation at what they considered an act of oppression, only desirous to express their disapprobation of the treatment which their fellows had received, merely for refusing to submit to a wanton invasion of their rights, immediately threw up their work, and on the refusal of Robb & Winebrener to re-employ the men, quit their service.[10]

As a matter of fact, the conspiracy trial that had been instituted to determine whether the men had overstepped the bounds of the common law by their concerted activity, under a doctrine to be mentioned again shortly, became in part a matter of trying the merits of the grievance. First the

[9] Reprinted by permission of the publishers from Commons, *Documentary History of American Industrial Society,* vol. 4, pp. 142–143.

[10] Reprinted by permission of the publishers from the same, pp. 143–144.

journeymen presented their side of the controversy to the jury, and then the masters followed with theirs.[11]

It is surprising that the first semblance of the modern collective bargaining agreement should have emerged out of such informal dealings as these. This is partly explained by the fact that unionization occurred first among the skilled craftsmen, whose skill was employed in a variety of ways and who were customarily paid by the job or piece. When they sought to engage in concerted action to raise their wages, it became necessary to revise the rates on a number of different types of work. And in order to make sure that all the members knew the prescribed rates on all the jobs they performed, a bill of prices had to be drawn up for their own use. It was such a wage list which union members in this period generally drafted after consultation among themselves and which they put into effect without consultation with the employers, simply notifying them that the new rates were now in effect. Here is the list for shoemaking trade in New York in 1805: [12]

Black Strap Boots, fair tops	$4.00
Black Strapping the top of do. [ditto]	0.75
Ornament Straps closed outside on do.	0.25
Black Strap Bootees	3.50
Wax legs closed outside, plain counters, fair tops	3.25
Cordovan Boots, fair tops	3.00
Cordovan Bootees	2.50
Suwarrow Boots, closed outside	3.00
Do. inside closed, bespoke	2.75
Do. inferior work, do.	2.50
Binding Boots	0.25
Stabbing do.	0.25
Footing Old Boots	2.00
Foxing New Boots	0.50
Foxing and Countering Old Boots	2.00
Do. without counters	1.75
Shoes, best work	1.12
Do. inferior work	1.00
Pumps, French edges	1.12
Do. Shouldered do.	1.00
Golo shoes	1.50
Stitching Rans	0.75
Cork Soles	0.50

[11] As given in the same, pp. 143–144, for the journeymen; and pp. 166–168, 236–237, for the masters. The decision in this case turned, of course, upon the question of conspiracy and not upon the question of which party was in violation of the agreement.

[12] M. A. Schaffner, *The Labor Contract from Individual to Collective Bargaining,* University of Wisconsin Bulletin 2 (1907), p. 87.

Thus written lists came into existence; however, these were not written agreements. They were merely statements of unilateral intent: the wage rates which the union expected to make good against the employers and for which its members had agreed to stand out if any employers refused to accept them. The disadvantages of this method of collective bargaining are apparent. True, workers were often able to impose their terms by a show of unity and a strike or threat of strike, but the terms, once so imposed, remained in effect only until the employers believed themselves strong enough to reduce the rates on the whole bill of prices or to nibble away at particular rates if the union seemed too weak to resist. There was nothing to preclude such action, for they had signed no agreement with the union. As early as 1806 we hear the plaint from journeymen shoemakers that because there were no signatures to the price list when posted, the employers made changes in it as they pleased.

This disadvantage applied as much in the case of the employers as in the case of their workers, and sometimes a particular wage bill would be jointly observed by informal agreement. Such an understanding did not prevent either party from taking unilateral action to change the whole bill, since there was no agreement on the duration of any list of prices, but it did mean that until such a concerted movement took place, the rates were to be respected. That is to say, it was a way of agreeing that a *standard* wage list should be observed at all times by the employers and workers in a given community, but it did not constitute anything more than a temporary agreement on what the standard rates should be. Despite the informality of such arrangements, we find a judge suggesting as early as 1827 that an understanding of this nature might constitute an "implied contract" and that a "mere difference of opinion" between the journeymen and their employers over the intent of such a contract might possibly be settled by civil action in court.

By the end of this period of beginnings, then, the practice of unilateral imposition of terms had, in a few trades and communities, given way to bilateral negotiation, and the drafting of one-sided terms of surrender had in some instances been replaced by two-party agreements. The change should not be overemphasized, however. Organized employee action of any kind was still far from common, and where it did occur, it was likely to be an elemental economic struggle of strike and lockout, without so much as the appointment of a negotiating committee. Ultimatum rather than conference was the prevailing practice among both unions and associated employers.

That this was the case in these early days is not surprising. For the most part, employers were unwilling to encourage the organization of workers by recognizing their "combinations," and negotiation would imply recognition and acceptance. Moreover, the very legality of union activity was in question. The common-law doctrine of conspiracy was invoked against the workers' organizations on at least sixteen occasions prior to 1842, and until 1834 convictions could be readily counted on. The most extreme form of this doctrine maintained that the very formation of a union for wage action of any sort was criminal. The modified form in which this doctrine held sway for more than a quarter of a century was directed not against union activity as such, but against certain union tactics, in particular the pressure that was brought against nonunion workers. The refusal by members to work alongside nonmembers was especially attacked in the courts. By 1834 the doctrine had begun to lose its hold, as evidenced by the first acquittal of unionists charged with conspiracy. It was not until 1842, though, that a decision of the Massachusetts Supreme Court in *Commonwealth v. Hunt* effectively removed the sting from this common-law rule. By virtue of the eminence of Chief Justice Shaw, who delivered the decision, it became the controlling case on the matter.[13] The conspiracy doctrine was subsequently exhumed on a few occasions, but it had ceased to be a major threat to unionism.

Refusal of employers to recognize the unions and the common-law doctrine directed against the unions do not explain fully, however, why unilateral imposition of terms was generally resorted to when either side organized. This practice apparently stemmed in some measure from a desire by each to maximize any tactical advantage. Unionists struck when they believed that economic circumstances so favored them that they could obtain the whole of their demand, without countenancing concession. This was usually in times of rising prices. On the other hand, employers would reduce wages when they believed the economic occasion was propitious for securing the whole of the reduction, without any need to placate their employees by compromise. This was usually in times of depression or unemployment.

Finally, the spasmodic nature of worker organization and employer counterorganization helps to explain the undeveloped state of their dealings. Perhaps more surprising than the lack of refinement of organized employee-employer relationships is the fact that in some few cases, even in the face of legal stigma, the method of negotiation and joint agreement had been discovered. It was far from firmly established, however; it might be used on one occasion only to be discarded on another.

The Tempering of Unilateral Action

The labor movement in America is frequently said to have begun in 1827, the year in which a number of separated craft societies first joined to

[13] This phase of the law of industrial relations is discussed more fully in Chapter 11.

establish a "trades' union." This organization, which now would be called a "central labor union" or an "industrial council," first appeared in Philadelphia, but workers in other cities soon saw the advantage of pooling their individual craft strengths. These central unions built up strike funds, which were used to support only those strikes that they had previously approved. There now appeared, as a result, a concern by trade societies with demands that other societies might attempt to secure. As long as a union acted alone, its demands were limited only by its own conception of what it might win. But with central labor unions and pooled strike funds, a union's demands, though still generally imposed unilaterally, had first to be screened by its sister unions if its members expected to receive strike benefits.

The procedure is illustrated in the records of the New York City General Trades' Union for the year 1835.

(March 12) The object of the meeting was principally to take into consideration the situation of the Cabinet Makers. Mr. Gillespie explained the nature of their case. It was to establish their new Book of Prices, the old Book, adopted in 1810, having been found deficient in various particulars; the new Book, he stated, was calculated, he thought, to obviate all the difficulties growing out of the old Book. After some further remarks from one or two more of the members of that branch of the business, the proceedings of the Meeting of the Cabinet Makers (heretofore published) were read. In these proceedings, the Cabinet Makers expressed their determination to unite in establishing a new Book of Prices. . . . A committee of seven was, on motion, then appointed, to confer with the Cabinet Makers, and requested to report at the next meeting. . . .

(March 25) The Committee appointed at last meeting to confer with the Cabinet Makers, reported, that they have met with the Cabinet Makers, who have explained the nature of their grievances. The Committee approve of their principles, considering them founded in justice, and recommend that the Convention sanction their strike. It was then unanimously resolved, that the contemplated strike of the Cabinet Makers, to establish their New Book of Prices, be sanctioned by this Convention, and that the Committee of Conference be continued to act with a committee from the Cabinet Makers during said strike. . . .

(April 24) Having now gone through with the business for which the meeting was called, the Delegates from the Cabinet-makers were requested to state the progress they have made towards establishing their New Book of Prices. They stated, that nearly all the employers have conformed to their wishes, but there are a few who hold out against the Journeymen. They also stated, that the Journeymen Cabinet-makers are grateful to the House-carpenters for their generous conduct in assisting to procure employment for the Cabinet-makers at their business, by which a large number were immediately employed;

also to the Ship-joiners and to the Piano-Forte-makers, who assisted them to procure employment at their respective branches, and otherwise encouraged them in their strike.[14]

Such a unilateral imposition of terms, however tempered by central union action, continued to arouse opposition in the form of employers' associations, usually informal and temporary. Where organization appeared on the part of both employees and employers, efforts at negotiations were sometimes made—collective bargaining, that is to say. We now encounter another form in which collective bargaining emerges: the case not of the small-scale employer in association with his fellows, but of the corporation with capital assets in the hundreds of thousands of dollars, numbers of employees sufficiently large to permit mass production, and factory conditions of labor. Now the workers of an individual company might organize for united action. Such activity was not limited to the large urban centers; it might occur wherever a single plant had workers in numbers sufficient for effective organization. It was the skilled craftsmen, many of whom had previously participated in unionism as journeymen workers for master employers, who generally initiated the action. In the conspiracy trials of the Thompsonville carpet weavers, we find a record of bargaining relations between a group of about seventy ingrain carpet weavers (out of a total force of one hundred) and a rug manufacturing company, in a small Connecticut town, that was doing an annual business of $150,000. The former president of the weavers tells the story of one attempt to reach agreement. It will be apparent from his recital that an individual grievance had prompted joint discussions and that these developed into negotiations for a change in general terms. The company at the time had a wage system in effect that, among other things, paid a premium if a piece was finished in a given time and inflicted a fine if it was not.

> Upon the 6th of July 1833, I was requested to call the shop together of which I was President. Mr. Taylor thought the opinion of the shop ought to be taken in relation to a grievance of which one of the workmen complained. One Boyle had complained that he had finished his piece within the time and could get no premium. William Keys also complained to me on the same day that he could not get a ticket, and that he had been much hindered in his work by poor filling. I called a meeting at 4 o'clock on Saturday and sent to Mr. Thompson [company agent]. The reason of the refusal to pay Keys was that he had not complied with the rule requiring a webb's notice [15] of his intention to leave the employment of the company. . . .

[14] Reprinted by permission of the publishers from Commons, *Documentary History of American Industrial Society,* vol. 5, pp. 232–237.

[15] A "webb's notice" was a notification given at the start of a piece of weaving that the man expected to leave upon completing it.

At the meeting on Saturday before mentioned Mr. Henry Thompson attended and consented to pay Keys, and that he might go away, but said he wished it distinctly understood that a webb's notice would be required thereafter. Mr. Boyle's complaint about not receiving the premium was also considered at this meeting, and Mr. Thompson said the premiums should be given up, and upon being inquired of if fines were to be given up also, he answered yes. Before the agent Mr. T. left the meeting, he was requested to raise the prices upon some difficult fabrics, to which he replied that he would refer them to the company who would soon meet. A committee of six were appointed to draw a petition, which was presented to the company at their next meeting.[16] An answer was returned by the company on the following day.[17] A meeting was then called in the High Shop and the answer

16

Thompsonville, July 23d, 1833.

To the Thompsonville Carpet Manufacturing Company.

Gent. We the undersigned, weavers in your employ, having had an interview with your Agent respecting some grievances which we complained of, we requested him to redress them, but received for an answer, that he had not any power in the matter, and was advised by him to make out a statement of them and present them before you at your meeting.

We therefore respectfully submit the following particulars for your consideration. The introduction of new and fancy fabrics are alike beneficial to all the employed, as well as the employer. But when there is additional labor, it is right the laborer should have remuneration for his extra work. Therefore you know for instance, that fabric lately introduced, called a double shot about, is a great deal more difficult for the weaver to get along with, and we think should be paid at one shilling per yard. The double grounds also should at least have one half cent additional as formerly, & the same for stripes with above two shuttles on the ground. To the above grievances we solicit your attention. Our requests are so moderate that we think they only want to be represented to you, to have them redressed.

17

The Thompsonville Company have this day received a petition from the weavers in their employ, soliciting an increase on the prices of weaving, and in answer, the Company request their petitioners will seriously consider the following facts.

The Thompsonville Company desire at all times to be on the most friendly terms with all persons in their employ. The Thompsonville Company, possessing a full knowledge of the present situation of the Carpet Manufacturers in the United States, are decidedly of opinion that the profits on the business are not such as to warrant any increase on the prices now paid for weaving; and the Company believe it will be most for the permanent interest of the weavers in their employ, to combine to work at present prices.

The Thompsonville Company believe their petitioners must be aware of

was read and was unsatisfactory. And the question was then put, "shall we make a stand or not?" It was determined to ask for an increase of wages on all kinds of fabrics, and the terms were agreed upon. The three ply weavers had never before made any complaint. We concluded to ascertain the views of those present by a personal vote, and each individual was asked "stand or not." Seventy said "stand," and but one made any objection, and he a slight one. Resolutions were then adopted [18] and a committee of which John Elder was one, was appointed to present them to the company. The meeting remained organized until the committee returned with a report that the company were not prepared to make any other alterations. Toward evening the Foreman (Mr. Ronald) came to the shop where we had assembled, and told us he was directed by Mr. Thompson to require us to leave the shop. I requested that we might be permitted to remain thirty minutes to finish our business, but he refused, saying he was ordered to shut the shops. We left the shop and went into Mrs.

---

the reduction which has already taken place in the duties on Carpeting, and that it is necessary for American Manufacturers to be able to meet Foreigners in the markets of this country. The duty on Ingrain and Venetian Carpetings formerly stood at 40 cts. per square yard, and in March last was reduced to 35 cts. per yard, and a further reduction of 3 cts. per yard is to take place January next, which will then make the duties 32 cts. per square yard. The Thompsonville Company would inform their petitioners that the styles of goods on which they ask an advance, command no higher price than other descriptions, and that the Company are obliged to make such styles as their customers order. The Company presume their petitioners must be satisfied that no favors have been shown to particular persons, but all have been placed on the same footing.

The Thompsonville Company believe that their petitioners will best promote their own interests by continuing to work as heretofore. By order of the President and Directors.—

GEORGE W. MARTIN, SECRETARY.

Thompsonville Company's Office, July 24, 1833.

[18]

Thompsonville, July 24th, 1833.

GENT. OF THE THOMPSONVILLE MANUFACTURING COMPANY.

We the weavers in your employ, having received your answer to our petition, when we immediately held a meeting, and came immediately to the following resolutions, viz:

1st. Resolved, That all plain grounds shall be paid as follows, at the rate of 15 cents per yard, and fines at 11 cents per yard.

2d. Resolved, That all stripes above two shuttles, and double whites, shall be paid 15½ cents per yard.

3d. Resolved, That all Double shot abouts shall be paid at the rate of 16½ cents per yard.

Metcalf's lot, where I was chosen President, and George Black Secretary. A committee of management consisting of nine was also appointed. . . .

On the next day Mr. Thompson requested me to call the men together in the yard at 2 o'clock P.M. which I did. They assembled and Mr. Thompson read a paper.[19] We went into the field and upon consultation refused to accede. On the morning following which was Saturday, at about 6 o'clock, Mr. T. handed me another paper, to which we were required to agree by Monday or to go in afterwards, if at all, at reduced prices.[20] It was determined to call a meeting that forenoon. I saw Thompson before the meeting and suggested some alterations, which I informed him I believed would render the propo-

---

4th. Resolved, That the three plies shall be paid at the rate of 30 cents per yard.

5th. Resolved, That we shall not return to work until the above grievances are redressed.

[19]

RULES AND REGULATIONS. All persons who enter the employ of the Thompsonville Company, will be considered as assenting to the following rules:

1st. Any weaver leaving the employ of the Thompsonville Company shall give notice of the same before commencing their last piece, the same notice shall be given by the company to the weaver.

2d. All weavers keeping a piece of Fine Carpeting over twelve days—a piece Super fine over fifteen days—a piece of three ply over Twenty one days—shall be liable to be discharged unless in case of sickness or some reasonable cause and which will only be allowed when duly reported at the Office.

3d. No reading of Newspapers or other publications will be allowed in any of the Weaving shops, and any one found so doing, will be fined One Dollar for the first offence and for the second discharged.

5th [4th] No smoking shall be allowed in any building belonging to the weaving department. Any man so doing, will be fined Five Dollars and forthwith discharged.

6th [5th] Any weaver wishing to be absent more than one day must give notice of the same at the Office.

[20]

Thompsonville Company's Office, July 25, 1833.

The Thompsonville Company inform the Weavers who lately have left their employ, that unless they return to work by Monday morning next, they will not after that day be allowed to enter the Company's employ on the same terms as heretofore. And all those who occupy Houses belonging to said Company are hereby notified to quit the same on Monday next, unless they return to work. By order of the President and Directors.

HENRY THOMPSON, AGENT.

sition acceptable. Mr. Thompson would not agree to any alterations. A meeting was held on that day in the field. The resolutions were again publicly read, and I explained what I had said to Mr. Thompson. Several present, among whom was Richard McDowell and James Taylor, reprimanded me severely, and said among other things that I was their servant and not their director. The question was then taken shall we accept the offer or stand permanently. The question was taken by personal vote, each being asked individually, and they unanimously said stand. . . . Early next week a committee meeting was held at William Taylor's room, at which about six of the committee were present. The object was, to provide funds for the support of those who had families and others in need. . . . During the third week Mr. Thompson asked us what we intended to do, whether we should go back and work or remain as we were. I told him our wages had been reduced & we wanted them increased. He said we should be ruined if we persisted. . . .

At a general meeting on Saturday a resolution was passed, or an agreement made that each one should be as active as possible in preventing weavers from coming there, and if any did come to notify them of the strike before Mr. Thompson knew it. . . .

At this point Henry Thompson, the plant manager, fills out the story. After recounting how the company had had three weavers arrested on conspiracy charges, he goes on to relate the final breaking of the strike:

On Sunday afternoon about the 27th of August, eleven men came from New York and stopped by direction, about a mile and a half below the village at Smith's tavern. They had been employed by the company to come to Thompsonville, and enter into the employment of the company as weavers. . . . The old weavers asked the new ones if they had come to take the bread out of their children's mouths. There was considerable conversation between the old weavers and myself on this occasion, and some harsh language. Conversed with McDowell and two or three old weavers in all at this time. About 9 o'clock in the morning, the eleven new weavers went into the shops. At about 11 A.M. three of the old weavers called upon me to know if I would receive a committee, to which I consented. Alexander and McGill came as a committee, and inquired if we would pay them now the same prices which we paid when they struck for higher wages. I replied we would pay them the same we paid the new weavers. They went away and held a meeting, then returned and asked if those in jail might return upon the same terms, and no example be made of any, to which I consented.[21]

[21] Reprinted by permission of the publishers from Commons, *Documentary History of American Industrial Society,* vol. 4, Supplement, pp. 26–35, 116–119.

There is indication, too, that this bargaining relationship between employees and company at Thompsonville had been continuous for several years prior to this strike of 1833. One of the weavers informed the court: "I was President of the shop in which I wrought, and had been for two years—most of the shops had a President. Business was ordinarily done with the President if of general interest. A mere private affair between the company and weavers the President and men had nothing to do with." [22]

With the advent of depression in the late 1830s, the union movement virtually disappeared. Many of the local unions, all the city councils, and the National Labor Union, which had sought to coordinate them, passed out of existence. A brief spurt of organization came in 1844, but it was not until 1850 that unionism regained its lost influence. And we find that as the unions come to life and seek wage advances to cope with the rising cost of living, collective bargaining practices are virtually right back where they were at the start of the period. The familiar method of unilateral imposition of terms reasserts itself.

As unions rebuilt their organizations, they relived their earlier practices. Local trade unions in the cities determined in consultation among their own members what wage they should enforce and notified their employers of change without even appointing a negotiating committee. Small-scale employers relearned the defensive procedure of counterorganization. For the most part they simply met by themselves to discuss their attitudes toward union demands. The larger companies pitted their growing power against their own skilled workers whenever the latter organized. In some few situations collective bargaining negotiations were attempted. Thus, after the hiatus in the union movement between 1837 and 1850, we find the same pattern that was evident in the opening of the twenty-five-year period. There is an air of familiarity about all this—we seem to be leaving exactly where we came in.

Conclusion

In one respect the period was an important stage of development in the process of collective bargaining in this country. It saw the rise of the championing of union-employer negotiations as a matter of policy. In 1833, at the very time when the Baltimore Master Hatters were charged with having unilaterally reduced the wages of their journeymen, they replied that they were only countering in the manner which the workers themselves had originated, but they added that fundamentally they, the Master Hatters,

> ... believe that in the regulation of the prices of labour, it is indispensable for their proper and fair establishment, that the different and

[22] Reprinted by permission of the publishers from the same, p. 59.

conflicting interests which are to be affected thereby, should mutually participate and co-operate; they believe that the mutual checks which the opposing interests of the parties, will on such occasions always put in motion, are as indispensable to a fair standard of fair prices, as are the checks and balances of a well organized government, both being essential to restrain man in his proneness to abuse power when stimulated by interest.

In 1834, on the occasion of a New York bakers' strike, a committee of well-known unionists issued a statement that looked forward to a time when "friendly conferences" would do away with the "necessity of those frequent strikes" that are detrimental both to the parties and to the public. In 1847 the editor of a workingmen's paper declared before an audience of workers: "It has always appeared to me, (and I have seen it acted upon) that a plain, friendly relationship and statement of facts on both sides would have reconciled both parties, with a little concession by each." [23]

These, however, were only straws in the wind. A majority of employers continued to oppose unionism, and to an important degree workers, because of the unwillingness of their employers to treat with them, were driven to a one-sided imposition of wages and working conditions whenever they were able. Nevertheless, during this period the number of both union officials and employers who had gained actual experience in the art of negotiation increased. Among their number, a few had become advocates of collective bargaining as a policy of union-employer relations. The idea of collective bargaining was gaining ground.

[23] Reprinted by permission of the publishers from the same, vol. 6, pp. 102–193; vol. 5, p. 308; vol. 8, p. 261.

A Historical Introduction to Collective Bargaining in the United States, 1850 to the Present

chapter 2

The movement toward collective bargaining was given impetus in the mid-nineteenth century by the stand of that remarkable reformer-publisher-politician, Horace Greeley. He espoused the jointly negotiated trade agreement in the editorial columns of the *New York Tribune,* the influential newspaper which he had founded. His espousal reflected his sympathy for the aspirations of organized workers and also his appreciation of a standard wage scale. He recognized that the competitive pressure of the substandard producer could be removed if all employers in an industry were obliged to abide by the same scale of wages. He became the first president of the rejuvenated New York printers' union, serving a term of one year. His influence was felt during the negotiations of 1850–1851, when the union sought to establish a pattern of negotiations in place of one-party dictation. Speaking at a union mass meeting in Tammany Hall late in 1850, Greeley asserted: "I do not agree that the journeymen should dictate a scale, but they should get the employers to agree to some scale. . . . I admit the right of the employers to participate in the adjustment of a scale, but . . . if they reject portions of the scale let them propose amendments and submit these to the arbitrament of fair men." [1]

Horace Greeley and the New York Printers

Greeley's efforts to institute bilateral dealings at this time failed because the employers could not associate effectively and agree upon counterproposals. Some of the employers were willing to enter into a collective agreement with the union, but others refused to have anything to do with it, charging that its operations constituted a usurpation of managerial authority.[2] As Greeley relates, the result was a return to the unilateral rule of the union. Defending the workers' position before attacks such as those appearing in the *Journal of Commerce,* he wrote:

[1] George A. Stevens, *New York Typographical Union No. 6,* New York State Department of Labor, Annual Report of the Bureau of Labor Statistics (1911), part I, p. 235.

[2] One of the most vociferous opponents of unionism at this time was perhaps the *New York Journal of Commerce.* With respect to this wage movement of 1850–1851, the *Journal* wrote on February 6, 1851:

> Quite recently the combination have raised the price of week hands to our price ($14), and have added 2 cents a thousand to the price of piecework, making 32 cents a thousand. They have enacted various other rules for the government of employers, which we shall adopt when we make up our minds to yield our independence, our self-respect, and the control of our own business, to the dictation of a self-constituted power outside of the office.

And on February 7, the *Journal* continued the attack as follows:

> Who but a miserable, craven-hearted man, would permit himself to be subjected to such rules, extending even to the number of apprentices he may employ and the manner in which they shall be bound to him, to the kind of work which shall be performed in his own office at particular hours of the day, and to the sex of the persons employed, however separated into different apartments or buildings? For ourselves, we never employed a female as a compositor, and have no great opinion of apprentices, but sooner than be restricted on these points, or any other, by a self-constituted tribunal outside of the office, we would go back to the employment of our boyhood, and dig potatoes, pull flax, and do everything else that a plain, honest farmer may properly do on his own territory. It is marvelous to us how any employer, having the soul of a man within him, can submit to such degradation.

From Stevens, *New York Typographical Union No. 6,* pp. 239, 240–241.

They do not claim the right of themselves to establish and regulate the prices even of their own labor, for they began by inviting the employers as a class to confer and unite with them in a free and friendly council, wherein the rates of compensation for all descriptions of journey work at printing should be established by mutual and general consent. Such a scale, once adopted, would have been binding on both parties until changed by mutual consent. A good portion of the employers responded to the invitation by holding one or two meetings, but concluded by simply rejecting (nineteen to fourteen) the scale proposed by the journeymen and adjourning without day. They suggested no modification, proposed no substitute; they gave the journeymen no ultimatum, no chance to understand what portions or provisions of their scale were deemed inadmissible, and what modification would render it acceptable. The only alternative practically offered to the journeymen was this: "Submit to work at as many different rates and under as many sets of regulations as the several hundred different employers in the city may see fit to establish and to change at their own good will and pleasure, or—help yourselves."

Thus repelled, the journeymen have waited, deliberated, reasoned, expostulated, and finally, giving ample notice of their resolve, fixed the first instant as the day on and after which their scale should be the common measure of their duties, their rights and recompense, while working as journeyman printers within this city. Most of the employers have acceded to their scale and the great mass of the work in our city is now executed and paid for in accordance therewith.[3]

[3] This defense is from the February 8, 1851, issue of the *Tribune,* as reproduced in Stevens, *New York Typographical Union No. 6,* p. 243. It is interesting to observe the notification given to the employers by the union, as reproduced in the same, p. 238:

TO THE TRADE: The following scale of prices has been adopted, after mature deliberation, by the New York Printers' union and, so far as their members are concerned, will be fully supported from the first day of February, 1851.

We submit these prices to the trade at large, and ask for them the support of journeymen and employers; because we believe them to be in every respect just and reasonable—because a number of the largest and best establishments in the city now pay them—because the recent great increase in the necessaries of life, and the general advance of wages by other trades, render these enhanced prices in our business imperatively necessary—because they will tend to the physical and consequently the moral improvement of printers—because they will protect good workmen against quacks, and thus become of pecuniary interest both to the employer and the workman, and because they will form what has been long needed in this city, a uniform and well-known tariff of wages.

With these brief, but we think cogent reasons, we submit the New York

Unions in other trades, too, now sought as vigorously as the printers to get employers to negotiate agreements. The New York journeymen tailors called a strike against their masters only after setting a meeting date "with the view to make arrangements with the bosses, but as none of the latter appeared, the meeting was adjourned." [4] Cognizant of the nature of the masters' opposition, however, the union adopted a somewhat less demanding bill of prices and repeated the offer to negotiate.[5] The silversmiths, organizing the same year, declared themselves in favor of bilateral dealings—"to conciliate, not defy, being their specific aim." [6] The bricklayers and plasterers, after reorganizing their unions, were willing to negotiate with employers even on matters affecting their constitution. The conciliatory offers by these unions, it should be noted, came during a period when the unions enjoyed an economic advantage conducive to winning their demands. By and large, however, these scattered efforts to substitute bilateralism for unilateralism in collective bargaining did not bear fruit.

This period is of special interest since we find for the first time a consistent, systematic exposition of the nature and obligations of a collective bargaining system. At the same time, we encounter a continuing reluctance or inability on the part of most unions and employers to depart from the old system of unilateral coercion. When one party's bargaining power of strategic position suggested advantages to be gained, unilateral negotiations usually prevailed. Both the old and the new methods were fighting for survival. Thus in 1853, when Greeley's influence within the councils of the printers' union was less marked, there was a reversion to the old practice, which evoked a protest from him. He pointed out that by "proceeding of themselves" the journeymen might be able to establish a temporary higher scale of wages, but the employers would not be obliged to honor it any longer than they had to. A crisp paragraph advocated a system of negotiations:

> We think the journeymen made a mistake in proceeding of themselves to fix a new and advanced scale of prices and then asking the

---

union scale to the trade; and by our signatures hereunto appended, do certify the following to be a correct transcript of the original copy.

[4] *New York Daily Tribune,* July 31, 1850.

[5]

To the Merchant Tailors of New York—Gentlemen, you are respectfully requested to attend a meeting of delegates from the Journeymen Tailors' Society to be held at the Shakespere Hotel on Monday, September 16, at ten o'clock, for the purpose of discussing the new bill of prices recently adopted by that body.

The same, September 13, 1850.

[6] The same, May 31, 1850.

employers to accede to it. They ought to have asked the employers to unite with them in revising the scale and adapting it to the existing state of things, and should have been prepared with statistics to show that the money value of labor has so changed as to render such revision just and proper. True, they have a perfect right to set a price on their own labor, but employers have the same right to determine what they will pay; and the object of a scale is (or should be) the establishment of a common standard to the avoidance of all controversy or caviling thereafter. Now we shall pay the new scale, reserving our right to determine at any time hereafter whether we can or cannot afford to persevere in doing so. But had the journeymen seen fit to ask a conference with the employers and had the scale been then readjusted with the assent of both parties, we should have felt bound to pay it until a modification had in like manner been agreed to by employers and journeymen, through their duly authorized representatives. And we fear the new scale is not likely to be paid, even pro tem, so generally as it would have been had the journeymen requested the concurrence of the employers in the modification, as they did when the scale was last revised three or four years ago.[7]

This chiding of his former union colleagues was followed on the succeeding day by a fuller statement of Greeley's philosophy of collective bargaining—perhaps the first such concisely ordered statement in this country. All the codes, propositions, resolutions, exhortations, and creeds of workers and their leaders of the preceding fifty years are succinctly gathered together here into a lucid exposition of the principles underlying the joint union-management trade agreement system. This statement stands as a landmark in the history of the development of collective bargaining in the United States.

1. We believe that the wages of Labor should be liberal—that the true interest of all classes requires this—and that they have generally been lower than they should be.
2. We believe that unregulated, unrestricted competition—the free trade principle of "every man for himself" and "buy where you can the cheapest"—tends everywhere and necessarily to the depression of wages and the concentration of wealth. Capital can wait—Labor cannot—but must earn or famish. Without organization, concert and mutual support, among those who live by selling their labor, its price will get lower and lower as naturally as water runs down hill. Consequently, we are in favor of trades unions or regular associations of workers in the several callings for the establishment and maintenance of fair and just rates of wages in each.
3. We believe employers have rights as well as journeymen—that they too should hold meetings and form societies or appoint delegates

[7] Stevens, *New York Typographical Union No. 6*, pp. 252–253.

to confer with like delegates on the part of the journeymen; and that by the joint action of these conferrers, fair rates of wages in each calling should be established and maintained.

4. We believe that the rates thus established are and should be morally binding upon all who see fit to engage in these callings respectively—that he who cannot afford them has no right to be an employer, and he who will not ought to be shunned alike by journeymen and customers—and that whenever employers or journeymen believe that the circumstances of their trade require an increase or reduction of wages they ought to assemble their own class and procure its sanction to a new conference of delegates as aforesaid and that its decision should be conclusive.

5. We believe that strikes, or refusals of journeymen to work at such wages as they can command, are seldom necessary—that proper representations and conciliatory action on the part of journeymen would secure all requisite modifications of wages without striking—and that the aggregate of wasted time, misdirected energy, embittered feeling and social anarchy which a strike creates is seldom compensated by any permanent enhancement of wages thus obtained.

6. We believe that the primary and most culpable authors of strikes and the mischiefs thence arising are those employers who refuse to unite in any efforts for the systematic adjustment of wages, but insist on fixing and paying such rates of wages as they choose, without reference to the established regulations or current usages of the vocation. If these would but desist from their evil practices, the claims of journeymen alone to regulate wages without asking the concurrence of employers would be easily proved untenable and speedily abandoned. While the journeymen's scales of prices are the only ones, they ought, for want of better, to be respected and adhered to. But to secure a conference and a mutual agreement as to wages, the employers in any trade have but to ask it. . . . If journeymen alone regulate the prices of labor, they will be likely to fix them too high; if employers alone fix them (as they virtually do under the free-trade system) they will as naturally fix them too low; but let the journeymen and employers in each trade unite in framing, upholding and from time to time modifying their scale, and it will usually be just about right.[8]

Horace Greeley's influence in the spreading of negotiation is impossible to assess. We do know that the columns of the *Tribune* disseminated the philosophy of union-employer negotiations in a manner never before attempted. He published such instances of bargaining as came to his attention. Characteristic of this educative influence is Greeley's reporting of informal negotiations between workers and employers in the manufacturing

[8] *New York Daily Tribune*, April 13, 1853. This statement will be found in Stevens, *New York Typographical Union No. 6*, pp. 621–622.

industries of Delaware County, Pennsylvania, which led to the adoption of a ten-hour day in that area:

> Here we see the whole question settled, so far as a large manufacturing district is concerned, without denunciation, bitterness or wrath, and without invoking the interposition of laws or politicians. The laborers simply consider the matter, resolve that sixty hours per week are as many as they think they ought to work, and they appoint a Committee to confer with their employers and submit to them the considerations which have impelled them to this conclusion. They urge that they need more time for intellectual and moral culture, for the training of their children, etc., than they can give after having performed twelve hours' labor per day in factories; and that, if they cannot earn their present wages by working ten hours, they are willing to take less. The employers meet in like manner, consider the respectful but frank suggestions of their workmen, accede to the Ten-hour System, and ask the workmen to use their best efforts to render the Reform universal. And thus the matter is happily and kindly adjusted—we confidently trust to the advantage of all parties. . . .[9]

Again, however, it is necessary to insert the warning that we must not think of collective bargaining as a continuously developing process in this country. As we have seen, it exists only with worker organization, and not until after the Civil War did unions acquire some permanency. Before that, organization made marked upsurges, only to be abandoned. So uncertain was the organizational foundation of the labor movement during these early years that the depression of 1857 nearly wiped out the local unions.[10] When unionism renewed its operations about 1863, as prices were rising as a result of the Civil War, most of the previous tendencies toward collective bargaining had disappeared in the six-year hiatus. As workers drew together to seek wage increases to offset the rising cost of living, they did not try to continue joint negotiations but returned to the old tried and true

[9] *New York Daily Tribune*, August 5, 1853. See also the same, May 16, 1854, for the account of a joint agreement on wages and other items reached by journeymen cigar makers and employers in a New York State convention in 1854.

Different views of Greeley's influence are provided by John R. Commons and Norman J. Ware. For the former's views, see especially "Horace Greeley and the Working Class Origins of the Republican Party," *Political Science Quarterly*, vol. 24 (1909), pp. 468–488. Ware's skepticism is expressed in *The Industrial Worker, 1840–1860*, Boston: Houghton Mifflin Company, 1924, pp. 21–22.

[10] John R. Commons et al. (eds.), *Documentary History of American Industrial Society*, Glendale, Calif.: The Arthur H. Clark Company, 1910–1911, vol. 9, p. 22.

system of unilateral imposition of terms supported by strike action. They reverted to "first beginnings."

Thus in 1864 the New York City printers first "decreed" a new wage scale and then passed a resolution "that on Sunday morning, August 14th, the members working in the various daily morning newspaper offices in the City of New York shall demand of the proprietors of the same whether they will pay the recently advanced scale so long as required by this union, and in case of refusal the employed in such offices shall promptly strike and refuse to resume work until their demands are fully acceded to, unless already acceded to unconditionally." [11]

This one-sided action aroused the opposition of Horace Greeley, the printers' old champion and former president but an ardent advocate of joint negotiations. Branding the proposed wage increase unreasonable, he asserted that the *Tribune* was not disposed to concede it. "Should we be coerced into doing it, it must be with the distinct understanding that we deem it unjust, and shall endeavor to escape from it at the earliest moment." His actions matching his words, Greeley retaliated by seeking to recruit printers who would be willing to work at less than the decreed union wages.

The Attack on Unilateral Demands

Generally, it may be said that opposition to the renewed unilateral union efforts came from three sources. First, there were those, like Greeley, who looked upon the unions' coercive efforts as unsuited to a cooperative society and who sought to replace them with a system of collective bargaining negotiations. Thus, even while trying to recruit a nonunion staff to counter the printers' 1864 wage decree, Greeley made clear his basic sympathy with organization and continued his educational drive on behalf of a trade agreement system:

> We are ready now and henceforth to unite with our fellow employers in appointing a committee of three or more persons to meet a like committee from the journeymen (we mean all the journeymen in our city), and any scale of prices and office regulations which may be agreed upon by a majority of each committee we will accept and abide by upon a distinct understanding that it can only be changed by the concurrence of two similar committees hereafter; but no scale will we recognize henceforth which is made by journeymen alone. If we are not entitled to at least an equal voice with our journeymen— much more with other journeymen—in the regulation of our office,

[11] Stevens, *New York Typographical Union No. 6*, p. 288. The whole story of this wage movement of 1864 is given in the same, pp. 279–295.

we will quit this business for some other wherein we shall have some recognized rights, some freedom of judgement and of action.[12]

The second source of resistance to unilateral action by the unions came from those employers who opposed unionism in any form. Their projected solution lay in the complete elimination of unions. For this purpose they sometimes formed "defensive" associations. They objected to union dictation and passed a series of resolutions as preludes to action.

> The "Moulders' Union" has made an attempt, and thus far a successful one, to dictate to and extort the most unreasonable terms from their employers all over the country. . . . They have undertaken to arbitrarily decide, not only as to what wages must be paid, but even as to the number of apprentices each shop is to employ, the kind and amount of work the laborers in our foundries may or may not be allowed to do, and to prevent any moulder from working in a shop who is not a member of their Union.
>
> . . . The members of the Journeymen Plasterers' Operative Society, through the columns of the public press, have given notice to the several boss plasterers of New York, that on and after the 1st day of February next [1864], they will demand twenty shillings per day, the main object of which, should they be successful in enforcing it, is to pave the way for more arbitrary measures, such as abolishing the present mode of lathing. . . .
>
> . . . The various departments of mechanical and other labor, dependent upon our inland lakes for employment, having banded themselves together by the most solemn pledges, under various titles of association, and under such organizations, have instituted various arbitrary rules of dictation, to both employers and owners, rendering themselves obnoxious and detrimental to every interest of those who contribute to their welfare.
>
> . . . No railway management can recognize as a right, any dictation, as to the wages they shall pay, the rules or regulations they shall adopt, or whom they shall or shall not employ; and societies used to prevent free action of either party [i.e., the individual employee and the company] in these particulars, if unchecked, would not only destroy all value in railroad property, but would strike a destructive blow to the commercial and agricultural prosperity of the entire country.
>
> . . . However laudable the motives may have been, in which these "Unions" originated, they have at length come to assume a dangerous attitude, and to act a disorganizing and ruinous part. For example: they assume to dictate to employers, and the employed, the rates of wages to be demanded and paid; what men may be employed, and what number of apprentices; who shall be discharged, and who re-

[12] *New York Daily Tribune,* August 20, 1864.

tained; when, and on what terms our establishments and business may be operated and carried on, or stopped, always vigilant to take advantage of the shifting conditions of business and work on hand and having apparently little or no regard to the justice or proprieties of the case, and enforcing their demands, as against the employers, by "strikes," and, as against workingmen, by both contributions and threats.[13]

After passing the resolutions, the employers' associations took action. They provided mutual support in resistance to strikes and circulated a blacklist of union members. Once the effectiveness of the unions was broken, disorganization would swiftly follow.

Strangely enough, the third source of opposition to union efforts at dictation lay within the unions themselves. The post-Civil War period saw a mushroom growth of national organization in the respective trades. Officers of these new national organizations soon found unilateral action by their constituent local unions an embarrassment. For one thing, it created adverse public reaction at a time when they were seeking to expand their influence in the national arena. For another, the local unions came to expect strike support from the national treasury, and irresponsible action in the field threatened the financial stability of the struggling national organizations.

Certain results of this three-pronged attack upon one-party imposition of wages and terms of employment should be noted. After a period of struggle over the question of local autonomy, the national unions placed limitations on strike action by the locals. The Moulders, for example, as early as 1865 required their local unions to follow specified bargaining procedures before striking. The printers first demanded that the national executive board approve strikes before benefits might be paid from the national treasury. By 1888 they found this insufficient control and required that local unions, to qualify for strike benefits, appeal to a national "organizer" before striking. This official then might intervene in negotiations to seek a settlement. Other examples might be added.[14]

A second result of the attack on unilateral demands was the encouragement of arbitration. Many people saw strikes—lockouts, too—as efforts to coerce a solution regardless of the merits of the dispute. With the outbreak of such coercive action following the Civil War, there was a widespread feeling that arbitration offered a means of substituting the reasoned judgment of fair-minded men for economic coercion. Joint boards of arbitration existed in shoe firms in Lynn, Massachusetts, about 1870. In 1872 the

[13] Reprinted by permission of the publishers from Commons, *Documentary History of American Industrial Society,* vol. 9, pp. 90, 102, 104, 107, 109–110.

[14] See Lloyd Ulman, *The Rise of the National Union,* Cambridge, Mass.: Harvard University Press, 1955, Chaps. 6 and 14.

Moulders required arbitration before a strike. A full membership referendum in 1876 supported this policy, but within two years it had to be abandoned for lack of employer cooperation. The preamble of the constitution adopted by the Knights of Labor in 1878 espoused "the substitution of arbitration for strikes, whenever and wherever employers and employees are willing to meet on equitable grounds." In the 1880s arbitration became popular in the building trades. A Chicago Carpenters' agreement of 1890 provided for a joint arbitration committee, headed by an umpire, with exclusive authority "to determine and definitely fix, from year to year, all working rules" and "any and all other subjects in which both organizations are interested." [15]

The development of joint negotiations, however, more than arbitration, gave promise of industrial order. The decreasing use of coercion is illustrated in the book and job printing industry in New York City. An association of employers calling themselves the Typothetae complained vigorously when the printers sought to institute a new scale by unilateral promulgation in 1869. It was said that "these men ask this advance as highwaymen solicited on the high road. They gave us no notice or time for a consideration of the matter. On Monday morning the new scale was presented, and on Monday morning it went into effect—that is, they all struck." [16]

The printers asserted: "We never have in any way intimated that we would not receive and listen to a committee from their august body," but nevertheless they made no move to open negotiations. Their good faith was further questioned by the employers' public declaration: "We were never consulted about the union rules and prices. . . . We hold that it takes two parties to make a bargain, and object to the enforcement of rules, in making which we have not even had the chance to express an opinion." [17]

The strike dragged on for about eight weeks. Finally the leaders of both groups met in informal and private conferences, and it was reported that "a spirit of mutual concession" prevailed. Only after three more weeks did the leaders reach a joint settlement and agree to a written agreement. It incorporated among its provisions the following: "This scale shall not be altered except by a call for a mutual conference between a joint committee of employers and journeymen, and no alterations shall take effect except upon one month's notice by either party or the other, unless by mutual consent." [18]

[15] M. A. Schaffner, *The Labor Contract from Individual to Collective Bargaining,* University of Wisconsin Bulletin 2 (1907), pp. 70–71.

[16] Stevens, *New York Typographical Union No. 6,* p. 297.

[17] The same, pp. 300–301.

[18] The same, p. 303.

The Spread of Collective Bargaining

Gradually, in one negotiation after another, collective bargaining made headway and gained acceptance during the closing years of the nineteenth century. The national agreement negotiated in the stove foundry industry in 1891 provided a major impetus. It brought to a close some thirty years of bickering and warfare between employer and employee groups. Under the new system, committees of three from the union and three from the employers were to meet annually to draft terms covering the organized portion of the industry. (It is to be noted that despite several particularly thorny issues, such as the apprentice ratio, these negotiating committees over the years proved eminently successful in settling their difficulties without strike or outside intervention.) Local disputes, affecting only a single plant and its workers, were to be settled by the immediate parties if possible, and in the event of continued disagreement the controversy was to be referred to the national presidents of both organizations; failing their agreement, a joint conference committee similar to the original negotiating committee was to serve as final referee. This system of negotiation persists to the present day, and it is one of the oldest continuous bargaining systems still operative.

The stove agreement has been hailed by Professor Perlman as inaugurating the era of trade agreements.[19] It is true that stable agreements had been negotiated before this both nationally (in iron, in 1865) and locally (in Chicago, in the bricklaying trade), but none matched this epochal agreement for scope or stability. Coming as it did as a climax to years of friction, it served as an incentive and guide to others.

The status of collective bargaining as the century drew to a close may be summarized in the findings of the first Industrial Commission. The negotiation process was no longer novel. It was employed in numerous individual establishments, in a number of industries on a local basis (such as the building trades and printing), and in ten or twelve industries on a national basis.[20] The last fifty years had seen the systematization of philosophy and practice. The danger of another hiatus in the union movement and hence in the collective bargaining system had been removed by more effective organization.

[19] Selig Perlman, *A History of Trade Unionism in the United States,* New York: Augustus M. Kelley, Inc., 1950, pp. 142–145.

[20] The Commission found some form of collective bargaining on a national scale in the following industries: iron and steel, tin plate, bituminous coal, stove molding, longshoring, pottery, the various glass trades, general foundry, printing, and machining. In the last three there was provision only for the interpretation and application of local agreements by a national joint committee. Several of these systems—notably iron and steel—were discontinued soon after the Commission's report.

Yet there were large sectors of the economy where unionism, with its adjunct of collective bargaining, was not welcome. Effective counterorganization, well financed, sought to prevent its spread. Indeed, the *relative* unimportance of collective bargaining at this time is to be emphasized. Only a small segment of the working force was organized into unions, and only a small minority of employers were willing to recognize unions for purposes of negotiation. In some cases companies and associations negotiated only if the circumstances of union strength or public pressure made it expedient. They just as readily and expediently threw over the union and resumed an independent course whenever the situation permitted. In most cases, however, they combined actively to combat the union, often resorting to industrial espionage, blacklisting, and supplying strikebreakers to one another.[21] The steel industry, with its large-scale organization, might have provided a stability of business organization beneficial to the trade agreement system. Instead it became a stepping-stone to the formation in 1901 of the "steel trust," the gigantic United States Steel Corp. The managers of this great concentration of capital combined their vastly expanded power to stamp bargaining out of their plants. In the same year, 1901, the employers undertook in earnest an antiunion offensive. The National Metal Trades Association adopted a policy frankly opposed to collective bargaining through unions. In 1903 the National Association of Manufacturers followed suit in its "Declaration of Labor Principles." Also in 1903, more than one hundred employers' associations joined to establish the Citizens' Industrial Association as a spearhead for the "open shop" drive, as the antiunion movement came generally to be known. If the collective bargaining movement had gained ground, it had also solidified its opposition.[22]

[21] The three practices "to which workingmen most frequently object," according to the Industrial Commission of 1898 in *Final Report of the Industrial Commission,* Reports of the Industrial Commission, vol. 19 (1902), p. 890.

[22] It is perhaps worth noting that where certain unions acquired a power greater than that of the employers they faced, the system of negotiations was sometimes abandoned for unilateral imposition of terms. The report in 1915 of the second Industrial Commission appointed by Congress (Commission on Industrial Relations) described a well-defined system of union control in the San Francisco building trades at that time which duplicated the system employed more generally almost one hundred years earlier. All decisions of individual unions on wages and working conditions required the approval of the San Francisco Building Trades Council before they could be imposed. Upon such approval, the union would inform the employers when the new scale or revised conditions would go into effect.

The president of the Building Trades Employers' Association described the system before the Industrial Commission:

> There is no collective bargaining in this city, as I understand the term. The system in vogue in this city is: The unions pass a so-called law raising

One other aspect of this half century of development should not pass unnoticed. The shift from unilateral imposition of terms to joint negotiation had an interesting consequence. Under the former system, unions attempted to enforce a wage scale or working conditions conceived in their own councils. Their "demands" were terms that they actually expected to win, and hence they were adopted only when the workers were themselves convinced of their feasibility and desirability. This was equally true of the employers. But when negotiations supplanted imposition of terms, a new approach—the bargaining, or "horse-trading," approach—arose. Unions asked for more than they expected to win so that in negotiations compromise would be possible without conceding what was actually sought. Employers did the same. And as the negotiators came to recognize this tactic, original demands and counteroffers were treated lightly. They served simply to disguise the true "demands," and one function of the bargaining process became the probing by one party for the actual expectations of the other —the resistance point beyond which concession would not be made without a stand.

An indication of the change in approach is the fact that the term "bargaining" did not come into general use until after 1900 and that "conciliation" was occasionally used before this. The newer approach has sometimes been condemned for introducing a huckstering element into the conduct of business enterprises. At the same time it must not be forgotten that the tactical proposal and counterproposal are a reflection of the passage from unilateral to bilateral determination of employment conditions, of the emergence of joint decision making by workers and managers in matters of common interest.

---

the scale of wages or changing the working conditions; that is referred to the Building Trades Council for their approval; if approved by the Building Trades Council, it is put in force; sometimes notice is given and again no notice is given in spite of the fact that the Building Trades Council say that one of their laws is that a ninety days' notice must be given before a change in wages or working conditions is put into effect. The employer has no voice whatever in making the above-stated rules; the employer's part consists in making what resistance he can; this resistance has met with no degree of success, excepting cases of housesmiths' trouble in the matter of eight-hour day in structural shops. Collective bargaining, as I understand the term, presumes discussion and consultation by the parties concerned before agreements are made. Here there is no such discussion. The so-called agreement is the ultimatum of one party which the other party has no choice but to accept.

Ira B. Cross, "The San Francisco Building Trades," in *Trade Unionism and Labor Problems*, John R. Commons (ed.), Boston: Ginn and Company, 1921, p. 484.

The Employee-representation Movement: 1900 to 1925

The scientific management movement, which had begun in the post-Civil War period but did not attract widespread attention until about 1910 in this country, seemed to pose a new threat to collective bargaining. By job standardization and time and motion study it promised to remove all disputes as to what constituted a fair day's work. The increased production resulting from greater efficiency, as well as the new incentive systems presumed to be psychologically founded, would permit the earning of higher wages. By this two-pronged approach, all the traditional disputes between unions and management would be solved scientifically, and there would be little room for collective bargaining, which might only disturb the "scientific" conclusions. The decisions in those areas in which labor for so long had been fighting for a voice would be removed to an impartial, objective set of judges—the efficiency engineers. Although the movement was not explicitly antiunion, it nevertheless carried a seeming danger to the collective bargaining movement.

The fight that the unions waged against this new philosophy constitutes one of the most absorbing chapters in the history of the American labor movement.[23] For our present interest, however, it is sufficient to note that this threat to union security proved a spur to more intensive union organization, increased missionary efforts on behalf of collective bargaining, and stimulated preliminary explorations into the field of union-management cooperation for production improvement. The promise of injury was thus not fulfilled, and the problem posed was partly solved in later years when the unions won the right to question the findings of a company's efficiency engineers and even to introduce their own engineers to check on the company's experts. As scientific management became better understood, those who applied it realized that broad areas of its subject matter required value judgment rather than scientific objectivism, so that the need for consultation, negotiations, and agreement had not, after all, been removed.

A far more serious threat to collective bargaining was presented by the employee-representation movement. The first plan placed in effect is sometimes said to have been that in a Pittsburgh lamp company in the winter of 1903–1904, although Filene's of Boston sponsored certain employee activities as early as 1898. The first use of employee representation in a company with a large work force came in 1915, when the Colorado Fuel and Iron Company, with 12,000 employees, instituted one such plan.

[23] A succinct statement of the opposing views will be found in Robert F. Hoxie (with Introduction by E. H. Downey), *Trade Unionism in the United States,* New York: D. Appleton & Company, Inc., 1921, Chaps. 12 and 13.

Although there were many variations among representation plans, the basic elements were the same. It was a "constitutional" system under which the employees in an individual company or plant, shop by shop or department by department, selected representatives to a "legislature," in which management was also represented. There were generally no separate meetings of the parties—indeed the concept of parties was sometimes disavowed by substituting for it the concept of workers and management as being, together, the citizens of an industrial community. Nevertheless, although workers' representatives were permitted to raise questions concerning wages and working conditions in assembly, final decision rested with management. The whole plan thus resembled a large grievance committee through which management could learn the complaints of the workers and, in turn, convey to them what was being done on their behalf. It was more a communication system than a means of joint decision making. The latter aspect was, however, stressed by leaders in the movement, and employee representation was made to appear preferable to collective bargaining, with which strikes, lockouts, violence, picketing, and such unsavory activities were associated.

Some of those in the representation movement sought to spread the idea that employee representation was a form of collective bargaining. Certain basic differences have been pointed out, however. The two systems may be compared as follows:

Employee representation	*Collective bargaining*
Employees may be represented only by fellow employees in the same company.	Employees may be represented by anyone they choose, whether or not in employ of the company.
Committee represents the employees of only one plant or company.	Union may represent a combined unit of two or more companies; a local union affiliated with a national organization is usually obliged to secure national approval of local contracts.
No provision for appeal over management decision. Independent action by employees not contemplated.	Management decision may be contested by strike action.
Usually initiated by management.	Usually initiated by employees.

Such differences have led those making special studies of representation plans to conclude that these are "distinct and conflicting systems" diametrically opposed in principle.[24] Certainly this was the view of the trade

[24] Carroll E. French, *The Shop Committee in the United States,* Baltimore: The Johns Hopkins Press, 1923, pp. 12–15. Paul H. Douglas also discusses the differences in "Shop Committees: Substitutes for or Supplement to Trade Unions?" *Journal of Political Economy,* vol. 29 (1921), p. 89.

unions, since employee representation by its very nature operated independently of them, while collective bargaining historically was dependent upon them. And in some respects, employee representation seemed to constitute a more effective, if less direct, threat to the collective bargaining movement than espionage, blacklisting, and strikebreaking pools; for if collective bargaining was still denied by the employers, they now offered a substitute, reputedly promising the same benefits.

Federal control of labor relations during World War I led to an expansion of the unions' influence, but at the same time it stimulated the employee-representation movement. Under the National War Labor Board, management was ordered to negotiate with its employees; but except in those companies that previously had established relations with "outside" unions, management was not required to deal with other than its own employees. This for all practical purposes meant employee representation, and in fact the War Labor Board encouraged and even ordered the establishment of such systems as a means of solving local disputes and relieving itself of a potentially greater case load.[25]

After the war, President Wilson assembled a National Industrial Conference composed of representatives of management, organized labor, and the public to work out a tripartite code of industrial relations that would facilitate the transition from war to peace. It was here that the clash between union-sponsored collective bargaining and management-sponsored employee representation became most sharply defined. The points of view are illustrated by the resolutions proposed by the two groups. That suggested by management representatives was as follows:

> *Resolved,* That, without in any way limiting the right of a wage earner to refrain from joining any association or to deal directly with his employer as he chooses, the right of wage earners in private as distinguished from government employment to organize in trade and labor unions, in shop industrial councils, or other lawful form of association, to bargain collectively, to be represented by representatives of their own choosing in negotiations and adjustments with employers in respect to wages, hours of labor, and other conditions of employment, is recognized; *and the right of the employer to deal or not to deal with men or groups of men who are not his employees and chosen by and from among them is recognized;* and no denial is intended of the right of an employer and his workers voluntarily to agree upon the form of their representative relations. [Italics supplied.]

Neither the public nor the union group was willing to accept this proposal, which would have fostered the employee-representation system as

[25] A comprehensive summary of the Board's position is contained in *Report of the Secretary of the National War Labor Board* (1920), pp. 56–67.

against the collective bargaining system by permitting the employer to insist upon the former and to deny the latter.

On the other hand, the union conferees proposed:

> The right of wage earners to organize without discrimination, to bargain collectively, to be represented by representatives of their own choosing in negotiations and adjustments with employers in respect to wages, hours of labor, and relations and conditions of employment is recognized.

Those in management would not entertain this resolution, however, as it would have required the recognition of "outside" unions. The President's conference broke on this issue and was adjourned without accomplishment.[26]

But if the struggle between these two systems remained unresolved in this period, the drama of that contest should not be allowed to blind us to a significant change. In a sense, the end of World War I marked also the end of an era of industrial relations. Wartime compulsory negotiation had stimulated the employee-representation movement. The postwar drive by organized labor to substitute collective bargaining for representation had motivated a spirited defense of the latter by the employers as a group. Having thus espoused a process of *collective* representation, even though not the process sought by the unions, many employers found it difficult to retrace their steps to individual bargaining. Some found it even undesirable. From this point on, labor relations would remain largely a collective matter. The only issue was the nature of the collective agency. The situation was neatly summarized in a statement in 1920 by Royal Meeker, U.S. Commissioner of Labor Statistics:

[26] The public group was willing to accept the union proposal, but only after it had entered a resolution of its own that sought to harmonize the two views:

> The right of wage earners in trade and labor unions to bargain collectively, to be represented by representatives of their own choosing in negotiations and adjustments with employers in respect to wages, hours of labor, and relations and conditions of employment is recognized. This must not be understood as limiting the right of any wage earner to refrain from joining any organization or to deal directly with his employer if he so chooses.

The management group refused to support this resolution since it would have required their acceptance of collective bargaining whenever employees preferred this to representation. On the other hand, the union men refused to accept it since it would have forbidden the closed shop. See the account given by Judge Elbert H. Gary, appointed as a public representative to the Congress, in *Review of Reviews*, vol. 60 (1920), p. 487; also *Monthly Labor Review*, vol. 9 (1919), p. 1342.

The huge majority of employers in this country are, and always have been, opposed to labor organizations. The President's First Industrial Congress came to a deadlock on the question of the right of employees to organize and to choose representatives to deal with management. The employer group in the conference must be taken as representing the majority of employers the country over. The speeches made by these representative employers were often difficult to understand, but their attitude of mind was never for a moment in doubt. They had been driven by hard experience to abandon individual bargaining with each employee and to accept collective bargaining, but they vigorously maintained their right to dictate the terms of the collective bargain. These employers conceded the right of workers to organize in a given plant and to be represented by representatives chosen from among the employees of that plant, provided the representatives so chosen were agreeable to the management of said plant.[27]

Throughout the twenties, employee representation remained a serious threat to collective bargaining. It was estimated that in the first half of that decade the movement embraced up to 1 million employees and acquired a "firm hold" in iron and steel, machine manufacturing, coal and iron mining, textiles, food products, and public service corporations and was making its entry into railroads and meat-packing.[28]

Legal Protection, 1925 to the Present

The first effective federal legislative protection for collective bargaining was passed in 1926. Its application was limited to the railroads, which because of their peculiar public interest had received special treatment in matters of labor relations since 1888. It was the failure of the Railroad Labor Board, established under the Transportation Act of 1920, to satisfy either the carriers or the railway brotherhoods that led to the Railway Act of 1926, which was further strengthened by amendments in 1934. The right of railroad workers to negotiate through representatives chosen at their own discretion was recognized, and the duty of railroad management to negotiate exclusively with the employees' representatives on matters of "rates of pay rules and working conditions" was fixed by law. These were requirements applicable only to the railroads, however. Not only did railroad workers enjoy a strategic economic position in the nation, but they

[27] Royal Meeker, "Employees' Representation in Management of Industry," *Monthly Labor Review*, vol. 10 (1920), p. 7.

[28] French, *The Shop Committee in the United States*, p. 29. Discussion of the employee-representation movement as a stimulus to the American Federation of Labor's union-management cooperation drive will be found in Chapter 18.

also were clearly engaged in interstate commerce, an activity under the exclusive authority of the federal government.[29] Under the Supreme Court's then narrow definition of interstate commerce, almost no other groups of workers could look to the federal government for aid in organizing or encouragement in bargaining. As in the past, all except railroad employees secured collective agreements only if they were strong enough to get recognition of their unions and to force bargaining. In most states, the law created further obstacles to union organization, providing the injunction as an easily secured device by which employers might stop strikes and break up union efforts to organize or to support economic demands. The Supreme Court in a number of cases between the turn of the century and 1927 also had greatly restricted union use of boycotts and strikes, holding them to be in violation of the Antitrust Act of 1890.[30]

The first attempt to extend the benefits enjoyed by the railroaders to employees generally came in 1933 with passage of the National Industrial Recovery Act, which sought to organize business along lines of "fair competition." Its supporters hoped that it would stimulate recovery from the deep depression. The famous Section 7(a) of that act simply required that every code of fair competition contain a guarantee of the right of employees to organize and select representatives for collective bargaining. It asserted no obligation on the part of employers to *recognize* unions, however, or to bargain with them, though a labor board created to administer this vague provision, after temporizing for some months, eventually read such obligations into it. Meanwhile, employee-representation plans mushroomed. They were not forbidden by the act, and managements attempted by means of them to head off workers' own union organization.

After Supreme Court invalidation of the whole NIRA machinery and the subsequent passage of separate legislation expressly and exclusively for collective bargaining, employees in all businesses affecting interstate commerce finally received rights matching those accorded railroad employees in 1926. The National Labor Relations Act of 1935, which did not take

[29] It should also be remembered that the brotherhoods were among the oldest labor organizations in the country and were practiced in the art of legislative lobbying. Their strategic economic position would have meant little in the absence of effective political organization. The potential strength of this combination of bargaining power and strategic position is exemplified in the events leading to the passage in 1916 of the Adamson Act, which established an eight-hour day on the railroads. See *Wilson v. New*, 243 U.S. 332 (1917); and Thomas Reed Powell, "The Supreme Court and the Adamson Law," *University of Pennsylvania Law Review*, vol. 65 (1917), p. 607.

[30] For a summary treatment of the restrictions applied to unions from 1900 to 1930, see Charles Gregory, *Labor and Law*, 2d rev. ed., with 1961 Supplement, New York: W. W. Norton & Company, Inc., 1961, Chap. 7.

practical effect until after the Supreme Court upheld its constitutionality in 1937, contained unequivocal guarantees of the right of employees to form into unions and engage in concerted activity, including strike action, without fear of employer reprisal. It also contained unequivocal prohibitions against interfering with union activity or refusing to recognize and bargain with unions.

The net implication of the National Labor Relations Act was that employee organization was a matter of concern to employees only and that the employer was required to accept in good faith whatever organization his employees established and to work with it. Consequently the old employee-representation plans now became outlawed. Such plans were established by the employer, not by the employees, and hence did not fulfill the new prohibition against employer control. Thus, by legislative action, what had begun as a major threat to collective bargaining in this country was now transformed into an aid to the unions; for in the organizing campaigns that swept the country after 1937, employee-representation plans, now rendered illegal, were sometimes found by the unions to constitute effective nuclei for new unions.

The revolutionary impact of this legislative protection to collective bargaining can be seen by contrasting the situation in 1932, just prior to the passage of the National Industrial Recovery Act, with the situation obtaining fifteen years later. It has been estimated that in 1932 only about 10 to 12 per cent of industrial workers were employed under collective agreements; from 7 to 8 per cent came under employee-representation plans; and approximately 80 per cent of all industrial workers were employed under individual contracts.[31] By 1960 approximately half of all employees in manufacturing were union members; nearly one-third in nonmanufacturing were union members; and even one out of every eight in government employment was a union member.[32] (See Table 1.) And employee-representation plans had passed from the picture. The change was particularly apparent in mass-production industries, where previously collective bargaining had been virtually unknown.[33]

In viewing these remarkable developments, we should not lose sight of

[31] *Collective Agreements,* International Labour Office (1936), p. 221.

[32] *Directory of National and International Labor Unions in the United States,* Bureau of Labor Statistics Bulletin 1320 (1961), table 7, p. 51. The number of nonmembers covered by agreements was roughly equivalent to the number of members not covered by agreement. See the same, Bulletin 1222 (1957), p. 16.

[33] A full discussion of this phase of the collective bargaining movement of the thirties is contained in Emily Clark Brown, "The New Collective Bargaining in Mass Production: Methods, Results, Problems," *Journal of Political Economy,* vol. 47 (1939), p. 30.

the legal repercussion of federal protection that is perhaps of most significance to collective bargaining. The doctrine of individual freedom of contract had in previous years been raised by the Supreme Court as a barrier to union activity.[34] Employment contracts executed by individual employees were accepted as superior to any collective agreement that sought to supersede them. Now, however, it was the *collective* contract that was given primacy. "Individual contracts, no matter what the circumstances that justify their execution or what their terms, may not be availed of to defeat or

Table 1   Union Membership as a Percentage of Total Number of Employees, by Industry, 1960

Industry	Percentage	Industry	Percentage
Transportation	100	Electric and gas utilities	47
Mining and quarrying	85	Stone, clay, and glass	42
Transportation equipment	82	Petroleum, chemicals, and	
Contract construction	79	rubber	39
Telephone and telegraph	55	Printing and publishing	38
Metals, machinery and equip-		*Nonmanufacturing*	29
ment (except transportation		Service industries	17
equipment)	55	Manufacturing (not classi-	
Food, beverages, and tobacco	55	fiable)	16
Manufacturing	51	*Government*	13
Furniture, lumber, wood prod-		Trade	7
ucts and paper	51	Finance and insurance	3
Clothing, textiles, and leather			
products	49		

Calculated from data in *Directory of National and International Labor Unions in the United States,* Bureau of Labor Statistics Bulletin 1320 (1961), table 7, p. 51; and *Statistical Abstract of the United States* (1963), pp. 224–225.

delay the procedures prescribed by the National Labor Relations Act looking to collective bargaining, nor to exclude the contracting employee from a duly ascertained bargaining unit; nor may they be used to forestall bargaining or to limit or condition the terms of the collective agreement." [35]

It is unnecessary here to review the impact of the decisions of the National Labor Relations Board on the bargaining process, since we shall examine that matter more fully later. It is sufficient to recall that the NLRB definition of collective bargaining since 1935 has included the doctrines (1) that the organization chosen by a majority of employees in a defined

[34] For example, see *Adair v. United States,* 208 U.S. 161, 28 Sup. Ct. 277 (1908); and *Hitchman Coal Co. v. Mitchell,* 245 U.S. 229, 38 Sup. Ct. 65 (1917).

[35] *J. I. Case Co. v. NLRB,* 321 U.S. 332, 337 (1944).

unit or jurisdiction is the exclusive representative of all employees in that unit [36] and (2) that the parties are obligated to negotiate in good faith with the intent of arriving at an agreement which, at the request of either party, must be reduced to a written contract. The old practice of unilateral imposition of terms has been declared contrary to public policy.[37]

The passage of the Labor Management Relations Act of 1947 confirmed the policy first endorsed in the Wagner Act of 1935 and made unmistakable the public's continued commitment to collective bargaining and the protection of workers' rights to organize "for the purpose of negotiating the terms and conditions of their employment." Further, through the act, the federal government assumed almost full responsibility for regulating unions' activities and collective bargaining except where these related to purely local affairs. The Supreme Court decided that the federal government had largely preempted the area of labor-management relations, having excluded state regulation in the detailed and often intricate provisions of the laws regulating collective bargaining and other union activities in any company whose business extends beyond a state's boundaries. Though Congress has made some attempt to enlarge the area of state jurisdiction over labor matters, collective bargaining has become largely an activity of national regard, and it is likely to remain so. Later legislation such as the Labor-Management Reporting and Disclosure Act of 1959 has demonstrated again the national importance of union activities and collective bargaining. The public interest affected by union-management bargaining is primarily that of the whole nation as defined by federal legislative acts and as administered by the National Labor Relations Board.

[36] For a brief examination of this doctrine of majority representation, see the Denver Tramway case, *Decisions of the National Labor Board* (NRA), August, 1933–March, 1934, p. 64; also *National Labor Relations Board,* Sen. Rep. 573, 74th Cong., 1st Sess. (1935), pp. 13–14, and H.R. Rep. 1147, 74th Cong., 1st Sess. (1935), pp. 20–22; and Lewis L. Lorwin and Arthur Wubnig, *Labor Relations Boards,* Washington-Brookings Institution, 1935, pp. 191–195.

[37] For a comprehensive examination of the Board's rulings, see its annual reports: The Labor-Management Relations Act of 1947 added obligations resting upon the union as well as upon the employer, established certain restrictions upon strikes affecting the national health and welfare, and revised the use of injunctions and the status of damage suits for breach of collective contract, but, with only minor exceptions, it did not modify the Board's interpretation of the meaning of the duty to bargain collectively as developed over a twelve-year period. The act did specify, however, that the duty to bargain involved the union as well as the employer; previously it ran only against the employer, although the Board had in 1947 ruled that refusal of a union to bargain in good faith relieved the employer of any obligation to bargain [*In the Matter of the Times Publishing Co.,* 72 NLRB 676 (1947)].

Conclusion

We have thus come some distance, in both time and accomplishment, since collective bargaining made its entrance on the American scene. The differences between the early efforts of workers to participate in a determination of the conditions under which they were employed and their efforts today should be neither exaggerated nor minimized. Our historical survey suggests, among other things, the persistence of the basic drive among employees to organize for an effective voice in the manner and terms of their employment. It does not support the notion that workers generally have been led to organize only on the basis of false promises or coercion. The historical perspective should likewise suggest the persistence of the basic problems engendered by the drive for worker participation—the difficulties of harmonizing the interests, rights, duties, and functions of organized employees, management, and the public. The problems we face today in these respects are not new ones, though they come in different settings and with different degrees of urgency.

Collective bargaining today is to be distinguished from union-management relations in the past not only in its bilateral character (in contrast to the earlier unilateral imposition of terms) but also in its incidence, its systematization, its continuity, and its acceptance. As we have seen, today it blankets under its coverage almost half of all industrial workers and has pushed its way, though slowly and hesitatingly, into new fields, such as white-collar workers and professional employees. Though widespread variation in procedure exists, certain dominant patterns have emerged: periodic negotiations for general terms—embodied in written agreements—and a separately organized system for settling day-to-day difficulties in the shop as they arise. Although collective bargaining relationships still have a mortality rating, they are becoming more and more entrenched, particularly in the larger companies, and the possibility that collective bargaining might pass from the industrial scene is no longer a live one. This is due partly to the fact that managements now recognize the need for collective dealing for reasons of efficiency if for no others; bargaining through representatives freely selected by employees has been accepted by some, though not all, managers as a feasible and desirable method of meeting that need. In all these particulars, the practices and results of earlier days appear more primitive and meager.

In some degree, the differences between the old and the present in industrial relations may be traced to changes within the labor movement itself. It has expanded its sphere of organization and influence from a few small sectors of a largely agrarian economy to every major industrial area of a large industrial economy. It has developed highly effective institutions which integrate locally, regionally, and nationally the efforts of its members and which are capable of being used offensively or defensively, politically or economically. It has built up through such devices as welfare and retirement funds strong bonds securing the members to their unions. It has accumulated property and funds that give its institutions a stability not based solely upon membership adherence. Thus the expansion and continuity of collective bargaining are due in large part to the expansion and continuity of the labor movement, and the systematization of collective bargaining is due in some measure to the systematization of union lines of authority, culminating in the national office.

But there are causes external to unionism that also help to explain the present strength of the labor movement as well as that of the collective bargaining movement dependent upon it. One is the increased size of industrial units. When a single plant brings together thousands of workers and a single company employs even hundreds of thousands, the individual must consent to be submerged completely in such bigness, or he must make himself heard through representatives. Although at first unionism was often regarded as a challenge to the freedom of action of the individual worker, there has come recognition that it is often only through association that the worker attains a degree of control over his own affairs. This belief is now reflected in legislative protection of the collective bargaining process, protection that Congress has continued to affirm.

Our attitude toward collective bargaining has also been conditioned by the increased helplessness of the individual worker in the face of economic disaster, a helplessness engendered by specialization in production. The individual has given up most claims to general ability or multiple skills, since mass production, with its material rewards, demands almost mechanical repetition of simplified operations. Ease of replacement increases competition for jobs in times of unemployment and reduces the fearful and the dependent to positions of subservience as they seek to retain their single means of livelihood, their wage-paying jobs.[38] In this situation some protection and a greater measure of certainty are afforded by common rules jointly negotiated. Thus changes in the economy itself, chiefly specialization and concentration in production, have established a fertile soil for the growth of collective bargaining. Moreover, since collective bargaining is

[38] "The reduction of all resource for life to a money income made the holding of a job imperative; and in the new circumstance the job was in the hands of an employer to give and to take away, without warning and even without explanation. As the Industrial Revolution became more conclusive in its effect, more and more individuals were cast into complete dependence upon the job...." Frank Tannenbaum, "The Social Function of Trade Unionism," *Political Science Quarterly*, vol. 62 (1947), p. 168.

consonant with our philosophical conceptions of representative institutions based upon consent of the governed, it has to a significant degree overcome the opposition understandably evoked from those who saw in it a threat to their own interests, and it has achieved popular, though not unqualified, support. Our changing economy has emphasized the need, and our evolving democracy has approved the means.

As collective bargaining has developed to meet the needs that called it forth in a democratic society, we have found that workers, union leaders, and employers are tempted to use it only for their own needs and requirements. Thus labor regulation has come full circle; the government again finds that protection of the public interest requires checks and limitations upon collective bargaining, bargaining tactics, and union activities. Unlike 100 or 150 years ago, collective bargaining is a well-accepted institution. Those who would restrict or regulate it must bear the burden of proof, but as in earlier times, legislation and court decisions still seek not so much to limit labor's freedom as to define public interest and welfare. Even those who most heartily endorse collective bargaining realize that it poses grave problems for an industrial economy, problems perhaps more serious than those with which it confronted the young industrial system of agrarian America earlier.

Our dependence upon continuity of production in vital economic units and the interdependence of the sectors of our economy make the *private* practice of bargaining more and more difficult. Its terms and its successes have become matters of wide public interest. Mindful of European experiences, many people have become fearful of the political use which might be made of the organized economic power of workers. These are issues that cannot lightly be disregarded. Yet their solution will be dependent upon adaptations, not abandonment, of the collective bargaining system. The movement of events has not disturbed the conclusion that Justice Holmes reached fifty years ago:

> It is plain from the slightest consideration of practical affairs, or the most superficial reading of industrial history, that free competition means combination, and that the organization of the world, now going on so fast, means an ever increasing might and scope of combination. It seems to me futile to set our faces against this tendency. Whether beneficial on the whole, as I think it, or detrimental, it is inevitable, unless the fundamental axioms of society, and even the fundamental conditions of life, are to be changed.[39]

Collective bargaining, developing over a span of more than 150 years, is a constituent of this process of social change through organization. Our

[39] Dissenting opinion from *Vegelahn v. Guntner*, 167 Mass. 92, 44 N.E. 1077 (1896).

historical sojourn should demonstrate that in this respect it is as much a *part of the growth* of the economy as, for example, the corporation and the "trust." It has interacted with the society of its origin, at once the creature and creator. We should not assume that its development in this process of social ferment is at an end. As our economy and its institutional members undergo further change, so too will the system of collective bargaining.

The Negotiation Process

Let us examine in some detail a number of aspects of negotiating conferences and become acquainted with the varieties of bargaining procedures. It is worth remembering that through these procedures some of the country's most important economic decisions are reached. A single agreement, for example, may add millions of dollars to the wage bill of one company; another may determine, in part at least, the rate of introduction of technological improvements in a basic industry; or several agreements may establish the systems of industrial discipline under which a high proportion of all the country's workers work and live. Moreover, the procedures employed by unions and managements have their necessary influence on the decisions which the parties reach.

Proposals and Counterproposals

Most agreements specify a date when they will expire and when the relationship expressed by the agreement will come to an end. A few agreements, however, provide for indefinite renewal of the old provisions until new provisions are approved. Such continuation of the parties' relationship has been helpful and mutually advantageous in at least one industry, bituminous coal mining, where bluster and strife were once common. According to an official of the United Mine Workers, the parties now have an "open end" agreement. By this we mean that it has no fixed termination date. It continues in effect until terminated on sixty days' notice by either party. This method allows greater flexibility to both sides. It also removes the pressure of an impending expiration date with the ominous threat of a strike after that date. Instead, it allows time for careful negotiations and discussions to ensure the best possible agreement. In addition, the union is able to take into account the current economic status of the industry and the effect of a wage boost upon the competitive position of that industry.

In the past decade, public impatience with crisis bargaining and the complexity of many issues raised by rapid technological change have convinced union leaders and managers in a number of other industries that they might gain some of the benefits secured by labor negotiators in coal mining. In early 1963 the auto workers and two of the large automobile companies set up study groups to explore difficult issues a year before formal negotiations were to begin. In the steel industry, union and management representatives have joined in a human relations committee since 1960 to recommend solutions to difficult nonwage problems. The committee has dealt with several touchy issues—the potentially explosive matter of plant-wide seniority, the cost of medical insurance, and renovation of the grievance machinery. A steel negotiator involved reported: "I think this [committee approach] promotes a mutual search for solutions instead of an atmosphere in which the union develops demands and the company defends against them."

In most negotiations continuous exploration of issues does not take place except through the grievance procedures. The parties meet more or less formally, laying on the bargaining table proposals and counterproposals. Since the union usually initiates the bargaining negotiations, it generally has to prepare a set of "demands" for submission to the company. Where a bargaining relationship is already well established, the demands or proposals may simply be suggested modifications of isolated clauses in the existing collective agreement. In other instances, a completely new contract will be presented, ready for signature, though not all paragraphs will have undergone change. This latter practice involves, of course, an examination of the entire document by the other party to ascertain what it is that has been changed, and why.

In a conference between representatives of a local union and a plant management, the process of drafting the union's proposal is not a particularly complicated one. Possible changes are generally discussed at stewards' and union meetings, with shop officers and members having an opportunity to make suggestions from the floor. Other unions sometimes post suggestion boxes into which members drop comments. In a few cases, members may be invited to submit their ideas by mail. The material received by any of these methods is considered by a committee, usually specially chosen for the purpose. It generally includes the elected officers and often contains representatives of each of the major departments or occupations represented in the membership. The proposal finally drawn up by this committee is sometimes submitted to the union membership for ratification before presentation to the employer.

In community, regional, or national negotiations, the business of drafting the proposal becomes more complex. In the first, the local unions involved often submit suggestions by their memberships to the district council or joint board or to the officials representing the union in negotiations, who exercise their own judgement in determining what should be included in, and what excluded from, the union's demands. Sometimes in order to satisfy the desires of all constituents, no demands are excluded except those actually conflicting with others, although the committee will decide which will be pressed in conference and which will be conveniently forgotten.

In national or industry-wide negotiations, the union's proposal is generally drawn up at a regular convention or in a special conference convened solely for that purpose. The local unions' wishes are made known through formal resolutions addressed to the conference or convention, and committees or subcommittees are appointed to consider all resolutions bearing on a particular phase of the collective agreement, such as wages, hours, seniority, and so on. Approval by the full conference, committee, or convention of the final draft is required.

The impression should not be given, however, that the union members usually take an active part in determining the demands to be pressed upon an employer.

Democratic participation in making up union proposals can lead to serious difficulties. The experience of the Communications Workers of America is illustrative. Prior to 1957 the union's collective bargaining program was discussed and decided by the annual convention on the convention floor. According to an officer of the union:

> Frequently, well intentioned but emotional speeches made at a union convention resulted in CWA's making demands in subsequent bargaining completely out of keeping with the then current economic facts of life. In addition, there was a tendency to be constantly changing national bargaining items which did not afford the opportunity of continued pressure year after year, in order to achieve worthwhile objectives which were not obtainable in a single year's bargaining. The inherent weakness of this method of determining national bargaining policy was compounded by the fact that CWA conventions

are public forums and detailed public records are kept. It cannot be otherwise in a democratic organization. However, as a result, our most intimate and strategic union discussions and decisions were available and were used by managements throughout the communications industry. Union negotiators came to the bargaining table completely in the dark with respect to what management had in mind.

To overcome the handicap of too much democracy in the formulation of its proposals, the CWA placed responsibility for working out its bargaining policy with a committee of sixty members elected by delegates to the national convention in special geographic and national bargaining unit caucuses.

In most other unions, too, experience has demonstrated the wisdom of giving the responsibility for bargaining proposals to the union officers, who may work with rank-and-file committees. They are responsible, that is, for the articulation of those demands which strike some balance between what they believe their members are most desirous of obtaining and what can actually be obtained. Other considerations may enter as well, but if it is a democratic union the officers must necessarily be guided either by what they infer to be the wishes of their constituents or by what they believe will be acceptable to them.

As control of union affairs has become centralized in the hands of the national office, the degree of discretion which local unions and even joint boards and district councils may exercise in drafting some bargaining proposals has become limited. This result has come about in a number of ways. The national union may prepare a standard contract, which becomes the basis for all local negotiations; it may adopt minimum standards in certain particulars; or it may require that certain standard clauses be inserted in all contracts negotiated by affiliated locals. In some instances, the national union must approve a local proposal before it can be presented to the employer. The curtailment of local discretion in major wage decisions is simply another manifestation of the union drive, formally noted by the Webbs about sixty years ago, to standardize the conditions of employment of all workers who are potential competitors for the job.[1]

We have been speaking here of the union's initial proposal. What of the employer who may wish to make "demands" upon the union or who is faced with the drafting of a counterproposal? Individual companies com-

---

[1] Sidney Webb and Beatrice Webb, *Industrial Democracy*, rev. ed., London: Longmans, Green & Co., Ltd., 1920, pp. 715–739. The object of such standardization is, of course, to prevent the exploitation of the weakest members of the group, which might serve to drag down the wages and conditions of their fellow workers. A more recent and limited study of the effects of centralization on collective bargaining is Robert R. France, *Union Decisions in Collective Bargaining*, Princeton University, Princeton, N.J., 1955.

monly leave this task to a specially selected bargaining committee, including at least one of the major operating officials. A company's position is generally outlined in discussions between top company officials or in executive committees; less frequently, nonoperating members of the board of directors may be involved. Where a company operates more than one plant, usually representatives from all plants will be heard before a company position is adopted. In some companies where an effective communications system is at work, representatives of particular departments will be given their say before the company commits itself by making an offer to the union. In a few large enterprises formal meetings of plant and departmental representatives will approach the size of, and perform the same purposes as, a union conference at which proposals are formulated.

In some bargaining conferences a trade association may represent a group of employers. In these cases a specially elected committee or the standing board of governors will usually formulate the association's position. There are, however, a few examples of employers' associations which hold conventions to draft proposals for industry-wide negotiations in a manner closely resembling that of unions.

Even this brief survey of the procedures employed in the preparation of a bargaining proposal suggests the tactical use to which they lend themselves. We may recall from our historical investigation that in earlier years the "proposals" which were drafted were not proposals at all, but demands which the party intended to enforce by unilateral action. They were thus adopted only after those concerned—the union membership or the employers—were convinced that they were feasible. It was only with the development of bilateral negotiations and collective bargaining as we know it today that unions and employers began to exaggerate proposals and counterproposals in the *expectation* that they would be forced to recede from an initial position. The tactical rationale of many union negotiators has been that the more they ask, the more they win, at least up to a point; company representatives have tended to offer little or nothing in the hope of discouraging their employees from expecting much more. Both have believed that bargaining meant compromise and that compromise meant receding from an announced position; therefore, in order to play the game, each set its announced position—the proposal or counterproposal—high or low enough to permit plenty of "compromise." Negotiations then involved, in part, the game of discovering what the other party really was after, its irreducible minimum, and its genuine demands.

The role of the proposal in the bargaining process when it is viewed as a horse-trading process is well enough understood by union and company leaders and by the rank-and-file workers. This is perhaps the most prevalent view. Despite such an understanding, the feeling-out operation involved in the initial proposal or counterproposal has its repercussions. It is not simply a harmless bit of bluffing. For one thing, the tactical use of the bargaining demand has been extended by union leaders because of the political nature of their organizations, with officers seeking reelection and organizing new members on the strength of "promises" which are fulfilled by being incorporated in bargaining proposals.[2]

Moreover, the emphasis upon the compromise nature of proposals has often discouraged a careful examination of the economics of the firm and industry preliminary to framing demands. Since with a tactical proposal, bargaining skill is at least as important as the economics of the case in determining what concessions are won and granted, the proposal may be drafted with only a lighthearted appreciation of the business situation; members of rank-and-file committees who are drawn into the proposal procedure may easily persuade themselves that they and their fellows are "entitled" to substantial concessions regardless of the economic position of the company. This is a matter important enough to be given more extended treatment in a later section of this chapter.

Finally, the tactics of the situation require that although the general union membership may understand that they will not win all that is asked for, they cannot be told just what does constitute the prize really sought. Concessions totaling a wage cost to the company of 50 cents an hour may be incorporated in a proposal and even adopted by membership vote, with the membership kept in the dark—for fear of informational leaks destructive to a bargaining position—about whether the union is prepared to settle for 5, 15, or 25 cents or any other amount. Union leaders may use this wide margin for settlement to cloak their ignorance of the economic basis for a wise decision. Under these circumstances, it may prove difficult for the union leadership to convince the members that they should accept a counteroffer representing a small fraction of what was demanded, for the members' expectation may have become fixed around a higher figure. Internal union friction and even a strike may be the result.[3]

[2] This aspect will be developed more fully in Chapter 8, Collective Bargaining and Its Politics: The Union.

[3] Abe Raskin, editorial writer for the *New York Times*, in an article analyzing the bitter, protracted newspaper strike in New York of 1962–1963, pointed out the pernicious role that inflated demands play during the strike:

> The submission of "pie in the sky" demands by the union developed exaggerated expectations among the strikers and helped engender the disappointment reflected in the initial rejection of the Wagner [compromise] formula. The publishers inadvertently added to this rank-and-file disappointment by overadvertising Mr. Powers' [the union president] official asking price. Long after he had cut his off-the-record figure in half, the publishers kept pointing to his formal call for a $38 package. At

In more recent years a few labor organizations have slowly and partially given up the use of the tactical proposal; their negotiators have experimented with proposals which closely approximate the demands which they believe the facts warrant. They do not change their demands unless they can be shown an error in their judgment. Those who subscribe to this type of proposal believe that it is more likely to gain prestige for the union, not only from the employer but also from the union's own members. Their reasoning is that management must inevitably be led to respect the sincerity of the unions and that their members will come to realize that the union expects to make good on its demands. This approach benefits from a union research staff to gather adequate data on which such "factual" proposals may be based, although it does not necessitate one. It also seems to call for less emphasis on rank-and-file expression of desired contract changes or, alternatively and preferably, education of union members in the economic state of their company, the industry, and the economy.

In some companies, as well, the tactical proposal has been abandoned for the proposal or counterproposal which is intended as approximately the company's best offer. There is in this substitution of a demand honestly intended for a demand expected to be compromised the suggestion of a reversion to the old unilateral demand—"take it or leave it." In a case before the NLRB, a union charged one company of reverting to unilateral, and thus illegal, bargaining because it eschewed tactical counterproposals, making a firm initial offer and refusing to budge unless the union could convince it that it was "factually" in error.[4] A firm, realistic offer by a company or a demand by a union is not necessarily a reversion to the older, unilateral kind of bargaining. The analogy is misleading if the genuine proposal is an effort to narrow the area of disagreement, to reduce the friction which is engendered by seeming unconcern for the other party, and to induce greater respect for one's own views, without being so convinced of one's "rightness" as to rule out the possibility of compromise.

---

one stage the union chief admonished Mr. Bradford [the publishers' chief negotiator]: "You've got people so convinced I want $38 that if I get $34 my members will say, 'where's the other $4?' "

And so it turned out, when an agreement was finally reached after 107 days of the strike. The members refused ratification on a first vote by a sixty-four-vote margin. Only after great effort were the officers able to persuade the members to approve the agreement at a meeting the following week. For the complete story, see the *New York Times,* April 1, 1963.

[4] The case involved the International Union of Electrical Workers and the General Electric Company's bargaining strategy popularly called "Boulwarism," after the former company vice-president, Lemuel R. Boulware, who first developed it.

The Negotiating Committees

The committee which represents the local union in bargaining has generally been elected by the membership specifically for that purpose, although sometimes permanent standing committees may be entrusted with the job. Those serving on the committee have usually been members of a proposal committee or conference of the type previously described, and almost invariably the local president is included. Some large local unions encompass within their membership the workers of a number of companies, and here negotiations are usually conducted by committees of men from the particular company involved, supplemented by a representative of the local as a whole.

Local unions do not stand alone in conducting their negotiations. In most cases a representative of some larger labor organization with which the local union is affiliated will participate, bringing in both a wider experience and a freedom from the employer-employee relationship. An "outsider" owes less respect to company officials and may as a result speak more freely and forcefully. Such a representative may be supplied by the community central labor union or industrial council or by a regional office of a particular union, but most commonly he comes as a field representative of the national union to which the local is directly attached.[5] Under this latter arrangement, there may be some question of the distribution of authority between the national and local union representatives. Shall there be local determination of all matters going into the local contract, with the national representative simply offering his expert assistance, or in an effort to establish common standards throughout an area or the industry, shall the national representative be given authority over the local negotiators?

In general, unions in this country have given local unions freedom of action within the confines of certain broad standards. National representatives participating in local bargaining sessions are expected to take their cues from the local officials. Although during the sessions the national representatives may do most of the talking and the local officials and rank-and-file members remain silent, the contributions of the local members should not be underestimated. Their real function is twofold: to supply information to the spokesman for the national representative during the conference recesses and to acquaint him with the probable membership reaction to some suggested compromise. They also carry information back

[5] It was primarily this injection of an outside man, representing not only the local group of employees but also workers in that trade or industry throughout the country—that is, interests which in the eyes of the employer were extraneous to the local situation—that led to the employee-representation movement discussed in Chapter 2.

to the membership on why certain clauses found their way into the agreement or why the union did not get all that the negotiators asked for.

The national representatives at local negotiations may exercise leadership, but even in some highly centralized unions the local committee refuses to accept their leadership and makes an independent stand. In that case the national representative must usually present the case to management as the local committee wishes it presented.[6] There are exceptions, however, and in some unions national representatives are given the authority to override local will, though such power is rarely exercised because of the recognized danger of political dissension and even wildcat strikes if unwilling acceptance of a collective agreement is compelled.[7]

In the case of many craft groups, such as workers in the building and metal trades, truck drivers, printers and garment workers, negotiations in the larger cities are conducted for all local unions by a joint board or district council, usually meeting with employers' associations. In regional negotiations a conference attended by delegates of all the locals in the area is usually called, which, after framing proposals, selects a negotiating committee.

National or industry-wide bargaining is usually conducted by the top officials of the national union in collaboration with representatives of the local unions. The presence of this local representation creates a problem which has been met by a variety of solutions. Shall local representatives come instructed by their memberships regarding their course of conduct in negotiations, or shall this be left to their discretion?

After some experimentation, most American unions have adopted the view that local instruction of delegates to national conferences leads to a provincial-mindedness that may sacrifice the good of the whole union to the special interests of a small group. To avoid this danger a variety of methods have been devised to choose those representatives from the local bodies who are to participate in industry-wide conferences. The Packinghouse Workers include in their negotiating sessions as many representatives from

[6] It should be pointed out, too, that participation of a national representative in negotiations does not itself imply approval of the resulting contract by the national office. As mentioned later, top union officers may refuse to approve a local contract even though a national representative participated in its making, though such an eventuality rarely materializes.

[7] For example, in the negotiation of 1961 with the American Motors Corporation, a majority of American Motors workers ratified the agreement which set up a profit-sharing plan, but the big and important Local 72 at Kenosha voted it down. Though the international officers could have declared the agreement duly ratified, they felt that political wisdom dictated a major "education" effort in the Kenosha local preliminary to a reballoting. On the second round, a majority of the Kenosha local, as well as of all American Motors employees, approved the agreement.

local unions as each local wishes to send. Small locals may have only one, but large locals may send five to ten, making an effort to represent workers in the various departments and operations of the plants.[8] Some unions follow the Glass Bottle Blowers Association in permitting the national president to appoint the local representatives, although—as in that union—this procedure has been questioned by some locals on the grounds that certain officers should be automatically selected as representatives or that the locals should elect special representatives. The American Flint Glass Workers' Union has followed the practice of using its executive boards together with its international offices in multiemployer negotiations. A number of unions follow practices similar to those of the Steelworkers. Each of thirty districts selects a number of representatives to be members of the 130-man international wage policy committee. The number selected in each district is proportional to the district's membership. The makeup of the committee thus reflects the different kinds of workers in the union—basic steel, fabricating, aluminum, ore mining production, and clerical. Interesting compromises have been worked out by the molders' union and the National Brotherhood of Operative Potters. In the former, the president selects three conferees from a list of nine sent in by the local unions, which for this purpose are grouped into nine districts. In the potters' brotherhood, the local unions elect representatives to one of three national contract conferences which are held for major craft divisions of the union.[9]

National and local union representatives thus appear together in virtually all bargaining conferences, from those in the individual plant (where national representatives supplement the local committee) to those blanketing a large part of the industry (where local representatives supplement the national officers).

The size of the union committee sometimes becomes an issue in itself. The more men on the committee, the more possible it becomes to secure representation of particular groups within the union. Also, the larger the committee, the more informed people there are to explain the final agreement to the members and to "sell" them on it if ratification should be necessary. Large committees are not always a boon to negotiations, though. They may become unwieldy; they are more difficult to assemble, more likely to become disorderly, and more given to discussion of individual

[8] Ralph Helstein, "Collective Bargaining in the Meat Packing Industry," in *The Structure of Collective Bargaining,* Arnold R. Weber (ed.), New York: The Free Press of Glencoe, 1961.

[9] The brotherhood is organized on an industrial basis, but locals are built on craft lines, with the exception of certain "mixed" locals. Designation of locals for election of conferees is intended to provide representation for all the crafts in the brotherhood. The three major divisions are Chinaware and Generalware, Sanitary Trade, and Tile, Porcelain, and Artware.

grievances or problems of interest to one group rather than to the union as a whole. A compromise sometimes adopted calls for the selection of a large "policy" committee, to which a smaller negotiating committee reports. Policy committeemen are kept fully informed of all developments; sometimes they even sit at the conference, although they do not participate. Of course, they must approve any agreement before it is submitted to the membership. They thus shoulder responsibility for the result and can generally be relied upon to "put the agreement over" with their own constituents.

The requirement of membership ratification, by majority vote, of any agreement reached by union representatives is almost universal. If the rank and file rejects the agreement, the committee is instructed to resume bargaining with the management in an effort to secure more advantageous terms.[10] In some instances a new bargaining committee may be selected to reopen negotiations.

The union membership will almost always give its bargaining committee full authority to call a strike whenever the committee believes such extreme action is warranted. This authority, which negotiators usually seek prior to the commencement of negotiations, means that the union committee may exercise full authority to reject all proposals for a collective agreement, while having no power to conclude an agreement without membership approval.

In some cases the local conference agreement must be approved not only by the membership but also by some governing body, such as the union's executive committee or the district council or joint board with which it is affiliated. A central labor union may have to give its approval in some instances, but very rarely nowadays. In virtually all cases it must be approved by the national union, which by this veto power over local commitments gains further power to enforce the "common rule," that is, those

[10] The director of personnel administration of a large industrial concern wrote in a letter to the authors in 1961:

> When a contract is negotiated by the bargaining team, it must be ratified by a union membership meeting. The key to this control has been exercised in some cases by the refusal of the business agent to call a membership meeting for ratification until he has been willing to submit a proposal that was acceptable to him. There have been a few instances where business representatives have called meetings to reject a company proposal in order to give the union bargaining representative a solid backing for his bargaining position.

Earlier testimony from both union and management men indicates that the use of membership rejection of proposed agreement to stiffen the demands of the union negotiating committee is not new. See Neil W. Chamberlain, *Collective Bargaining Procedures*, Washington, D.C.: American Council on Public Affairs, 1944, pp. 40–41.

standards which it deems too important to the union's welfare to allow their undercutting in any locality.

In community (city-wide) negotiations, where agreements are concluded by committees representing joint boards or district councils, an agreement may require the approval of the board or council and sometimes, in addition, of the memberships of the local unions involved. In the case of regional or national negotiations, it is more common to give conferees the power to conclude agreements, though this is by no means true of all unions. Opposition to such centralization of authority has not been lacking.[11] Nevertheless, just as power over internal union affairs has steadily moved in the direction of the union's national headquarters, despite sporadic protests, so too has the power to conclude general labor agreements been accumulating in the hands of the national officers.

Certain advantages may inhere in requiring rank-and-file approval of the collective agreement. In national unions and in large local unions, leaders may become more and more removed from actual working conditions, making the agreements which they negotiate less acceptable to the workers who must live under them. The requirement of membership approval is likely to bring this condition into the open. Moreover, in unions plagued with factional disputes, not to have membership approval is to run the danger of branding an agreement with the stamp of officials whose leadership may not be accepted by an important bloc within the union. Union responsibility to adhere to the provisions of the contract may be easier to maintain if the contract is definitely tied to the rank and file by majority approval.

Generally speaking, workers are more likely to respect the obligations of an agreement to which they have given specific assent. It may also be argued that where the union's bargaining proposal is of a tactical nature— that is, where it does not represent the terms for which the union is actually

[11] The Pacific Coast paper industry provides an interesting example of such opposition. In the first (1934) negotiations between what came to be known as the Pacific Coast Association of Pulp and Paper Manufacturers and the Pacific Coast Association of Pulp and Paper Mill Employees, the employers insisted that the union representatives be fully empowered to bind their respective locals. In the 1935 conference, some union delegates came instructed by their locals and thus without full authority; employers halted negotiations until all union delegates were given unrestricted power to consummate an agreement. By 1937 some local unions had become so insistent that the employers reluctantly consented to submit the conference agreement to the local memberships for approval, with the understanding that a majority vote of all the members collectively (that is, of all local unions) would constitute ratification. In that and succeeding years, individual locals have voted to reject the agreement but have abided by the favorable majority vote.

willing to settle and where these terms are not made known—membership approval of the proposal becomes relatively meaningless, only a gesture of solidarity, and ratification of the final agreement remains its only means of indicating satisfaction or dissatisfaction with the union's bargaining program.

Despite the validity of these arguments, significant objections may be raised to the policy of limiting the authority of union negotiators by requiring a majority membership approval of the agreements which they conclude. The men who attend the conference and hear the case presented by the other party and who, in the light of that presentation, see cause to modify or refine their own positions have the benefit of information—sometimes confidential—which is not available to the general membership. Ratification by the rank and file therefore means that those with less information on which to base their judgment may reject an agreement even though it constitutes the most satisfactory settlement possible under existing conditions. Moreover, it sometimes happens that the number voting on the question of approval of the agreement is so small as to be unrepresentative of the membership as a whole, opening the possibility of rejection of an agreement reached by the union's ablest negotiators on the strength of the vote of an uninformed minority. Such an occurrence, though admittedly infrequent, serves to lessen the respect of company representatives for union organization, convincing them of the lack of "responsibility" of union membership. The union's negotiators are thus placed at a disadvantage in subsequent negotiations, since the company might justly question the degree to which the union's representatives in fact represent their membership.

Not without basis, some employers have also pointed out that where skillful negotiators have extracted from the company every possible concession but the union membership has nevertheless rejected the agreement, the company is placed in the undesirable position of having to make further, "impossible," concessions or of facing a strike. If in the effort to avert a strike the employer grants additional favors, the union membership may accept this victory as a pattern for subsequent negotiations, rejecting future conference agreements in the expectation of winning other concessions when bargaining is reopened. One company negotiator reported that from 1960 to 1962 he had experienced and noticed elsewhere "an unusual number of cases in which the bargaining committee reached agreement and recommended it to the members only to have it vigorously turned down. This obviously places both the company and the union committee in a very embarrassing position and results either in a serious strike or in a better settlement. It is a development which disturbs me greatly." Another able negotiator for a large manufacturer also commented unfavorably on the rising trend of rejections of agreements by union members in the late fifties and early sixties: "We must have responsible negotiations for the stability of the firm and labor relations; allowing relatively uninformed members to overthrow the hard work and careful study and bargaining of company and union experts just doesn't make sense. I do not see how we can continue to offer the agreement to the rank-and-file for their rejection or approval on whims."

The requirement of rank-and-file approval is time-honored, however. It goes back to the earliest organized efforts of workers in this country to influence their terms of employment. This custom of an earlier day perhaps carried greater meaning then, when the number of workers involved was small and easily assembled. In negotiations today where these same circumstances obtain, the old arguments in favor of membership approval retain their validity. But in negotiations involving not only large numbers of employees but also those employees scattered in more than one plant of the same company or in more than one company, the arguments against the requirement of membership approval attain almost conclusive force.

Under these conditions it is probable that collective bargaining would profit from a placement of full authority in the hands of union negotiators. Of course, certain precautions have been suggested by those favoring such a course. First, negotiators must be wary of making inflated demands, since these may encourage the members to expect more than can be secured. Second, and as an accompaniment of the first, an educational program for the membership is needed in order to acquaint them with the economic conditions in which bargaining is to take place, a program preferably coupled with well-planned economic research. Third, in order to secure union negotiators most capable of understanding and evaluating issues brought forth at the bargaining table, their appointment by the union president rather than election by rank and file would seem desirable, since such a procedure would presumably stress ability rather than popularity as the basis for choice. And fourth, in order to maintain the responsibility of union officials to the membership, assurance of periodic democratic elections within the union should be provided. This last condition is now largely met by the Landrum-Griffin Act of 1959, providing for regular secret-ballot elections.

Let us turn our attention now to the company negotiators. Here practice is almost as varied as with the unions. Nevertheless, it is probably true that companies today are more and more placing responsibility for collective bargaining on line executives, such as the president or operating vice-president. Industrial relations directors frequently participate in the larger corporations, but primarily as advisers and consultants.

Just as labor unions have introduced into conferences representatives of organizations with which they are affiliated, so many companies, particularly the smaller ones, have been assisted by "outsiders." These may be staff members of general employers' associations or representatives of trade associations of which the company is a member. In some few instances such associations may take over completely the conduct of negotiations, or its representatives may form a majority on the negotiating committee.[12] When a number of employers band together into an association and bargain jointly through it, more formal procedures must be adopted. Occasionally the bargaining committee consists of a representative of each member of the association, but, as in the case of local unions in national negotiations, the resulting committee may be unwieldy in size. A smaller committee is therefore generally chosen by the group, either by election or by appointment of the president or manager of the association.

In the same way that labor unions have sometimes sought to secure representation of occupations or departments on their negotiating committees, so many employers' associations have given specific representation to special-interest groups within their membership. Thus the labor committee of the Massachusetts Leather Manufacturers' Association is selected from all the branches of the industry covered by the association—calfskins, kid leather, side leather, sheepskins, and splits. The labor committee of the United States Potters' Association is intended to give representation to Eastern as well as Western members, to china as well as semiporcelain manufacturers, and to small as well as large plants. A former president of the San Francisco Employers' Council expressed a view still maintained by the council: "Where the employers' bargaining unit is composed of a number of units of the industry with special problems, it is advisable to have a

[12] An example provided by the Glass Container Manufacturers' Institute, which represents the major container manufacturers and suppliers of materials and negotiates major agreements for some sixty-two members. The institute, incorporated in 1945 to promote the industry's varied interests, represents thirty-five manufacturers of glass containers, six manufacturers of closures (bottle caps, stoppers, and corks), and twenty-one suppliers of raw materials or equipment used in making glass containers or closures. Of these sixty-two member companies, fifty-six are in the mainland United States, one is in Puerto Rico, four are in Canada, and one is in the Philippines. Institute member companies located in the United States produce more than 90 per cent of all domestic bottles and jars.

Each company that is signatory to a labor contract has one member on the institute's committee on labor relations. This group, in turn, elects a negotiating committee of six, which, with the institute's director of labor relations and members of the institute staff and council, works out contracts with the two principal unions. On the West Coast, a single contract covering most of the other employees is arrived at in meetings with the Glass Bottle Blowers Association. Elsewhere, contracts for these small groups of other workers are negotiated individually by each company.

representative of each unit on the committee; for example, in our restaurant negotiations, we negotiated a master contract on behalf of the dairy lunch houses, cafeterias, A and B restaurants and tea rooms. A representative of each of these types of services was included on the committee."

The degree of authority held by management's bargaining agents to bind the company varies considerably from instance to instance. Full power to commit the company to agreement reached in conference is most commonly found when the president is on the negotiating committee. When the president is not a member, the committee may be empowered to make decisions on minor matters but be obliged to refer important questions to the president or an executive committee. In some companies all concessions by management representatives are subject to final approval by higher authority. If the negotiators have too little authority for the negotiating responsibilities they face, collective bargaining suffers, to the detriment of both management and union. In a study of bargaining in the trucking industry, it was charged that "in too many places the task of setting policy for an area-contract negotiation was delegated to third and fourth echelon managers." The result was that in many industry associations, top managers defected from the associations' labor policy, causing a breakdown of the industry front.[13] In certain industries, such as automobile parts, railroads, and coal, unions have at times complained that the discretion of management negotiators has been limited by the influence of "outsiders" such as bankers or important customers.

Despite the fact that the negotiating committees of many companies must thus secure the approval of officials above them before making binding commitments, this process of ratification is generally less formal and less difficult than is the case with the unions. Close collaboration between interested officials is usually maintained, so that the conference agreement is likely to be one that has already received the sanction of those in authority. This difference in the case of ratification is made possible because ultimate union authority rests with the membership at the base of the organizational pyramid, while company authority is concentrated at the apex.

The problem is not so simple when negotiations for a company are conducted on a plant-by-plant basis, however. An official of the company —vice-president or industrial relations director—may sit with plant management, guiding negotiations and rendering the more important decisions in line with general company policy, or plant management may be left to

[13] See the report of A. Ewing Greene, Jr., past chairman of the American Trucking Association's industrial relations committee, entitled *Collective Bargaining in the Trucking Industry* (1962). A reprint of the official summary is found in *Collective Bargaining, Negotiations and Contracts,* Washington: Bureau of National Affairs, 14:51 (February 1, 1963).

negotiate alone but with the necessity of referring decisions on the more important issues to the central office for approval. This latter policy may introduce considerable delay into the agreement-making process, and union negotiators have sometimes become impatient with the lack of authority displayed by plant management in such situations. The following verbal exchange, which occurred in one bargaining conference, is illustrative. The union was asking for a 10-cent-per-hour increase, and the plant management had tentatively offered to compromise at 7 cents, provided it could secure the consent of top company officials.

Union Representative   You said: "Would you take 7 cents for a compromise" . . . isn't that right . . . "subject to the approval of the company?"

Plant Representative   That's right.

Union Representative   And you say the company wouldn't approve that?

Plant Representative   Yes. And, as I've said before, I'm quite sure that the record will show that I offered that subject to the approval of the company, as you yourself have mentioned.

Union Representative   That's the way I remember it.

Plant Representative   I said that it had to go back to the company for their approval.

Union Representative   That's right . . . you did say that . . . but if you people can't bargain up here . . . if you have to go back every time you offer something . . . why don't you bring them up here . . . and let's thresh it out right here. If you have no authority to offer anything, that would seem like the thing to do.

Plant Representative   We have offered . . . and when it comes to trading, you said yourself you didn't have the authority to offer to accept the 7 cents . . . that you'd have to go back to your men.

Union Representative   That's right . . . sure!

Plant Representative   Suppose they had told you: "No, we're going to stick to the 10 cents." You would then have had the same situation I was in.

More commonly, however, a plant management whose authority is limited will not suggest a counteroffer until it has already received the sanction of top company officials. This practice, however, obviously does nothing to expedite agreement.

In contrast to the centralized control, some companies have granted extensive authority to individual plant managers in their collective bargaining relations with the union. In such cases, as one industrial relations executive remarked, the plant managers may be considered "the ultimate authority in their own plant labor relations, answering for their policies with their jobs." This practice, with respect to the negotiation of the general terms of union-management relationships, is on the decline, however. Increasingly, union and management representatives are negotiating on a company-wide basis, establishing the terms of wage changes, pension benefits, length of workweek, health and welfare provisions, union security, and grievance procedures. Since experience has demonstrated the wisdom of not trying to settle all matters affecting labor through centralized bargaining, increasingly unions and management are conducting bargaining sessions at both the company-wide and the local plant levels. The local supplementary negotiations deal with such subjects as wage differentials among job classifications, seniority arrangements, work sharing, administration of layoffs, scheduling of hours and vacations, and time-study procedures.

Supplementary local negotiations have the merit of allowing those union leaders and managers who are best informed about particular issues to resolve them. They also help assure local people that their problems will not be ignored or swept aside in the rush and trouble of settling the large, overall issues. In recent years local negotiations have proved to have some serious drawbacks, however. A settlement at the national level does not necessarily mean that strikes will be avoided at the local plant level. In both the automobile and the steel industries, companies have been plagued with local strikes for weeks after the general master agreement has been ratified.

The director of industrial relations of one of the major rubber companies wrote privately:

> Our company-wide agreements cover only partially many subjects which are dealt with in their entirety in the national agreement in many other industries. As you know our master contract has a very considerable supplement attached to it at each of our many plants, and this supplement is negotiated after the master contract has been signed and ratified. I must say that over the years we have wondered whether this double exposure to strikes first on the national level and then at the local level was justified.[14]

[14] To meet some of the problems and dangers of local along with national bargaining, officials of the Ford Motor Company responded in 1961 as follows:

> In view of the scope and number of local negotiations which were to take place at plants and parts depots and the expected emphasis by the UAW, certain procedures were followed which were felt to be extremely helpful. Detailed instructions were sent to all Company locations explaining which issues were to be discussed locally and which were to be discussed nationally in the Company's view. The rationale for the Company's position on the various issues was also explained in order that discussion could take place as to why an issue was local or national. This aided in reducing disputes at the main bargaining table and, more importantly, provided a common approach to local negotiations at the various Company locations. Very beneficial, from Ford's standpoint, was the establishment of a large telephone center with direct lines for each Com-

Negotiations conducted at both the company-wide and the local levels result in some of the same complexities which negotiators for employers' associations face. Since they bargain for memberships, sometimes of considerable size, the impact of the agreement upon the association's members must always be considered.[15] In some associations, the negotiated agreement becomes binding upon members only if they individually sign it. Under such an arrangement, the member may elect to accept or reject the terms reached in conference; the association which represents him has no power to compel his acceptance of the agreement reached with the union, and any compulsion to force the member's adherence to its terms must be brought by the union itself. On the other hand, a number of associations delegate full binding authority to their bargaining representatives, so that members are automatically committed to any conference agreement.[16] In between these extremes, there are various degrees of authority: limitation of discretion on certain vital issues; limitation of discretion within a broad framework; or requirement of ratification by a majority vote of the membership or the board of directors or—in rare instances—by a unanimous membership vote.

Division of managerial authority or failure to clarify the limits of authority of management's negotiators has sometimes been as annoying to union representatives as the latter's lack of binding authority has at times been to management. Not only is any agreement delayed, but the union may find itself in the position of shadowboxing, not knowing whether its views are reaching those who have the power to say "yes," and even reduced to the necessity of calling a strike to secure consideration. This sort of situation was revealed in one National Labor Relations Board case, where an editor

---

pany Division which kept up-to-date contacts with the plants. This provided liaison with the main bargaining table so that the status of local negotiations was always available on a moment's notice.

[15] This is a matter to be examined in Chapter 9, Collective Bargaining and Its Politics: Management.

[16] In 1960 a clothing manufacturer closed his New York plant and surreptitiously moved all equipment and unfinished garments to a new plant in Coffeeville, Mississippi. An arbitrator found that the manufacturer was bound by the provisions of the Market Agreement of 1957–1960, which had been negotiated and signed by the New York Clothing Manufacturers' Exchange, Inc., and the New York Joint Board of the Amalgamated Clothing Workers of America. The manufacturer had been a member of the exchange when the agreement had been entered into and had continued his membership up to the time he left New York. See *Jack Meilman*, 34 LA 771. The arbitrator's decision was later upheld by a justice of the New York Supreme Court. *The New York Times*, October 20, 1960. For other similar cases, see *Sidele Fashions, Inc.*, 36 LA 1364 (1961); and *Judy Bond, Inc.*, 38 LA 1711 (1962).

of a newspaper had been sent in to negotiate for the publisher. In his subsequent testimony before the Board's examiner, he stated: "At no time throughout the negotiations was I ever under the delusion that I had any authority to sign a contract." When asked what he did have the power to do, he replied: "I don't know. I was never told." The trial examiner reported further: "The terms of a proposed contract were discussed and certain agreements were tentatively reached. Management's representatives, however, refused to initial such clauses as were tentatively agreed upon. The meeting adjourned with representatives of management again promising they would attempt to ascertain the extent of their authority." [17]

Conference Organization

Collective negotiations, particularly in smaller companies, are sometimes conducted without formal organization. Other bargaining sessions have been organized more systematically. The chief purpose of this more formal constitution is to provide a moderator who, even though he is a member of one of the partisan groups, is given the task of bringing some procedural order into negotiations, which otherwise may easily break down into a series of undirected and sometimes impertinent arguments. Where the number of representatives is large, a chairman may be necessary, if only to preserve order by recognizing speakers. A perceptive negotiator and labor student mentioned recently that he has noted a subtle change in the organization of bargaining conferences:

> Up until the last decade bargaining sessions were widely regarded as the province of the union and the union spokesman tended to be the dominant figure in the sessions. Now, with the unions' very strong interest in protecting the status quo, I observe more of a tendency for the session to be regarded as a joint affair, but with the management spokesman tending to act as chairman, to the extent that function is performed at all.

Because a moderator chosen from among the bargainers does not have to be neutral, occasional use has been made of an impartial chairman. This practice is more common abroad than in the United States. It occurs in this country most frequently when a conciliator is brought into the picture and acts as a chairman, though not formally selected to fill that role. Officials of the Federal Mediation and Conciliation Service or of state mediatory agencies are called upon to help, particularly in negotiations between managers of smaller companies and local unions. Unfortunately the conciliator is usually introduced only after an impasse has been reached, and he is thus

[17] *In the Matter of Republican Publishing Co. et al.*, 73 NLRB 1085, 1102–1103 (1947).

placed at a decided disadvantage. Not only must he perform the customary chairmanship tasks of preserving order and encouraging agreement through procedural devices, but he must as well attempt to provide a solution to end the deadlock. Conciliators are in almost unanimous agreement that the earlier they participate in negotiations, the more likely they are to succeed in helping the parties reach agreement. They become more familiar with the issues and thus are better prepared to suggest compromise solutions; also, a neutral party capable of exercising to the greatest advantage the functions of conference chairman may steer the conference to agreement—avoiding deadlock altogether—by suggesting and enforcing procedural devices which avert argument. These devices may include appointing a subcommittee to investigate a particular question and report back to the full conference, supplying the conferees with information they may not have at hand, or calling in outside expert opinion to settle factual disputes.

In addition to the chairman, a conference secretary is sometimes appointed, though less frequently. Generally, each party will name one of its own members to take notes, although sometimes no record of any sort will be made. At the other extreme, court recorders are sometimes hired to make a verbatim transcript of proceedings. Although once favored and used in a fair number of negotiations, verbatim transcripts are much less popular today. A complete record was usually made so that future arbitrators could refer to it for an interpretation of what the conferees really meant when they finally agreed upon some clause, just as federal courts turn to the *Congressional Record* to interpret the intent behind legislation. A conference record was to help establish beyond dispute just what agreements or commitments the parties might have made that were not reflected in any written contract. The keeping of verbatim records has drawbacks, however. The insistence by only one of the parties upon such a record often has been considered by the other to be suggestive of distrust, arousing a feeling of antagonism. Other objections have been based on the belief that frankness is inhibited when every remark goes into the record and on the discovery that the verbatim account is not always useful in interpreting the meaning of contract provisions but all too often requires a "secondary interpretation" itself.

The use of joint conference subcommittees for a variety of purposes is one organizational device which has proved particularly helpful. The spokesman for a large manufacturer explained the role of subcommittees in negotiations in this way:

> The role of the subcommittee varies substantially, based on the bargaining situation. But in any major situation today [1962] where there are complex employee benefit plans involved, it would seem almost imperative to arrange for subcommittees in order to make meaningful progress. Aside from the formal subcommittees of the

main national negotiating team which were established on highly technical issues such as pensions, insurance and supplemental unemployment benefits, there were times when it was advisable to establish committees to discuss issues affecting a group of company locations or a group of company employees. For example, certain company and union personnel joined together to discuss and attempt to resolve an issue of the assignment of certain type of work in parts depots. The issue was not common to all company employees but was more or less common at all parts depots. Certain issues involving skilled maintenance and construction employees throughout the company were discussed in subcommittee meetings. While the meetings of these subcommittees did not necessarily lead to agreement on these issues, reports were issued to the main table ultimately leading to resolution of the issues.

The manager of labor relations in another large firm pointed out the bennefits of subcommittees but also indicated a trouble point:

> They are particularly helpful in solving knotty or highly technical problems of the agreement. We may agree on the pattern in our top-level negotiations without fixing the details. The major task of the technical subcommittees, then, is to apply the principles we had negotiated to the particular context. This has led to some disagreements, primarily as a result of the efforts of union technicians to apply "frosting to the cake," in the words of the union president.

Subcommittees have also been fruitfully used when issues prove to be too comprehensive or complex to allow of settlement during the conference itself but can be deferred to postconference deliberation. In this latter use, the subcommittee's agreement sometimes requires the ratification of the original conference or a succeeding conference before being submitted to the union membership or before becoming effective.

Conference Procedure

In the actual negotiations between the bargaining parties, there may be no ordered procedure or only a very informal procedure. This is particularly true of local negotiations. Describing his own experience, one union representative remarked: "There is no order at a conference. If the boss wants to go fishing, the union goes fishing with him. If he wants to talk about baseball, you talk about baseball. If the union is strong, the reverse may be true." This lack of procedural plan is in part due to a belief by some that any semblance of parliamentary order makes the conference stilted, puts every man on his guard, and renders agreement more difficult. Nevertheless, most bargainers have developed certain broad patterns of negotiating to which they adhere.

Preliminary informal meetings of the bargaining parties have occasionally been held to establish the order and scope of bargaining conferences. More informally, there is sometimes only an agreement between the parties on the order in which issues shall be discussed.

Especially in large-scale negotiations, the conference may begin with an opening statement by leaders on both sides, perhaps with a general discussion by other participants. This opening session sometimes offers the only real opportunity for including all conferees in the negotiations, if their number is large, the actual bargaining then being delegated to a subcommittee. Such preliminary discussion is usually followed by a presentation of specific proposals, most often by the union, since it is usually the union which is pressing for changes. This presentation consists of a reading of the desired terms followed by a brief justification. If the other party has not yet had an opportunity to consider the demands or prepare a counterproposal, there follows an adjournment to allow for this. Upon resumption and a reading of the counterproposal, bargaining will begin in earnest.

When the chairman of each committee knows within what limits it may make concessions, this bargaining may take place across the table in open meeting. The more common procedure, however, is for the side receiving a proposition to caucus following conference discussion, in order to prepare its response. These caucuses may consume a large part of the conference time. A national official of one union has added that frequently there is more wrangling in the committee caucus than there is in actual negotiations between the two parties.

An issue which cannot be settled after an initial discussion is generally tabled for the time being. In the course of agreement on other matters, some settlement of the tabled proposition may become apparent, or, in the light of other concessions, the party which had proposed it may withdraw or compromise it. In reaching a conference agreement, unit voting is almost invariably employed; that is to say, each party votes as a group. In reaching agreement within the group, sometimes a unanimous vote of all committeemen is required, while in other cases a simple majority is sufficient.

As agreement is reached clause by clause, some negotiators begin the construction of the new contract, so that the progress of the conference is clearly indicated. Until the conclusion of the entire contract and its approval in its entirety by both parties, however, any agreement upon particular issues is recognized as only tentative, for the clauses of a contract may be interrelated. The settlement of one may affect the determination of another, and a concession on one clause won early in the conference may be traded for a concession on another, more important issue sometime later.

Use of Economic Data

In discussing the proposal procedure and the choice and authority of the negotiating committees, we had occasion to inquire into the effect of the procedures employed upon the use of relevant factual information. We have observed how the abandonment of unilateral imposition of terms and the resort to bilateral negotiation introduced an element of horse trading or huckstering into decisions concerning the conditions under which workers would be employed. We have also seen that bilateral negotiation does not require gross exaggeration and that in some few instances attempts have been made to rest joint decisions more solidly on an economic basis by taking account of the pertinent data. We may now profitably inquire more fully into the general question of the use made of information concerning the economic circumstances of the business or industry in arriving at collective agreements.

It is of course true that in *all* collective bargaining, *certain* economic data inevitably intrude as considerations, either to one party or to the other or to both. Such data may be the average wage paid to workers in a company or industry; changes in the cost of living; the total additional cost entailed by a specific wage increase; the per unit labor cost of production, additions to that cost which a wage increase necessitates, and possible consequent effects on sales price; comparative wage structures of competing companies; or the profit position of the company. Our question, however, involves the extent to which such information plays a role in the conclusion of the trade agreement. Are such economic data admitted as factors controlling the settlements reached, at one extreme, or are they ignored in the bargaining process?

The experience of negotiators has been widely varying on this score. Both extremes of opinion are represented, but the consensus falls somewhere between. There are those who from their experience contend, as one industrial relations manager does, that the economic fact "doesn't amount to a damn in helping to reach an agreement. The real basis for agreement is the fear that there will be trouble otherwise." Similarly, an international representative of one union has declared: "High wages and better working conditions are not won by argument, but by the only weapon workers have—the right to strike. All the data and arguments presented don't convince the employer. The union is willing to show why it makes certain demands, but the basic question is not how strong a case the union presents in argument, but, will my plant operate or will it not?"

Other negotiators, although unwilling to deny that factual data have some significance in collective bargaining, stress their limited value. One coal operator and frequent official of the Appalachian coal conferences has said that factual data are of value in keeping wage demands within competitive limits—"in preventing the union from making such excessive demands that substitute fuels will be given a boost"—but that in helping to determine just *what* wage increase shall be asked and granted, they are of no significance. The executive vice-president of an Eastern manufacturing corporation, in somewhat the same vein, says: "The statistical facts of the case may not warrant the terms of the final agreement, for there are many points which influence the final results. Nevertheless, without factual information the results may easily be less satisfactory to all."

Perhaps the most prevalent attitude among both union and company representatives is that the role of factual data in negotiations is not as significant as it deserves to be, though the use of these data is increasing and will probably continue to increase. Sensible administration or even establishment of many of the new pension, health, welfare, and unemployment programs requires detailed statistics and much factual information. As important, perhaps, is the fact that such programs also generate statistics which have uses elsewhere in bargaining.

Economic data undoubtedly deserve a place of greater importance in negotiations, and the adequate collection of pertinent information might well encourage greater reliance upon it in concluding the trade agreement. At the same time, it may be asked why, if some negotiators have found the use of such factual information valuable in helping to reach agreement, has its use not become more widespread, and, as a result, why has not the accumulation of adequate pertinent data been more stimulated? The answers to these questions are to be found in the manner in which economic data have largely been employed in collective bargaining.

With few exceptions, they have been injected into negotiations by one of the parties as an argument to bolster its position; they have seldom been introduced by both parties as the basis for arriving at agreement. After deciding on its bargaining position, each side makes selective use from among available data of whatever will support its demands. There is seldom any consideration given to a procedure whereby each party contributes relevant information which will add up to the total situation in which the joint decision must be made. Facts are regarded as "bargaining cards" to be played or withheld as tactical considerations warrant. One company negotiator stated:

> Over the past twenty years the use of and reliance upon economic and statistical data in negotiations has grown very rapidly. As nearly as I can tell, both sides are making much more use of objective materials, statistics, and survey information. At the same time, however, it is my impression that such materials appear less and less at the table. Each side is better prepared and the other side knows he is. Each holds its own data to itself. They are reluctant to use data

jointly or any other objective materials for they may not support the positions that they have already taken.

In thus referring to facts as argumentative weapons in one approach and as grounds for agreement in another, no suggestion is intended that agreement flows naturally out of the facts of a case; often argument arises as to what facts are relevant. Even with complete agreement on all the facts, disagreement is likely to emerge over their interpretation. Nevertheless, if collective agreements are to have any basis in rational calculation, continued and increasing resort to the available pertinent data is to be encouraged. If instead of combating one alleged fact with another the parties would seek preliminarily to establish jointly what the facts are, agreement could be reached with fuller knowledge of the consequences, or individual positions could be maintained with greater assurance.

Some of the obvious—and important—consequences of the policy of using facts as arguments (as in a debate) rather than as a basis for agreement (as in a government commission) have been the following: (1) discouragement of the development of adequate research facilities by both employers and unions, since "factual argument"—however unreliable—may be secured simply by resort to the many partisan sources available to both groups; (2) development of an attitude of disrespect toward all economic data, since they are regarded only as arguments to be supported if they turn in favor of the bargainers or rebutted or ignored if they weigh against them; and (3) placement of the bargaining relationship primarily upon the basis of crude economic strengths in antagonism, thus postponing a more mature union-management relationship.[18]

[18] Alfred Beret, president of the American Federation of Hosiery Workers, declared in 1963 that the following statement, made almost twenty-five years ago, reflects the thinking of the union officers today and is "as currently applicable and appropriate as it was in 1940":

> It must be rather evident to all those who have been actively participating in negotiations with employers that today conditions have introduced a factual basis for negotiation and labor relations to an extent that some of the methods used by old-time labor leaders would be laughed out of existence if attempted. It is the purpose of having a research department to record accurately all such information as will serve the membership of the union in their attempts to analyze and more intelligently evaluate those problems which come before them.
>
> Statistics and statistical compilation in themselves serve no end and can establish no formula for the solution of problems other than offering the means for the evaluation of economic policies or the analysis of our economic problems. It is quite possible that the information assimilated, tabulated and analyzed by the research department may in many cases displease individuals or local unions. To do otherwise than to record

The economic data developed by union and management research organizations and presented at the conference table have usually been intended less as a basis of agreement than as a point of attack. This "factual argumentation" in collective bargaining has resulted not only in the destruction of much of the value of such data as are obtainable but also in the denial to the other party, where this is possible, of such data as may support its case, however pertinent these data may be. Unions have often maintained that they have a moral right to secure from companies information, generally of an accounting nature, concerning their financial position, although this "right" has frequently been denied by management.[19] The denial of this information may be viewed as a negative form of "factual argumentation." At the same time, one reason why managements have declined to submit company data to union representatives has been that they fear that union negotiators will distort such data to provide factual argument rather than use them in a genuine effort to arrive at demands which are economically justified.

The long-run economic effects of this method of using economic data may be disadvantageous to both parties involved. This method may also have an immediate effect upon the bargaining process itself. This, primarily, has been to inject into negotiations disputes over facts, in addition to the disputes over interests with which collective bargaining is primarily concerned. Negotiations may become weighed down with lengthy and meaningless arguments over the validity or invalidity of several conflicting

---

accurately and analyze honestly, however, would be folly, and to attempt to please any one person or group of persons would mean merely a waste of time, effort and money by this Federation in maintaining a research department.

[19] A spokesman of the Ford Motor Company replied as follows when asked about the use of cost data in labor negotiations:

While Ford attempts to place costs on union demands wherever possible, these costs do not form the sole basis for Company positions inasmuch as it is felt that the matters to be bargained over are the wages and benefits to be provided to employees represented by the union in light of sound business judgments and economic and public policy. Discussions purely on the basis of costs can result in management abdicating its responsibilities to its employees by allowing the union to dictate benefits, provided the costs are not too high. Management's responsibility goes far beyond determining how much it will pay for its work force.

Since internal studies often appear self-serving, reference is often made to studies conducted by governmental agencies and other neutral sources. It is questionable except as they support the general philosophy of the parties, how much of a role such studies play in resolution of the issues involved.

sets of figures purporting to explain the same situation. On occasion, such debate has actually descended to the level of a juvenile street argument. Moreover, it is fully as pointless, since neither party is interested in eliciting the facts of the situation but only in destroying the other's position to support its own.

While in a few rare instances economic studies made by one of the bargaining parties independently of the other have been accepted by both as a valid basis of negotiations, the net result of treating fact as argument has been to discredit independent studies. Each party lacks confidence in the data which the other supplies, to the extent that even when union representatives complain that companies deny them access to their books, they will sometimes add that the figures they do obtain are usually untrustworthy. It is not surprising, then, that there are those who maintain that in arriving at agreement, factual considerations are of little significance.

The disadvantages of such misuse of economic data have not gone entirely unnoticed by those immediately involved. Because the need for facts as a basis for negotiation and agreement is great and because it cannot be satisfied by independent collection of information of unquestioned validity, attempts have occasionally been made to secure an agreement on the pertinent facts of a situation. By this process of factual accord, both bargaining parties reduce the area of conflict, expediting and facilitating agreement on issues of interest. Such determinations of fact may take the form of attempts to reconcile conflicting sets of data prepared by the bargaining parties independently; agreement on a source of data to be accepted by both groups as authoritative; establishment of joint fact-finding commissions, either permanent or *ad hoc* in nature; or joint employment of impartial third-party investigators.

There is no doubt that a number of negotiators, both union and employer, are becoming interested in the possibilities of the factual approach to collective bargaining. At the same time, while encouraging such an approach, some employers have not recognized that this attitude on their part involves a moral obligation to supply the unions with such company records as will permit the drafting of factually based proposals, provided, of course, that the union has established its own good faith. Little can be done by either party without a sympathetic response from the other.

A factual basis for collective bargaining probably offers considerable hope for a more smoothly functioning employer-union relationship, but it guarantees no millennium in which the lion shall lie down with the lamb. As has been noted, divergent interpretations of jointly determined fact will still provide conflict, and disagreement will arise over the relative weights to be accorded various economic considerations. Moreover, it is apparent that data are useful only insofar as procedures are devised and accepted for making use of them. As yet such devices as the joint conference for exploring and agreeing upon the relevant data are not common.

Perhaps the basic impediment to the use of economic facts in reaching agreement lies in the conception held by the parties of the nature of the bargaining process itself. We shall examine this question in a later chapter.

Resolution of Deadlocks

Despite the most earnest efforts to reach agreement, there may come a time in any bargaining conference when each party feels that it has compromised as much as is feasible, and deadlock may ensue. In an attempt to get negotiations off dead center, the conferees may resort to mediation. In mediation, a neutral third party enters the negotiations, and if he secures the confidence of both groups, he hears from each, privately, its version of the reasons for the impasse and the circumstances under which it may be willing to make further concessions. To the neutral agent the negotiators may be willing to confide an inclination to yield ground, provided the other party gives way too. Learning the true resistance point of each, the mediator may be given the key to agreement. In other conferences one or both groups may have maneuvered themselves into positions from which they can retreat only with loss of prestige, and the intervention of the mediator provides an opportunity for each to give ground, in response to the suggestion of a disinterested outsider, without seeming to yield to the other.

Despite a feeling on the part of some union leaders that an appeal to a mediator to intervene is a sign of weakness, indicating a willingness to make further concessions and an inability to rely on one's own strength, and despite the belief on the part of a number of employers that governmental conciliators are biased in favor of organized labor, there has been a greatly increased acceptance of mediation by both groups in the last twenty years. Some international unions now require their chartered locals to use the Federal Mediation and Conciliation Service before dissolving the bargaining conference, and some collective agreements provide for the calling in of a mediator should a deadlock be reached in negotiations for the subsequent agreement.

If mediation fails or if the issues in dispute are so sharply drawn that the negotiators feel a resort to mediation would be fruitless, the two parties may sometimes agree to arbitrate their differences. There has been some increase in the use of this method of reaching agreement, though it is still uncommon. A few unions maintain a staff of experts whose chief function is to assist local unions in the preparation and presentation of their cases before arbitration boards, and some industries have established their own arbitration councils.

Many negotiators, probably a majority, still frown on the arbitration of contract terms. Some union representatives claim that arbitration boards consciously or unconsciously are usually biased against labor, and some employers believe that the arbiter customarily settles disputes by "splitting the difference," so that the union must always win concessions, and the employer must always lose. Companies sometimes oppose arbitration on the grounds that it grants control of company policy to an outside agency, thus representing an improper delegation by management of its responsibilities. Both groups have charged that arbitrators are seldom versed in the economic and technical aspects of the company or industry, so that their decisions are necessarily ill-advised. Some have claimed that agreement upon the arbiter is as difficult as agreement upon the issue in dispute and that the cost of arbitration proceedings is an impediment to its use. A frequent criticism by union representatives is that the delay involved sometimes postpones settlement for such a length of time that the morale of the union membership may be broken.

If all possible efforts at agreement through direct negotiation or mediation have failed and if the parties are unwilling to accept settlement by arbitration, the resolution of the deadlock will usually come through strike or lockout. Examination of this exercise of bargaining power will, however, be reserved for a later chapter.

The Final Agreement

Our brief examination of the history of the collective bargaining movement in this country revealed that most early agreements were oral. The National Labor Relations Board has outlined four situations in which this is most likely to be the case: where the business is small and the employer-employee relationship is one of close, personal contact; where as a result of mediation both parties verbally agree to accept a conciliator's memorandum of the settlement as a statement of the terms to be observed; where the company agrees to adhere to terms embodied in a contract signed by the union with another company; and where the employer, out of opposition to the union, refuses to accord it the recognition which a signed agreement would entail.[20]

The widespread employment of collective bargaining after 1937, aside from legal requirements growing out of a Supreme Court decision and the Taft-Hartley Act,[21] inevitably led to the greater use of the written agreement. Among the reasons for the prevalence of the written agreement are

[20] David Saposs, *Written Agreements in Collective Bargaining* (*Digest of Testimony at Hearing in Case of Inland Steel Co. v. Steel Workers Organizing Committee*), NLRB Research Memorandum 2 (1938), pp. 11–12.

[21] *H. J. Heinz Co. v. NLRB,* 311 U.S. 514 (1941); National Labor Relations Act, as amended, Section 8(d).

the following: (1) It introduces a sense of stability into the bargaining relationship, giving each party the assurance that the other does not intend to deny its word; (2) with the development of the union-management relationship, the subject matter sometimes becomes so comprehensive and frequently so technical that its very preservation is dependent on a reduction to writing; and (3) efficient application of the agreement in the settlement of individual grievances of employees requires a reasonably precise statement of the terms to be applied.

It is this last aspect to which we shall next turn our attention. We have examined the practice of negotiating the collective agreement, and we shall now consider the issues about which union leaders and managers negotiate —the subject matter of collective bargaining.

The Subject Matter of Collective Bargaining

chapter 4

Labor and management have usually determined for themselves the appropriate subject matters of collective bargaining, and most of our discussion will be concerned with the arguments over, and problems resulting from, their determinations. A brief consideration of the public policy issues involved is worthwhile, however. Increasingly in recent years Congress, the NLRB, and the courts have felt a necessity to consider the appropriateness of some collective bargaining subjects. Their action has almost always been a pragmatic response to public pressures and needs rather than the implementing of a certain view of what collective bargaining should be. Having given not only legal sanction but also a measure of encouragement to collective bargaining, the federal government is expected by the public to assume some direct responsibility for matters handled through bargaining.

Government Influence on the Content of the Agreement

When Congress passed the Wagner Act, no one saw any need to regulate the content of labor agreements or to determine the appropriateness of bargaining subjects. The then chairman of the Senate Committee on Education and Labor expressed a nearly universal viewpoint: "All the bill proposes to do is to drag them [the union negotiators] to the door of the employer and say, 'Here they are, the legal representatives of your employees.' What happens behind those doors is not inquired into, and the bill does not seek to inquire into it." [1] By 1947, when Congress enacted the provisions of the Taft-Hartley Act, many lawmakers and citizens had come to believe not only that some inquiry into the bargaining matters beyond the door was wise but also that some limitations and regulation were necessary. Union membership had increased over four times, and union influence had grown even more. Through collective bargaining, union leaders had been able to gain benefits for workers, but they had also learned to use it to protect and increase the strength of the union organization.

Union security provisions such as the closed shop, the union shop, involuntary checkoff, and hiring halls had long been a part of American collective bargaining, but the rapid growth of unions in the late thirties and forties and the newness of their challenge to accepted business institutions alarmed some people and among many others raised doubts whether collective bargaining should be subject to no restrictions except those upon which the parties agreed. The new Taft-Hartley Law limited future union security measures, prohibiting outright the closed shop. It also attempted to regulate several other collective bargaining matters which particularly excited public attention. It made illegal "featherbedding" arrangements, and it limited the purposes for which welfare funds could be used and specified their administration. The act also required that sixty-day notification be given of expiration of an agreement. Later, in the Labor-Management Reporting and Disclosure Act of 1959, Congress made "hot cargo" agreements illegal. (If the management of one firm agrees not to handle the goods of a struck or banned firm, that is, treats them as "hot cargo," it thereby applies indirect economic pressure on that firm, reinforcing the union's direct pressure.) These prohibitions and regulations have not been wholly effective in accomplishing the aims of those who proposed them. Nevertheless they suggest that as a matter of public policy, Congress may declare certain subjects inappropriate for collective bargaining if public interest will be served thereby.

The issue raised most frequently about the subject matter of collective bargaining is not the degree of legislative restraint on it, but rather the degree of freedom unions enjoy in bargaining over matters seemingly far removed from the direct relationship of union and management. Managerial spokesmen often discuss the appropriateness of subject matter in terms of an invasion of management prerogatives or an encroachment over the

[1] Senator David I. Walsh, *Congressional Record,* 74th Cong., 1st Sess., May 16, 1935.

right to manage. The National Labor Relations Board and the courts have also ruled at various times that management must bargain with union representatives over such topics as Christmas bonuses,[2] stock-sharing plans,[3] and the relocation of a plant.[4] The Board has also ruled that bargaining must prevail in matters of safety rules, work clothing, retirement and pension plans, profit sharing, merit rating systems, and the subcontracting of specialized operations previously performed by the company's own employees. Despite its many rulings, however, it has not set forth any principle or standards to guide either union or management negotiations. Its reluctance to do so is not surprising, for the parties involved in negotiations have never been able to agree on any line dividing appropriate and inappropriate subject matters, although they have tried.

Management Attitudes

At one time businessmen argued that the determination even of wage rates should be left to "market forces," personified in the individual employer. For example, in 1853 the editors of the *New York Journal of Commerce* asserted:

> Suppose the Printers' Union should succeed by a forced violation of the law of demand and supply in driving the price of composition up to a figure beyond what the profits of the business would bear, what would be the consequence? One consequence would be that it would crush weak establishments and throw the hands employed in them out of business. Establishments which do but just live at the old prices would die at the new. The men thus discharged would seek employment where they could find it; and might perchance be glad to take "$2 a day and roast beef," if they could not get $2.87½ as demanded by the union. If, however, a reaction were not produced in this way it would be in another. For, if such enormous prices could be realized by typesetting, thousands would think it just the business for their boys to learn and in a few years the market would be glutted with an over-supply of hands. Men who violate the laws of nature, even in a matter of trade, are sure to be punished for it sooner or later by the operation of those laws, if in no other way.[5]

Nearly a century later the president of General Motors expressed himself in very much the same way. At a time when the United Automobile Work-

[2] *18th Annual Report*, National Labor Relations Board (1953), pp. 73–74.

[3] *Richfield Oil Co.*, 110 NLRB 356 (1954), enforced C.A.D.C., January 26, 1956, 37 LRRM 2327.

[4] *Diaper Jean Co.*, 109 NLRB 1045 (1954).

[5] George A. Stevens, *New York Typographical Union No. 6*, New York State Department of Labor, Annual Report of the Bureau of Labor Statistics (1911), part I, p. 251.

ers were seeking to bargain over a pension plan which the company had earlier unilaterally instituted, he remarked:

> If we consider the ultimate result of this tendency to stretch collective bargaining to comprehend any subject that a union leader may desire to bargain over, we come out with the union leaders really running the economy of the country; but with no legal or public responsibility and with no private employment except as they may permit. . . .
>
> Only by defining and restricting collective bargaining to its proper sphere can we hope to save what we have come to know as our American system and keep it from evolving into an alien form, imported from East of the Rhine. Until this is done, the border area of collective bargaining will be a constant battleground between employers and unions, as the unions continuously attempt to press the boundary farther and farther into the area of managerial functions.[6]

Attempts had already been made to define and restrict collective bargaining, but with no success. At the end of World War II, in 1945, President Truman called a National Labor-Management Conference at which employers and union leaders tried to draft a statement of principles defining management's "right to manage." The employers proposed to exclude a large number of subjects from collective bargaining, including, among many others, product manufactured, location of plants, plant layout, method of production, distribution, financial policies, prices, job duties, size of work force, work assignment, production standards, number of shifts, and maintenance of discipline.

The union men replied that while they agreed that "the functions and responsibilities of management must be preserved if business is to be efficient, progressive, and provide more good jobs," they considered it unwise to build a fence around the rights and responsibilities of each party. To make such a sharp division would create "much unnecessary strife," as each side would be tempted to invade the other's domain.

In asking union leaders to restrict the area of collective bargaining in the mid-forties, employers were sentimentally harkening back to an earlier and simpler day when their word had been the law of the shop. Their longing was understandable, but their sense of realism was faulty. Unions had long interested themselves in, and bargained over, virtually all the areas enumerated by the employers in 1945. As long ago as 1869, the miners' union was concerned with the price of coal, for price fluctuations changed their earnings. The United Mine Workers experimented with various devices, including support of federal legislation, to secure some measure of control over the industry's price policy and thereby protect the wage rate. Other ex-

[6] The *New York Times*, March 24, 1948.

amples abound. Unions in the printing trades have organized foremen since at least 1889; clothing workers have for years assisted in setting production standards; and the building trades unions have for decades acted as their industry's employment agency. During the Great Depression, hosiery workers had even helped determine the investment policies of the firms with which they negotiated.

Rather than trying to rely upon some basic statement of principle to define the appropriate subject matter of collective bargaining, many employers insist upon a so-called "management's rights clause." Some are very brief, such as the following:

> All the functions, rights, powers and authority which the Company has not specifically abridged, delegated or modified by this agreement are recognized by the union as being retained by the Company.[7]

Others are longer and more detailed: [8]

> The parties to this agreement recognize that they are engaged in a common endeavor in which each of them has separate and distinct responsibilities which both of them are obligated to meet in a manner consistent with their mutual overriding responsibility of the community as a whole.
>
> The Union recognizes and respects the obligation of management to obtain for the Company's stockholders a reasonable return on their investment and to assure the continued growth and prosperity of the Company. The Company recognizes and respects the obligation of the Union to help its members to protect and advance their welfare and to obtain for themselves and their families a fair share of the fruits of their labor. Both parties recognize that they can best fulfill their separate obligations to stockholders and employees, respectively, by conducting their relations with each other on a cooperative basis that will make it possible to offer consumers a growing volume of high quality products at a reasonable price.
>
> To achieve these ends, each party recognizes that it must respect the proper functions of the other.
>
> The Union recognizes the right of management to maximum freedom to manage consistent with due regard for the welfare and interests of the employees.
>
> Specifically, the Union agrees, in order to clarify its recognition of

[7] Great Western Sugar Co. and Grain Millers, 1964, quoted from *Collective Bargaining Negotiations and Contracts,* Washington: Bureau of National Affairs, 65:11–12.

[8] The clause is from the 1961 agreement between the American Motors Corporation and the United Automobile Workers. It is interesting because it was elaborated at the time the parties entered into a "progress-sharing" arrangement. The clause was designed to underscore management's intention not to open the door to joint management.

management functions belonging exclusively to the Company, not to request the Company to bargain with respect to the following:

1. Any change or modification of management rights clauses contained in the several working agreements with the respective local unions.
2. The right to determine the products to be manufactured, their design and engineering, and the research thereon.
3. The right to determine all methods of selling, marketing and advertising products, including pricing of products.
4. The right to make all financial decisions including but not limited to the administration and control of capital, distribution of profits and dividends, mortgaging of properties, purchase and sale of securities, and the benefits and compensation of non-union-represented personnel, the financing and borrowing of capital and the merger, reorganization or dissolution of the corporation, together with the right to maintain the corporation's financial books and records in confidence. This right includes the determination of general accounting procedures, particularly the internal accounting necessary to make reports to the owners of the business and to government bodies requiring financial reports.
5. The right to determine the management organization of each producing or distributing unit and the selection of employees for promotion to supervisory and other managerial positions.

None of the foregoing shall be deemed to modify or limit any right secured to either the Company or the Union in the National Economic Agreement or the several Local Working Agreements.

The Union hereby agrees to relieve the Company from any obligation to bargain or negotiate with respect to any of the matters mentioned in the preceding paragraphs as matters with respect to which it will not request the Company to bargain.

The Company recognizes, however, that decisions made pursuant to the exercise of the management rights set forth above may have impact upon employees. The Company, therefore, recognizes that it is a proper function and a right of the Union to bargain and the Company agrees that it will discuss and bargain in good faith with the Union at the latter's request, with respect to the impact of such decisions upon wages, hours, and other terms and conditions of employment or upon the convenience, welfare, interests, health, safety, security and dignity of employees and their families. The Company will continue its past practice of advising and consulting with the Union in advance of the effectuation of decisions having an impact upon such matters. The Company further agrees that it will refrain from assigning to unrepresented employees operations or functions presently performed by represented employees at the location.

Insistence by the Company upon full compliance with this agreement and with the management rights clauses in the said several Working Agreements shall not be an objective of or reason or cause for any strike, slow-down, work stoppage, walk-out, picketing, or other exercise of force or threat thereof by the Union or any of its members; nor shall insistence by the Union upon full compliance with this agreement and the provisions of the National Economic Agreement or the several Local Working Agreements be an objective of or reason or cause for any lockout, or punitive, discriminatory or disciplinary action or other exercise of force or threat against any employee; provided, however, that nothing in this paragraph shall be deemed to modify or limit any right secured to either the Company or the Union in such agreements.

This Management Rights Clause shall remain in full force and effect, as long as the Progress Sharing Plan as set forth herein or as hereafter amended shall not have been terminated.

Although managements usually see in the "rights" clauses a declaration of their existing or residual rights, the student of labor does not consider them to be a resolution of the problem. Residual rights must be exercised in a manner consistent with the other provisions of the agreement, or, as the Ford-UAW agreement reads, "subject only to such regulations and restrictions governing the exercise of these rights as are expressly provided in this Agreement."

The agreement limits residual rights in three ways. First, the contents of the agreement may expand from one negotiation to the next, regardless of the wording of a management's rights clause in the previous agreement. Indeed, a rights clause is itself subject to negotiation and renegotiation. Second, the intent of a management's rights clause depends on the intent of the entire agreement. Managers may insist that they retain in writing an unfettered right to schedule production, for example, but in scheduling they will still have to bargain with the union over hours of work, starting time, overtime, shift changes, transfer of employees, seniority arrangements, and pace of work. After such bargaining, the claim to a unilateral right to schedule production may be rather empty. Moreover, some authorities see in the recognition clause, which acknowledges the right of the union to represent the employees, a commitment entitled to equal consideration with a management's rights clause; the two may be viewed as complementary. Such acknowledgment sometimes limits authority which managers believe they have protected by "specific wording."

Third, as long as there is a no-strike pledge in the agreement, it is hard to prevent any worker complaint from being processed through the grievance procedure, right up to arbitration. The grievance is of course subject to the terms of the agreement—a worker complaining that he has been unfairly treated is unlikely to secure remedial action unless there is something in the agreement to support his case—but it is through the grievance process (in which an arbitrator is sometimes used in the final stage) that the judgment is made whether the grievance is covered by the agreement. That determination is partly a matter of interpretation and—as we shall see in examining the grievance process later—also to some extent a continuation of the bargaining power relationship between the two parties. For these three reasons a management's rights clause can scarcely be considered to resolve the question of what issues are bargainable, even at a given point in time, and certainly over time.

The National Association of Manufacturers has pointed out that employers themselves are partly to blame for loss of management control. Through lax administration, poor enforcement of agreements, ill-advised and poorly prepared-for arbitration, loose supervision, and hasty or meager preparation for negotiations, managers have encouraged unions to exert their influence and have allowed them to assume areas of control.[9]

The Right to Manage and the Scope of the Agreement

A common assertion of managers is that their right to make business decisions free from collective bargaining is based upon property rights. Acting as the trustees or delegated representatives of property owners (i.e., stockholders), they have the right and, indeed, the duty to organize and direct machinery, materials, and money. A union which seeks to force management's agreement to increase output, modify price policy, adopt different accounting conventions, or make a different line of products is said to be trespassing upon the legal rights of private property. Such a line of argument, while possessing surface plausibility, overlooks the important fact that the property basis of management carries no duty on the part of others to *be* managed.

The trouble with property ownership as a conferrer of authority is that it gives command only over *things*. This involves no special difficulties in a society of small property holders and individual proprietorships, for control over things is all that is needed to produce for, and sell in, the market. But when business enterprise assumes a corporate form and requires the cooperation of large numbers of people performing specialized functions, control over things ceases to be sufficient.

Except in the case of authoritarian relationships (for example, in the military services in this country and in totalitarian societies generally abroad), people can be managed and directed only with their own consent. While property rights carry with them a power of disposition of goods, they do not carry an equal power to use those goods *if* the cooperation of others

[9] *Do You Still Have the Right to Run Your Plant?* National Association of Manufacturers (1962).

is necessary to that use. Cooperation, without which the property right is reduced to a power of disposition, cannot be commanded. It can be won only by consent. And there is no legal compulsion upon the workers to cooperate. There is no legal statement of the terms on which cooperation must take place. The definition of those terms is left directly to those parties involved, and there is nothing in the law to stop the union from demanding as the price of the cooperation of its members a voice in some matter previously independently determined by management. Since property rights do not mean that one has command over others, management *may* find it essential to share its authority as a means of inducing cooperation in order to maintain the value of a going business. Over time, it becomes customary to share authority, in order to win cooperation, in certain recognized areas of business decisions—wages, for example, or hours, or perhaps the speed of assembly lines.

Thus the right to manage and direct others does not flow out of legal rights but must be granted by those very people who are managed and directed; the price of the grant may be that management must yield its independence in certain matters of business operation. What matters? *Potentially* none would seem to be excluded—whatever matters are deemed important to those whose cooperation is being sought.

The determination of the appropriate subject matter of collective bargaining is apparently not a matter of fixed principle. The inclusion of new matters in collective agreements is simply evidence of changing social relationships. Even when the NLRB and the courts require bargaining over certain issues, management does not have to surrender functions or areas of control to unions. Certainly Ford and General Motors did not grant the UAW its demand for profit sharing in 1958 just because the issue was bargainable. A management need not agree to union demands if it is willing to resist. After a 113-day strike in 1945–1946, General Motors not only maintained control of pricing in which the union wanted to share but also forced acceptance of a wage increase lower than that recommended by a government fact-finding board. This illustrates that managers do not get their way or maintain their "rights" by wishing. They must bargain forcefully with unions and must realistically measure the cost of maintaining their "rights" against the willingness and ability of the unions to insist upon their demands.

Over time the union's views—and management's—concerning what is or is not of direct interest to employees undergo change, not solely because of "enlightenment," the shift of political influence, or boundless greed, but because social and economic conditions and institutions change. The General Counsel of the NLRB, Arnold Ordman, observed in 1963 that the content of collective bargaining changed

... not because of the zeal or the perversity of labor or management, but rather because of the simple economic fact that our industrial complex is growing. The ramification of domestic industry, the interlocking of corporate interests, the rapid rate of industrial growth both here and abroad pose competitive problems and marketing problems which sit alongside management's negotiators at every bargaining session. The impact of technology and the constantly rising curve of productivity per man-hour fashion a spectre of increasing unemployment which haunts every negotiator for labor.[10]

As a result of such changes as those mentioned by Mr. Ordman, organized groups of workers may come to feel keenly that some aspect of business management in which they have no voice affects their interests vitally.

If in future years the automobile workers, for example, come to feel more strongly than they did in 1945 and 1946 that automobile prices directly affect their wages and welfare, they may make a stronger stand and win some direct influence in the price policy of General Motors. There is no reason to believe that they might not sometime be as successful as the coal miners in an earlier period in influencing prices if they feel as great a concern about it.[11]

Changes in the bargaining unit or shifts in market control and competition may lead unions to insist upon broadening the scope of bargaining. For example, it may be impractical for a single small firm to undertake an extensive advertising program to expand sales, but numerous small companies, bargaining collectively with the union, may respond to union pressure for a promotional campaign to which all contribute and from which all benefit. This has, in fact, happened in the New York City women's clothing industry. Workers in the individual firms would be likely to feel that company advertising plans are of no direct interest to them because they seem so meager in size and effect, but pitched on an industry basis they may be of importance because of their greater impact on sales, output, and employment.[12]

[10] From an address, "Progress and Accommodation," before the Section of Labor Relations Law, American Bar Association, August 13, 1963.

[11] In 1962 Nunn-Bush Shoe Co., an innovator in the area of guaranteed annual pay, concluded an agreement with the independent Industrial Union of Master Craftsmen, which requires its officers to consult with union leaders on contemplated changes in wholesale prices. Formerly, the company was required only to notify the union men, who could then attend conferences on price changes. See *Collective Bargaining Negotiations and Contracts,* Bureau of National Affairs, July 20, 1962, p. 53.

[12] Some economists fear that prices are just such a matter, in which control will become possible on an industry basis where not possible on a company

Though collective bargaining has expanded into new areas, particularly during the last thirty years, one need not conclude that the only limit to enlargement of the scope of bargaining is that imposed by management. Unions are political bodies responsive in varying degrees to their constituents. Union members tend to be apathetic about voting unless they have a complaint. In this respect they act like typical American voters, who more often vote against than for a candidate.

Union officials, therefore, prefer to avoid issues which can give rise to intraunion disputes and which force them to take sides against any members. Union negotiators might find that attempting to influence the location of a new plant would be politically unwise. Members in one existing local might want the new plant located near them, while another union local might argue for a place closer to it. The same kind of difficulties could arise if union officers helped decide the product mix; some members would be hurt, and some would gain. How could an elected officer choose among his members without incurring more disfavor than favor?

In the daily shop work of job assignments, skill classification, production standards, and maintenance of discipline, union officers show little desire to join in managing and in initiating action; they prefer to retain their freedom to protest management's decisions and to stay out of the cross fire of criticism and avoid the wounding resentments of their own members.

Unions have not pushed massively and inexorably into vital policy areas.[13] They have pushed when they could and when it was in their clear interest to do so, advancing when management was careless or weak and retreating when management aggressively resisted them. When unions do enlarge their powers, it is almost always in those areas where they have long been established: wages, hours, and conditions of employment.[14]

We shall now turn our attention to some of the matters which have

---

basis. Union and management, it is believed, will combine to raise wages and prices—both benefiting at the expense of the consumer (see Chapter 15).

[13] "Under Perlman's Theory of the job-conscious nature of trade unionism, one would expect union participation in plant decision-making to be limited to subjects closely related to the size and administration of the job territory. Despite the extension of collective bargaining to new industries and the rise of industrial unionism since the theory was formulated, our data give strong support to this view." M. Derber, W. E. Chalmers, and M. T. Edelman, "Union Participation in Plant Decision-making," *Industrial and Labor Relations Review*, vol. 15 (1961), p. 99. Also see M. Derber, W. E. Chalmers, and R. Stagner, "Collective Bargaining and Managerial Functions: An Empirical Study," *Journal of Business*, vol. 31 (1958), pp. 107–119.

[14] The four paragraphs above were adapted from an article by James W. Kuhn, "Encroachments on the Right to Manage," *California Management Review*, vol. 5 (1962), pp. 18–24.

found their way into collective agreements. To write of these in detail would require a lengthy volume in itself. We shall be content here to survey in the most summary fashion some of the ways in which the union, through the bargaining process, has affected the conduct of business in the United States. It goes without saying that not all the provisions mentioned are to be found in every agreement, and indeed it would be the unusual agreement which covered all the topics listed. The matters discussed below are to be regarded as taken from a composite of many agreements from many industries.[15]

In the light of the above discussion, one should expect that the matters in which unions have most successfully gained the right of participation are those which bear a direct and immediate relationship to the work environment and economic security of employees. It is true that if one wished to make a thorough canvass, he could uncover instances where a particular union, in specific circumstances, has negotiated with a company even on such issues as depreciation policy, the quality of the product or service, capital financing, and the location of the company. But these represent situations which are still unusual, and no further mention will be made of them. Our interest at the moment runs simply to the customary and usual subjects of collective bargaining.

Provisions Affecting "Personnel" Policy

For the most part, these are matters which are normally considered to be of a "personnel" nature—employment, transfers, promotions, discipline, and the broader issues of wages and hours. What should be of interest, however, is the scope of the union's interest in these matters. We shall also discover that unions are now dealing effectively with problems directly connected with the production process where these have been demonstrated to have a substantial impact upon the security and job satisfaction of the employees—problems such as the content or requirement of a job, methods of operation, and rates of operation and work loads. Finally, it is worth noting that some of the concessions won by unions and incorporated into collective bargaining agreements may appear to be minor victories since they perhaps do nothing more than state in writing practices which the

[15] Those who wish to examine in greater detail the subject matter of collective bargaining may consult *Collective Bargaining Negotiations and Contracts* and *Labor Arbitration Reports,* reporting services of the Bureau of National Affairs. See also *Union Contracts* and *American Labor Arbitration Awards,* reporting services of Prentice-Hall, Inc.; and Sumner H. Slichter, James J. Healy, and E. Robert Livernash, *The Impact of Collective Bargaining on Management,* Washington, D.C.: The Brookings Institution, 1960.

company had already been following. The significant consideration in these cases, however, is that the practice then becomes a matter of agreement and thus is no longer subject to exclusive control by management. The union has won its point that that particular matter is one on which it has a right to be consulted before changes in practice are made.

Let us examine first the manner in which the union has made its impact on hiring and employment policies. In some cases, particularly where some of the industrial unions in the mass-production industries have been involved, it has been agreed that no individual will be discriminated against because of race, creed, color, nationality, or religion.[16] In addition to their interest in the personal characteristics of job applicants, unions have also been concerned with applicants' professional qualifications, largely as a means of reducing job competition. By weeding out those who cannot surmount certain hurdles, the union can help to maintain the prestige and status of various skills. With respect to some occupations, such as that of telegrapher, where professional competence is not only important but measurable, there has been joint agreement on qualifications—stated in terms of license held; experience; and minimum speeds for perforating, transcribing signals, aural reception, hand sending, and so on—which must be possessed by new employees. Apprenticeship programs to promote the professional competence of new employees and employees seeking advancement to higher-rated positions have been established jointly by unions and management in some companies, involving such determinations as the length of the training program, the ratio of apprentices to journeymen, and the supervision and assignment of apprentices.

Collective agreements sometimes place other limitations on management's freedom to hire employees in the labor market. This is obviously the situation when the union serves virtually as an employment office for the company, as in the building trades and longshoring. Some agreements proscribe new hirings before certain conditions have been met. Most important in this connection is the provision concerning employees possessing seniority, that is, a company service record of more than some defined length of time, such as six months. If they have worked within the past one or two years before being laid off, they will be called back to work in the order of their seniority before any new man is employed.

In filling vacancies, managers may also be obligated to give preference to employees who prefer the vacant job to their own, to former employees who have lost their seniority standing, or to experienced workers or union members whether or not previously employed by the company. Occasionally an agreement will specify that for some period of time, such as six

---

[16] In other instances, without entering into written agreement, some unions have insisted upon excluding certain minority groups or limiting their employment to quotas or to specified jobs.

months prior to the introduction of laborsaving methods or machinery, no new employees will be taken on in the job classifications or plants or offices affected. The purpose is to absorb employees already on the payroll who otherwise would be laid off.

After workers are hired, they must be assigned to some job. Unions usually take no special interest in an employee's original assignment (unless it involves the placement of a new man, without special qualifications, in a position superior to qualified employees with seniority); however, questions of the reassignment of workers are often subject to joint decision in important particulars. Provisions with respect to transfers may be classed as prohibitive (those foreclosing management from taking certain kinds of action) or operative (those prescribing the nature of the action which management must take under certain given circumstances). In addition there are some clauses which rest discretion with the employee.

Prohibitive agreements include provisions that no employee may be reassigned without his consent; that employees with specified company seniority may not be transferred against their wishes from one plant or locality to another; that employees of one major department of the company shall not be assigned to jobs in another department except for temporary periods— such as two weeks—in an emergency, or when arranged with the local shop committee; or that temporary assignments of employees carrying them outside of their locality may not exceed some specified period.

In the operative agreements, which determine how transfers are to be made, seniority is a commonly accepted factor, sometimes modified to preserve some discretion on the basis of a man's ability. The rule to which unions have generally sought to secure agreement is that where employees desire to make a change to a given opening, the employee with the greatest seniority shall be chosen; where employees prefer not to change, the one with the least seniority is to be selected.

As has been mentioned, some assignment provisions allow employees to exercise discretion under stated circumstances. Thus when a class of work is transferred from one department to another or from one plant to another, employees may be given the option of transferring with the work or being assigned to other work for which they are qualified within the same department or plant. Again, in the event of changes in operating methods, employees may be given a choice of retraining to meet the demands of the new methods or transferring to a different job.

The assignment of employees to particular shifts (day, afternoon, or night), to particular machines (as in the hosiery industry, where knitters are responsible for the care of their machines and resent being moved from one on which they have lavished their attention), or to particular runs (as in the case of truck or bus drivers) may also be a matter of joint concern. Sometimes written clauses cover the matter, and other times the parties rely upon unwritten understandings which can be interpreted and applied through the grievance procedure.

Unions likewise participate in the determination of procedures governing layoffs. In cases of dismissals because of lack of work, the union must in some instances be notified in advance and given the reasons for the contemplated action. Occasionally management is required to forgo any further subcontracting of work which can be performed by its own employees. In a number of companies, arrangements have been mutually worked out for a reduction in force in a series of steps. For example, first the probationary, temporary, and one-year employees are dismissed; then there is a sharing of work down to some specified number of hours; then follows—as a last resort—the laying off of workers. In the designation of those workers to be cut from the payroll, seniority is sometimes applied strictly, while in other companies it may be accepted as the major governing factor but with consideration also given to ability, physical fitness, or family status. The importance accorded seniority is a tribute to the effectiveness of the union, for it has often been opposed by management on this issue. In the words of one union representative: "A company will naturally put the emphasis on the ability to produce. We say that a person with the longest service contributed more to the building up of that particular company, and, therefore, has more equity in his job."

One difficulty in applying the seniority principle when laying off employees has concerned the question of whether a senior employee may "bump" the man next below him or whether an employee displaced from his regular job shall be given the job of the man with least seniority in the department. The first alternative leads to a series of "bumps" in a falling domino fashion, while the second obviates the disturbance of employees in the intermediate classifications. In any event, it is clear that at a time of layoff a number of transfers may be required. To smooth this difficult period, joint conferences of union and management representatives are sometimes provided for, at which both parties review the schedule of transfers in advance of its effective date.

Employees dismissed because of lack of work usually must be notified in advance. By agreement, the period of notification varies from one day to perhaps one week. Increasingly the principle of severance pay, with the sum graduated on the basis of length of service, has been accepted. In some instances reduction in force due to mechanization or technological change has been hedged by various provisions for reabsorbing those displaced, retraining displaced workers to fit them for the new skills required or for other suitable employment, or giving lengthier advance notice.

Another subject of collective bargaining, of direct and immediate interest to employees, is promotions. Promotions may be considered a form of hiring, the recruiting being from among the present employees. Some managements have retained the discretion to determine whether a particular job shall be filled by hiring from outside or by promotion from within, but many unions have successfully urged the latter policy. Once managers have decided that a vacancy is to be filled by promotion, a "bidding" procedure is called for by some agreements. Thus a common arrangement in the electric utility field is the provision that vacancies within the bargaining unit be posted by management for a specified period of time, during which interested employees may "bid" for the job. This procedure ensures that no interested employee is overlooked and that uninterested employees are not considered. Whether or not an agreement calls for a bidding arrangement, there remains the necessity of determining which of a number of employees is most deserving of the promotion. In general, it may be said that unions have consistently sought to have this question answered on the basis of objectively measured seniority, while managements have attempted to make the primary determinant their appraisals of relative ability. The result of this conflict of opinion has been a variety of clauses calling for the consideration of seniority in varying degrees. In some instances, the parties have simply agreed that seniority shall be a "factor" in selecting employees for advancement. In others the seniority element receives greater emphasis through the provision that when two or more candidates for a job have demonstrated "substantially equal" qualifications, the employee with the longest company service shall be chosen, provided he is able to do the work within a reasonable breaking-in period.

Despite the wording of promotion clauses which appear to place primary emphasis on relative abilities, in actual operation seniority frequently becomes the controlling consideration. Unions have been able to secure this desired objective in some cases through their successful insistence, before grievance arbitrators, that management be able to demonstrate *by objective standards* that a junior employee is more qualified than one with greater seniority before it may promote him. Devising a practical system that operates on objective measurements is a problem which the reader might consider for a little while to convince himself of the difficulties involved. It is in part because seniority is a completely objective standard, though not necessarily of ability, that unions have resorted to it as the principal yardstick in such matters as promotions.

In the area of disciplinary control over employees, unions have been especially successful in establishing a joint interest with management. Of 400 representative agreements examined by the Bureau of National Affairs, 82 per cent specified the grounds for discharge, nearly three-quarters detailed appeals procedures, and over one-half spelled out the procedures to be used in making a discharge.[17]

---

[17] 46 LRRM 23, 24 (1960).

In general, management retains the right to impose penalties "for proper cause," while the union has the right to protest through the grievance procedure. The two parties have built up a body of disciplinary doctrine through decisions in the grievance procedure. As a consequence of arbitrators' decisions in this area, there has grown up the closest approximation to "common law" to be found in industry. The analogy should not be pressed too far, but it does not involve much distortion.

In matters of discipline, perhaps the first question customarily raised by unionists is whether "just cause" exists for imposing a penalty. Here it is important to ascertain whether the employee knew that his conduct was improper and subject to penalty. Knowledge on the part of the offending employee of the standards of conduct being enforced may be shown in several ways. The management may have posted rules covering the conduct in question. In some cases, certain standards are considered to be understood or implied, even in the absence of general promulgation, such as prohibition of assault upon a fellow worker or theft of company property. In other instances, an employee might know that his conduct was improper, having received an individual warning on a prior occasion. Some cases involve insubordination—the refusal to carry out an order given by a person possessing the appropriate authority.

In connection with the issue of whether the employee could be expected to know that certain conduct will evoke discipline, other subsidiary questions may have to be answered. Was the language of the notice, warning, or order clear and free from ambiguity? Has the particular standard been required of all employees, or have some been discriminatorily treated in the sense that they have been held to standards which were overlooked in the cases of others? Have rules been systematically enforced so that employees could reasonably expect that they are still effective? We all know of the existence of certain municipal ordinances which remain on the books even though they are never observed. Similarly, sometimes plant rules—such as "no smoking"—are commonly disregarded, so that an employee, without warning, could not reasonably be expected to believe that they would be enforced.

These are only some of the questions which are raised in appraising whether an employee was disciplined for proper cause. In answering them, general rules are being hammered out in arbitration; these rules become as important a part of the collective bargaining relationship as if they were spelled out in the agreement itself.

Certain procedural requirements customarily have to be observed in the meting out of discipline, though there is no uniformity among companies. Some of the contractual provisions or arbitration decisions require that the offense for which an employee is being punished be specified, so that he may properly prepare a defense if he so chooses. Sometimes there must be notice not only to the employee but also to his union representative (the counterpart in industry of the accused's right to counsel), followed by a hearing. For an arbitrator to rule that findings must conform to the charges made is not unusual. If an employee has been charged with theft, for example, but the findings do not substantiate the charge, discipline for theft will not be upheld even though the evidence indicates excessive absenteeism. Discipline cannot be justified by evidence unrelated to the original charge. Occasionally arbitration decisions have upheld the principle that an employee may not be punished twice for the same offense—the substantial equivalent in industry of the rule against "double jeopardy" to be found in our civil courts—as well as the principle that an offense committed sufficiently remotely in time cannot be used as the basis for later punishment— the industrial equivalent of a statute of limitations.

Finally, there is the question of the reasonableness of the penalty. Even if there is cause for discipline, it may be that the penalty invoked is excessive—discharge for a minor infraction, for instance. In earlier times agreements often stipulated that if an arbitrator found that the offense was as charged, management's judgment concerning the appropriate penalty was not to be challenged. In general now, however, an arbitrator is free to determine whether a penalty "fits the crime." Sometimes the question of the nature of permissible penalties is raised. The customary punishment is discharge or suspension for a specified period of time. Are other penalties available, however, such as demotion or fines? In some situations the former may conflict with the seniority provisions of the agreement, while in other cases legislation may prevent the levying against workers of fines to be paid to the company.

Wage and Hour Provisions

Wages represent one of the more traditional fields of collective bargaining, and it is to be expected that the impact of unions here has been an important one. Again it should be held in mind that the variety of provisions in agreements makes it difficult to speak of general practices. We shall describe arrangements which are prevalent and which give a fair approximation of what is to be expected. The system (or lack of system) under which each individual was paid his individual rate has largely disappeared in recent years; now workers are likely to be grouped together under particular classifications to which wages or wage brackets are attached. In an automobile plant, for example, despite the fact that employees on an assembly line are performing varied operations, they may all bear the designation "assemblers" and receive the same rate. In some plants the number of such classifications runs high, and each classification is paid its particular rate. The union may challenge the classification of a particular job through the grievance procedure, claiming, for instance, that a man who is operating on a subassembly line and who is therefore classed as "assembly —minor" is actually so closely integrated with the main assembly process that he should be classed as "assembly—major" and paid the (higher) rate for the latter classification. In some companies the question of the rate or rate range appropriate for a particular classification is subject to question in the grievance procedure, whereas in other bargaining systems such matters may be brought up for consideration only at the time of negotiating a new agreement.

More and more, however, management has been introducing job evaluation into the setting of wage rates. Under job evaluation, each job or classification is weighed on the basis of a number of "factors," such as the amount of training or experience necessary to learn the job, the hazard involved, the pleasantness of the working conditions, the responsibility entailed, and so on. By examining each classification on the basis of such factors, a score is given to it, and on the basis of the score, each of the job classifications is placed in what is usually called a "labor grade." The number of labor grades in any company varies; there may be nine such grades in one company and fifteen in another. Each grade embraces a numerical range, so that all job classifications which have been scored somewhere between 80 and 90 points, for example, might be placed in labor grade 3. All jobs which fall within a particular labor grade are paid the same basic wage rate. Where such systems of job evaluation have been introduced, the union is usually privileged to raise grievances on the grounds that a particular job has not been correctly rated, that is, that it should have a higher score and should be moved into a labor grade paying a higher wage rate. In the periodic negotiations for a new agreement, the union may also question the appropriateness of the wage intervals between labor grades, claiming perhaps that there should be a difference of 4 cents an hour between grades rather than 5 cents, or vice versa, depending upon whether the union conceives the differential to be unfair to the less skilled or the more skilled employees.

The relationship of occupational wage rates to one another is generally referred to as the "wage structure" of a plant. For the most part, the wage structure is taken as given. As we have seen, it is subject to alteration if the worker can show that one rate is inequitable in the light of other rates (the factor of equitable comparison, discussed in a later chapter) or that a mistake has been made in the classification or rating of a job; it is also subject to alteration if the content of a job is changed. Despite grievances concerning such inequities, the wage structure, on the whole, retains a certain fixity from year to year. The wage question with which unions and managements are most concerned is the wage *level*. Each has a definite interest in the size of any increase or decrease that is to be applied to all the rates which make up the wage structure, negotiating at length, for example, on whether to raise all rates by 10 cents an hour, by 12 per cent, or by some other figure.

We have been speaking of hourly or time rates, but it is also true that workers may be paid on an incentive, or piece rate, basis, the earnings of each fluctuating with his output. What his production must be in order to provide him with a "fair" return is customarily determined on the basis of company experience or time studies. Here again the union may enter a plea on behalf of the worker that the incentive or piece rate is too "tight" and that he must produce an excessive amount in order to receive the earnings considered to be fair. Usually, too, a base rate is provided which constitutes a guarantee to the piece rate worker that when output falls through no fault of his own, he will have some minimum return.

Most agreements contain a number of other provisions with respect to wages which can only be touched on here. In many cases where a rate range is attached to a classification, a worker's progression from the minimum rate to the maximum is dependent upon a demonstration of increasing ability. This is the system known as "merit rating." If a union believes a worker has been unfairly passed over when such merit increases were awarded, it may present his case in the grievance procedure. Differentials and bonuses are sometimes given for certain operations; for example, night-shift workers may receive from 5 to 10 cents more than those on the day shift, or a bonus may be paid for work that is considered hazardous, such as handling toxic chemicals or entering areas of heavy radioactivity. Some agreements spell out in considerable detail the rate to be paid to workers who are temporarily transferred to jobs carrying a different rate. In such cases an agreement may provide, for example, that if the transfer does not exceed three days the workers shall continue to be paid their regular rate but that after three days they shall be paid the higher of the two rates involved.

The subject of hours is also important in any collective agreement. Uniformly the normal hours of work per week are a negotiated matter. In some companies the normal hours, perhaps 35 or 40 per week, apply to all employees. In other companies the number of hours varies with the classification of employees, so that an employee may have a normal week of perhaps 30, 35, 39, 40, or $45\frac{1}{3}$ hours, depending upon his classification. In most contracts the union has established some restriction on the scheduling of the workweek. This may range from the binding commitment that regular manufacturing operations shall be confined to five consecutive days, Monday to Friday, inclusive, except for certain operations designated as "continuous," to a provision which simply states that the employee's workweek shall be a calendar week beginning at the start of the Monday shift.

Hours or days worked outside of those so specified are paid for at penalty rates. Changes in shift hours may sometimes be made only after advance notice to, or discussion with, the union.

Equalization of hours among employees is a principle which has become widely established in one form or another. One application of this principle has already been noted in the discussion of layoffs, that is, providing for the part-timing of employees down to some specified number of hours, such as thirty-two per week, before any employees with seniority are laid off. Extra work in periods of part-time operation may be apportioned equally among employees, either to spread the burden or to share the additional income.

Unions have also been concerned with the question of what constitutes hours of work for purposes of pay. Among the items for which an employee may receive pay, by agreement, are "call-in" time, when workers report for duty without previous notification that work is not available; rest periods; lunch hour; time spent preparing tools and equipment; time spent changing clothes; time involved in returning from distant assignments; and time occupied in receiving instructions at the commencement of the working day.

Determination of the hours or days for which employees will be paid special "penalty" rates is a matter which has received considerable attention from unions. The Fair Labor Standards Act has supplemented their efforts in this respect by requiring the payment of overtime rates under specified circumstances. Collective agreements often go beyond this legislation, however, requiring penalty rates not only when more than eight hours have been worked in a day or forty hours during a week, but also, in a number of companies, when work is performed on Saturdays, Sundays, or holidays, regardless of the number of hours worked during that week. This has at times given rise to the arrangement known as "overtime on overtime," where a worker may be paid $1\frac{1}{2}$ times the regular rate for working Saturday and Sunday because he has already worked forty hours in that week and where, in addition, he will claim $1\frac{1}{2}$ times the resulting rate just because it is Saturday and Sunday on which he is working—days that carry special rates, regardless of the number of hours previously worked that week.

Just as there is a question as to what are to be considered hours worked for purposes of pay, so is there a question as to what are to be considered days worked for purposes of overtime. Some agreements require that a holiday falling within the regular workweek be counted as a day regularly worked in computing the amount of penalty pay which may be due employees; similarly, a day of illness or an absence otherwise excused may occasionally be considered.

The more thorny overtime questions concern the "right" of employees to work overtime and their obligation to work overtime. The first is raised by virtue of the fact that work beyond hours defined in the agreement as "normal" is compensated at a higher rate, so that at times employees regard it as a concession to be sought, a lucrative arrangement for augmenting income. Consequently, the union may seek to apply the same objective standard on which it so frequently relies, seniority, and establish the principle that where overtime is desired, it shall be awarded to those employees possessing the greatest seniority. In other cases, it may seek to establish a worker's right to any overtime in connection with his particular job or machine.

At times, however, overtime may loom as a disadvantage, particularly if there has been no prior notice to the employee. When the foreman comes around at four o'clock in the afternoon to inform his men that the job must be finished that night—"everybody stays"—there may be grumbling from those whose plans for the evening have thus been disarranged. Because of such occurrences, some unions have sought to make the working of overtime voluntary, with no obligation resting upon the employee to work beyond his normal hours. As yet, however, this provision has not obtained general acceptance.

Fringe Benefits

The area of personnel administration sometimes loosely blanketed by the term "employee advancement policies" is one in which union activity has been increasing in recent years. Almost all agreements now contain provisions for vacation plans, describing the duration (usually in accord with length of service), the requirements for eligibility, the method of computing payments, and such miscellaneous issues as whether an additional day is to be received for each holiday falling within the scheduled vacation. Provisions for paid holidays have also become widespread, and the number allowed has been increasing. Here there are sometimes special rules concerning eligibility for payment, covering such questions as whether an employee who is temporarily laid off or who is ill or otherwise excused is entitled to holiday pay. In many cases agreement has been reached that, except under specified circumstances, an employee must report on the working day before and after the holiday in order to receive compensation for it.

Jointly negotiated welfare programs are now commonly a part of labor agreements. The number of workers covered by negotiated health and insurance plans increased from an estimated seven million in 1950 to over fourteen million by the end of 1960. Comparable estimates for the number of workers covered by pension plans were five million in 1950 and eleven million in late 1960.[18] A number of welfare programs contain provisions

[18] Dorothy A. Kiltner, "Health, Insurance and Pension Plan Coverage in Union Contracts," *Monthly Labor Review*, vol. 85 (1962), pp. 274–277.

for sick leave, group insurance, death benefits, and increasing severance pay. The last named is usually a lump-sum payment upon the termination of employment, the amount depending on the length of service. Unions have been very successful in establishing or joining in the operation of pension plans since the late forties.

In the matter of the health and safety of employees, unions have generally been content to leave responsibility with management, reserving the right to prod and criticize where they believe provision has been inadequate. In a number of cases joint safety committees have been organized, occasionally with effective results. On matters which have been of particular concern to workers, however, contract clauses may make specific the action expected, for example, the supply of goggles, gloves, or other protective work clothing at no expense to the employee. If sanitation has been unsatisfactory, the union may insist on a provision for the employment of a sufficient number of janitors to ensure "proper housekeeping." Since such clauses are commonly subject to arbitral determination of whether intent has been complied with, they are more than innocuous expressions.

The Effects on Production Policies

In a sense, a system of classification of business decisions which draws a line between personnel administration and production policies is making an artificial distinction. The two are inseparably related. The assignment of employees, the selection of individuals for promotion or layoff, the system of discipline, and the effect of wages and other forms of remuneration as incentives are all inextricably tied up with the production process. Nevertheless, by custom we have come to think of production as related to the mechanics of the process. It determines the specific job requirements, the functional relation of jobs in a sequence leading to an end product, the determination of the factor (input) requirements, and so on. Regarding production, we say that we are less concerned with the disposition and treatment of individuals and more attentive to the arrangements which we assume would be necessary regardless of which individuals occupy particular assignments or how they feel about their place in the organization. Such an approach, while at times useful, can lead to obviously incorrect conclusions. Perhaps the primary value of the field of study now characterized as "human relations in industry" has been to reveal the areas in which personal and organizational elements have so vital an interaction that neither can be ignored. The relation between personnel and production matters will become apparent as we now turn briefly to issues which have generally been considered to belong to the latter category.

In general, collective agreements contemplate, in the words of one impartial chairman, "that management shall instruct the employees as to the work to be performed, and that . . . the employees shall perform the work which they are instructed to do." Despite this principle, the question frequently arises of whether a workman may "properly" be called upon to perform certain operations as part of his job. The conception of division of labor has a firm hold upon union philosophy. As long as duties required have fallen within the description of the classification covering the worker, there has been only infrequent and spasmodic resistance by employees to work assignments. There is often opposition, however, to the performance of duties which the employee conceives to be outside the requirements of his job classification. This is an issue to which variant solutions have been offered, both in collective bargaining and during the arbitration stage of grievance settlement. In most situations where managers change the content of an employee's job or rearrange his duties—actions frequently necessary in the production process—the employee's only basis for protest is whether he is properly classified. It may be, for example, that new duties added to the old now warrant his being reclassified at a different rate, even though a foreman does not agree.

At times, however, unions have taken a firm stand against a rearrangement of job duties where this involves loss of employment. Some have opposed the telescoping of jobs that results in unemployment for some. Examples are the reduction of the number of men in the engine crew on the railroads, where technological change has reduced the need for the full-time services of the fireman, and the reduction of the dock crews because of increased mechanization in the loading of ships. More frequently issues affecting the number of men on a job have not involved a reassignment of duties, however, but rather the determination of how many men are to be employed on a specific operation. The brewery workers may argue in negotiations that two men are required to man a truck because of the manifold duties, whereas the employers may counter that one man can satisfactorily drive, deliver, and take orders. Some electrical workers' unions have insisted—at times successfully—that a line crew be composed of a specified number of men, for the sake of safety. And finally, the question of the number of men required for a particular operation in turn often leads to the further issue of the work load or rate of operation per man. At times the content of a job, the number of men on an operation, and the rate of operation are so interrelated as to become a single problem.

Standards or rates of operation constitute one of the areas of production control in which the union's interests have been militantly affirmed. In most companies, unions have won the right to protest production standards, with protest customarily resulting in a retiming of the process involved. Managements have not always been willing to submit disputes in this area to arbitration, however. Indeed, only in the exceptional company do unions participate in the original determination of work loads or operating speeds.

They continue to press for such participation in several key industries, nevertheless.

Much has been said of unions' opposition, resulting from a fear of consequent unemployment, to technological changes in the production process. Contest over the actual introduction of improved machinery and methods has now largely been relegated to the past, however. While unions retain their concern for the immediate unemployment effects, they have within recent years sought to meet the problem not by opposing change but by controlling its timing. Occasional arrangements have been made for new technological processes to be accompanied by provisions looking to the reabsorption of those workers who may be displaced—by carrying them on the payroll for some specified period of time subsequent to adoption of the new methods, in the hope that through normal turnover a place may be made for them; by retraining; or by granting severance pay to ease the transition between jobs.

Conclusion

We shall conclude here this most summary treatment of some of the subject matter of collective bargaining agreements. It is an interesting exercise to explore the various approaches to standard problems which have been adopted by unions and managements in different situations. Such an exploration can best be undertaken not simply by referring to clauses in the agreements themselves but by studying grievance cases as they appear in arbitration reports. Arbitrators customarily summarize and evaluate the positions of the respective parties as they relate to daily problems, thus providing a view of the agreement provision. One becomes aware, too, in such a study, of the "exceptional" provisions embracing an area of business operation not often covered by collective bargaining, which in some particular instance has become an issue vitally affecting the welfare of the workers. We do not generally think of collective bargaining as being concerned with the location of a plant, for example, and yet under some circumstances unions have reached agreement with employers binding the latter not to change the location of their operations during the lifetime of the agreement.[19]

If any conclusion can be reached as to the "appropriate" subject matter of collective bargaining, then, it is that one cannot label certain matters as bargainable and exclude others as beyond the union's interest. Such labels do not often stick. With changing economic, social, and political relation-

[19] This has been true of unions dealing with employers operating small shops with a slight capital investment, who have sometimes in the past removed almost overnight to a location outside a unionized area in hope of escaping the union scale of wages.

ships, issues which were once of no concern to the workers, presumably because they were beyond their control, or those not immediately affecting their welfare become of direct interest, with the possibility of control discovered or created. One may question whether the impact of the union on any given sphere of business operation is desirable or undesirable, just as one may wonder whether the influence of a trade association is beneficial or not, but this is a question to which the answer cannot be readily found simply by dividing all business matters into the two classifications of those which are bargainable and those which are not bargainable.

The difficulty which some people encounter in thus accepting the possibility of the expanding influence of unionism is that it poses the further insistent question: Where will it all end? To this no answer can be supplied, despite the dogmas of conservative despair and radical determinism. We may be sure, however, that the efforts to make the process of change *end now* are foredoomed to failure. Energies may be more effectively expended in directing the course of changes which are prompted by evolving social relationships than in seeking to halt them. The issue then becomes less one of *whether* the unions should be heard on certain matters of business operation than one of how well considered their proposals are. Management cannot defend its conceived interests simply by turning a deaf ear on particular topics and repeating "no," for the bargaining power of unions at times will permit such a rude reply to be overridden. Nor are unions likely to make good for long their "right" to joint control if the effect is to ignore other interests than their own. It is through discussion and mutual persuasion that the best chances lie for determining the workers' "proper" interest in the conduct of the business organization on which, in varying degrees, they and others depend for their livelihood.

The Nature of
Collective Bargaining

chapter 5

Efforts to define the nature of a thing often lead to sterile argument. Concepts necessarily reflect points of view, but in the social sciences there is usually limited opportunity to "test" their reliability. In economics, for example, much can and has been written, but inconclusively, about the meaning or nature of "capital," "rent," "interest," "value," "money," and like terms. Such discussion is not purely of academic interest. It is not true, as is often maintained, that any definition is as good as another as long as it is used consistently. How people define collective bargaining—that is, how they regard it—will in part determine the practice of collective bargaining.[1]

We shall not here be concerned with all the purposes or functions which collective bargaining *might* serve. We are concerned with its character as it is found in the United States, with what might be called its "generic nature." We are not interested at the moment, for example, in the fact that at times collective bargaining has been made an instrument of political party advancement or that some political creeds advocate its use for this purpose.

[1] In this sense, definition need not be actual verbalization. An employer or union official may have a conception of collective bargaining which affects his practice of it even though he has never reduced that conception to words.

108

Thus Communists have not disguised their belief that trade unions in a Communist regime are instruments of the state and that in a non-Communist country they should be converted into agents for the party's interests. There are adequate grounds for believing that some trade unionists in the United States have accepted this view. It is not arguable, however, that collective bargaining is essentially a method of gaining political control, even though it may on occasion be utilized for that purpose.

Collective Bargaining and the Common Rule

Through collective bargaining, agreement is reached on the general terms governing all employees within the bargaining unit. Variations among employees in certain particulars may persist, as in the wage differentials between workers in different occupations and even between workers performing the same job but having different skills; in the hours assignments; in the preference for promotion; and so on. But such variations are permissible because (1) they are deemed of too little importance to require general regulation, (2) they are differences above some minimum or below some maximum standard which is generally applicable, or (3) they are brought about by the general standard itself, as when one employee is preferred over another because of superior ability or long service.

Collective bargaining, then, seeks an agreement whose terms not only prescribe uniformity of treatment of employees but also allow diversity and permit variation of treatment. Some terms may, for example, set uniform standards of disciplinary action applicable to all, while others, such as those governing layoffs, allow diverse treatment according to seniority. Still other terms permit management to vary its rewards to workers within certain discretionary limits, as in the case of promotions. It may be free to promote as long as there is no discrimination on the basis of union activity, race, religion, or politics. Theoretically the agreement also establishes certain areas wherein employees may be treated individually, without regard to uniformity, standards of deviation, or discretionary limits, since most agreements specifically recognize the rights and powers of management in certain matters as complete and unimpaired—the so-called "management's rights clauses." In practice, however, an unbounded right of individual rule as opposed to general rule is more an illusion than a reality, since such areas of managerial independence are always bounded by the proviso that they are subject to any limitations imposed elsewhere in the agreement. Discretionary boundaries are thus imposed, even though they may not much hamper the freedom of management in the particular areas enumerated in the management's rights clause.[2]

[2] Thus the Labor-Management Relations Act of 1947, Section 9(a), allows

Despite these differences in the form of the collective bargaining rules, they all remain *general* rules. If deviation in treatment among individuals is permitted, the bases for deviation or the limits of discretion are *generally* applicable. The collective agreement is, in fact, a collective of "common rules." It is the result of a collective bargaining effort which seeks to eliminate competition among workers and to enable the group to participate in the determination of the conditions of employment.

Whenever there were fewer jobs than applicants and no organization among the workers, the neediest and most desperate of the jobseekers were likely to underbid their competitors simply to obtain *some* job and *some* income. It was not a ruthless employer who brought about this situation, but rather the operation of individual competition in the labor market. Competitive pressures threatened the standard of living of all workers, of course, not just the underbidders. To meet the threat, workers had to agree on the minimum terms which might be accepted by *any* worker, regardless of his personal willingness to accept less. "The competition of master with master for labor is not so keen that it is not neutralized and more than neutralized by the competition of laborer with laborer for work; and by combination the laborer tries to do away with the suicidal competition of laborers with each other." [3] The elimination of individual competition was achieved through the device of the common rule, replacing individual terms with general terms in all the important particulars on which employment might turn. The common rule became the collective agreement.

The common rule was developed through collective action, but of course it could be applied without negotiating an agreement *with the employer*. Simply by agreeing among themselves to the minimum terms which any of them would accept, workers could establish the common rule. As we have seen in an earlier chapter, this indeed was the method first attempted. Suffering from some grievance or believing themselves entitled to an increase in wages, workers would come together and take an oath, sometimes with hand on the Bible, that they would not work for terms less than those they decided upon among themselves. The disadvantage of this procedure, however, was that if new or migrant workers came into the community, they had to be persuaded or coerced to join in the oath. Capitalizing on this weakness, the masters would advertise for workmen in newspapers in nearby communities. Owing no allegiance to the local common rule, such imported employees often proved effective in reducing wages and acting as strikebreakers. A further difficulty lay in the fact that despite an oath, the financially weakest workers would sometimes be forced to accept the mas-

---

management to bargain individually with any worker as long as the settlement does not conflict with the collective agreement.

[3] John Davidson, *The Bargain Theory of Wages*, New York: G. P. Putnam's Sons, 1898, pp. 167–168.

ters' terms, thereby precipitating a general abandonment of the common rule. Strike benefits were very early inaugurated in the American labor movement to guard against such defections, but they were sometimes insufficient. As long as the employer remained free to ignore the common rule whenever he was able, the rule remained in danger.

Greater protection for collective bargaining and insurance of uniform action among workers were provided by the device of the closed shop. If the employer could be forced to hire only those workers who were members of the union, then the union could safeguard its common rules whether the employer agreed to them or not. The departure by any worker from the terms jointly agreed upon in union meeting could be punished by expulsion from the union; if the employer hired only through the union, the expelled worker could be restored to employment only by admitting his error and paying a fine or by moving to another community in which the union was not as strong. The effectiveness of this system is evidenced in the history and growth of the International Typographical Union, which has relied from its inception upon the closed shop to safeguard its common rules.[4] In general, however, employers have resisted the closed shop as the primary support of any common rules, since such a system could too easily deny them any voice in the making of those rules.

Because of the difficulties of enforcing uniform terms by unilateral action, organized workers finally began to use collective bargaining as a means to secure an agreement. When an agreement was negotiated and accepted by *both* union and employer, the threat from needy unemployed or competing workmen was eliminated for the life of the agreement. The employer as well as the workers agreed to the minimum terms which were to be applied to all, regardless of their willingness to work for less. The employer benefited by assurance of stable labor costs and labor conditions while the agreement remained in effect. Moreover, the process of collective bargaining leading to the joint agreement not only permitted the safeguarding of the terms of employment but also provided an opportunity for the workers, through their representatives, to have a voice in the conditions under which they worked. The purpose of collective bargaining and of the common rule thus expanded from one simply of protection to one of participation as well.

Regarded from this point of view, collective bargaining gave rise first to the common rule and, out of that, to the collective agreement. Thus the nature of the agreement is illuminated by the nature of the common rule and the bargaining out of which it developed. In probing that nature, we may use as a basis for analysis the relationship of the collective interests

[4] This reliance explains the determined fight made by the ITU against the enforcement of the Labor-Management Relations Act clause banning the closed shop.

which brought the agreement into existence and the individual interests of the employees. We are now concerned with the collective as against the private, with the group as against the individual, and with the general as against the specific. In this examination we shall necessarily be led to consider the whole of collective bargaining—the grievance process as well as the determination of the common rules—since the settling of grievances involves, among other things, the application of the rules to particular situations and cases.

The problem with which we are now dealing can be set forth more concretely. It is sometimes said that the grievance process is a means of meeting individual needs and resolving the tensions of individual employees. Such means and resolutions transcend the collective agreement and extend collective bargaining, for they must take into account the entire range of human emotions and sentiments, which are evoked in the industrial community no less than in any other community. Since one presumes that no agreement can be foresighted and comprehensive enough to provide for all contingencies provoking grievances, the adjustment procedure must fill the breach by seeking solutions to these personal problems. That no provision is made for the terms of settlement in the agreement is irrelevant. Such problems remain and "cannot be exorcised by pronouncing them out of contract bounds." [5]

The soundness of this line of thought should not, however, blind us to the question it raises but does not answer. Granted that individual grievances may have an important effect upon harmony in a shop and that all situations likely to provoke grievances cannot be anticipated in the agreement, it is also true that the provisions of the agreement do not always *successfully* solve the grievances which they *do* embrace. And if "the sense of injustice of aggrieved workers runs deeply to the very center of their being," [6] the same reasoning which suggests the advisability of seeking solutions to personnel problems even if not covered by the agreement also suggests the possible desirability of seeking better solutions than those which may be permitted by applicable clauses of the agreement. Arbitrators have thus frequently been asked to disregard the "technicality" of a contract and meet the "human" and production problems involved in grievances. One outstanding arbitrator has declared that "the quality and success of the administration of the agreement is not measured by the degree of compliance with it, but rather by the degree to which it aids the achievement of just and harmonious production. . . . The labor agreement looks to

[5] Isadore Katz, "Minimizing Disputes through the Adjustment of Grievances," *Law and Contemporary Problems,* vol. 12 (1947), p. 259. This article presents a well-reasoned version of the above argument.

[6] The same.

continuous performance . . . and continuous association in a common enterprise from which both parties must derive their shares." [7]

What then becomes of the common rule? What is the nature of collective bargaining when the forms of its agreements may be abandoned or applied from case to case? Here we encounter the issue of the relationship of the collective to the individuals composing it. In analyzing this problem we shall discover that the manner in which the collective agreement is regarded is tied closely to the way in which one views the bargaining process. One may examine the nature of collective bargaining and the agreement from three viewpoints. While they are not necessarily conflicting, they focus upon different aspects and suggest divergent answers to union-management problems and public policy conclusions. These viewpoints are that collective bargaining is (1) a means of contracting for the sale of labor, (2) a form of industrial government, and (3) simply a system of industrial relations. We shall discuss each of these in turn.

The Marketing Concept and the Agreement as a Contract

The collective agreement historically has been a statement of the terms on which a company's employees collectively are willing to work. It has, of course, been distinguished from the labor contract, under which an individual *commits* himself to perform service for a period (sometimes of indefinite duration) for a specified remuneration. Failure to honor this commitment may render a person liable to a damage suit for breach of contract. The collective agreement commits no one to give service but merely assures that when service is given, it shall be rewarded as provided for in the agreement. Even this legal distinction, however, does not attempt to disguise the fact that the individual labor contract constitutes little more than acceptance of the collective agreement by employees and that for most practical purposes the individual labor contract has been replaced by the collective agreement.

Collective bargaining thus may be viewed as the process which determines on what terms labor will continue to be supplied to a company by its present employees or will be supplied in the future by newly hired workers. The primary emphasis which is generally given to the wage scale serves to reinforce this view, since it suggests the money exchange, which is the most prevalent basis for contract. A union demands on behalf of its members that the employer raise wages by a specified percentage or by so much per

[7] Shulman, *Conference on Training of Law Students in Labor Relations,* vol. 3 (1947), pp. 663–664. See also Morris L. Ernst, "The Development of Industrial Jurisprudence," *Columbia Law Review,* vol. 21 (1921), p. 155.

hour or rescind an announced wage cut. If its demand is not met, a strike is threatened. If there is no agreement on the price of labor, no sale will be made. Employees are willing to continue to sell their individual labor only on terms collectively determined, and collective bargaining is the process by which the terms of sale are ultimately settled.

If the money basis for the collective contract suggests most strongly a sale of labor, it does not exclude the possibility that other terms may also be insisted upon and granted. A union may demand not only a given wage scale but also sanitary improvements, shorter hours, longer lunch periods, a seniority system, a vacation plan, and sundry other items as the price of the labor of its members. But regardless of the variety of such demands and their nonmonetary nature, they still constitute the terms of sale of the labor which is collectively controlled by the union. Collective bargaining remains a means for employees to sell their manpower through a common agent.

As already noted, collective bargaining originated as a means of enforcing a common bill of wages, and the forerunner of the modern trade agreement was a simple price list setting forth the amounts to be paid to every worker for a particular job. Such a list today would be called the "piece rates." At least as early as 1827 in this country, it was suggested that a bill of prices setting forth an agreed-upon schedule of piece rates in the tailoring trade might contain the necessary elements of a contract. A Philadelphia recorder, during a trial alleging conspiracy on the part of the journeymen tailors, referred to such a schedule as an "implied contract" and intimated that its violation might be made the basis for a civil action.[8] For a variety of reasons, however, legal recognition of the status of the agreement was delayed. For one thing, there was considerable doubt about the legal status of the union, one of the contracting parties. The conspiracy doctrine in its extreme interpretation cast suspicion upon the union's very right of existence, and in a later period there was considerable confusion over the legal personality of an unincorporated association. Again, union-employer agreements were often regarded as simply gentlemen's understandings, statements of intention, or memoranda, and thus no more enforceable than the minutes of a meeting. The fact that the terms of employment might be accepted only after unilateral action by one of the parties enshrouded the process in an atmosphere of coercion quite contrary to the voluntarism presumed to accompany bilateral contracting.

Nevertheless, as the negotiated and written collective agreement became more customary, its close kinship to a contract became increasingly evident. Its voluntary nature was now considered to be preserved by that very coercion which earlier had beclouded its character; it was argued that the

---

[8] Reprinted by permission of the publishers from John R. Commons et al. (eds.), *Documentary History of American Industrial Society,* Glendale, Calif.: The Arthur H. Clark Company, 1910–1911, vol. 4, pp. 253–254.

privileges of strike and lockout were alternatives to contracting, for the exercise of bargaining power might or might not lead to acquiescence in proffered terms by the other. It was the bargaining which preceded or accompanied such coercion that gave new color to the use of coercive force.

There is thus no indication that the written trade agreement originated as a contract. In time, however, it borrowed the form of the contract, and as its use spread it became more and more related to the contract. Legal discussion of its enforceability used the contract as an analogy. The final report of the Industrial Commission in 1902 was quite explicit in its identification of the mechanics, if not the end result, of collective bargaining and contracting: "It should be clearly understood that the process by which employers and employees, directly and without the intervention of outside parties, agree upon the terms of the labor contract is precisely similar in nature to the process of bargaining between two parties regarding any other contract." [9] The report went on to deplore the fact that collective agreements were not given the legal standing of "other" contracts.[10]

Its peculiar nature became the subject of legal analysis.[11] In 1931, after a survey of reported decisions, one specialist reached the conclusion that a collective agreement was "something more than a custom yet something different from a contract for the breach of which damages is the normal remedy." [12] Increasingly, collective bargaining was being accepted as a

[9] *Final Report of the Industrial Commission,* Reports of the Industrial Commission, vol. 19 (1902), p. 834.

[10] The same, p. 856: "Not a few persons believe that the system of collective bargaining would become much more effective if the terms of trade agreements were made legally binding in the same way as the terms of other contracts."

[11] Among articles in the law journals dealing specifically with this subject are the following: William Gorham Rice, Jr., "Collective Labor Agreements in American Law," *Harvard Law Review,* vol. 44 (1931), pp. 572–608; J. Blumberg, "Nature, Validity and Enforcement of Collective Bargaining Agreements," *New York University Law Quarterly Review,* vol. 11 (1933), pp. 262–269; H. C. Johnson, "An Analysis of the Present Legal Status of the Collective Bargaining Agreement," *Notre Dame Law Review,* vol. 10 (1935), pp. 413–443; G. T. Anderson, "Collective Bargaining Agreements," *Oregon Law Review,* vol. 15 (1936), pp. 229–253; T. R. Witmer, "Collective Labor Agreements in the Courts," *Yale Law Journal,* vol. 48 (1938), pp. 195–239; and M. A. Pipin, "Enforcement of Rights under Collective Bargaining Agreements," *University of Chicago Law Review,* vol. 6 (1939), pp. 651–672.

[12] W. G. Rice, Jr., *Harvard Law Review,* vol. 44 (1931), p. 604. Rice's judgment was based on his inability to uncover any case where damages had been awarded for a breach of the agreement except as the agreement was considered to form part of an individual contract, for the breach of which or fortuitous interference with which suit had been brought.

marketing process which resulted in a contract. In 1935, a leading labor economist testified before the Senate Committee on Education and Labor: "Now, collective bargaining has a well-defined meaning, the basis of which is cooperative marketing of labor. That is all it is. This is the basis of it." To elaborate, he compared the marketing of labor to the marketing of eggs, likening the grading of eggs for market to the grading of skills by the unions.[13]

A study made in the office of the solicitor of the U.S. Department of Labor revealed that by 1941, despite variations in state judicial practices, it was "possible to make a collective bargaining agreement that will be enforceable in the courts just as other contracts." [14] The contractual elements of voluntary agreement, a consideration for both parties, and means of enforcement were all presumed to be present. Finally, the Labor-Management Relations Act of 1947 threw open the federal courts to damage suits for violation of collective agreements, thus guaranteeing a judicial forum for such suits regardless of variations in state practices. The contractual status of the agreement was thus assured. Though union leaders were not entirely happy with the assurance, many of them have often inclined to the marketing theory of collective bargaining and have implicitly suggested that the agreement was a contract. The following exchange between John L. Lewis, then president of the United Mine Workers, and Charles O'Neill, chairman of the organized coal operators, which occurred during a collective bargaining session, reflects the marketing attitude.

> *Lewis* Mr. O'Neill and his associates presumably want some miners to work for them after July 1. Well, what have they to offer?
>
> *O'Neill* We would like to know what he [Lewis] wants us to pay. What is his price? We do not know. If we cannot find that out, we

[13] *National Labor Relations Board, Hearings on S. 1958,* 74th Cong., 1st Sess. (1935), pp. 873–875. In 1947, an attorney specializing in labor law testified at the House hearings on the Taft-Hartley Bill:

> I define bargaining as a process by which one person, if he wants something, approaches the man who has got it, and offers a price for it, and they use all of the arts of bargaining to reach an agreement. We had the process in this country in the old days when we did horse trading. We do it now when we trade in the old jalopy on a new car. We go to the dealer. We do some bargaining. And people, when they bargain, they use all sorts of wiles and arts and devices and techniques to get what they want.

Amendments to the National Labor Relations Act, Hearings on H.R. 8, 80th Cong., 1st Sess. (1947), vol. 4, p. 2733.

[14] David Ziskind, *The Law behind Union Agreements,* U.S. Department of Labor (1941), p. 2. (Mimeographed.)

cannot bargain or haggle or do what is done as he says in the market place. We want to go to the market place. We want to know what each seller has to give us and what he wants for it.[15]

There is an intimate connection between the marketing theory of bargaining process and the view of the collective agreement as a contract. Both come from the same ethical mold or from similar ones. Collective bargaining as a marketing process is based on a conception of the need to remedy a bargaining inequality which oppresses the individual worker. The philosophy of individualism which pervaded the political and economic theory of the nineteenth century assumed maximum mutual advantage when two or more people voluntarily entered into a "bargain" or contract. That assumption was negated, however, when the bargain was not made voluntarily but out of necessity, and to many it seemed increasingly clear that under most circumstances the individual worker was faced with the need of concluding some wage bargain. His alternatives were usually so restricted that only a casuist could consider his acceptance of a contract for employment voluntary.

The uncertain turn of the business cycle, the pressure of immigration, the cityward movement of farm population, and the spread of mechanization and mass-production techniques all seemed to create a perpetual competition for jobs, which placed employment at a premium. With little or no savings, the individual worker had scant means for sustaining a search for alternatives to proffered employment, at however low a wage. As one individual worker competing with innumerable other individual workers, he took what the employer set. The "bargain" was not between equals; the contract was forced by circumstances which seemed always to weigh upon the employee to the advantage of the employer. The unbalanced situation could be summed up in the phrase "labor's disadvantage." [16]

---

[15] *In the Matter of Inquiry in the Bituminous Coal Dispute,* Stenographer's Minutes before the Federal Mediation and Conciliation Service, June 22, 1948.

[16] W. H. Hutt, *Theory of Collective Bargaining,* London: P. S. King & Staples, Ltd., 1930, pp. 5–8. John Mitchell has likewise set forth the principle of labor's disadvantage in "The Economic Necessity of Trade-unionism," *Atlantic Monthly,* vol. 113 (1914), pp. 161–170, reprinted in *University of North Carolina Record,* Extension Series 40, no. 182 (1920), p. 22:

> Since the workingman has little or no money in reserve and must sell his labor immediately; since, moreover, he has no knowledge of the market and no skill in bargaining; since, finally, he has only his own labor to sell while the employer engages hundreds or even thousands of men and can easily do without the services of any one of them, the workingman, if bargaining on his own account and for himself alone, is at an enormous disadvantage.

It was this imbalance which collective action was designed to right. "The province of trade-union action is the strengthening of the position of the laborer as a bargainer, the enabling him, in particular, to resist that pressure of circumstances of which employers might be ready to take advantage." [17] This result could be achieved since by common action workers could prevent themselves from being played off one against the other. For this reason union members bitterly condemned the nonconformer and the nonunionist from the very inception of the labor movement. His independence, coupled with his bargaining weakness as an individual, threatened the position of all who had banded together. By using the device of the common rule, the employees collectively could insist that if an employer were to hire any of their number, he must offer no less than a standard minimum. While the employer might dispense with the services of any single employee, he could not dispense with the services of all. He was faced with the necessity of complying, of compromising, or of temporarily suspending operations in an effort to wear down the resistance of his employees.

The collective action by the workers did not create additional employment alternatives, of course. What it did was to accept the situation of limited alternatives but seek to restrict the employer's ability to profit from it.[18] It accomplished this by increasing the bargaining power of the workers relative to that of the employer. "The object of trade-union policy, through all the maze of conflicting and obscure regulations, has been to give to each individual worker something of the indispensability of labor as a whole." [19]

Perhaps too easily does the theory of collective bargaining as a marketing process assume that collective action of unions has *restored* some original equality of bargaining between workers and employers—an equality

[17] John Davidson, *The Bargain Theory of Wages,* New York: G. P. Putman's Sons, 1898, p. 268. One of the outstanding union leaders in the past, John Mitchell, president of the United Mine Workers, has similarly declared: "Trade unionism starts from the recognition of the fact that under normal conditions the individual, unorganized workman cannot bargain advantageously with the employer for the sale of his labor." *Organized Labor,* American Book and Bible House, 1903, pp. 2–3.

[18] Collective bargaining is, of course, not the only program sponsored by the labor movement. The union has used other devices to attack the lack of employment alternatives. In earlier years, organized workers unable to wrest from their employers terms which they felt justified founded cooperative workshops of their own. These efforts at self-employment, with only a few exceptions, proved ephemeral. More recently unions have turned to a political program for governmental provision of the number of jobs necessary to full employment when private industry fails to do so.

[19] Davidson, *The Bargain Theory of Wages,* p. 267.

that was taken to characterize their relationship under the philosophy of individualism. Aside from the tenuousness of this assumption, there is little to suggest that collective bargaining has established (or reestablished) an equality of advantage between management and workers. It has done so only in the sense that it is as difficult for one as for the other to dispense with some bargain if both are considered collectively. To the extent that an employer finds it a hardship to duplicate his entire staff of employees, a collective bargain is necessary to him, as it is to his employees, whereas under individualistic bargaining an agreement was necessary only to the employee. The questions of who occupies the more strategic position and who possesses the greater bargaining power remain to be answered, however.

Not only does the marketing concept of collective bargaining fail to focus attention upon these questions, but it also suggests that the agreement between the parties is strictly and definably limited. It constitutes the sum total of obligations of all parties to it. Running for a specified period of time, there is no requirement upon anyone to make further concessions or modify its terms during that period.[20] In the bargaining conference the union has marketed the labor of its members. The terms which it has secured are set forth in a binding contract.

The contract is now enforceable in courts of law,[21] though as a matter

[20] Whether such a requirement was involved in the obligation to bargain of the National Labor Relations Act had been a moot point until the revisions of the Labor-Management Relations Act of 1947 ruled specifically in the negative, at the same time asserting the contractual nature of the agreement, as has been noted, by its provision for federal jurisdiction in damage suits. The NLRB has held, however, that during the life of the agreement bargaining may be required with respect to matters which had not been discussed before or included in the agreement. See *California Cotton Cooperative Association,* 110 NLRB 1494 (1954).

[21]

(a) Suits for violation of contracts between an employer and a labor organization representing employees in an industry affecting commerce as defined in this Act, or between any such labor organizations, may be brought in any district court of the United States having jurisdiction of the parties, without respect to the amount in controversy or without regard to the citizenship of the parties.

(b) Any labor organization which represents employees in an industry affecting commerce as defined in this Act and any employer whose activities affect commerce as defined in this Act shall be bound by the acts of its agents. Any such labor organization may sue or be sued as an entity and in behalf of the employees whom it represents in the courts of the United States. Any money judgment against a labor organization in a

of practice the courts are seldom called upon to perform such a service, for most agreements contain within them their own means of enforcement—the grievance procedure. Only in the event of failure of this procedure to dispose of a dispute over the contractual obligation of the parties may that resort be had to the courts. Thus when the agreement is regarded as a contract, the grievance procedure *must* be viewed as a means of enforcing the contract. It may serve other functions as well—the settlement of disputes not otherwise provided for, for example—but its judicial function cannot be escaped.

Construction of the agreement as a contract leads naturally to its strict interpretation and application. Its terms represent the bargain struck. Pressure for deviation from its provisions to accommodate what are claimed as special circumstances is likely to be looked upon as only a scarcely concealed and inadmissible continuation of the same power tactics which led to its signing as a term settlement. To permit departure from the agreed provisions would be to encourage a constant rebargaining of the agreement throughout its lifetime. As a legal instrument, its clauses are expected to be honored for their period of effectiveness. Mutual agreement upon modification, while possible, is frowned upon for the same reason.

There is the further danger that to permit a loose construction of the bargain will set a precedent. What was intended only as an exception may become the rule. Moreover, if in the course of applying the terms some unanticipated consequence should create a problem for one party or the other, there is opportunity to amend the offending provision upon expiration of the agreement, at the time of renegotiation.

Considered in this light, the common rules become more or less rigid commandments. The settlement of a grievance is not governed by the circumstances peculiar to an individual's situation; moreover, settlement is not conditioned by special circumstances common to a class of cases. Settlement depends exclusively upon the rule as spelled out in the agreement, and the rule is to be applied without discrimination to all who come within its terms. The occasional injustice which may result is felt to be more than compensated for by assurance of performance, by stable employee-management relations, which come about when all concerned know what can be expected—the certainty of the consequences of particular actions or of the sequence of particular events. The primary purpose of the *common* rule is preserved by its even application.

---

district court of the United States shall be enforceable only against the organization as an entity and against its assets, and shall not be enforceable against any individual member or his assets.

Section 301(a) and (b) of the Labor-Management Relations Act of 1947, 61 Stat. 56, 29 U.S.C. § 185.

It does not follow that because the agreement is looked upon as a contract, grievances not covered by its terms will be necessarily disregarded. Such grievances may be settled between the parties without benefit of common rule. Nevertheless, there does follow a presumption that the agreement embodies *all* the obligations of the union-management relationship, and numerous agreements have specified that the grievance process may be directed only to alleged violations of the agreement.

The Governmental Concept and the Agreement as Law

Primarily because the marketing theory of collective bargaining seems to deny continuity in the bargaining relationship (as contrasted with a simple employer-employee relationship), a considerably different approach has been suggested. The contractual nature of the bargaining relationship is admitted, but the contract is viewed as a "constitution," on the basis of which is reared an industrial government for the plant, the company, or the industry (that is, for the bargaining unit). The need for some balance of bargaining power is accepted, but that balance rests firstly on the mutual dependency of the parties and secondly, and derivatively, on the power of each to "veto" the acts of the other.

The industrial constitution is written by the joint conference of union and management representatives which convenes periodically, "and the result of these conferences is always the same, an agreement of some kind, verbal or written, which, because of the mutual power to veto, must necessarily be a compromise." [22] The principal function of the constitution (or trade agreement) is to "set up organs of government, define and limit them, provide agencies for making, executing, and interpreting laws for the industry, and means for their enforcement." [23]

Prof. Sumner Slichter of Harvard University expressed this concept in one of the most widely quoted paragraphs in the literature of industrial relations:

> Through the institution of the state, men devise schemes of positive law, construct administrative procedures for carrying them out, and complement both statute law and administrative rule with a system of judicial review. Similarly, laboring men, through unions, formulate policies to which they give expression in the form of shop rules and

[22] William M. Leiserson, "Constitutional Government in American Industries," *American Economic Review,* vol. 12, Supplement (1922), p. 61. This article remains perhaps the most systematic exposition of the governmental approach to collective bargaining and has been chiefly relied on here to present that view.

[23] The same.

practices which are embodied in agreements with employers or are accorded less formal recognition and assent by management; shop committees, grievance procedures, and other means are evolved for applying these rules and policies; and rights and duties are claimed and recognized. When labor and management deal with labor relations analytically and systematically after such a fashion, it is proper to refer to the system as "industrial jurisprudence." [24]

In common with other governments, the industrial polity has its legislature, its executive branch, and its judiciary. The legislature consists of the shop and grievance committees, which meet as often as needed to supplement the basic laws of the trade agreement. The latter, because it is basic in its nature, cannot be expected to provide for all contingencies in the day-to-day operations of a business. New problems often arise which must be met before the trade agreement or industrial constitution can be amended. Local union committees meet with management to solve these problems, but such legislation as they enact must not, of course, conflict with the fundamental law of the agreement.

The agreement applies, of course, only to that business unit for which it has been drafted, and in the areas of operation which it covers it supersedes all other regulations and requirements. "Legislation," that is, a supplementary agreement, conflicting with its terms has no standing, just as congressional actions may be struck down if they do not conform to the Constitution. Any injury sustained as a result of such a violation of the basic agreement is customarily redressed, and applications of the agreement which are found faulty will be similarly treated. An early study of collective bargaining in the Chicago clothing industry pointed out the close analogy between collective bargaining and federal constitutional law, sorting the decisions of impartial chairmen (arbitrators, equivalent to a supreme court) into categories labeled "scope of the government," "jurisdiction of the industrial courts," "special immunities of the workers' representatives," "general immunities of industrial citizenship," and so on.[25] Agreements subsidiary to the basic collective agreement and in harmony with its terms must be similarly honored and may be similarly classified.

The right of initiative, within a framework of legislation, characterizes the executive branch. This authority is vested in management. Changes in methods of production, introduction of new machinery, determination of the products to be manufactured, scale and timing of production, standards of quality, and organization of personnel in such matters as assignments to jobs, transfers, layoffs, and promotions—these are typical areas in which the agreement either specifically or tacitly recognizes management as the

[24] Sumner Slichter, *Union Policies and Industrial Management,* Washington, D.C.: The Brookings Institution, 1941, p. 1.

[25] Leiserson, "Constitutional Government in American Industries," pp. 66–75.

executive office. It must accord with all the rules; it must lie within the boundaries jointly defined. Management may initiate a layoff, but it must proceed in line with any agreed-upon requirements concerning notice, designation of the employees to be laid off on the basis of seniority, part-timing of remaining employees, and so on. Management may discharge an employee for disciplinary reasons, but only after meeting jointly determined standards such as adequate warning, timely action, and a fair hearing.

The action taken by management may fail to comply with such statutory or constitutional requirements. Management may be uncertain about the precise nature of the standards to which it must conform. The actions of the shop committee may conflict with the basic agreement. To settle such issues, judicial machinery is needed. It is provided by the grievance procedure, culminating in arbitration, which for this purpose must be distinguished from the grievance procedure when employed to supplement the agreement—a legislative function. Questions of rights established under the contract which have been denied in practice are referred to joint tribunals, consisting of an equal number of union and management members. Compliance with procedural requirements is reviewed, as are the merits of the case. If injury is discovered, redress is made. In some instances these judicial officials sit as a court of equity, determining whether generally accepted conventions of fair dealing have been complied with. In other instances they interpret the meaning of the agreement for the guidance of the parties, and their ruling remains authoritative unless some future joint conference overrules it by amending the agreement. The details of this process will be explored in the next chapter.

To establish and maintain such an industrial government, with its three branches, continuity of the founding organizations must be assured. The government rests upon the management and the union jointly, and the passing of either means the end of the government. Continuity is far more significant under this approach to collective bargaining than under the marketing theory, for under the latter, collective terms may be negotiated periodically, with the organization of the workers lapsing between such "sales" without any necessarily harmful effect; under the governmental approach, however, the lapse of the industrial government between the constitutional conventions (that is, conferences to renegotiate the agreement) would be disastrous because it would result in the suspension of the process of jointly conferring on problems of mutual interest as they arise in the shop, the process which gives life and meaning to the bare bones of constitutionalism in industry.

In a manner that the marketing theory does not, the governmental theory of collective bargaining stresses the need for an exclusive representative of the employees in the bargaining unit. In contracting, a union may without difficulty negotiate terms applicable to its members only, leaving the remaining employees themselves to associate for similar purposes or to contract individually. The idea of competing sellers of labor, whether collective sellers or not, contains no anomaly. But a government—industrial or otherwise—which competed with other governments in the same jurisdiction for its citizens and subjects would present something new under the sun. Two parties may compete for control of a government, but the government itself is not duplicated except in a state of rebellion.

To fulfill its function, a government must have power to discipline its subjects in order to obtain compliance with its laws. Such a power is negated if the subjects may escape such discipline by the simple act of renouncing citizenship (that is, membership in the union) while remaining within the same jurisdiction, as either unattached employees or members of a rival union. The concept of joint government in industry moves one inexorably to accept the need for a single exclusive agency whose laws and judicial enforcement are uniform throughout the industrial area included in the bargaining unit, affecting all employees in that unit whether they are members of the union or not.[26] That is to say, the sovereignty of the industrial government must not be impaired.

Indeed, it is the emphasis on an exclusive government within a single bargaining unit which suggests the ethical principle underlying the governmental approach to collective bargaining. That principle may be stated as the sharing of industrial sovereignty. It has two facets. In the first place, it involves a sharing by management with the union of *power* over those who are governed, the employees. In the second place, it involves a joint defense of the *autonomy* of the government established to exercise such power, a defense primarily against interference by the state. Both stem from a desire to control one's own affairs.

With respect to the insistence by the union, as representative of the employees, on a sharing with management of the power to direct the lives of the employees, the effort proceeds along lines of establishing rules, regulations, or "laws" which are *mutually* acceptable—which have the approval of the employees, through their representatives, and are satisfactory to the employer. The power to promulgate such laws and to exercise such con-

---

[26] In our society, founded as it is upon democratic principles, this need for an exclusive rule-making agency in industry has found its expression, in our labor legislation, in the doctrine of majority representation (see Chapter 2). Under this doctrine all employees in the bargaining unit are given an opportunity to express their preferences among competing unions. The union which receives the largest vote, provided it receives a majority of the votes cast, is then designated as the exclusive representative of *all* the workers, whether they are members of the union or not, and unites with management in collective bargaining. The terms of the collective agreement are binding upon all employees in the bargaining unit.

trol—sovereignty in one sense—is no longer a prerogative of management but of union and management jointly, in the collective bargaining conference. "Government by discussion enters into industry (as it did in the state) when the ruler can no longer arbitrarily force obedience to his laws, and must get the consent of those who are to obey the regulations." [27]

Whereas this aspect of the sharing of sovereignty concerns participation in control, the second aspect concerns limitation of control by others. Management and union join in opposing the intervention of third parties in the settlement of their own industrial (governmental) problems:

> Organized groups may be regarded as having political attributes: they exercise a kind of private government over their members. In this relationship they have generally proved very impatient of any interference by the courts and have tried, in many instances, to establish in practice a more or less complete immunity from legal actions. The bylaws of trade unions, cooperatives, trade associations, and fraternal societies often prescribe limitations which prevent the appeal of domestic controversies to external agencies, and the courts will not interfere in intra-corporate affairs, for example, with the same readiness that they will adjudicate disputes between unorganized persons. Group autonomy is impossible where government intervenes continually in these domestic disputes. [28]

But it is not only the group governments of the trade union or the corporation, acting singly, which argue such immunity from outside intervention; it is equally the government which is jointly established by them, based on collective bargaining, which claims the privilege of nonintervention.

The antipathy to outside interference has been modified in the years since World War II to the extent that there is permitted a more widespread participation by government conciliators in negotiations which threaten to break down, even though the conciliators have no authority to impose a settlement. Voluntary arbitration of the terms of a new or renewing agreement is still not common, and any suggested adoption of systems of compulsory arbitration, even in restricted areas such as public utilities, is met with intense opposition from union officials and management alike.

Freedom to compose its affairs and relations in whatever manner and by whatever means it desired was deemed by management, when it possessed undisputed sovereignty in its industrial sphere, to be an essential ingredient of a liberal society. Now that the union has wrested a share of that sovereignty, it joins with management in claiming that an ethical principle of self-determination bars the intervention of others into this area of private group decision. The parties jointly assert an autonomy over their group affairs.

[27] Leiserson, "Constitutional Government in American Industries," p. 60.
[28] James J. Robbins and Gunnar Hecksher, "The Constitutional Theory of Autonomous Groups," *Journal of Politics,* vol. 3 (1941), pp. 12–13.

They share sovereignty over internal matters, and they defend that sovereignty from external interference.

Yet both management and unionists have learned the usefulness—perhaps even the necessity—of asking outsiders to sit as "judges" (arbitrators) of disputes that arise under the "constitution." While the parties customarily attempt to limit the arbitrator's jurisdiction, he is not often in fact limited. Complex, poorly drafted, or ambiguous contract provisions and the myriad unforeseen industrial situations that arise at the place of work result in the need for much interpretation and discretion. Justice Douglas wrote in a famous decision:

> The collective agreement . . . calls into being a new common law
> —the common law of a particular industry or of a particular plant
> . . . [and] arbitration is the means of solving the unforeseeable by
> molding a system of private law for all the problems which may arise
> and to provide for their solutions in a way which will gen-
> erally accord with the variant needs and desires of the parties.[29]

We may recall that common law is often referred to as judge-made law, which is to say that it is the application of principles which find their source elsewhere than in the written law of constitution or legislative statute but which by force of cumulation and precedent can be stated with a consistency, logic, and vitality that no other form of law has in greater degree. While the source of such law may be the courts, it may be traced further—in Justice Holmes's famous words—to "the felt necessities of the time, the prevalent moral and political theories, intuitions of public policy," [30] which find their expression through the courts.

The common law thus has an underlying basis of social morality which in time, however, is translated into objective standards carrying a normative rather than a moral quality. "In other words, the standards of the law are external standards, and, however much it may take moral considerations into account, it does so only for the purpose of drawing a line. . . . What the law really forbids, and the only thing it forbids, is the act on the wrong side of the line, be that act blameworthy or otherwise." [31] This objectification can, however, be overstated, for the "line" is not sharply drawn but is perhaps more like a strip, on each side of which an act is, objectively, legal or illegal but within which an act may be either, depending upon whether there is a more subjective appraisal of morality than of normality. Nevertheless, for a number of situations to which the principle applies, the strip is no different from a line, for they will fall on one side or

[29] *United Steelworkers of America v. Warrior and Gulf Navigation Co.,* 40 LC 66,629 (1960), 70,813–70,814.

[30] Oliver Wendell Holmes, Jr., *The Common Law,* Boston: Little, Brown and Company, 1881, p. 1.

[31] The same, p. 110.

another in any event; and moreover, the effect of weight of precedent is to narrow the strip, in some cases by hammering out specific exceptions to the principle or special classes of cases. The purpose of such objectification is to remove the necessity of probing intent and to permit ascertainment of compliance with the law on the basis of facts which are relatively more easily established. It matters not if a man *intended* well if his action, resulting in injury to others, departed from standards of permissible conduct; nor, conversely, is it significant that a man sought to inflict harm if his action was within the bounds of allowable behavior. In the absence of written standards of permissible action, the concept of "prudent" or "average" conduct may be resorted to (in Holmes's time, more frequently than in ours, a concept given content in specific situations by a jury of "average" citizens).

Now, in the same manner that a body of common law has grown up in society at large, so has a body of industrial common law been reared within our individual business concerns. Grievances not susceptible to settlement by application of the terms of the agreement may be resolved by referring them to some base of morality, stemming from the "felt necessities" of business operation juxtaposed to prevailing ethical standards and shared concepts of justice.[32] In time such moral determination is translated into normative standards—the drawing of the line or blocking out of the strip on either side of which an act is, on the face of the facts and regardless of intent or purpose, permissible or not permissible, a justified or unjustified grievance. In the union-management relationship this drawing of the line (or strip) is carried on by joint committees, and in the event of disagreement they often vest judgment in an individual or board of arbitration whose accumulating decisions serve the same purpose.

The origin of the term "common law" goes back to the days when in England the kings' courts established a judicial superiority over the numerous lesser jurisdictions of a previously decentralized kingdom, thus permitting the universalizing of legal principles and the consequent elimination of variant doctrines. In the same way, the development of industrial common

[32]

> [The] labor arbitrator's source of law is not confined to the express provision of the contract, as the industrial common law—the practices of the industry and the shop—is equally a part of the collective bargaining agreement although not expressed in it. The labor arbitrator is usually chosen because of the parties' confidence in his knowledge of the common law of the shop and their trust in his personal judgment to bring to bear considerations which are not expressed in the contract criteria for judgment.

Justice Douglas, majority opinion, *United Steelworkers of America v. Warrior and Gulf Navigation Co.*, 40 LC 66,629 (1960), 70,813.

law in a plant or company through joint grievance procedures has encouraged the development of standard principles of employee-management relations throughout the plant or company, to a considerable extent eliminating the diversity of practice between shops or departments. The plant or company has become the "kingdom" throughout which the "law" of personnel policy has been made common. But the universalizing process has not stopped here. There has been a strong tendency for those aspects of industrial relations which are not covered by specific individual agreements to accumulate a body of principles which become standard not only throughout the company but throughout industry. This result should not be surprising when we recall the nature of common law and the fact that it had its origin in the prevalent ethical concepts and the requirements of experience. The former are sufficiently similar throughout our society to provide a common basis for the standards governing employee-employer relations generally, and the business necessities are, if not equally similar, sufficiently so to tend in the same direction.

The area of industrial discipline provides perhaps the most favorable example of this action. One has only to examine a collection of grievance arbitration decisions to become aware of the recognition of common principles of judging whether an employee has been justly penalized. Without attempting a preciseness of formulation which perhaps is not possible, we may recognize the widespread acceptance of such objective standards as the promulgation of rules or the issuance of orders which the employee may reasonably be expected to know of and to understand before he can be disciplined for their violation; procedural requirements such as the specification of the offense for which punishment is imposed and the opportunity for discussion, investigation, and a fair hearing, with the accused employee permitted the counsel of his union representative; a substantial equivalent of the ban on double jeopardy and something akin to a statute of limitations; evidential requirements as to weight and burden of proof; the limitation of managerial discretion by standards of what constitute reasonable and permissible penalties; and so on. Such principles will commonly be insisted upon by employees and their union agents and enforced by arbitrators or umpires, regardless of whether they find expression in the agreement or not.

We have thus made a distinction between the constitutional or statutory law of industry and its common law. In the former, the agreement establishes the terms of the employee-management relationship, and individual cases are governed by those terms. In the area of common law, where no written standards control, it is the mutual recognition of the requirements of morality and the needs of operation which provides the basis of decision and ultimately the norms of action. In the case of the written rule, bargaining power—the superior strength of one contestant over the other, management in one instance and the union in another—determines the nature of the particular relationship. In the case of the unwritten rule, the relationship is less localized and takes its roots in prevalent *social* customs, outlooks, and folkways. Deviation from terms of the written rule may be difficult—logic prevails—but deviation from the unwritten code is less difficult if that code is founded on an expectancy simply of reasonable behavior under given circumstances. To repeat after Holmes, the life of such a system of prescribed conduct stems not from logic but from experience.

The sharpness of such a distinction becomes blunted upon reflection, however. In practice there is less difference between the two systems of law, for the *interpretation* and *application* of the statute (or the agreement) must proceed from the same individuals who look to the institutional setting—even though sometimes tardily—for guidance in construing what actions may reasonably be required of people in their relations with each other. The same ethical forces which help to determine the common law continue to operate even when standards of behavior have been reduced to writing, and these serve to mold the law in operation. As Holmes has suggested, the primary function of the statute is to induce the judges to lay down a rule of law; it serves to influence, and it becomes a "matter of fact" to be weighed along with all the other facts in a case.[33] It does not often, however, furnish ready-made answers to specific problems, except perhaps in those cases where such an answer would probably have been reached anyway. In applying a seniority clause which recognizes greater merit and ability over length of service, the determining of what constitutes greater merit and ability, of what indicates such superiority, and of whose judgment is final may be based less on logical derivatives from the seniority clause of the agreement than on the experience and morality of the time and place. And in time such moral judgment becomes normative judgment, leading to objective standards which in fact replace the written rule of the agreement.

But if there is this tendency, as seen by those who hold the governmental or jurisprudential view of collective bargaining, the reliance upon experience as one of the bases of judgment means that the drive to universalize is held in check. There are two influences at work, seemingly contradictory in nature: one, the effort to establish the *common* rule, standards which establish the same liability for reasonable behavior on the part of all within the social unit; and the other, the reliance upon the logic of the situation rather than the logic of the rule to determine cases which seem to warrant special treatment even though falling within the rule. This is the universalizing as opposed to the individualizing principle, with sufficient recognition of the latter—the *extraordinary* justice which was the basis for the early system of equity—to make the former more acceptable.

[33] Holmes, *The Common Law,* pp. 150–151.

For those who accept this view of the collective agreement there is not the same urgency for a strict adherence to its provisions as for those who consider it a contract. Deviations are permissible and at times even desirable; there is more emphasis upon reasonable conduct and less upon logical consistency, without at the same time belittling that virtue. Departures from the common rule, if founded in the requirements of experience and morality, are looked upon as preserving rather than destroying the common rule; the rule becomes less brittle as it is made more flexible.

The Concept of Industrial Relations (Industrial Governance) and the Agreement as Jointly Decided Directives

The governmental concept of collective bargaining proceeds by analogy. It likens the system of union-management relations to "the constitutional forms well known in modern states." [34] There is, however, no need for such analogy. The nature of the bargaining process is explainable in terms appropriate to its own industrial setting—it is a method of conducting industrial relations, a procedure for jointly making decisions on matters affecting labor. This view is not antithetical to the governmental approach, but it discards the analogy to *state* government and builds upon the fact of *group* government. It recognizes that in every institution or organization some governmental form is necessary. The presence of the union allows the workers, through their union representatives, to participate in the determination of the policies which guide and rule their work lives. The expressed willingness or unwillingness of union leaders to participate in making "business" decisions and administering shop rules is entirely irrelevant. The fact that time and again union leaders have disavowed any interest in becoming decision makers is immaterial. Collective bargaining *by its very nature* involves union representatives in decision-making roles.

The bargaining conference that negotiates the agreement exercises final

[34] From Prof. F. S. Deibler's comment on Leiserson, "Constitutional Government in American Industries," p. 88. Deibler goes on to say:

> From a sociological point of view, I suppose, it is correct to emphasize group action and to show how similar sets of circumstances tend to develop similar institutions, whether these influences are operating within the larger social group or within that group represented by the employer-employee relations. The significant thing in this study, as I see it, is not the kind or form of institution that is developing, but the fact that an orderly procedure in disposing of conflicting interests has been devised and that one should analyze that procedure to see what changes it imposes upon the relations of the parties thereto.

and binding authority in those areas with which it concerns itself. Union representatives meet with owner representatives to reach joint decisions which are incorporated in a written agreement and which cannot be overruled or rescinded for the period of agreement, except by another joint conference possessing similar authority. Union representatives alone are powerless to modify its terms; owner representatives (those whom we designate as management) are equally without authority to alter the joint agreement. It is subject to change only by *mutual* agreement of these two groups of representatives.

The agreement thus becomes a set of directive orders, a guide for administrative action within the firm. It provides a framework bounding the discretion of managers and unionists alike. At lower levels of company and union there may be further negotiations, carried on within the framework of the collective agreement; plant officials and a local union leader, for example, often negotiate subsidiary agreements within the permissible discretionary limits of the master agreement covering all the plants of a company. Or at the other extreme, a shop foreman may collaborate informally with a union steward by working out a private understanding as to how they will handle recommendations for promotions, within the terms set forth in the collective agreement. In some instances a local union leader may join with lower-level managers to establish and carry out policies on which the master agreement is silent. For example, an agreement may say nothing about transfers, but the plant superintendent—within the limits of discretion allowed him—may locally negotiate a transfer policy with the workers' representatives. In these and other transactions where the union leaders participate in making managerial policy they must be responsible to their superior union officials and mindful of their rights and duties under the agreement if they are not to threaten the whole structure of functional organization within the company.

Union leaders and workers want some means of assuring the enforcement of the decisions in which they participate and of questioning those decisions made by managers which they may come to feel are unsatisfactory. The grievance procedure, described in the previous chapter, is the instrument by which the union and workers can test whether the limitations on managerial discretion have been observed in practice. (As also noted in the last chapter, it may be used as well to continue bargaining, binding management further or loosening the bonds stipulated in the agreement.) The agreement may, for example, establish the policy that in scheduling vacations, the employees' wishes shall be considered. Those applying this policy are not forced to acquiesce in the employees' desire. They retain discretion in the final scheduling, but they are obligated procedurally to entertain the requests of the workers and substantively to accommodate such expressed preferences where feasible. Failure to give consideration to employees' wishes can be made the basis for complaint, and the union may force compliance with the agreement, appealing to arbitration as a last resort. An appeal to the strike is possible, but usually both union and management have found arbitration to be a better method of settling disputes over compliance with the explicit and assumed provisions of the agreement.

In every business—indeed, in any organization—there are, however, numerous *implied* directives which take their place alongside those which have been made specific. An eminent labor scholar, Archibald Cox, has pointed out:

> There are too many people, too many problems, too many unforeseeable contingencies to make the words of the contract the exclusive source of rights and duties. One cannot reduce all the rules governing a community like an industrial plant to fifteen or even fifty pages. Within the sphere of collective bargaining the institutional characteristics and the governmental nature of the collective-bargaining process demand a common law of the shop which implements and furnishes the context of the agreement. We must assume that intelligent negotiators acknowledged so plain a need unless they stated a contrary rule in plain words.[35]

If the operations of the business are to go forward, persons in administrative positions must thus often interpolate or infer the policies that they invoke. They must so act because they have been given no clear directive and no firm limits to their discretion. Though they do not possess final authority, they must proceed on the basis of what they believe those who do possess such authority expect of them. Sometimes the inference is easy to make and unlikely of error. Other times it may not be so clear and may be more likely to contain error or, at a minimum, to result in disparate administrative policies throughout the company. Despite this danger, the process of administrative interpolation cannot be eliminated. The agreement does not—cannot—spell out all the rules and provisions which the union and employer jointly expect to be observed in daily operations. All aspects of the organized employee relationship cannot possibly be anticipated. After outlining the most important provisions, the best that can be done is to suggest the general principles of fairness and cooperation which are intended to guide *all* decisions. Decisions made (generally by some member of management, less commonly by a union official) in accordance with assumptions which the other party questions may be challenged in the grievance procedure, just as in the case of decisions made in accordance with the more definite standards of the agreement. Settlement of these

[35] "Reflections on Labor Arbitration," *Harvard Law Review,* vol. 72 (1959), p. 1402.

questions by means of the grievance procedure assists in clarifying intentions which may otherwise remain vague and uncertain.

Where the union is involved, there are thus two kinds of provisions for management to observe—the known written provisions of the agreement and the assumed guides or standards in which union interest is implicit but not always actively expressed. The difference between these two sets of guides results primarily from the greater precision and universality of the one over the other and only secondarily from any delimitation of the union's fields of interest. Their purpose is the same: to supply a basis for action and decision which is acceptable to both the union and the employer in those matters where mutuality is admitted and discretion required.

Once we recognize the sameness in purpose of the explicit provisions set forth in the agreement and of the rules which must be assumed, we can see the agreement in its proper perspective. It becomes not a binding legal document, but rather a guide to workers, union leaders, and management. As such it should be subject, first, to all the flexibility required for the accomplishment of its intended objective and, second, to all the limitations required for the attainment of this end. But it is the operating requirements of production in conformity with the mutual interests involved in production that are decisive; the *application* of the agreement provides its significance and reveals its nature.

Deviations from the provisions of the agreement are permissible if the parties agree they are necessary to gain the objectives for which the provisions were themselves drafted; deviations may also be defended if they pose no threat to the standards set forth in the agreement. In effectively performing their administrative activities, both managers and union leaders must depend upon reasonably continuous guides and understandings. Their decisions must be reasonably consistent in application. If deviations are so frequent or so important as to threaten a still desired provision or if they raise doubt about the standard itself, they vitiate the function of the agreement. Departures are sometimes desirable for operational reasons, though, and they can be countenanced as long as they do not create such a danger. In the terms we have previously used, application of the common rule is determined by operational requirements. The presumption in favor of the common rule may be rebutted by special circumstances which indicate that a special solution is preferable.

We are indebted to Prof. Harry Shulman, for some years umpire for the Ford Motor Company and the United Automobile Workers, for an elaboration of the place of arbitration in the grievance procedure under such a conception of the nature of the collective agreement:

> Unlike litigants in a court, the parties in a collective labor agreement must continue to live with each other both during the dispute and thereafter. While they are antagonists in some respects, they are

also participants in a joint enterprise with mutual problems and mutual interests. The smooth and successful operation of the enterprise is important to the welfare of both. A labor dispute submitted to arbitration is not a controversy as to a past transaction, like the typical law suit in which each litigant desires to win, and, win or lose, to wind up the litigation and have nothing more to do with the matter. A labor dispute submitted to arbitration is a mutual problem which affects the future relations of the parties and the smooth operation of their enterprise. The objective of the parties, notwithstanding their contentions in advocacy, must be, not to win the immediate contentions, but to achieve the best solution of the problem under the circumstances. An apparent victory, if it does not achieve such a solution, may boomerang into an actual defeat. An award which does not solve the problem and with which the parties must nevertheless live, may become an additional irritant rather than a cure.

This means that the parties' approach must be radically different from that of litigants. A litigant does not care whether he wins his law suit because the tribunal understood the problem and made a wise judgment or because the tribunal was actually confused or was influenced by wooden technicality, or irrelevant or emotional considerations. But the parties in a labor dispute submitted to arbitration, seeking an award with which they must both live harmoniously in the future must seek not merely a victory but a wise and enlightened award based on relevant factors and full understanding of the problem. And they must, therefore, seek to have the arbitrator know as much as possible about their enterprise, their interests in it, and the problem involved.[36]

The ethical principle underlying the concept of collective bargaining as a process of industrial governance is that those who are integral to the conduct of an enterprise should have a voice in decisions of concern to them. We may call this the "principle of mutuality." It is a correlate of political democracy; as Brandeis pointed out, "collective bargaining is today the means of establishing industrial democracy—the means of providing for workers in industry the sense of work, of freedom, and of participation that democratic government promises them as citizens." [37]

---

[36] Justice Douglas took judicial notice of the difference between labor agreements and the usual contract in the *Warrior* case: "When most parties enter into a contractual relationship they do so voluntarily, in the sense that there is no real compulsion to deal with one another as opposed to dealing with other parties. This is not true of the labor agreement. The choice is generally not between entering or refusing to enter into the relationship, for that in all probability pre-exists the negotiations." *United Steelworkers of America v. Warrior and Gulf Navigation Co.*, 40 LC 66,629 (1960), 70,813.

[37] Louis D. Brandeis, *The Curse of Bigness,* Osmond K. Fraenkel (ed.), as

Mutuality recognizes that property is the basis for authority only over property. Authority over men requires consent. Defining authority within the enterprise thus involves defining areas of joint concern within which decisions must be sought by agreement. As conceptions of what corporate activities vitally affect workers' interests expand, so too does the area of joint concern. And as the area of joint concern expands, so too does the participation of the union in the management of the enterprise.

The principle of mutuality is often misunderstood. It is sometimes suggested that advising with the union, before managerial decisions in certain areas are made, constitutes primarily a sop to the union itself, rather than a direct advantage to the workers. If the managerial decision is of benefit to the workers, it is argued, why should consultation be necessary, unless it is designed to support the notion that management benefits are only "bread and circuses" to delude the workers and that only through the union can lasting advances be made? [38]

If the owner-appointed management on its own initiative wishes to grant paid vacations to its workers, why should it not be free to do so without bargaining with the union? The answer lies in the mutuality of concern with such a policy. On what basis shall vacations be granted? To what extent, if at all, should employees with long-term service benefit over those with short-term service? On what basis should compensation be granted—average earnings (if so, over what period?); straight rates, with overtime included; with extra pay if holidays fall in the vacation period? Is it possible that employees would prefer less vacation if more paid holidays were granted, or would they prefer a less liberal vacation plan if more liberal retirement policy were provided? On what basis shall vacations be scheduled? What if the company cannot spare key workers when their planned vacation period arrives? Should employees be required to take their vacations during periods of layoff, whenever those may occur? Can vacations be split? All these and numerous other questions can be raised upon the introduction of a vacation system. They *can,* of course, be answered by owner-appointed management acting alone, but whether such answers best meet the desires of the employees, balanced against the needs of the business, cannot be assured unless there is opportunity for the workers to discuss such matters through their representatives. This means a process in

---

projected by Clarence M. Lewis, New York: Viking Press, Inc., 1934, pp. 70–95.

[38] This is the viewpoint expressed in "Improvement in Terms of Employment as an Unfair Labor Practice," *Harvard Law Review,* vol. 54 (1941), pp. 1039–1040, and it is the view of those managers who espouse or practice "Boulwarism," a management approach developed in the 1950s by Lemuel R. Boulware of General Electric. The company's slogan which accompanied the approach was "Do right voluntarily."

which the workers, by representation procedure, join in managing the affairs of concern to them.

The principle of mutuality does not compel agreement before action can be undertaken. It constitutes no injunctive process operating against continuity of the business. It requires only discussion in good faith with an intention to reach agreement if at all possible. If there is no meeting of minds, however, solution must come, under existing institutional arrangements, through a contest of economic power. "Absent a contractual waiver of [the right to strike] mutuality requires, and collective agreements are to be construed as contemplating, that if the employer is left free [after negotiations] to impose revisions in employment terms without regard to the desires of the employees, the latter are entitled to a comparable degree of freedom of action, namely, the peaceable withholding of their service, in order to protest, or to secure the nullification of the employer's action." [39] The fact that managerial decisions in business operations may be reached through such pressure devices, as an accepted method and procedure, is one of the phenomena distinguishing our economic society from most others, both historically and to a lesser degree contemporaneously.

Finally, the determination of the areas of joint concern, within which the bargaining process operates, involves a process of progressive definition.[40] In part that definition may be supplied by law, through labor legislation, and through administrative rulings and court decisions.[41] Much more importantly, however, it is provided by agreement between the parties themselves. The same process by which agreement is reached in areas of mutual concern also decides the boundaries of those areas. Definition may not be easy, and it may be forthcoming only after strike or lockout. But this process of defining the areas wherein joint agreement shall be sought is itself a matter for joint agreement, and it is subject to the same procedures.

Summary and Conclusions

We may briefly summarize these three views of collective bargaining as follows.

The marketing concept looks upon collective bargaining as a means of contracting for the sale of labor. It is an exchange relationship. Its justification is its assurance of some voice on the part of the organized workers in

[39] *In the Matter of Massey Gin and Machine Workers,* 78 NLRB 189 (1948).

[40] See Chapter 4, The Subject Matter of Collective Bargaining.

[41] The Supreme Court has now declared that the law requires bargaining over some issues. Neither party can refuse to complete an agreement just because the other party will not meet its demands on a "mandatory" issue. See *NLRB v. Borg-Warner Corp.,* 34 LC 71,492 (1958), 356 U.S. 342.

the terms of sale. The same objective rules which apply to the construction of all commercial contracts are invoked, since the union-management relationship is concerned as a commercial one. If a situation is covered by the terms of the agreement, the answer to the specific problem is logically derivative from the agreement.

The governmental concept views collective bargaining as a constitutional system in industry. It is a political relationship. The union shares sovereignty with management over the workers and, as their representative, uses that power in their interests. The application of the agreement is governed by a weighing of the relation of the provisions of the agreement to the needs and ethics of the particular case. Interpretation of the terms follows from the logic of experience and morality, so that the agreement becomes in fact molded to the dominant operational needs of both parties and their social setting, rather than the reverse.

The industrial relations concept views collective bargaining as a system of industrial governance. It is a functional relationship. The union joins with company officials in reaching decisions on matters in which both have vital interests. When the terms of the agreement fail to provide the expected guidance to the parties, it is the joint objectives, not the terms, which must control.

As has already been suggested, it would be erroneous to consider these three approaches as sharply distinguished from one another or as mutually exclusive. We may profitably inquire into the relationship between them.

1. To some extent, they represent stages of development of the bargaining process itself. Early negotiations were a matter of simple contracting for the terms of sale of labor. This characteristic predominated until the establishment, in the first part of this century, of systematic relationships in the clothing industry, with striking use made of the office of impartial chairman. These developments led to elaboration of the governmental theory. The industrial relations approach was foreshadowed by the union-management cooperation programs after World War I. Its more recent statement can be traced to the National Labor Relations Act, which established a legal basis for union participation in the decision-making process; to the subsequent sudden organization of mass-production industries along industrial lines; and to the resulting necessity for hammering out a conception of union-management relations which explicitly explored their relative authorities and responsibilities. Development of theories of the nature of collective bargaining thus mirrors the evolution of the bargaining process.

2. To some extent the three approaches constitute stages of *recognition* of what collective bargaining is. The governmental nature of collective bargaining existed long before the statement of that theory. Joint industrial governance was evident very early in the history of the collective bargaining movement in this country, for employers were not slow to complain

that unions were usurping some of their powers. It has, however, taken students and practitioners of labor relations some time to recognize these aspects of the bargaining process, which existed almost from its inception. There are still some who refuse to accept collective bargaining as actually constituting a system of joint governance in areas of mutual concern. This delayed recognition is traceable to the existence of larger institutional patterns and our conception of the social structure as a whole, by which we have been conditioned to look upon certain groups as playing certain roles and as a result of which we have difficulty in adjusting our thinking to changed situations.

3. To some extent, these three approaches to collective bargaining represent different conceptions of what the bargaining process should be. As such, they express normative judgments. There are those who believe that the contract system of negotiations provides the greatest freedom of relationships. Others accept the governmental system as establishing law and order in industry. Still others regard the industrial relations system as suggesting a means of integrating union and business activities in a way that can be congenial to both organizations. It should be clear, however, that the motive for accepting any of these theories does not affect their validity or invalidity.

4. To some extent these three views of the nature of collective bargaining suggest different emphases on various aspects of collective bargaining. In the usual bargaining relationship today, as we have seen, a contract *does* link the two parties together and establishes the terms on which that link shall be maintained. There are certain circumstances under which the agreement may be given legal force. The bargaining process *is* a species of government suggestively analogous to the modern state; to use the grievance procedures jurisprudentially is assuredly to make a valuable contribution to collective bargaining. The union *does* join with company officials in making certain decisions. All three aspects of collective bargaining can thus be simultaneously maintained, but each provides a different emphasis, stresses a different guiding principle, and can influence the nature of actions taken by the parties. In part that emphasis is supplied by society at large, through its governmental instruments, the result of which over the years has been to transform the agreement into a legal contract. But the parties to the bargaining process themselves supply a more important interpretation in their practices and policies. Which approach is stressed will be, in the final analysis, determined by the view one adopts of the nature of the bargaining process and the bargaining agreement.

There is profit in differentiating these three conceptions of the nature of collective bargaining. In the examination of problems of industrial relations, they will be found to serve as useful tools of analysis, suggesting different possible solutions to the same problems. Moreover, they provide guides in the study of union-management relationships. The marketing approach points to a study of the law of contract and principles of a price-oriented economic system as fruitfully applicable to bargaining systems. The governmental approach suggests a study of government, political party relationships, and the nature of authority as most pertinent to the bargaining process. The industrial relations concept suggests the study of business processes and industrial organization as a means of getting to the roots of problems of collective bargaining.

The distinctions which have been made in this chapter are not simply abstract issues of academic interest alone. They lead to differences of procedures which may be vitally significant in determining the degree of success or failure of the bargaining relationship. Only a few will be mentioned here, but others will be developed in greater detail in Chapters 6 and 17.

The marketing approach stresses the presence of alternatives, however limited, to any given union-management relationship. If there is no agreement on terms, no sale of labor is made. Further, those who see the agreement as a marketing contract are generally reluctant to process through to arbitration grievances which fall outside the scope of its terms; for them, the contract represents the whole of the bargain struck, and the employer retains undiluted discretion in, and control over, all other matters. Thus the grievance procedure must adhere rather rigidly to the clauses of the agreement, and grievances are judged on the basis of what is required by the contract. To submit under union pressure to arbitration on issues other than those embraced in the agreement would be to surrender more than the bargain calls for.

Under the jurisprudential and industrial relations approaches, the parties in the grievance procedure are free to modify the terms if the occasion warrants, though with due care not to destroy the intent of the agreement and the standards it provides. Grievances are decided on the basis of what is required by the circumstances, of which the agreement is only one—although a very important one.

The governmental and industrial relations approaches stress the continuity of a given relationship. They regard collective bargaining as a continuous process. The distinction between grievances covered and those not covered by the agreement becomes blurred. In the former, there is a system of law to cover each contingency; in the latter, union interest in the rules and regulations affecting workers is recognized as not exhausted by the requirements of the agreement, since all contingencies cannot be anticipated. As a result the grievance procedure is available for disputes over issues not mentioned in the agreement.

Under the marketing concept, withholding of data, distortion of fact, or capitalizing on information unknown to the other may be viewed simply as shrewd bargaining or sales technique. Under the governmental concept, it may be difficult to determine whether particular data should be considered to be part of the "government's" official records, accessible to both parties, or to be campaign material, a matter of party politics. Under the industrial relations concept, all relevant data become necessary to an informed joint decision; while this concept does not assume automatic harmony between the two parties, it does emphasize the need of cooperation.

The marketing approach contemplates relationships based on voluntary contracts which are two-party affairs. But it looks upon the courts as the final arbiter of the meaning of the agreement, and it accepts the possibility of such judicial intervention as desirable to the preservation of the system of collective bargaining. The governmental approach looks to the autonomy of the industrial government, presuming nonintervention by others. The general availability of the courts for enforcement of the terms is regarded as a detriment rather than an advantage, not only because it invades the sovereignty of the enterprise, but also because it leaves judgment up to those to whom the experience of the enterprise is unintelligible. A permanent umpire is more likely to overcome the latter objection.

Because of these and other significant differences in results, it would appear worthwhile when appraising the industrial relations issues of our times to keep in sight the fact that the nature of the bargaining process is not simple and unchanging. Its characteristics and functions may, on the contrary, be difficult to place, since these, as well as the institutional setting, are subject to growth and adaptation. Of one thing we may be fairly certain, however. The legal, economic, and political significance of collective bargaining as it has evolved and is evolving today will be obscured if we continue to treat it as though its nature were not—or should not be—substantially different from that of the collective bargaining of previous generations.

More important results of differences of interpretation, affecting the role of the bargaining process in society at large, will be reserved for later examination. We shall now turn our attention to collective bargaining as the parties carry it out in the shop and at the place of work.

Grievance Procedures

chapter 6

After agreeing to the general terms which are to govern their relationships, managers and union officers do not break off the collective bargaining process. It continues on a daily basis at the place of work. First of all, they must settle any differences of opinion which arise concerning meaning and interpretation of the various provisions of the agreement. Second, they must agree on how to apply the general terms to changed, unforeseen, and specific situations. Third, as the time period of agreements has been lengthened and their coverage has been extended to cover tens of thousands of workers in many different locations, union officers and managers have had to deal realistically with worker (and foreman) demands for local adjustments and modifications of the basic agreement.

The Growth of Adjudication under the Agreement

In the early years of collective bargaining in this country, union leaders and employers did not differentiate the process of formulating a basic agreement from that of adjudication, administration, and adjustment under the agreement. As we have seen, on occasions negotiations would begin with a problem arising under the agreement and lead to a strike over the agreement itself.[1] Though these problems arose daily and each was a potential dispute, the parties made little attempt to establish any procedure by which they might regularly and peacefully settle them. Employers dealt with their unions only as long as the basic agreement was being negotiated; they recognized no continuing relationship. The reason is easy to understand. As long as the general terms were fixed by unilateral action and were respected only while the other party was on the upper end of the economic seesaw, there was no *mutual* interest in the continuity of those terms. At least one party always looked forward to modifying them when its bargaining power and strategic position permitted. The process of modification might proceed on a day-to-day basis, by a nibbling away at the application of the general terms. If union members believed that an employer was not complying with the terms of employment, as they understood them, they could support their contention only by the same show of strength which had won those terms in the first place. Moreover, the establishment of any regular, continuous relationship with the union would have implied an acceptance of the union which many employers were unwilling to grant.

Trade unionists and employers gradually developed the jointly negotiated and written trade agreement by which they abided for a fixed period of time. As the development proceeded they began to appreciate that the process of adjudication and adjustment under the agreement was fundamentally different from the process of making the agreement itself. The threat or use of a strike by the union or of a lockout by the employer might be necessary to *reach* the basic agreement, but a show of strength to *enforce* or *interpret* it was redundant as long as the parties dealt with each other in good faith. The earlier "agreements," which were often only oral understandings or demands imposed by one party, were too unstable to permit any regular handling of disputes. The existence of a jointly written fixed-period agreement, however, allowed the parties to set up a regular procedure for dispute settlement. It consisted simply of a meeting of union and employer representatives in conference when a dispute arose about some provision of the agreement. They then settled the dispute on the basis of the "rules" already laid down in the agreement, not on the basis of the relative bargaining advantage enjoyed at the moment by the employer or the union.

In many instances, union and employer representatives were able to agree finally on the way to apply some general provision of the agreement to a particular situation and thus avoid forceful action by one party or the other. However, this procedure did not always work. Not infrequently the two parties would find themselves in deep disagreement over how the

[1] See Chapters 1 and 2.

jointly agreed-upon terms of employment were to be applied or interpreted in a particular case. Such a disagreement appeared only to leave each party the unhappy alternatives of enforcing its own view with the threat of strike or lockout or of giving in. For rational men a third choice existed, though, and by the end of the nineteenth century, union and employers often chose to arbitrate their disputes. They learned through experience that when an arbitrator was chosen to act as judge between their disparate views, settlement of day-to-day shop disputes could be guaranteed, with neither party sacrificing too much. Usually they bound the arbitrator to rule only in accordance with what he understood the parties had meant when they had negotiated their agreement. Consequently, an arbitrator was not expected to be able to depart very far from the intent of either party. He was looked upon as a kind of strict constructionist judge who would refer to, and was limited by, the terms of the agreement.

All parties benefited from the special procedure for interpreting and applying a collective agreement. Previously, if a worker claimed that he was not being paid the wage called for by the schedule of rates, while his employer insisted he was, and if his fellow workers felt that he was thus being unjustly deprived of his due, the controversy was likely to boil up into a strike involving the entire shop and the whole union. We may recall how the journeymen tailors working for Messrs. Robb and Winebrener in Philadelphia in 1826 struck when six men were discharged for insisting upon a job rate for a lady's pongee riding habit, a rate to which they thought they were entitled under a bill of prices drawn up by the union and agreed to by the employers.[2] Under the later procedure of settling the dispute according to the "rules" of the agreement, such a strike could have been averted. If the union members and the employer had not been able to agree upon what the appropriate wage rate should have been for the job, the matter could have been referred to arbitration. The workers would have continued in their jobs even though receiving a rate which they considered less than their due, secure in the knowledge that if an impartial arbitrator upheld their view as correct after reviewing the facts, they would be fully recompensed. The settlement procedure, including arbitration, assured continuity of production for the employer and uninterrupted work for the workers. At the same time, neither party stood in danger of material loss if the arbitrator's decision went against it, for that decision was to be limited by his understanding of the parties' original intentions.

Benefiting from the assurance of continuity in production and work in the face of disputes under the agreement, union members and employers were encouraged to extend the settlement procedure. They began to use it where individual workers were involved in disputes which could not be

[2] See Chapter 1.

settled by reference to the agreement but which involved more general and commonly recognized principles of equity. If a worker was discharged for faulty work or improper conduct, for example, he and his fellow workers might believe that the cause was insufficient to warrant the penalty or that the penalty was unreasonable. He and they might even protest complete innocence of the alleged offense. Though the agreement might be silent on the subject of the worker's rights, or the union's, in such a case the issue could be referred on its own merits to a conference between union and employer representatives and, if necessary, to arbitration. The referral could be made without risking strike, lockout, material cost of interrupted work and production, or loss of principle.

As the distinction between disputes over the general terms of a collective agreement and those arising after an agreement was made became better understood, the means used to settle the latter came to be known as the "grievance procedure." [3] Through it employers and union officials sought to solve the problems of individual workers as well as to settle disputes over the application and interpretation of an agreement's general terms. When they employed the grievance procedure for judicial and administrative purposes, they disavowed the use of their organization's bargaining power or strategic position to force a decision favorable to themselves. In effect, they agreed to seek solutions to particular problems on the basis of standards already jointly recognized, such as those spelled out in their agreement, or on the basis of equity values borrowed from a commonly shared legal and social heritage.

In contrast, when they approached their negotiations of the basic agreement, they had no mutually accepted standards or principles available to guide their decisions. Each party then tried to wrest concessions from the other on the basis of its economic strength. If agreement was reached at all, it was more the result of relative power than of common principles.

Although sometimes useful, arbitration was not a necessary part of adjudication through the grievance procedure. As noted above, even without it, employers and union leaders could approach disputes under an agreement in the spirit appropriate to their settlement. The epochal national agreement in the stove industry in 1891 did not include arbitration as a step in its explicitly devised grievance machinery. Indeed, most grievances have always been adjusted directly by union and employer representatives. But if not essential, both parties have found through experience that arbitration is the only effective means of *ensuring* some mutually acceptable

[3] This term seems to be of at least as recent origin as the term "collective bargaining." The Industrial Commission does not use the expression in its report published in 1902, but by 1911 it had gained currency, probably through establishment of such "boards of grievances" as those in the clothing industry, to be mentioned shortly.

disposition of grievances amenable to judicial judgment and at the same time of promoting continuity of production and work for the life of the agreement. The agreement by union and employers to use arbitration was almost the *sine qua non* of their acceptance of a formal, explicit grievance system; the spread of such systems can almost be measured by the use of grievance arbitration.

Some indication of the gradual resort to arbitration following its late start is provided by the Industrial Commission in its final report of 1902:

> While thus local collective bargaining as to the general conditions of labor is seldom carried on by any very formal system, a large proportion of the local agreements themselves provide more or less formal methods of conciliation and arbitration, as regards minor disputes concerning the interpretation of their terms, usually by joint arbitration committees. Such committees are either temporary—being chosen by the parties to a particular dispute—or, somewhat less commonly, they are permanent, being chosen by the parties to the agreements as such, and having authority to settle all disputes arising during their term of office. Such permanent committees are found especially in those trades where both employers and employees are strongly organized.[4]

In its study of collective bargaining in the United States, the Commission reported that although employers and union men differentiated between disputes over the terms of agreement and disputes arising under the agreement, with few exceptions they had not established any special procedures for dealing with the latter. Grievances were handled locally, though "such local machinery does not usually rest upon definite agreements between employers and employees but is either a matter of custom or governed by the rules of the separate organizations."[5] Certain regional agreements made special provisions. A noteworthy example of this occurred in the Illinois bituminous mines, where the state coal operators' association had hired a special commissioner whose sole duty was to assist in the settlement of disputes under the agreement. However, the agreement did not permit arbitration, and if the parties could not peacefully come to a settlement themselves, they were free to use the strike or lockout.

There was acceptance and use of a grievance procedure "in those trades where both employers and employees [were] strongly organized," as the Commission reported, but one must remember that total membership of all unions in 1902 was only about 10 per cent of the "total employed workers."[6] Few traders were completely organized, and in many important

---

[4] *Final Report of the Industrial Commission,* Reports of the Industrial Commission, vol. 19 (1902), p. 838.

[5] The same, p. 842.

[6] "Total employed" is based on nonagricultural employment and refers to all

industries, such as coal mining, steel, railroad, textiles, shipping, and meat-packing, employers had defeated union organizing attempts, were fighting unions, or had scarcely recognized a union's right to represent workers. Where employers and managers resisted and resented a union's existence, they were unlikely to agree to any terms, let alone establish permanent consultative machinery, with or without arbitration as its capstone. Even after the Wagner Act of 1935 required recognition of unions and bargaining in good faith, many employers for a time refused to accept arbitration of grievances. They contended that vesting final judgment in an outsider deprived managers of their right to make their own decisions. By 1945, however, when union membership was over 50 per cent of total employed workers,[7] management representatives were able to give general endorsement to the full grievance procedure. The President's Labor-Management Conference of 1945 unanimously recommended that all labor agreements specify a complete procedure for settlement of grievances, including arbitrations.[8]

Grievance Handling at the Place of Work

During World War II, both managers and union leaders developed their grievance systems and learned to use arbitration of grievances at the insistence of the War Labor Board. The procedures insisted upon by the Board had been distilled from "the best practices of employers and unions, developed through years of collective bargaining and of trial and error." [9] It was this cumulative experience of almost half a century which emphasized the desirability not only of third-party arbitration but also of immediate, initial attention to grievances by men at the place of work. These men had the intimate knowledge of the complaints necessary to provide prompt and equitable settlement and thus to ensure workers a practical enjoyment of their rights under the agreement.

The first grievance procedures had grown out of the demands of workers and union representatives that employers live up to the terms of the agreement. The roving business agent of the building trades union, the walking delegate on the docks, and the shop steward of the craft union thus came to

workers except those in occupations and professions in which there is little, if any, union organization or in which strikes rarely, if ever, occur. *Handbook of Labor Statistics,* Bureau of Labor Statistics (1950), tables E-1 and E-2, pp. 139, 142.

[7] See definition above.

[8] The *New York Times,* November 30, 1945, p. 17.

[9] From a statement of the National War Labor Board issued July 1, 1943, quoted in *The Termination Report of the National War Labor Board,* 3 vols., vol. I, pp. 65–66.

assume the informal roles of policemen.[10] The importance to the union and to collective bargaining of local policing and prompt settlement of most grievances at the place of work was, in the first instance, not widely appreciated by either unions or employers and certainly not by the public and labor students. In the early years of this century, grievance procedures were established in two major industries, anthracite coal and clothing, but the feature publicized as most exemplary was arbitration.

As a consequence of the Coal Strike Commission's award in the famous strike of 1902, the anthracite industry established procedures for the adjustment of disputes. Since the mine operators had bitterly opposed and fiercely fought recognition of the United Mine Workers as the miners' representative, it is not surprising that their opposition should have carried over to the newly devised grievance procedure. The procedure applied to all anthracite mines and provided a top board to settle disputes under the agreement award, but it did not provide for bilateral grievance adjustment in the mines themselves. This was a serious weakness, for the operators could easily evade local compliance with the agreement. They denied the union any right to police their performance, insisting upon direct settlement with the individual employee of any issues voiced by him.

Not until 1912 was this flaw remedied and a comprehensive five-stage procedure set up. When a miner had a grievance, he was first to discuss the matter with his foreman in the mine. Failing a satisfactory settlement there, a local grievance committee of three fellow employees (commonly local union officials) met with company representatives. If still no agreement was reached, the two district members of the top board of conciliation— one for the union and one for the company—sought resolution of the dispute, and if unsuccessful they referred the matter to the full board of conciliation, consisting of three members each for the union and the company, elected by districts. In all these steps the attempt was to settle the issue by bilateral discussion, which of course did not guarantee settlement. Such an assurance was provided, however, in the final stage—decision by an "umpire" chosen for each case as needed.[11]

Unions' and employers' recognition and use of a grievance procedure

[10] Sidney Webb and Beatrice Webb, *The History of Trade Unionism,* London: Longmans, Green & Co., Ltd., 1950, pp. 304–306, 489; and H. A. Millis and R. E. Montgomery, *Organized Labor,* New York: McGraw-Hill Book Company, 1945, p 251.

[11] In practice, however, the parties so frequently selected one of three men (Carroll D. Wright and Charles P. Neill, both former United States Commissioners of Labor, and former United States Circuit Judge George Grey) that it may almost be said that they made use of permanent umpires. Edgar Sydenstricker, *Collective Bargaining in the Anthracite Coal Industry,* Bureau of Labor Statistics Bulletin 191 (1916), p. 97.

that offered a reasonable hope and the practice of prompt and equitable settlement of disputes significantly affected collective bargaining. As never before, it became a democratic, continuous process. The lowest union member, the shop steward, and the foremen could participate daily in its operation, not only the union leaders and top managers.

The impact on miner-operator relationships has been reported by one who made a study of the system after its first ten years of operation. Noting that the extended series of stages of discussion was designed to encourage settlement by the parties themselves and "to eliminate as far as possible the element of arbitration," this investigator commented:

> At the same time it must be remembered that the average individual mine worker naturally looks upon the enterprise process of settling disputes as a series of appeals from the decisions of his employer or of his employer's representatives. He has been accustomed to look for compulsion from his employer, and at one time his only method of appeal from his employer's decision was the strike. The new method of "conciliation" is to him a means by which he can refer his employer's decision to some other authority.[12]

No figures are available on the number of grievances which were discussed prior to inauguration of the formal system of 1903, but it is clear that they were rarely aired.[13] And although the number of grievances processed is not a sufficient indication of the health and vitality of employee-employer relationships, the large increase in the number of grievances occurring after 1903 suggests that complaints which miners previously would have silently nursed were now being brought into the open, talked about, and settled. In the ten-year period ending in 1913, 253 cases were presented to the board of conciliation. Of these, the board refused to entertain 5; 32 were settled by the parties between themselves before the board proceeded to a hearing; and another 89 were withdrawn by the complainant, often indicating informal agreement. Seventy-eight decisions were rendered by the board, and 49 disputes had to be submitted to an umpire. Wage issues predominated throughout the period. The unwillingness of the employers to accept the union is indicated by the fact that charges of discrimination against workers for union activity made up the second largest grievance category.

Perhaps even more publicized than the procedures for dispute settlement instituted by the anthracite coal award was the permanent grievance system adopted in the clothing industry in the years before World War I. Formal adjustment procedure was established in the Hart, Schaffner and Marx Company, in Chicago, following a strike in 1910, and it is sometimes said

[12] The same, p. 89.
[13] The same.

to be the first successful experience in working out a "comprehensive plan for the adjustment of labor disputes in an individual business concern." [14] A market-wide strike in the cloak, suit, and skirt industry of New York City in the same year was terminated with the Protocol,[15] a landmark in the history of union-management relations, which among its provisions contained the plan for a board of grievances and a board of arbitration. This elaborate system covered an employers' association (the Cloak, Suit, and Skirt Manufacturers' Protective Association, whose membership was made up of numerous small-scale shop owners) and nine local unions of the International Ladies' Garment Workers' Union, known collectively by the name of their central body, the Joint Board of the Cloak and Skirt Makers' Unions. The four-step grievance procedure gave the individual worker or shop owner the opportunity to present his complaints to immediately available grievance representatives and to appeal the grievance through the succeeding steps if he was dissatisfied with the disposition of his case. If the case was important enough, it might finally be taken to the three-man board of arbitration, one of whose members was a neutral representative.

By their example, the grievance procedures used in the clothing and anthracite coal industries greatly influenced the American approach to dispute settlement under collective agreements. The older unions in the twenties and the mass-production unions in the thirties sought to establish the basic grievance procedure—several successive steps through which a worker and his representative might appeal his grievance if necessary to a final hearing and decision by an outside party. The nature of the usual appeals procedure can perhaps be better appreciated by tracing through the various steps of an actual case.

Believing that he had unjustifiably been denied the opportunity to work on a regular working day, Joe Parcy informally complained to his foreman, Lee Madison. Madison told him that nothing could be done. It was a tough break, but there was no violation of the agreement and thus no remedy. Dissatisfied with the answer, Parcy sought out his shop steward, J. D. Nettler, and together they drafted a formal grievance:

> On January 4, 1964, I came to work on my regular shift. But for reasons beyond my control, due to icy streets, the city buses

[14] Thomas Tongue, "The Development of Industrial Conciliation and Arbitration under Trade Agreements," *Oregon Law Review,* vol. 17 (1938), p. 270.

[15] A most interesting account of the strike and subsequent negotiations is contained in Alpheus T. Mason, *Brandeis: A Free Man's Life,* New York: Viking Press, Inc., 1946, chap. 19. Louis D. Brandeis, later an associate justice of the United States Supreme Court, was largely instrumental in the acceptance by both parties of the terms of the Protocol.

which are my only means of transportation made it impossible for me to get here before 7:50 A.M., fifty minutes after starting time. My home was contacted by supervision, and was informed that I was on my way. When I arrived I was not admitted to the plant for they had called somebody to replace me. I feel the whole thing is unjustified and am asking to be compensated for 8 hours lost time at the rates provided for in Article 8(d)(1) [the reporting pay provision] [16] of the agreement.

Representative of Local No. 2   Complainant
s/J. D. Nettler   s/Joseph Parcy

Three days after Nettler filed the grievance with Madison, he and Madison and Parcy met to discuss the matter. Although he was sympathetic to Parcy's loss, Madison pointed out that he could not run the packaging department shorthanded, storm or no storm. After waiting nearly forty-five minutes, he had called in another man who lived across the street from the plant. By waiting for Parcy, the company had lost money, and he could not see that it was right for it to pay out more. Though he did not discuss his underlying concern at the meeting, Madison knew that any pay awarded to Parcy would put him over his allotted budget for the final packaging inspection job. He was anxious not to incur any extra labor costs in his department, for the company had been pressing its foremen to keep within their budgets and offering bonuses to those who trimmed costs below the budgets. Nettler replied that if Madison was going to take such a hard-nosed stand, they would turn the grievance over to the chief steward and take it to Mr. Coppers, department superintendent.

Several days later, Parcy, Nettler, and Madison met with the chief steward and Coppers in the latter's office. They reexamined the matter carefully, arguing at length about the exact time that Parcy reported in and that his replacement was called, but agreeing in general about the facts of the case. Coppers said that he had gone over the matter with Meyers, an assistant in the industrial relations department, and that neither of them could find any violation of the agreement in the way the supervisors had handled it. "It is admitted that transportation was difficult on the morning involved," he wrote in his answer after the meeting, "but this has no bearing on the fact that jobs must be covered. I feel there is no justification for this request for lost time, and it is therefore rejected." In order to be fair, he suggested that he would be willing to let Parcy work to make up the

---

[16] Article 8, "Reporting for Work Pay": "When an employee reports for work at his regular shift time without having been notified to the contrary by his foreman . . . and is not assigned work, he shall be paid for one-half the normal shift at the rate of 75 units per hour at the base rate or at the hourly rate customarily paid to him."

hours he had lost but not at overtime; Coppers, too, did not want to add any extra labor costs in his department. After some heated discussion, the chief steward and Nettler rejected the suggestion. They pointed out that Parcy could legally work the hours only as a fill-in over the next few months during weeks when, because of layoffs, he would work fewer than forty hours. Further, there would be seniority complications and no end of trouble.

The grievance was appealed to the third step, where the plant grievance committee and the director of industrial relations and two of his aids considered the matter at their next regularly scheduled meeting. They called in Parcy and Madison and questioned them carefully. After they had left the meeting, the grievance chairman, who also happened to be the chief steward, argued that Parcy had acted in good faith and that the company ought to show its good faith. Simply to dismiss the grievance would be pretty shoddy treatment for a loyal, long-service employee. He pointed out that "the boys" knew about the case and would take careful note of the company's decision. "We think it is a question of whether you think penny pinching or loyal workers are more important to the _____Company. We've always said Room 313 [the accounting office] really runs this place. If you turn Parcy down, it'll prove it."

The director granted that the situation was "rather unusual, where Parcy, through no fault of his own, arrived after a replacement had been arranged to take his place. There is no contract violation in denying him work, though, under the circumstances of this particular day. . . . However, considering the worker and his efforts to meet the shift schedule, the company feels that he should not be unduly penalized." The director proposed that if the union would agree that the case was an unusual one and in no way established a precedent, the company would agree to compensate Parcy four hours of reporting pay, the allowance due men who are called to work on days when no work is available.

Parcy was still dissatisfied, but the chairman told him that the grievance committee did not feel it would make sense to spend $500 to take the case to arbitration on the chance of winning only $10 pay. Upon the advice of the committee, Parcy felt he had no choice but to accept the settlement.

This case illustrates the most conspicuous elements of a typical griev- ance procedure. At each of several succeeding steps, the grievance may be appealed to higher-ranking officers who are less likely to be involved in the case and better able to judge it on its merits. In the first step a single union representative (usually called the "steward") meets with the foreman to try to settle the problem at its source. The final bilateral discussions commonly take place between the union's plant grievance committee and the com- pany's industrial relations officers, who meet regularly in an effort to solve problems before grievances arise and also to settle grievances brought to them. The activity here might be likened to that of a professional fire department that not only helps put out fires but also seeks to prevent fires before they start. The lower steps are more like a voluntary fire department, available only when called.

Agreements generally provide for four steps, though some may list as many as six.[17] The number does not increase proportionally with the size of the company, for promptness is an essential characteristic of successful grievance settlement, and a multiplication of steps in a large company where thousands of grievances are filed annually would lead to an intolerably expensive procedure if delay were to be avoided.

Variations in grievance procedures are common as union and management negotiators seek to meet the requirements of special circumstances and experiences. One agreement may require answers to grievances within twenty-four hours, and another may require answers within ten days; some agreements may allow oral answers, and others may require written ones; and one agreement may define grievances narrowly, while another will permit any problem or complaint to be processed through the formal procedures. To handle some grievances, such as those involving major piece rate changes and discharge cases, a union and management may agree to skip the lower steps. These important cases go immediately to the only officials who have the final authority to decide them in any case.[18] Small union locals may bring a representative from the national union in at an early step to give them expert guidance and help; large union locals often have grievance representatives expert in particular areas—health and welfare compensation, unemployment benefits, time study, apprenticeship, or job classification—who meet with the appropriate company experts to try to settle outside of the regular procedures the often knotty grievances arising from particularly intricate and specialized provisions of the agree-

[17] "Grievance Procedures in Union Agreements, 1950–51," *Monthly Labor Review,* vol. 73 (1951), pp. 36–39.

[18] In the printing trade a special processing of discharge cases is sometimes used, in which the printers in a particular shop, organized into what is known as a "chapel," pass upon the equities of the situation, without the participation of the employer, who—as well as the discharged employee—may, if he wishes, appeal the chapel's decision to the local union. From the local union, either party may appeal to a special bipartisan committee or to the national union office, depending upon the particular agreement prescribing the procedure. There is some historical basis for this device, for the institution of the chapel predates unionism, having for several centuries, with employer acquiescence, existed as a form of social government in the shop. Also, the printers were among the first craftsmen organized into unions in this country, early developing a deep-seated belief in their right to determine work relationships among themselves as long as they observed the correlative duty of delivering a fair quality and quantity of work to their employers.

ment. Almost every company and union has a joint safety committee that tries to settle safety complaints before they go to the regular grievance procedure. In the building trades, where several craft unions represent workers, a joint agreement is sometimes negotiated that sets up a joint grievance procedure.

The Significance of the Procedures for Workers

Although all the grievance steps specified in agreements are described in nearly equal detail, they are not of equal importance when rated by the number or kind of grievances recorded and settled. As in other appeals procedures, the parties process fewer cases in each succeeding step, the less contentious, more routine being settled first. By far the largest portion of grievances never progress beyond the first step,[19] and probably even more complaints are never even formalized in writing. Despite the fact that by far most settlements take place at the lowest grievance steps and informally even before that, union and management officials alike frequently belittle their importance. Union men often complain that the steps below the industrial relations level are mere formalities, and company officers admit that foremen and lower supervisors usually rely upon precedents in answering grievances and that they frequently consult with the officers before answering other grievances of whose import they are not sure.

The bulk of grievance settlement may look like "mere formality" to the union and company officers who deal with grievances at the top levels. The grievances that engage *their* skill and interest often involve complex and novel matters of policy and interpretation of past settlements. But just because the chief company and union grievance handlers emphasize those issues (and the top-level procedural steps where they are resolved), the other and routine grievances are not therefore insignificant. Certainly they are not unimportant to the workers who originate them, nor do they prove to be unimportant in the whole grievance process. Focusing attention and concern on grievance arbitration and the step immediately preceding it tends to distort one's understanding of the grievance process. It demeans the work carried on in the lower steps and magnifies unduly that performed

[19] G. Allan Dash, Jr., "Bargaining through the Grievance Procedure," *The Collective Bargaining Agreement in Action*, American Management Association, Personnel Series, no. 82 (1944), p. 4; Gerald G. Somers, *Grievance Settlement in Coal Mining*, West Virginia Bulletin, ser. 56, no. 12-2 (1956), p. 9; *Arbitration of Labor-Management Grievances*, Bureau of Labor Statistics Bulletin 1159 (1954), p. 3; T. V. Purcell, *The Worker Speaks His Mind on Company and Union*, Cambridge, Mass.: Harvard University Press, 1953, p. 222; Melville Dalton, "Unofficial Union-Management Relations," *American Sociological Review*, vol. 15 (1950), p. 614.

in the higher, so that the whole grievance process appears to be dominatingly judicial in nature.

Adjudication is an important function of the grievance process. While workers can expect a measure of impartiality in the upper stages of the grievance process, which are removed from the conflicts and tempers of the shop, arbitration by a neutral carries even greater assurance of equity. Workers value such judgments as protection against unjustified managerial action; adjudication assures a man the opportunity for a full hearing and recompense if he demonstrates that management infringed on or denied his rights.

The advantage of judicial judgment is also its limitation; it protects a man's rights after management has acted—not before. The compensation provided by a grievance award may not be at all appropriate to the injury done. That foremen should ignore the interests and rights of workers and give only tardy recognition to them can be an affront to the workers' dignity and self-respect. Workers thus seek through the grievance process not just compliance and compensation after the act but consultation before.

Many of the written grievances on record in company and union files indicate a desire by workers to have a hearing and a chance to express their feelings and opinions and to offer their knowledge. The complaints are often vague and unrelated to the agreement; but however they are written, the foremen are required to meet with the grievers and their stewards and to consider the matter respectfully and carefully. The consideration that foremen, supervisors, and company officers must give to grievances probably helps explain why workers do not look upon the grievance process as a failure even though management rejects by far the largest proportion of all grievances and complaints. Even when grievance answers are less than impartial, as is the case sometimes at the lower levels, workers may be partially satisfied just to have had an opportunity to express their views, to be listened to, and to hear directly and immediately the supervisors' arguments. The discussion may range far afield from the official complaints, giving the grievers a chance to bring up other matters not properly treated in a formal complaint. Thus the formal procedures merge into informal methods of treating shop problems.

The formal grievance procedure ensures workers and their representatives a chance to approach managers if informal relationships break down. Workers are able informally to advise foremen and company officers and consult with them. Union representatives and managers need to consider jointly the problem of applying and interpreting customs, precedents, shop rules, and general provisions of the agreement. One probably cannot separate in fact the administrative function from that of adjudication since the work is performed through, and under the cover of, the judicial grievance procedure, but formally one may usefully make the distinction.

Union representatives in the shop can become highly competent and knowledgeable in the administration of the collective agreement and industrial relations. Some companies agree to retain key union stewards as full-time representatives, paid fully or in part from the company payroll, in recognition of the important and useful personnel service they render. Whether paid by company or union and whether full or part time, the chief stewards and division committeemen handle grievances constantly. They become familiar with all parts of the plant, meeting managers and workers at every level and getting to know the individuals of importance in the company bureaucracy. They can aid managers or hinder them no little bit. Whether they are originally intended to or not, union representatives at the place of work participate to a surprising degree in activities that managers publicly insist are strictly their concern.

Union representatives have helped administer such matters as subcontracting arrangements, programs for improving use of machines and installing equipment, job classification plans, and incentive pay systems. Union representatives typically help administer seniority provisions, "bumping" rights in layoffs, seniority claims to preferred jobs, shifts and location, priorities in transfers, and order of recall as work picks up. All are often extremely complex problems and are well suited for joint administration, as many managers recognize.

To join managers in resolving any issue which discriminates among workers on the basis of personal judgment, not objective criteria, puts union representatives in an uncomfortable position, though, and in these instances they prefer to lend their advice informally; they serve openly only on those administrative committees that deal with relatively uncontroversial issues such as safety, apprenticeship, absenteeism, and community fund drives.

By joining in such administrative duties, unions have extended their influence beyond the compliance and judicial purposes of the grievance process, but they have kept within its original spirit. When properly carried out, both functions contribute to stable, peaceful relationships between union and management during the life of an agreement. Such a relationship does not just happen; a successful grievance system makes large demands upon the effort, honesty, patience, and understanding of men in management and the union. Both parties must work to see that grievances, problems, and complaints are handled responsibly. Foremen must be willing to admit their mistakes; stewards cannot push grievances simply to enhance their political reputations, nor push worthless grievances out of weakness. Industrial relations officers and members of plant grievance committees must not duck the tough decision unfavorable to their side by passing the buck to an arbitrator. Neither can they concentrate all settlements in their own hands. To do so militates against prompt action and can lead to settlements that show little understanding of conditions at the place of work.

The Grievance Handlers and Fractional Bargaining

Both union and management need to have informed representatives available at all times to handle grievances as they arise. For the system to work only occasionally and spasmodically would defeat its basic purpose. When complaints are unattended, grievances remain unsettled, and problems go unsolved; workers become disgruntled, and tension rises in the shop. Foremen and stewards need to know the agreement reasonably well and to be kept up to date on arbitration decisions and high-level settlements. They need to understand the procedures, supplying answers, conducting inquiries, and remedying errors in accordance with the rules and provisions of the agreement. Training is vital and experience helpful in providing representatives who can handle grievances in an informed way.

To ensure the availability of grievance settlement, unions must provide an adequate number of representatives at the place of work. (In large industrial plants there may be representatives of one kind or another for every twenty to fifty workers.) Typically, the workers themselves elect stewards or committeemen from among the ranks of their own department or work group. If one of them should quit or be discharged or promoted, the workers can replace him at a new election. But if he is laid off in slack times, with the probability that he will be called back in a few days or weeks, there is little point in calling a new election to replace him; at the same time, in his absence, his constituents would be without representation. He would also be absent in case of overtime work if, because of low seniority standing, the foreman could not ask him to stay. To meet the requirement of availability, most unions insist upon, and most managements agree to, superseniority for all union representatives. As long as any of his constituents are at work, the representative will be kept at work too, regardless of his seniority rank.

Being at the place of work, however, does not help a representative to handle and investigate grievances unless he has some freedom to leave his job and move about appropriate areas of the plant to talk with workers, other union officers, and foremen. Agreements almost always guarantee representatives the right to interrupt their jobs, after notifying their foremen or supervisors, to take care of grievance duties. For time spent off the job on legitimate grievance work, the union, the company, or both jointly reimburse the representatives at their regular rates of pay.

Shop representatives must be more than merely available if they are to be effective. They must feel free to challenge management with no threat of retaliation. For this reason, union members fiercely defend their shop representatives, resisting any management attempts to limit their activities or to discriminate against them. As a result, workers and union leaders sometimes defend a representative's behavior even when it is of a kind which would receive little or no defense if engaged in by a rank-and-file employee. Although they are not immune from company discipline, able and active shop stewards and committeemen can maintain a position at the place of work, more or less independently of management. Their independence, influence with the workers, and administrative duties (formal and informal) give them a position of importance in the shop. Often they become secondary or even equal centers of power in the shop, sometimes rivaling the foreman and his line superiors. This development of the shop representatives when mixed with the democratic politics of the shop and the dynamics of work flows, production schedules, and shop technologies significantly alters the basis and function of the grievance process.

Two assumptions underlie the premise that peaceful grievance settlement can be assured if union leaders and managers fulfill the prerequisite of continuous, responsible, and informal good-faith handling of grievances. The first is that the negotiators of the collective agreement are in fact the representatives of all the workers and supervisors. The only two relevant organizations are the local union and the plant management. The second assumption is that in adjudicating, interpreting, and applying the terms of an agreement, the daily negotiators are guided by the same relative bargaining power that they or their party either suffered or enjoyed in the fixing of the terms of the collective agreement.

The assumptions are valid only as long as workers can expect and are willing to fulfill their job demands through the regular union organization and will accomplish their work goals in accordance with the regulations set forth or agreed to by the official company negotiators. These assumptions are often invalidated, though. The technology in many industries enables small groups of specialized workers to interfere with the production of a whole plant or a complete assembly-line operation. Their bargaining power is thus often greater than that of the local union, for the loss they can inflict upon management is as great as that which the local union can impose. Yet the cost of the demands for their few members is usually much smaller.

Likewise, some technologies and changing work conditions give foremen an advantageous bargaining position from time to time, enabling them to get adjustments of work rules or to negotiate with the shop representatives for more freedom to assign, transfer, promote, or rate workers. Special conditions, therefore, put the parties in the shop in positions of strength— and weakness—which provide the opportunity for them to bargain for benefits not secured in the collective agreement.

Furthermore, members of work groups and shop foremen often feel free to grasp this opportunity since they may feel a greater sense of responsibility to settle their own shop problems than to settle those of the wider organizations. The centralization of personnel and industrial relations authority in staff groups tends to insulate shop foremen from a sense of responsibility to company policy. And in large industrial unions where work groups of many different skills and varying work interests are enrolled, the diverse workers not infrequently develop a greater sense of loyalty to their own groups than to the union. Thus it is that where once the grievance procedure seemed to promise peaceful settlement of disputes arising after the collective agreement was signed, in some situations the basis for the promise has been so undermined or weakened as to make the promise only conditional.

One finds throughout American industry, and particularly in the great mass-production plants, the occasional to frequent use of disruptive bargaining tactics, subtle sabotage of production, overtime bans, slowdowns, and even wildcat strikes. A close study of the relationship between workers and foremen at the place of work reveals that each party applies pressure on the other to force or to induce settlements favorable to itself. What was supposedly eliminated and made unnecessary by the grievance procedure in fact still exists or has reappeared in the guise of judicial and administrative settlement of disputes and problems.

Shop controversies leading to bargaining in the grievance process arise from a number of sources. One source is the range of discretion that is permitted both by provisions of the agreement and by shop rules. For example, foremen can discriminate through discipline and commendation of workers or through assignment of work among a crew. The line between allowable and improper discretion is a fine one, but workers and foremen daily measure it so closely that only slight changes are significant to them. Under the agreement, supervisors are usually allowed in emergencies to perform work normally done by a member of the bargaining unit. Union representatives and foremen may define an emergency quite differently in different cases and may bargain over which criteria apply in different situations. Or an agreement may grant workers "reasonable time for personal needs." When production schedules lag, foremen may decide that a "reasonable time" is noticeably shorter than when work is slack. Workers may feel that a "reasonable time" varies with *their* needs, not the foreman's.

Another source of local shop bargaining controversies is the agreement which fixes only the *method* or *standard* of settlement, but not specific settlements themselves. In the case of piecework rates, bargaining is essential since a rate of exchange is set between a subjective element and an output of a given product.[20] There is no reason to expect that a company time-study man and the workers will automatically reach the same judg-

[20] Hilde Behrend, "The Effort Bargain," *Industrial and Labor Relations Review*, vol. 10 (1957), pp. 503–515.

ment as to the proper effort for a given output. Other bargaining issues arise if workers become dissatisfied with changes in their condition and see ways of exerting pressure to secure remedies. Under long-term agreements, workers probably feel increasingly the need for introducing a flexibility that allows them to adjust the agreement and its provisions. Rapídly changing technologies, employment opportunities, and economic conditions can quickly make fixed agreements intolerable if there is no chance for modification and adjustment.

The largely informal bargaining that is conducted under the cover of the grievance procedures should not be confused with the collective bargaining that produces the overall agreement. Rather than the whole collectivity of the local union, only groups of workers and their representatives—fractions of the plant work force—engage in grievance bargaining. For this reason, the term "fractional bargaining" is appropriately and usefully applied to it. Individual workers or single shop representatives do not typically conduct fractional bargaining, for only under unusual circumstances would an individual be able to exert enough pressure upon supervisors to force them to bargain. An individual's grievance has a fair chance of being considered on its merits. The grievance of a work group is just as likely to be considered on the merits of the group's bargaining power as upon the merits of the grievance. Since the response of a group of workers to a settlement may be a matter of pressing concern to foremen racing to meet a production deadline, expediency may, and often does, temper considerations of merit. A foreman can ignore group demands only at his own risk. His advance, bonuses, and job security depend more on getting production out or cutting unit costs than on following the provisions of the agreement. If a work group wishes some special privileges for its members in terms of pay, seniority, hours, or work load, a foreman may well be tempted to agree in the face of a threatened walkout or slowdown if the cost to him is not too high. That the cost to the company in other departments may be high indeed may not weigh heavily with him.

Shop representatives, as well as supervisors, approach group grievances differently from the way they approach the grievances of individuals; when grievances affect more voters, they have a higher political potential for elected representatives. A shop steward may be a union officer and legally bound to act only in the interests of the whole union, but politically he holds his position on the suffrance of his work group, and he must be responsive to it before he can be responsible to the larger organization. Thus only the upper, less involved union and management organizations can afford the luxury of not recognizing work groups. Foremen and shop stewards must contend with them. They do so, not because they are irresponsible men, but because they do not always have practical alternatives.

Work groups existed before there were grievance procedures and even before there were unions;[21] the flow of production and its technology have long grouped workers of similar skills, fostering among them common interests and a sense of self-identification that may be stronger than identification with the union.[22] The rise of unionism and the development of the grievance procedure, however, have given work groups a protected position, continuity, and unity of action that they did not enjoy before.

With no union to protest, managers could hire, fire, and discipline workers at will without having to answer to anyone. Any workers or group of workers who withheld or who were suspected of withholding cooperation lost their jobs. Any continued, organized opposition or resistance to management was nearly impossible. Now that the collective agreement limits the authority of management, workers can more openly group themselves around the privileged shop representatives and collectively act in their own interests. Under the protection of the agreement, they can with greater immunity engage in activities that earlier would have brought penalties. Using organized tactics, they can now force foremen and even higher managers to bargain with them, and sometimes they gain their narrow, parochial demands, uncompromised by the conflicting demands and needs of other groups just as deserving.

Paradoxically then, collective bargaining and unions have helped to strengthen the identity and power of fractional groups. Grievance procedures and the presence of the protected shop steward have favored the growth of a power center at the place of work—within, though not necessarily an integral part of, the local union. The procedures and the protection are not alone responsible for the power center, but they have given it new direction and allied strength. They have given workers an opportunity to organize themselves into semiautonomous groups in the shop, to which they show loyalty before they do to the union.

Understandably, neither top union leaders nor management officials have shown much enthusiasm for recognizing the autonomy of work groups and the legitimacy of their fractional bargaining. Such recognition might encourage a kind of anarchy within the union, corrupting the broader loyalties of the members and shop representatives and benefiting a few work groups in a strong bargaining position at the expense of others less advantageously situated. For managers, fractional bargaining has two obvious consequences. First, it leads to interruption of production, for even where workers seldom engage in work stoppages and more overt tactics, they can subtly disrupt production as they apply pressure to foremen. Second, fractional bargaining can bring about confusion and conflict in

[21] Stanley B. Mathewson, *Restriction of Output among Unorganized Workers*, New York: Viking Press, Inc., 1931, pp. 15–127.

[22] See Leonard R. Sayles, *Behavior of Industrial Work Groups*, New York: John Wiley & Sons, Inc., 1958.

company policy if foremen in different parts of a plant or company settle grievances in different ways. In time the integrity of the collective agreement itself can be destroyed, to the detriment of union and management.

Notwithstanding the undesirable consequences of fractional bargaining over grievances, the value of the grievance system is not destroyed. Many, if not most, grievances and problems arising during the life of an agreement can be, and usually are, settled peacefully and equitably. Further, even fractional bargaining has advantages that one should not forget. Shop determination of such matters as worker rotation in jobs, overtime assignment, seniority in job placement, and local variation in other matters such as job classification and even pay rates can be advantageous, allowing large firms to adapt more expeditiously to local opportunities and immediate circumstances. When tools, machines, and techniques change rapidly, as they do in many American industries, managers and union leaders need to explore and consider more than one approach in coordinating the efforts of men and the rhythm of machines. Stability and peace are not the only characteristics of good industrial relations. The industrial process presents us with so many variables and unknowns that flexibility and experimentation should also commend themselves.

Besides the benefits that can accrue to the firm and union from fractional bargaining, there are benefits for workers too. In the daily informality of the work group, workers probably have a better chance to participate in decisions, to be heard, and to make their influence felt than in even the local union. If workers gain increased satisfaction from participation in the bargaining maneuvers and if a meaningful industrial democracy is thereby encouraged, the dimming of the utopian promise of peaceful settlement of *all* disputes may not be too high a price to pay. The grievance system in practice promises less, and yet at the same time more, than those who developed it foresaw.[23]

[23] The issues involved in fractional bargaining are explored at greater length in James W. Kuhn, *Bargaining in Grievance Settlement*, New York: Columbia University Press, 1961.

Bargaining Power

chapter 7

The concept of bargaining power is at the same time useful and tricky. The term is widely used and appears to be self-explanatory, having no need of further definition. Supplying content to the many definitions of bargaining power is not always easy, however, and we shall discover that what seems simple may be deceiving in its appearance.

Bargaining power has generally been regarded as the ability to control the setting of wage rates, sometimes within given limits. A "pure theory" of collective bargaining has been developed which approaches the problem of wage determination with only this (implied) definition of bargaining power, one of the best-known examples of this probably being the theory of Prof. A.C. Pigou. It will be instructive to consider his model as an aid in developing a clearer idea of the nature and significance of the concept.[1]

Bargaining within a Range of Indeterminateness

Pigou assumes that when union and management are bargaining about a change in the wage scale, there will be a given wage above which the union

[1] This summary is taken from Pigou, *Economics of Welfare,* 4th ed., London: Macmillan & Co., Ltd., 1938, pp. 451–461.

will itself not want to press, for fear that unemployment will result. At the same time, there will be a wage below which the employer will not want to set his wage scale, in the belief that if he does, he will lose a needed part of his labor force. That is to say, the fact that an excessive wage increase will lessen the demand for labor and that an excessive wage decrease will lessen the supply of labor sets boundaries to the wage bargain. These boundaries enclose a *range of indeterminateness*. It is impossible for a settlement to take place outside this range. It is equally impossible to say where within this range the bargain will actually be struck. However, for the union there will be, with some lower limit, a wage which it would be prepared to accept rather than strike; and for the employer there will be, with some upper limit, one which he would be prepared to accept rather than face a strike. These limits are their respective "sticking points," above or below which they will not move without first taking a stand. If the employer's upper limit lies above the union's lower limit, there is established a *range of practical bargains,* within which it is possible for agreement to be reached by negotiations. An agreement is possible because the union will accept any wage within this range rather than strike, and similarly the employer is prepared to accept any wage within the range rather than be subjected to a strike. If the employer's sticking point lies below that of the union, a strike will be inevitable. The employer will fight before he grants a wage *above* a figure which is *below* that which the union is prepared to accept without taking a stand. Table 2 shows these relationships.

Given a range within which practicable bargains can be made, no strike need take place. Nevertheless, there remains the question of where within such a range the concluding bargain will be struck. Each of the parties will seek to push toward the other's limit, and in the process of bluff and bluster by which this result is sought, they may find themselves involved in overt conflict which neither wants and which both know is unwarranted.

The range of indeterminateness thus sets voluntary limits to the exercise of the parties' bargaining power, and relative bargaining abilities will influence the wage settlement within that range as the bargainers negotiate and finally fix upon a particular rate. The parties will comprehend the limits of the range of practicable bargains only through their estimate of relative bargaining powers, which would include, of course, an evaluation of the cost of a strike.

Other writers besides Pigou have assumed such ranges of boundaries to the bargain. John R. Commons introduced the concept of "limits of coercion," a range of bargains bounded by the alternative bargains open to buyer (employer) and seller (union).[2] *Within* such limits or ranges there is room for the play of bargaining power and negotiating ability. Despite the au-

---

[2] John R. Commons, *Institutional Economics: Its Place in Political Economy,* New York: The Macmillan Company, 1934, p. 331.

Table 2 *

a		b	
$2.75	Union's maximum (upper limit of range of indeterminateness)	$2.75	Union's maximum (upper limit of range of indeterminateness)
2.50	Employer's maximum (upper limit of range of practicable bargains)	2.55	Union's minimum
2.35	Union's minimum (lower limit of range of practicable bargains)	2.45	Employer's maximum
1.75	Employer's minimum (lower limit of range of indeterminateness)	1.75	Employer's minimum (lower limit of range of indeterminateness)

* In column *a*, an agreement can be reached without strike between $2.35 and $2.50, since within this range both parties would prefer any settlement rather than accept a strike to secure a more advantageous rate. In column *b*, however, no such range of practicable bargains exists. The minimum wage which the union would accept, rather than strike, is above the maximum wage which the employer would grant rather than face a strike. What wage will actually be settled upon here depends on the outcome of an economic fight. All that can be said is that it will fall somewhere within the range of indeterminateness, as the union would not want any wage higher than the upper limit of this range, and the employer would not want a rate lower than the lower limit.

thority of such economists, the conclusion seems unavoidable that the notion of a range of bargains is probably fallacious. It obscures rather than clarifies the more important concept of bargaining power.

First, any limits which may be imposed by reason of the impact of a wage rate upon the supply and demand curves of labor are not even known to the parties. If these limits are to be located at all, it is in experience. A range of indeterminateness such as assumed by Pigou is not itself determinate. Second, while there may be tentative sticking points held in mind by the bargainers, one of the functions of their negotiations and one of the uses of bargaining power is to make a demand which appears unreasonable at first take on greater respectability as the alternatives to its acceptance become more obvious. During the months following World War II, the idea of wage increases of 30 per cent sounded shocking at first, but in many instances became more "reasonable" in the course of negotiations. In later years, the startling demand for a guaranteed annual wage became reasonable and acceptable as a supplemental employment benefit. After long negotiations, managers also found noncontributory pension plans to be less radical than they first took them to be. The same could be true of proposed wage cuts of, say, 10 per cent following a period of prolonged prosperity which trailed off into a recession. If, then, there is any "range of reasonableness" or "range of practicable bargains" or "limits of coercion," they will be established through negotiations and in the very process of agreement. As will be shown shortly, the same forces which operate to set the wage *within* such a range, if one is assumed, must also operate to set the range itself, and since these are simultaneous processes, there is no point— or method—of distinguishing between them.

Apparently, there is nothing to be gained by approaching the concept of bargaining power through a process of first establishing limits to its exercise. Wage rates as well as other matters of the bargaining conference are determined by the direct play of bargaining power. But what is bargaining power? Can it be given a more precise and usable definition than simply the ability to control wage rates? Let us observe briefly what some authorities have had further to say about it.

Bargaining Power as the Ability to Exploit and Impose Costs

Professor Commons, one of the great pioneers in the field of labor studies, concluded: "Bargaining power is the proprietary ability to withhold products or production pending the negotiations for transfer of ownership of wealth." [3] This definition purports to be a generic one, applicable to the determination of scarcity values throughout the economy. It bears the defect of Commons's preoccupation with the significance of property rights in capitalistic society, since it rests bargaining power solely on ownership without respect to the economic circumstances in which that ownership is enjoyed. The *proprietary* ability to withhold production through strike or lockout may be unaccompanied by *actual* ability, that is, power. As Professor Knight has pointed out, "freedom to perform an act [which embraces proprietary ability] is meaningless unless the subject is in possession of the requisite means of action, and . . . the practical question is one of power rather than formal freedom." [4] The right to strike cannot be equated with bargaining power. At the very least, there are degrees of effectiveness in the use of the asserted right, a fact which is commonly conceived as material to bargaining power though without significance to proprietary ability.

Prof. Henry Simons, a thoroughgoing economic liberalist in the classical

[3] The same, p. 267.
[4] Frank H. Knight, *Freedom and Reform,* New York: Harper & Row, Publishers, Incorporated, 1947, p. 4.

sense, defined bargaining power as monopoly power and related it to organization.[5] For him, bargaining power was group restraint over individualistic action. As such it constituted a departure from the normative ideal of the perfectly competitive economy and had no rationale except intended abuse for group advancement. Bargaining power may thus be accepted on its face as power to exploit, and an increase in bargaining power represents an increased capacity to exploit. This narrow approach to the problem may be maintained only on the premise of an atomistic society endowed with all the attributes of a perfect economy. If we abandon such curious, if time-honored, assumptions, we may justifiably admit producers' interests (in the broad sense of all those engaged in the production process) as well as consumers' interests, and voluntary association regains its respectability.

If we admit the nonexistence of perfect competition, bargaining power, however ultimately defined, bears some relation to ability to realize one's desires. Consequently, one may expand "bargaining power" by improving knowledge or increasing mobility, among other methods which can hardly be labeled monopolistic and exploitative. There is something inadequate about a definition of bargaining power which condemns all group activity for possessing it in any degree.

Prof. Sumner Slichter, one of the foremost of modern labor economists, wrote: "Bargaining power may be defined as the cost to A of imposing a loss upon B." [6] This description appears to be defective, however, in suggesting either that the objective of one party is to impose a loss upon the other (rather than secure an advantage for itself) or that a loss to B may be identified with advantage to A.[7]

Prof. John T. Dunlop has conceived of bargaining power as the relative ability of two contracting parties to influence the wage, in the light of all prevailing factors.[8] Prof. Charles E. Lindblom accepted Dunlop's conclu-

---

[5] Henry C. Simons, *Economic Policy for a Free Society*, Chicago: The University of Chicago Press, 1948, pp. 129, 154.

[6] Sumner Slichter, "Impact of Social Security Legislation upon Mobility and Enterprise," *American Economic Review*, vol. 30, Supplement (1940), p. 57. The idea is repeated in "Good Bargains and Bad Bargains," *Collective Bargaining Contracts*, Bureau of National Affairs (1941), pp. 46–48. This same approach has been elaborated by Joseph Shister in "The Theory of Union Bargaining Power," *Southern Economic Journal*, vol. 10 (1943–1944), pp. 151–159.

[7] The criticism that this definition implies that bargaining power must always be exercised at a [positive] cost is hardly well taken, however. Cost may obviously be considered in a negative sense. Thus Pigou in his *Economics of Welfare*, p. 454, has pointed out that under given circumstances a strike would represent negative cost to a union or to an employer.

[8] John T. Dunlop, *Wage Determination under Trade Unions*, New York: The Macmillan Company, 1944, p. 78. Dunlop distinguishes between "deter-

sions in broad outline but refined them to the proposition that "bargaining power is best defined to include all the forces which enable a buyer or seller to set or maintain a price." Like Dunlop, he included as factors determining bargaining power (1) the tastes, goals, and motives of the parties; (2) skills in techniques of persuasion and coercion; and (3) competition from other buyers and sellers. Bargaining power is thus not regarded as ability to set aside competitive factors; competitive factors may be used or manipulated to enhance bargaining advantage.[9]

Concession and Resistance in Bargaining Power

Finally, special attention should be directed to the concept of bargaining power implicit in Professor Hicks' analysis of wage setting under collective bargaining.[10] He starts with the proposition that the willingness of the employees to undertake a strike and of the management to resist a strike depends upon what is to be gained by such sacrifice. The *duration* of the strike, in particular, will be governed by the relative return. The steeper the wage increase sought by the union, the more likely the employer is to be willing to face a long strike; and the more willing the union to undertake a long strike, the greater the potential gain. On this assumption one may set up for each employer a schedule of wage changes which he would be willing to pay rather than face a strike of given length; the wage changes and strike durations would vary directly. At each point on the schedule the anticipated cost of the strike and the anticipated cost of the wage concession balance. The schedule would indicate that the employer would be willing to grant any lower wage increase rather than face a strike of the associated duration, whereas he would prefer to meet the strike rather than grant a higher wage. Hicks calls it the "employer's concession schedule." One may draw a similar schedule for any union, showing the length of time its members would remain on strike rather than allow their wage to fall below a corresponding rate. For any higher wage, they would forgo a

---

mining" and "resultant" concepts in such a manner as to establish a definite relationship between the degree of bargaining power and the level of the wage rate, the latter simply measuring bargaining power by the resulting wage without reference to the forces causing it.

[9] C. E. Lindblom, " 'Bargaining Power' in Price and Wage Determination," *Quarterly Journal of Economics*, vol. 62 (1948), pp. 402–403. Because of this necessity of embracing within it all forces entering into wage determination, Lindblom concludes that "the concept of bargaining power is shown to be a blunderbuss rather than a refined tool of analysis."

[10] The presentation here is taken from J. R. Hicks, *Theory of Wages*, New York: The Macmillan Company, 1932, chap. 7.

strike; at any lower wage, they would make a stand. Such a schedule may be thought of as the union's "resistance curve."

These two curves are diagramed in Figure 1. *OE* represents the wage which the employer would have undertaken in the absence of union pressure. *EE'* is his concession curve. At any point on that curve the costs of the given wage increase and the costs of the strike of the associated duration are equal. The employer's curve levels off at some rate, since above this rate the employer would prefer to close down the business. *UU'* is the union's resistance curve, at any point on which the sacrifice of accepting a lower wage rate matches the costs of striking for the indicated length of time. The union's curve generally will join the wage axis on the left-hand side, since there is usually some rate above which it would not push for fear of employment repercussions, and, on the right, the curve will meet *EU'*, since there is some length of time beyond which the union would simply be unable to carry on a strike but would have to settle on the employer's terms, that is, wage *OE*.

At some point, *P*, the employer's concession curve and the union's resistance curve will cut each other. The associated wage rate, *OP*, represents the best possible bargain for both parties, for at any higher wage demand, the employer would prefer to entertain a strike. This preference is based on the belief that the employees would not hold out for as long as would be necessary to make the strike as costly to him as the demanded increase in the wage bill. At any wage less than *OP*, the union would not have extracted its maximum bargaining advantage; the employer would have been willing to pay more, in the belief that the employees would have stayed out longer before accepting less. A prolonged strike caused by his holding out for a lower wage would be more costly to him than settlement at the higher rate.

Thus the task of the negotiators is to identify point *P*. If the bargaining is skillfully conducted, a strike not only will be avoided but could not possibly do either party any good. Strikes represent a miscalculation by either party of its own or the other's bargaining power, on the strength of which the concession and resistance curves are drawn. "There is a general presumption that it will be possible to get more favorable terms by negotiating than by striking." [11] Moreover, time is on the side of the employer past some point in a strike. As the strike continues, the employer is interested only in the cost of the remainder of the strike, and since the union's staying power begins to decline from the first day of the strike, with the passage of time its resistance curve moves to the left, reducing the highest wage that the union negotiators can obtain. That is to say, the concession and resistance curves are conceived as drawn at a moment in time. They do not

[11] The same, pp. 144–145.

Figure 1. Hicks' bargaining schedules.

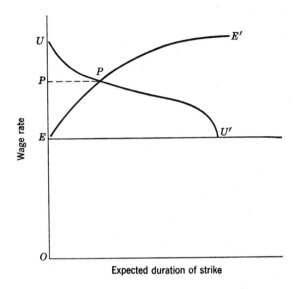

"last" throughout the duration of the strike, showing that when the strike goes into its sixth week, for example, the union will be prepared to take a wage of so much, and the employer will be prepared to grant a wage of so much. These curves represent the wage which would be accepted by both parties rather than face *future* strikes of given (i.e., anticipated) duration. They are thus presumably being redrawn throughout the period of the strike, in accord with the changing expectations of the parties.

Of course, conditions may change to improve the union's bargaining position. Such an occurrence presumably would bring forth a new point *P*, which the union bargainers would strive to reach. Other things remaining equal, fighting it out to the bitter end *must* simply mean going back on the employer's terms. Except for occasional resort to the strike to keep employers mindful of the power of the union or to improve the cohesion of the members, a strike "arises from the divergence of estimates [of employer and union] and from no other cause." [12]

One criticism of the conception of bargaining power implicit in Professor Hicks' analysis is that, like the other cited definitions, it proceeds solely from the standpoint of price and wage determination. Although the concept of bargaining power which Hicksian analysis suggests has been useful, one needs to modify it, including in it more than the wage factor. The importance of bargaining power in fixing *all* the conditions under which the cooperation of economic partners takes place must not be slighted. We are

[12] The same, p. 147.

concerned with group power in terms of both theory and policy, and bargaining power has its greatest relevance to groups. It concerns the whole of group relationships and the process of group agreement. Simply listing the components of *wage* determination as tastes, skills, and competitive forces is to say little about the total relationship between the parties which collective bargaining seeks to establish and maintain and which is established and maintained on the basis of relative bargaining power. Even for the economist, price is not the only interest. The nature of economic organizations (including intergroup relationships) through which economic activity proceeds is at least as much a subject of interest to the economist as to the political scientist, and that interest cannot be satisfied by exclusive attention to price or wage issues. Bargaining power relates to the organized economic relationship (for our interest, between management and union), which has as only one of its functions the determination of prices and wages.

The Costs of Agreeing and Disagreeing

The view of bargaining power as an effective force behind the whole collective bargaining relationship and the process of intergroup agreement is the one adopted here. Broadening Professor Hicks' implicit concept, we may define bargaining power as the ability to secure another's agreement on one's own terms. A union's bargaining power at any point of time *is*, for example, management's willingness to agree to the union's terms. Management's willingness in turn depends upon the cost of disagreeing with the union terms, relative to the cost of agreeing to them.

If the cost to management of disagreeing with the union is high relative to the cost of agreeing, the union's bargaining power is enhanced. (If a strike is very costly to management and the union's terms are quite inexpensive, the union's chances of getting its demands are improved.) If the cost to management of disagreeing with the union is low relative to the cost of agreeing to the union's terms, the union's bargaining power is diminished. (If sales are off and production is being cut back anyway, a strike may be relatively inexpensive compared with the cost of the union's demand. In such a case, the union's chance of getting its demands are not good.) These statements in themselves reveal nothing of the strength or weakness of the union relative to management, since management might possess a strong or weak bargaining power to press its own terms. Only if the cost to management of disagreeing with the union's terms is greater than the cost of agreeing to them and if the cost to the union of disagreeing with management's terms is less than the cost of agreeing to them is the union's bargaining power greater than management's. More generally, only if the difference to management between the cost of disagreement and agreement on labor's terms is proportionately greater than the difference to labor between the costs of disagreement and agreement on management's terms can one say that labor's bargaining power is greater than management's.

Bargaining power defined as we have done here is not an inherent attribute of the parties or some absolute "amount" of power available for any and all bargaining situations. The parties may change it as they use different tactics to influence each other.[13] The passage of time also may bring changes of bargaining power for unions and management as economic conditions shift or as public opinion and governmental influence mobilize for or against one of the bargainers.[14] Bargaining power changes too with the nature of the demands made, the costs of agreement and disagreement being relative to the demands. In general the greater the demand, the greater the resistance to it and therefore the less the bargaining power.

The word "cost" is here being used in a broad sense, as disadvantage, thus including pecuniary and nonpecuniary costs. Not all costs can be reduced to a common denominator, of course, but in making decisions some sort of balance *must* be struck, even with respect to incommensurate matters, if decision is to be made and action undertaken. The very incommensurability of certain issues makes possible the changing of minds that might be unpersuaded if all significant issues could be reduced by an economic calculus to a numerical balance or imbalance.

There is some use in dwelling on this point briefly. Previously we said that a major difficulty with definitions of bargaining power has been the fact that they have dealt with only one issue in the bargaining process, wages, and that numerous other issues not reducible to a dollar scale of values are also involved. The sort of balancing of costs which is contemplated in the definition of bargaining power just given does not require measurement of costs in any arithmetical sense, however. The balancing of incommensurable items may be accomplished in the same way that oranges may be balanced against apples on a consumer's indifference map. What these costs of agreement and disagreement may be to the bargainers cannot

---

[13] Prof. Carl Stevens suggests that shifts and changes of tactics should be viewed as the use of existing bargaining power to gain objectives rather than as ways of changing the magnitude of bargaining power. "On the Theory of Negotiations," *Quarterly Journal of Economics,* vol. 72 (1958), p. 93, footnote 2.

[14] Prof. A. Cartter adds a "time term" to his bargaining model, adapted from J. Pen's model in "A General Theory of Bargaining," *American Economic Review,* vol. 42 (1952), pp. 24–42. He believes that "time automatically tends to bring about a settlement, for the passage of time gradually increases the [cost of disagreement] . . . for both parties." *Theory of Wages and Employment,* Homewood, Ill.: Richard D. Irwin, Inc., 1959, pp. 123–126.

be known precisely enough to permit balancing, except through the exploratory process of negotiation. Through negotiating, the feasible and infeasible combinations become apparent.

Several points are to be noted about this definition of bargaining power: (1) It takes into account the total situation, not only the striking or resistance capacities of the parties, but the economic, political, and social circumstances insofar as these bear upon the cost of agreement or disagreement. In fact, there appears to be no meaningful way in which a union's striking power, for example, can be separated from surrounding economic and political forces. (2) It allows for the real possibility that bargaining power may shift over time. It is not static, but dynamic. Even within brief periods of time, relative positions may change considerably as the parties maneuver for advantage in the bargaining process. (3) The concept of bargaining power, which is here oriented toward a group decision-making process, is not exclusively tied to two-party negotiations. Although in this analysis we shall primarily be interested in the union-management relationship, the concept is equally applicable to situations involving joint decisions of more than two parties. (4) If agreement is reached, it must be on terms which for all the parties concerned represent a cost of agreement equal to, or less than, a cost of disagreement. (5) If disagreement persists, it must be because of terms which for at least one of the parties concerned represent a cost of disagreement equal to, or less than, a cost of agreement.[15] (6) Bargaining power for any party may be increased by anything which lowers the relative cost of agreement to the other party or raises the relative cost of disagreement.

In elaborating this concept of bargaining power, let us first turn our attention to the factors which influence the cost of disagreement, following which we shall consider the determinants of the costs of agreement.

In terms of an agreement process, the most meaningful view of the costs of someone's disagreeing with you on your terms is that person's conception of the costs. His prediction or estimate of the cost to him of disagreeing with you is conclusive with him. He may be either right or wrong, of course, as he may discover during negotiations or as you may be able to convince him. Consequently, bargaining power becomes in part a matter of

[15] Professor Stevens points out that two parties may fail to reach a settlement and continue bargaining even though one may enjoy a greater coefficient of bargaining power than the other. The reason is, he explains, that there is not only a necessary condition for settlement, the *existence* of an "acceptable" settlement, but also a sufficient condition; i.e., the parties must be informed and aware of the possible settlement. Disagreement could thus persist because the parties are unaware of their available route to settlement. See *Strategy and Collective Bargaining Negotiation,* New York: McGraw-Hill Book Company, 1963, pp. 21–22, 169.

influencing the psychological reactions of the negotiators; one may use the tactic of sheer bluff, but it is also possible to influence another's estimate of the cost of disagreeing on your terms by a straight factual approach if you believe he is operating on an unwarrantably optimistic estimate.

Union Tactics and the Costs of Disagreeing

The most widely recognized tactics are those by which one party seeks to make the cost of disagreement on its terms high to the other. The union uses the strike, withholding labor until its terms are met; the employer uses the lockout, withholding employment until his terms are met. Regardless of who initiates either action, *both* parties are subjected to costs, of course. When a union conducts a strike aimed at closing an employer's business operations, the employees must also bear a cost—their loss of wages. The employer's estimate of how long his employees will submit to their loss of wages will partly determine his estimate of the duration of the strike and consequently the cost to him of rejecting the union's terms. Similarly, in the event of a lockout the employer, while initiating action, is himself equally subjected to some loss from cessation of operations. The losses may be those of present profits, for example, or perhaps even of future profits through loss of customers. The union's estimate of how long the employer will or can stand such a drain will affect, in part, its estimate of the cost of refusing to agree on his terms.

As a result, each party has made efforts to increase the effectiveness of these tactics and to render itself immune to the tactics of the other. The efforts have centered primarily around the union's seeking to strengthen the strike weapon and management's seeking to weaken it. In some of the earliest recorded turnouts of journeymen, we find evidence of the use of strike benefits to lengthen the staying power of the workers and thus increase the cost to the masters of disagreeing with them. Strike benefits were used at least as early as 1805, in the strike of the Philadelphia shoemakers, and in the 1827 conspiracy trial of the Philadelphia journeymen tailors, there was even an attempt made to buy off strikebreakers with strike benefits. On the other hand, employers throughout the years have generally sought to limit the union's interference with members who sought to return to work or nonunion workers who sought to replace the strikers.

The tactical aspects of conducting strikes have been carefully and thoroughly explored by both unions and management. Each attempts to conduct itself so that maximum costs fall upon the other party while only minimum costs are imposed upon itself. The timing of a strike, for example, can be a matter of considerable importance. A strike against an automobile firm just after it has invested in retooling for a model change and when it is ready to begin its competitive sales campaign for the new model would probably be more effective than at any other time of the year. The printing unions in New York for many years timed the expiration of their agreements with newspaper publishers to coincide with the beginning of the period of heaviest advertising, between Thanksgiving and Christmas. A strike at that time would cause the greatest loss of advertising revenues to the papers. Also, a strike by the Hatters in the first part of the year, before Easter, would cause a more serious loss to hat manufacturers than a strike in the summer.

Under some conditions striking workers may find that the costs of a strike decrease over time rather than increase. For example, in the state of New York, unemployment insurance becomes available to strikers after eight weeks. Two months after the beginning of the long New York City newspaper strike of 1962–1963, the average striker was receiving enough strike benefits and unemployment pay to total $120 weekly, a payment comparable to his regular take-home pay. In the long steel strike of 1959, federal, state, and local government benefits and relief provided the striking steelworkers with at least $22,750,000 worth of aid. Full records might well have disclosed the total government assistance to have been in excess of $45 million, according to the union's secretary-treasurer.[16] Or, if other related jobs are plentiful, strikers may find work elsewhere and feel little pressure to agree with management's terms.

The very structure of unions is in part determined by strike effectiveness. One advantage of the craft union structure is the key position which skilled workers frequently play in an enterprise, coupled with the relatively low wage bill which they entail. A strike of a handful of powerhouse employees may close down an entire plant, involving the employer in a substantial cost of disagreeing on their terms, whereas because of their small number the cost of agreement may be negligible in comparison, even if they demand an "outrageous" pay increase. The cost of disagreement to the employer can be materially reduced, however, if striking craftsmen can be replaced, and here enters one powerful incentive for craft unions to exercise control over *all* workers with given skills and training who might provide replacements for the striking craftsmen.

In the case of unskilled or semiskilled workers, there is little possibility of gathering under one union all those who could substitute for striking employees. The very lack of skill increases the opportunity for substitution. At the same time that it becomes easier for the employer to find substitutes for any given semiskilled worker, growth in the size of industrial establishments makes it more difficult to replace an entire body of employees. Here an industrial union shows greater strike effectiveness by being able to take away from the employer virtually his whole working force in event of

---

[16] The *New York Times,* September 19, 1960.

disagreement. Unsurprisingly, therefore, the industrial union has its greatest strength in large plants rather than small shops, since in the latter the possibility of the employer's replacing the whole staff of employees in event of strike still remains.

In addition to the strike as a bargaining weapon, the device of picketing has been developed to a high degree of usefulness by the unions. This generally serves to support a strike, though it may be used independently. A picket line advertises a strike and strengthens it insofar as members of other unions refuse to cross it, whether they are engaged in their personal or their employer's business. The picket line has acquired an almost religious significance to many union members, so that its violation takes on aspects of sacrilege and taints the offender. In the presence of such dogma, it becomes possible for even a small group of employees to isolate the company from the economy, inflicting a cost of disagreement upon the company out of all proportion to their significance to its operations. As a single instance, the refusal of 371 photoengravers to accept a settlement similar to that won by the nearly three thousand typographers after a 3½-month strike in New York in 1962–1963 continued the strike for nearly an additional week. The picket line of the photoengravers, like that of the typographers earlier, kept some seventeen thousand newspaper unionists idle at a time when they were ready to work and kept newspapers from approximately thirteen thousand newsdealers anxious to stock the main item of their sales.[17]

The cost to the employer of disagreement with the union is thus in some instances dependent upon the union's ability to provoke sympathetic action by unionists in other establishments or other trades. Striking workers frequently seek the support of the powerful Teamsters brotherhood, which by reason of its strategic function of delivering supplies and removing finished products can sometimes bring enormous pressure upon an employer.

In addition to the picket line, a means by which unions in the past (less frequently today) sought to increase the cost to the employer of disagreeing with them by arousing outside support was the secondary boycott. This has now been outlawed by the Taft-Hartley and Landrum-Griffin Acts, though unions occasionally still covertly resort to it. The boycott itself is a time-honored tactic. Through the boycott, unions encourage others to have nothing to do with a struck company or its sympathizers. The "we do not patronize" list is the best-known example of such action. Since the primary boycott is virtually restricted to instances where the employer is selling directly to the public and since the effects of the boycott campaign are often slow in making themselves felt, unions often attempted to extend the boycott to secondary sources of influence. Through the secondary boycott,

[17] The same, April 1, 1963.

the striking union would bring pressure upon a sympathizing union in a related company to strike, too, even if the latter union had no dispute with its employer. The intent was to force the second employer to seek to mediate a settlement of the original dispute in order to solve his own difficulties. In some instances the union would bring pressure directly upon a second employer, without going through the latter's union; it might throw a picket line around his premises and thus persuade his workers to refuse to enter the plant. The nature of the secondary boycott can perhaps be most easily grasped by referring to Figure 2, in which the arrows indicate directions of pressure.[18]

In not all cases is it or was it necessary for the second union actually to strike. The first union might declare the goods produced by the primary employer, A, "banned," "no go," or "black." By doing so, it might persuade union members at other plants working for other employers to refuse to handle them. Employer A would quickly find his usual markets cut off or reduced, or the primary union, A, might picket a secondary employer, C, and by pressing him, apply indirect pressure to employer A. The following case, related in a Senate debate in 1959, illustrates the technique and its effectiveness:

> The Barbers Union in a dispute with the Terminal Barber Shops, Inc., located in the Waldorf-Astoria Hotel, picketed entrances to the Waldorf-Astoria Hotel. The evidence shows that for a few days business went on as usual, and then the Teamsters Union recognized the picket line and refused to deliver supplies to the Waldorf-Astoria. There were no linens brought in. There was no milk. There was no food. Supplies could not go out. The greatest hotel in the country was about to come to a standstill. . . . As a result, the management of the Waldorf-Astoria Hotel had to say to the concern which had leased the barbershop space, "You will have to yield. If you do not, we cannot renew your lease." [19]

Such overt labor actions as strikes, picketing, and secondary boycotts may be accompanied by violence. The literature of industrial relations has been filled with recitals of bloody conflict and even death, as employers and

[18] The Teamsters have recently begun to use the tertiary boycott as a means of evading the legal restrictions on the secondary boycott. By applying direct pressure upon shippers to induce their organized truckers not to deal with unorganized truckers, the union can gain leverage. The line of coercion runs from organized to unorganized carrier via the shipper as a third party. Ralph James and Estelle James, "Hoffa's Leverage Techniques in Bargaining," *Industrial Relations*, vol. 3 (1963), p. 79.

[19] Senator Curtis, *Congressional Record*, Senate, April 24, 1959, p. 5955, quoted in the *Legislative History of the Labor-Management Reporting and Disclosure Act of 1959*, vol. II, 1959, p. 1178.

Figure 2. Secondary and primary boycotts.

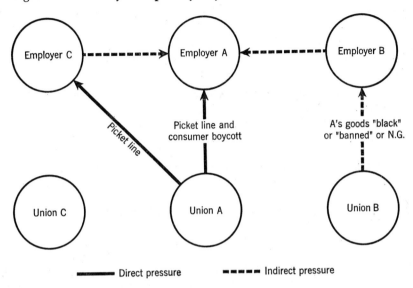

unionists have sought grimly to make good their efforts to keep the price of disagreement high for each other. Strikers have sought to stop back-to-work movements, and employers have sought to use strikebreakers.[20] More significant than the possibility of violence is the fact that the reliance on overt tactics for increasing bargaining power has had its repercussions on the very governmental form of the unions. Effective and efficient use of these tactics often necessitates a tightly held leadership operating on authoritarian and military principles. Democracy within unions can be afforded only between contests with the employer. From the time the agreement is reached on the demands to be made upon the company until those demands are surely won or lost, union leaders argue that the actions of members must be firmly controlled to restrain the weakest of the individual strikers from capitulating or providing leverage for the employer to split the striking organization.

If the above tactics are the more dramatic methods by which a union attempts to impose upon management a high cost of disagreeing with it, more subtle ways of imposing costs have been discovered. One primary cost of disagreement may simply be the refusal of the other party to coop-

---

[20] A peculiarity of American labor law is the requirement that employers recognize and bargain collectively with a union certified by the NLRB only as long as there is no strike. Once the union strikes, the employer is free to bargain individually with any worker he can get to accept employment. Back-to-work movements thus threaten the strike, strikers' jobs, and even collective bargaining itself.

erate in the daily tasks of production. Such lack of cooperation has sometimes taken on organized aspects, in the form of slowdowns.[21] One industrial relations manager described how on-the-job pressure may create a
cost of disagreement that brings results. He relates the experience he and
his New York electrical company had in trying to get workers to accept
new work methods and new wage rates:

> We needed the changes if our control panels were going to be
> competitive. In recent years other firms had caught up with our sales
> and it was a question whether we could stay in this part of the
> business. No serious opposition to the new standards developed until
> we got to the panel-wiring department. As soon as we put in the new
> standards the production from all fifty men dropped from a third to a
> half. Now they knew the old standards were too loose and they knew
> we had to raise them. . . .
>
> We'd raised them 25 units and we might have been off 5 units
> either way, maybe. But they accused us of making it too tight and
> wanted us to cut back 10 or 12 units. On the average the wirers had
> been making from $2.61 to $2.80 an hour and a few of the fast ones
> made as much as $3.20. Now they were making only $1.60 to $1.80.
> For five months they refused to work overtime too. That was allowable
> under the contract unfortunately. Well, I can tell you, our production
> schedules were really being hurt. They finally gave up the overtime
> ban but kept on with the slowdown for another four months. We
> couldn't fire them because they're too skilled and replacements are
> hard to get. Besides we needed that production. Finally we gave in
> and dropped 12 points to get out of our tight production corner.

Noncooperation as a cost of disagreement need not always assume an
organized form, however. Resentment over management failure to concede
some point which employees deem of little moment to management but of
considerable significance to themselves may result in unpremeditated holding back. Even such a little matter as refusal of the right of employees to
smoke on the job, where no safety or efficiency reason for refusal appears
to exist, may create a resentment which finds its expression in early quit-
ting, lingering in the washroom for an illicit cigarette, or any of a number
of outlets for private aggression. The failure of agreement between unions
and management, both across the bargaining table and down in the shop,
developing simply from incentive to noncooperation probably engenders an
attitude of latent hostility that makes future agreement more difficult and
more costly.

The threat to management of a loss of cooperation in production loses
much of its potency as a cost of disagreement if management believes that

[21] See Richard S. Hammett, Joel Seidman, and Jack London, "The Slow-
down as a Union Tactic," *The Journal of Political Economy,* vol. 65 (1957),
pp. 126–134.

its employees have already developed an antagonism leading to loss of on-the-job cooperation. The loss becomes a "sunk" cost, so to speak, something which having already been lost cannot be lost again. Only if the employer is made to believe that cooperation can effectively be reestablished by conceding his terms does its loss add to the employees' bargaining power. Loss of cooperation may be a strong bargaining card for the union before it is played, but once played it has much less effect because further disaffection will add only marginal future costs of disagreement to the employer.

Management Tactics and the Costs of Disagreeing

The discussion, so far, has run in terms of the union's power to make disagreement with its terms costly to the employer. It is here that the dramatic actions of industrial relations are encountered. But managements and employers, too, are able to make costly the workers' disagreement with their terms. In the past, their methods of achieving this often bore a more precise resemblance to those of the union than at present. The so-called "La Follette hearings" in the United States Senate in the period from 1937 to 1939 on the violation of free speech and the rights of labor by companies and employers' associations resulted in thousands of pages of printed testimony on the use of violence and intimidation in opposing employee organization for collective bargaining. The boycott was matched by a blacklist and sabotage by the *agent provocateur*. These forms of pressure have now been rendered illegal by various legislative acts, but the decisions of the National Labor Relations Board continue to reveal intimidatory actions by some managements designed to render the unions' disagreement with them costly, such as discharge for union activity, encouragement of rival unions, or even closing of plants!

By far the most common method by which management can increase the cost to the union of disagreeing is by withholding the employment of the latter's members except on terms agreeable to management. The unionists' alternative to agreement becomes the lockout and thus a loss of jobs and income. If sales are low and customers' inventories high, as was the situation for steel in June, 1959, employers may decide that the cost of a work stoppage would be considerably lessened. The steel industry that year was able to produce nearly $3\frac{1}{2}$ million tons more steel, even with its plants closed down for 116 days, than it produced the year before, and only $6\frac{1}{2}$ million tons less than the year after. Employers do not have to wait for market conditions to lessen the cost of a work stoppage; in a number of industries—air transportation, railroads, newspaper publishing, and Hawaiian sugar growing—employers have developed strike insurance. In 1960, for example, the Long Island Railroad sustained a twenty-six-day strike and was greatly aided by insurance benefits received amounting to about $50,000 a day.[22] Two years earlier, six major airlines agreed to a mutual assistance pact under which they would pay a struck airline any increased revenues received as a result of the diversion of passengers or freight. In the first eight months of the pact, the airlines paid out over $9,500,000, a large portion of that sum going to Capital Airline.[23] From strike insurance, several of the New York newspapers that ceased operation in the prolonged 1962–1963 work stoppage, either because they were struck or because they locked out their employees, received a total of $2,250,000.[24] In the New York work stoppage the ITU called a strike against only four of the newspapers, but the managers of the four other papers in the city also suspended operations, locking out their employees. They thus imposed a greater burden upon the striking union, requiring it to provide strike benefits for a larger number of members, and they also denied work to many other members of other printing trades unions.

The lockout, as presently practiced, is not a distinct action from the union's strike but, rather, constitutes a way of looking at the same action from another point of view. At contract renewal time, the employer insists on a reduction in wages. The union rejects this decision, and the employer withholds agreement on any other basis. The union calls out its members rather than accept it or, alternatively, seeks a wage increase. The employer refuses it and insists that wages be kept at existing levels. The union strikes to secure its objective, and the employer refuses to reinstate the strikers except on the old wage scales. Thus the initiative in setting off the action rests with one or the other, but the resulting action involves simultaneously a withholding of labor and a withholding of employment. The relative cost to each of disagreeing with the other will depend upon a variety of conditions, including the economic and political circumstances in which the parties find themselves. But the costs are relative—the dollar loss of income to the workers cannot be laid alongside the dollar loss of income to the company because a dollar of income has a different value in each case.

Moreover, the cost to the employees may be more than simply temporary loss of income. It may involve an actual loss of job, through replacement either by other workers or by machines. And the cost to the union as an organization may be loss of members and even of bargaining rights.

Finally, each party may resort to public opinion and political pressure to add to the other's discomfiture. By picketing, newspaper advertising, press releases, or radio speeches each may try to arouse the public to express disapproval of the other's course of conduct, in the hope that the pressure

[22] *Business Week,* September 17, 1960, p. 144.
[23] The *New York Times,* September 9, 1960.
[24] The same, April 1, 1963.

of governmental officials, social disapproval, and loss of public favor will constitute a further disadvantage which the other will be unwilling to incur. The uncertainty and diffuseness of public response and the difficulty of making social pressure articulate render such tactics of questionable value, however, except under unusual circumstances, such as when the public's own welfare or convenience is involved or when a particular controversy is converted into a question of general principle (whether "one man is more powerful than the United States government," for example).

Public support is most effective when aroused through public leadership. If governmental officials can be persuaded that it is in their own best interests to intervene in a labor dispute, whether because of concern for general welfare or because of political debt to one of the bargaining parties, the result may be to focus sentiment which previously was diffused. Pressures upon one or the other of the parties will be multiplied as fellow employers or fellow unionists fear that public disfavor, as expressed through elected officials, will lead to greater costs to themselves. If it is an intransigent employer who is publicly castigated by the President or governor, there may be concern generally among employers that a political climate unfavorable to management is being created. If it is a recalcitrant union which is condemned by a state or local official, other unionists may worry that legislators may be moved to introduce bills designed to control strikes which affect public health, safety, or comfort. Thus the cost of disagreement can become generalized, spreading from the particular parties in dispute to others more remote. Nevertheless, governmental pressure may involve costs specific to one or the other of the bargaining parties—perhaps a loss of government contracts to a company or an injunction against the union.

These are all relatively intangible costs, but they are of the sort which are becoming more and more important to employers and unions both. The size of bargaining units, the intractability of settlement, and the serious consequences of strikes in our interdependent economy have increased the tendency for governments—local and federal—to intervene in disputes to protect public welfare. The effects of such intervention will ultimately make themselves felt in the political sphere, in the kind of government which is elected and the kind of social legislation which it sponsors. These are matters which are vital to the future strength if not the actual survival of the respective interest groups. It has been said, for example, that unions restrained themselves prior to the 1948 election in the hope of securing a government committed to the repeal of the Taft-Hartley Act and that the stubborn action of some single union, such as the United Mine Workers, aroused their antipathy because of the fear of adverse effects upon their major design; thus the cost of disagreeing with their employers had become considerably enlarged because of their political objective, with a consequent relative increase in the bargaining power of the employer. The East Coast dock workers were persuaded to agree to a settlement of a thirty-four-day strike in early 1963 when government officials made clear that legislation setting up compulsory arbitration for maritime disputes was likely if the strike did not end. And in fear of similar legislation, union officers and government leaders urged the rail unions and railroad managements to settle their difficult controversy over firemen on diesels without resort to a strike.[25]

Bargaining Power and the Costs of Agreeing

Our discussion is by no means intended to be an exhaustive analysis of the costs to one of the bargaining parties of disagreeing with the other, on which relative bargaining powers partly rest. It does indicate, however, the way in which the strength of one party is in part dependent upon the other party's cost of disagreeing on its terms. The further determinant of one's bargaining strength is the cost to the other of *agreeing* with it on its own terms. As we have seen, it is the relative cost to the bargaining opponent of agreement and disagreement on one's own terms which establishes one's bargaining power. Let us turn next, then, to a brief consideration of some of the costs of agreement. This is a matter which is no less complex than the costs of disagreement. For convenience we shall dissect it into three subcategories: (1) direct costs of concessions, (2) secondary costs of concessions, and (3) nonmarket costs of concessions.

From the definition of bargaining power used here, it is evident that the higher the monetary demands, the higher the costs of agreement to the party on whom the demands are made, and the weaker the bargaining power of the demanding party (with some modification that will be shortly noted). The definition thus stresses that bargaining power is *relative* to what is being bargained for. A group's bargaining power may be weak relative to one set of demands, whereas the *same group's* bargaining power may be strong relative to a different set of demands. Since the different demands affect the costs of disagreement and agreement to the other party differently, bargaining power varies with the demands.

[25] In a warning speech to labor in April, 1963, Senator Wayne Morse, a friend of labor, said that he doubted very much "that, *barring another transportation emergency,* the Congress and the Administration will go the route of turning all maritime disputes, or all transportation disputes, over to compulsory arbitration. . . . [The hearings now under way in the House on such bills] are more than anything else an opportunity for a lot of people to express their opinion about unions for the public record." The same, April 6, 1963, p. 46. (Italics supplied.) While Senator Morse was reassuring his listeners, he was also warning them that a major strike could bring punitive congressional action.

The direct costs of agreement will generally be tied up with specific money costs. How much will a wage demand increase the wage bill, or how much will be added by a more liberal vacation plan or group insurance program? Here the amount which is directly added to the year's budget will be the most pertinent consideration. In addition to the amount of the direct costs, the duration of the increases and additions will also be pertinent. If a company believed that a wage increase once granted would extend for only one year or if a union believed that a wage cut once instituted would be withdrawn at the end of the year, there would be less resistance than one usually finds to wage changes. Experience has convinced managements that once a pay increase is granted or a union's demand gets written into the collective agreement, it is there to stay. At any rate, it will not easily be removed. Similarly, unions have acquired the belief that a "backward step" can be retraced only by repeating the struggles they have once gone through.[26] For either bargainer, then, the cost of agreement may not be the monetary loss simply for the period for which the agreement is reached, but for some indefinite period beyond. If the wage cost of agreement is limited to a definite time, it will be because one of the bargainers is willing to accept the costs at a later date of forcing a readjustment. These future costs, properly discounted, must be added in as part of the cost of the present agreement.

In the case of retroactive agreements, it may be not only current and future direct costs which must be computed but also past costs. This is particularly important in the case of pension agreements. Under them, employees now at advanced ages may become eligible for minimum pensions within perhaps as little as five years, without any fund having been

---

[26] An effective statement and examination of the rationale of this position are to be found in Prof. Henry C. Emery's article of years ago, "Hard Times and the Standard Wage," *Yale Review,* vol. 17 (1908), pp. 251–267. Speaking of the unionists, Emery concluded (pp. 266–267):

> What they dread most of all is a reduction of wages, not so much because they unreasonably refuse to make any sacrifices when the whole community is suffering, but because they believe, and they think they know from experience, that a reduction of wages once made is very difficult to restore. . . . When the manufacturer cannot pay standard wages and run full time at a profit, let him curtail his production, let some men be discharged, but let the level of wages continue intact. Then, when the readjustment comes, there will be no need of a fight, but, automatically, as the demand for products increases, the capitalist's self-interest will send him again in search of more labor.

The primary difference in this respect between the time when Emery was writing and today is that unions now are less inclined to await the "readjustment" but, rather, tend to compel it.

set aside in the past for that purpose. It becomes necessary to establish such a fund at the present time, as though the pension system had already been operating over a period of years. These are not, of course, past costs in any literal sense, since payments must be made in the present or future; part of the cost of agreement is these liabilities incurred in prior years without having been calculated or provided for earlier.

Direct costs may not be easy of computation. In some instances nothing but guesswork is possible. What will be the cost in relaxed incentive or foremen's morale and authority if greater control over discipline is granted the union or if straight seniority is recognized in layoffs and promotions? What will be the cost in reduced output if union stewards are given the right to challenge time studies? What will be the cost of a severance-pay plan? The number of jobs regularly available depends upon the state of technology and the level of general business activity. The former cannot be accurately forecast for more than short periods, and the government's changeable willingness to push and maintain full-employment measures determines the latter. The acceptance of such costs *may* be nothing more than an exercise in optimism, and their rejection a reflection of pessimism. One needs to examine the terms of agreement realistically; they may promise gain as well as cost, and both ought to be evaluated. Disciplinary systems in which unions participate can improve morale. Employee representation in time studies sometimes facilitates their acceptance. To the extent that such results are possible, the cost of agreement may be restrained and even reduced.

The secondary costs of one party of agreeing on the other's terms present problems of a somewhat different nature. In the first place, if more than one union exists in the company, the concessions won by one of them are likely to provide precedents which the others will insist on following.[27] A wage increase is not likely to be awarded to one union and denied to others in the same plant. Similarly, where a union is negotiating with a number of competing firms, it is often obligated to grant to all firms whatever concessions it may grant to any individual firm. This is the so-called "most-favored nations" arrangement, to borrow a term from international tariff agreements, under which the most favorable terms conceded to one buyer must be generalized to all. The direct cost to the union of agreeing with an employer on a 10-cent wage reduction may thus carry with it a secondary

---

[27] After the ITU, Local 6, and the New York newspaper publishers' association reached an agreement in 1963 on a benefit package of $12.63, the other printing unions demanded and got the same-sized package. "The stereotypers, the mailers, the deliverers and all the other crafts evaluated every offer with slide-rule care to make sure that it added up to exactly the $12.63 in total benefits the printers had received." The *New York Times,* April 1, 1963.

cost of an equal reduction in all other plants in the same trade or industry in the competitive area.

A secondary cost to the employer is likely to be the impact of improved terms for those in the bargaining unit on those who are outside the bargaining unit. If the pay or vacation plan or pension system of rank-and-file production workers is improved, such conditions must also be improved for foremen and higher levels of management, entailing further costs.[28]

Some companies make a practice of retaining percentage pay differentials between levels of authority, with foremen receiving a specified differtial over their highest-paid workers, with second-line management receiving a stated differential over the foremen, and so on up the ladder. In such situations it has sometimes become a standing joke that the union wins pay increases for management. Thus secondary costs of agreeing with the union must be added to the direct costs of such agreement.

The change in production costs as a result of wage adjustments and the change in prices and the resulting changes in product demand constitute what is unquestionably the most important secondary cost. These changes should perhaps be considered direct costs, since their calculation is necessary before one can even determine changes in the total wage bill. The degree of slack in the employer's cost structure and the degree of competition in his product market will be highly relevant considerations to both parties in determining the cost of agreement on the other's terms. If added costs can be absorbed without affecting price or if reduced labor costs are simply compensatory and do not lower price, secondary effects on demand for the product can be ignored. If, however, price changes result from labor-cost changes, the more competitive the product market, the more significant will be the secondary results. The greater the elasticity of demand facing the individual seller, the more marked will be the response to his price changes, either up or down.[29]

Lastly, there are nonmarket costs of agreeing to the other's proposals. These are factors which are not associated with the cost-price relationship but which generally involve "matters of principle." One example concerns the union's status. On the one hand, if managements entertain some objec-

---

[28] In late 1962 Kaiser Steel and the United Steelworkers concluded an agreement on a unique monthly productivity-sharing plan which promised considerable benefits to the workers. Two months later Kaiser found it desirable to extend the plan so that supervisors and other nonunion employees might also share in the benefits.

[29] Those interested in pursuing this aspect of bargaining power with some theoretical elaborateness, though according to a different definition of bargaining power, are referred to Dunlop, *Wage Determination under Trade Unions*, chap. 5.

tion to the very presence of a union in their plant and conceive of them as being inimical and undesirable from either a personal-interest or a social point of view, the cost of agreement with the union will be to establish that which they would prefer to eliminate. Such recognition of the union has in point of history (until perhaps the late 1930s) been one of the costs of agreement which American employers generally have been most reluctant to assume. On the other hand, to a union which is fighting to gain the support and adherence of employees in a given plant, the cost of agreeing on management's terms may be to brand it as ineffectual and even venal. "Selling out" to management is a phrase of opprobrium sometimes applied literally as well as figuratively; the result may be that hard-won members or employees on the verge of signing up with the union will fall away, and the organization will collapse.

Another "matter of principle" over which unions and management contest with vigor is the union shop. Managers express their opposition to the union shop in terms of their interest in preserving individual freedom to join or not to join a union. This is not the only reason they are reluctant to require all employees to become union members. Compulsory membership under a union shop would ensure the union a larger and steadier flow of dues income than if employees joined and paid dues voluntarily. The hard-to-measure effect on a union's bargaining power is real and significant according to many managers. The spokesman for a large aircraft company stated that his firm's objection to compulsory union membership was that it "increases the strength, the resources and striking power of the union." [30] The vice-president of industrial relations for a large electrical manufacturer provided a similar reason for his company's refusal to agree to a union shop: "We don't want that money from non-members going into the union treasury." [31]

There is also a tactical cost of agreement, associated with the principle of the opening wedge. A union or management may object less to the direct or secondary costs of some particular proposal than to the possibility of its being used as a springboard for some future demand which they are totally unwilling to consider. Unions have been antagonistic to any grievance or arbitration review of expulsions from the union which automatically entail discharge from employment under a union security agreement. They oppose such reviews, not because of a fear of having a few employees reinstated to their jobs against the wishes of the union, but because of a much deeper fear that this will establish a precedent for outside intervention in union affairs, thereby threatening the union's bargaining power.

[30] *Wall Street Journal,* January 4, 1963.
[31] J. W. Kuhn, "Right-to-Work: Symbol or Substance?" *Industrial and Labor Relations Review,* vol. 14 (1961), pp. 587–594.

In some instances, managements have been hesitant about agreeing to the participation of unions in the description and classification of jobs, contemplating the danger that this might lead to the union's insistence on discussion and agreement prior to any reassignment of duties among employees and open the possibility of establishing "job jurisdictions" as binding as craft jurisdictions. Such examples might be multiplied. Here the cost of agreement includes an admission of interest by the other party in an area which is sought to be retained with exclusive discretion.

There are indeed certain principles which unions and managements may adhere to so firmly that they constitute creeds with deep ethical or moral roots, the compromise of which will scarcely be considered. In some such instances the cost of agreement may be viewed as infinite. Some managements have closed down their plants rather than give in to the union, and some unions have allowed their organizations to disintegrate during a protracted strike rather than agree on management's terms. In these situations the cost of agreement on the other's conditions is set so high that presumably the cost of disagreement on those same conditions could not be raised to top it. The cost to management of agreeing on the union's terms, for example, would be regarded as so great that the union would be unable to make the cost of disagreement any greater. In such a situation the union's bargaining power would be weak relative to its demands.

Conclusion

When bargaining power is viewed in this manner, it follows that it may be altered in one of two ways: (1) by changing the cost to the other party of agreement on one's terms or (2) by changing the cost of disagreement. Generally speaking, the union may increase its bargaining power either by *increasing* the cost to management of *disagreeing* on the union's terms or by *reducing* the cost to management of *agreeing* on the union's terms. This conclusion is subject to an important modification, however. A union or management may not always be able to alter one of these determinants of its bargaining power independently of any effect on the other determinant. One cannot always assume that a union will automatically increase its bargaining power by reducing the cost to management of agreeing on the union's conditions. Bargaining power and its two components are relative to particular proposals. If a union were to reduce its wage demands from 10 cents to 2 cents, for instance, such action would *tend* to lessen the cost to management of agreeing with the union; hence it would seem to increase the union's bargaining power relative to the new demand. But before one could arrive at such a conclusion, it would be necessary to observe the effect of this action upon the union's membership. By reducing the prize to be gained, the union may have weakened the desire of its members to fight for it. Whereas the employees might have been willing to strike for a 10-cent-an-hour increase, they may decide that 2 cents an hour is not worth fighting for. In any event, if management believed such to be the effect, it would conclude that the cost of disagreeing with the union even on the latter's reduced demands would have been substantially lessened. The union's bargaining power relative to the revised terms it was seeking would depend upon management's revised estimates of the costs of both agreement and disagreement. The result might as well be weaker bargaining power for the union as stronger.[32]

Our analysis of bargaining power reveals the fallacy of attempting to equalize bargaining power by legislation. Bargaining power is dependent at least as much upon what each party is seeking as upon each party's coercive ability, and what the parties seek is largely beyond the control of legislation, except with respect to specific issues. Indeed, as we have seen, coercive power—the erecting of costs of disagreement—is only relative to the objective being sought. One cannot conclude, however, that legislative control over bargaining power is not feasible or desirable. In a given social context, certain forms of making disagreement costly become inadmissible. Management's use of the blacklist and injunction has thus been largely outlawed. Under the Labor-Management Relations Act of 1947, the union's resort to the secondary boycott was rendered illegal in interstate commerce. And in the Labor-Management Reporting and Disclosure Act of 1959, Title VII, Congress attempted to prohibit "hot cargo" boycotts and to restrict picketing where unions use it to extend their organizational influence. There is now wide questioning of the union's privilege to strike under certain circumstances. In some states strikes have been banned in public utilities. In some situations, as on the railroads or airlines or where the President determines that national health and welfare are involved, a waiting period may be required before a strike is permissible. In these

---

[32] At the same time, even should management conclude that the workers would be unwilling to strike for the 2-cent increase, its careful appraisal of the situation might lead it to believe that its refusal to grant even this "measly" pay raise (as the workers might regard it) would involve intangible costs of disagreement in the form of distrust, hatred, or noncooperation, rendering disagreement more expensive than agreement. An astute union leadership would point out such a possibility, but regardless of whether or not it did, as long as management recognized this element it would enter into a calculation of the union's bargaining power. Of course, if neither group considered this possibility, it would not enter at all into determination of the union's bargaining power. *Bargaining power is a subjective concept*—and a complex one.

instances legislative action has reduced the power of one or the other of the parties to make disagreement with its terms costly.

The view which one takes of the bargaining process itself will in part determine what limitations are considered acceptable. To those who regard collective bargaining as a marketing procedure, involving the sale of labor services, the strike and lockout, for example, may be upheld as necessary to a freedom not to contract, as an alternative to a forced sale or purchase. On these grounds, limitations on these rights might be opposed in principle. On the other hand, those who look upon the bargaining process as the basis of a group government or as an industrial relations system might, on these grounds, conclude that the strike and lockout, as instruments of bargaining power, are not necessary in principle even if unavoidable at the present. Possibly the bargaining parties may develop more refined methods of giving the unions power to make managerial disagreement with them costly, and vice versa; these methods may be, hopefully, more in keeping with functioning group governments or the operational requirements of the economy. If the end purpose of the bargaining process is an agreement which is voluntarily accepted by those who are party to it, it is at least possible that this objective may be as effectively accomplished, at least in certain situations, by means other than the strike or lockout and without any greater degree of compulsion. It is a question of whether our ingenuity is sufficient for the task.

The problem of strikes and lockouts as exercises in bargaining power may be looked at in another way. These are means of making one party's disagreement with the other more costly, thus increasing bargaining power. But as we have seen, bargaining power may also be increased by reducing the cost to the other party of agreeing with you. The reduction may be accomplished by methods other than simply lowering the demands which are made. Two unions may make the same wage demands, for example, one being satisfied to leave the problem of meeting them up to management, but the other offering its cooperation to help make the wage concession less costly. As our analysis indicates, agreement will come when the costs of agreement are less than those which are entailed by disagreement. If it is possible systematically to reduce the costs of agreement by improved methods of collective bargaining, it may follow that such methods of making disagreement costly as the strike and lockout will simply find less frequent use. Without being banned, they would thus disappear as a major problem. Occasional resort to them would be acceptable as that measure of tolerance for private group disagreement and breakdown which seems unavoidable in a democratic society. There is much to recommend this view, and we shall have occasion to explore its possibilities in considerably greater detail in Chapter 16.

Throughout this chapter mention has been made of costs to the union and management. A moment's reflection will reveal, however, that since "union" and "management" are simply abstract entities, in this context collections of individuals, costs will be estimated differently depending upon the influences which bear upon those doing the estimating. This is a question that involves the political structure of each union and company. In the next chapter we shall examine how the political factor enters into the bargaining process.

Collective Bargaining and Its Politics: The Union

The union is a political [1] system, and the aggregate of interests which are represented by management constitutes another political system. The decisions which they jointly reach in the bargaining process are in part dependent on their respective political characteristics. It will prove fruitful to center discussion around two essential ingredients of any political system, the issues of authority and responsibility. We shall be concerned with the derivation of the authority of the leaders and the nature of their responsibilities. Let us turn first to the union.

Democracy in Shop Elections

The union as a political system offers opportunities for careerists. In blue-collar unions, an official position carries with it the promise of ad-

[1] It will be readily observed that the word "political" is loosely used in this and the following chapter to include phenomena not strictly embraced in that term. "Political" as used here relates simply to the noneconomic influences upon two centers of economic activity and decision making—unions and managements.

vancement and a respectability and prestige worth striving for. With the growth of national organizations, the shop steward does not have to limit his aspirations to a local presidency; he can look forward to state or regional office or a special staff function from which a successful campaign will take him to the general executive board. The higher offices are rewarding assignments in their importance, if not in their pecuniary return; they customarily involve supervision over some vital aspect of the union's affairs, collaboration in the formation of central policy, or participation in the union's supreme court of appeals. The presidency of the national union may even come within reach. Thus the steward working in the shop may entertain the hope of eventually gaining one of the influential offices of our contemporary society. Union offices sometimes lead to political positions in local and state governments and appear to be becoming an avenue to federal appointment, though seldom to elective federal positions. It is not surprising, in view of the status now attached to union officeholding, that there should be some workers who aspire to union office and seek their preferment within that organization rather than through business advancement.

Since a union office is commonly won through election, the would-be officer must first become a candidate, and he has to win votes. Though sometimes unopposed, he usually has election rivals. Once elected, he must retain the support of his constituents in order to be returned to office. To accomplish these results he must convince his fellow workers of his capacity to do things for them which they would like to have done. The obvious vote catchers are a pay increase, reduced hours, and better working conditions. These become campaign "promises" to attract support, and if the candidate is elected he will feel some compulsion to try to make good on his promises in collective bargaining negotiations. In some instances the promises are impossible of achievement, and the result is likely to be a disillusioned electorate or a leader who fights to get as much of the impossible as is possible.

Further, in line with American custom, unions do not require members to vote. Abstentions are usually numerous, and to have a minority of the electorate carry an election is far from uncommon. Those most sure to vote are the members who are against a candidate, voting "agin" rather than "for" also being a common American practice. Aggrieved bloc voting and abstentions make candidates particularly vulnerable to any group displeased with either their promises or their fulfillments. Both practices also foster volatile changes in voting, of which local union officers are constantly aware.[2] These are facts of political life which are familiar to Americans from an early era.

[2] Leonard R. Sayles and George Strauss, *The Local Union,* New York: Harper & Row, Publishers, Incorporated, 1953, chaps. 10 and 16. The authors point out that high turnover of local union offices is prevalent throughout unions.

The political nature of unions thus leads to a rather continuous importunacy, affecting what the union's demands shall be in collective bargaining as well as what it is satisfied to accept. The standard method by which the union leader evidences his responsibility to his constituency is by seeking from management general gains, such as a wage increase or a vacation plan, or specific benefits for particular members, such as in the settlement of grievances. His appeal for votes customarily runs in terms of what he plans to obtain for the members if elected.

The success of such election appeals is indicative of the members' preferences and strongly influences union proposals. One local candidate may run on a platform pledged to support the national officers in demands for pensions and retraining benefits, for example, while his opponent might urge that the union demand a straight 30-cent-an-hour increase. Although the election of one of the candidates would not settle the nature of the bargaining demands actually made, it would provide a measure of members' expectations. Such contests for membership support on the basis of their self-interest occur at all levels of authority within the union. Note the appeal for votes in this handbill circulated by an employee who was campaigning for the job of local union president.

Members of Local 440, I.U.E.!

Election of officers will be this Friday. If you want leadership and ability vote for Joe Pucci. If Local 440 is to meet the challenge of the new management we need a strong, experienced president. The Admiral [company president] says he's going to cut costs and raise efficiency—Joe Pucci will see to it that he doesn't cut jobs and raise hell with our hard-won standards.

Joe Pucci knows how to win for the workers—he is an experienced Chief Steward in the Fabricating Department, the plant's largest.

(1) Between October, 1960 and June, 1963, he won over $13,000 in back pay through grievances he initiated or handled. In the last six months alone he has won $5,000 in back pay.

(2) Of the 12 cases he has taken to arbitration he has won 10. No other department has so high a proportion of wins.

(3) The Fabricating Department has filed more grievances against management trying to take away our contractual rights than any other department.

Joe's philosophy is:

(1) To tell his men what the facts are. He has regularly distributed grievance reports to all stewards in his department and interested members.

(2) He does not trade off grievances and would fight any steward who tried to.

(3) He is not afraid of telling a man if he is wrong, but if he is right, and his case is just, Joe Pucci will sit on the door of the I.R. Department until the grievance is settled.

(4) He doesn't let technicalities entangle him—he is out to solve problems, not to be a contract lawyer—and he does solve grievances—he does serve the members.

His Record Proves It!

His stand on out-of-classification work is this: As long as the company is willing to pay regular rates to first grade wiremen to work on relay adjustments we should allow it.

(1) Second grade wiremen have nothing to fear. Under the government contract overtime will be unlimited and nobody will lose any work.

(2) No second grade wiremen will lose jobs because of layoff. The government wants and needs as much of the work as F.T.C. [the company] can provide.

(3) If F.T.C. does not do the work, it will have to be subcontracted to Kellog. Joe is in favor of our people getting the work and the pay.

(4) He will fight to keep all of the AK-10 Relay work [with the loose piece rates] here in any case.

Vote for Experience, Ability and Your Best Interest—Joe Pucci.

(Vote against Frank-Merriwell contract finishes, bumbling arbitration, and weak leadership.)

The Electorate's Influence on Bargaining

Political campaigning may affect bargaining conferences and negotiations as well as union demands. Intraunion factionalism based on rival candidacies may raise antagonisms among the representatives at the bargaining table and lead to splits or at least a lack of cohesion in pursuing bargaining strategy. A management official in the New England leather industry observed: "Internal union politics creates dissension in the union negotiating committee frequently during a discussion of the merits of an employer's counter-proposal. . . . The followers of the union political adversaries are unwilling to be placed on the spot, so to speak, and subjected to criticism on the floor of the union meeting if either group takes a stand contrary to the views of the other."

Decisions and actions which affect various work groups or workers with special interests in different ways can cause serious political troubles within a union. Prof. Leonard Sayles was one of the first to point out how different seniority plans can cause dissension within a union and serious political problems for local leadership.[3] In a large Midwestern plant, a local union secured the right to have its officers sit with management representatives on the skill classification board. The board determined what jobs were to be

[3] "Seniority: An Internal Union Problem," *Harvard Business Review*, vol. 30 (1952), pp. 55–61.

classified as skilled. The rating was a desired one because it protected workers from being "bumped" by semiskilled workers in time of layoffs. Every group with even a faint claim of being skilled clamored for the desirable classification, rocking the union with intrigue and dissension. The local officers found the political pressures unbearable, being able to satisfy only a few work groups and having to make many unhappy. Within eighteen months the local renegotiated the agreement and withdrew from the classification board. Thereafter the officers involved themselves in the more politically appealing work of grieving management's "impossible and unreasonable" classifications.

The fact that the membership ultimately holds within its power the giving of union office means that at times it can force its leaders to conform to its wishes, even when the leaders are opposed in principle. Officials have admitted pushing for agreements which they believed to be unfair to the company because they felt their members demanded them. It has been said that in the Cleveland building trades during informal negotiations preceding actual bargaining, union representatives in some years have readily agreed that wage rates were as high as could be reasonably expected but have then gone on to point out that their members would nonetheless ask for increases, inquiring of the employer representatives: "What are we going to do about it?"

Management negotiators have good reason to take such a question seriously, for agreements are usually not completed until the members approve them, and approval is by no means automatic. Disapproval can be seriously embarrassing to the negotiators and politically dangerous to the union leaders. In recent years rejection of negotiated agreements has ceased to be uncommon. The Federal Mediation and Conciliation Service estimates that in over 750 situations in 1962, rank-and-file union members rejected settlements negotiated and approved by their leaders. The director of the service, William Simpkin, pointed out that the rising number of contract rejections is a disturbing factor in labor-management relations. He said that they "introduce an uncertainty and instability in negotiations, which, if continued, will be detrimental to the bargaining process." [4]

Several examples of settlement rejections by union members illustrate the problem. In 1963 the New York Typographers rejected an intricately negotiated agreement and continued their long 100-day strike another two weeks. An insurgent faction of the union president's "hard-line party" derided the economic benefits as too niggardly and the protective clauses as too weak.[5] Two years earlier, the musicians of the New York Philharmonic had walked out on strike when presented by their local officers with a signed agreement. They protested that they had not participated in the

[4] The *Wall Street Journal,* June 3, 1963.
[5] The *New York Times,* April 1, 1963.

negotiations. In 1961 the big Kenosha local of the United Automobile Workers rejected the profit-sharing agreement laboriously worked out by the managers of American Motors Corporation and UAW leaders. The vote caused consternation at the national offices and a demand for a revote. Approval was won the second time, but only after a concentrated effort by union officers to "persuade" the members to reconsider.

Union officers do not always have a second chance to present their case to members. However responsibly they may act or want to act, they can never forget that they hold office at the pleasure of their electorate. Consider the case of the president of the Studebaker local of the UAW in the period from 1953 to 1955. The company had asked in 1953 that the union approve new wage standards so that labor costs could be cut. Studebaker was no longer competitive with the Big Three automobile companies, and it was running heavy losses. Company negotiators argued that if adjustments were not made, the plant would soon have to close. The union turned down the request, but Horvath, the local's president, began an intensive study of costs and the automobile market. He concluded that Studebaker was indeed in trouble and that wage adjustments were needed.

He felt secure in his position, for he had received 71 per cent of the vote in the last election, while his major opponent had received only 18 per cent (90 per cent of the membership had voted). After conducting many study meetings and after a long program of explaining the need for cutting costs in 1954, Horvath won for the company the right to cut rates an average of 14 per cent, to reduce fringe benefits, and to put in "competitive work standards" where justified. The vote was a lopsided 5,371 to 626, but ominously for Horvath over three thousand members—40 per cent of the total—did not cast ballots. The company and newspapers across the nation hailed him as a "labor statesman," however.

Inside the local, many members charged that he was a management stooge and a sellout artist. In March, 1955, the company suddenly introduced the new "comparable wage standards," and worker resentment flared. Horvath charged the company with bad faith in acting so precipitously with no prior warnings, and his opposition charged him with conspiring with management. In July, his opponent, who had earlier received only about one-quarter as many votes as Horvath, won 56 per cent of the vote and became the new president.

If local officers find that they have maneuvered themselves into an untenable position, they can sometimes withdraw without loss of face by calling in national union representatives. An official of one of the railroad brotherhoods explained the possible procedure: If the general chairman, who is the local negotiator and an elected official, realizes that it would be wise for him to give ground on certain union demands but finds it difficult to do so without loss of prestige, he might have the national office advise him to yield, providing him with the "out" that *he* would have stood firm, but the national office overruled him. In other cases the local officers may be in a position to demand and secure fuller support from their national officers, even though the latter disapprove of the cause. A high officer of the United Automobile Workers admitted that local strikes were sometimes approved by the national office only because it was known that they would be called anyway and because it would discredit the national's authority and diminish the prestige of its officers if such strikes were called in the face of their opposition. The intricacies of local-regional-national politics in the large union cannot be explored here; they do, however, have their bearing upon the bargaining process.

The existence of special-interest groups within the union, usually of an occupational or regional nature, further complicates the political life of union officers. The aspirations of all must be respected, even if these conflict or if substantial blocs of votes may be lost. Particularly in an industrial union, a number of grades and varieties of skills may be represented, and some of these occupational groups seek preferment over others. One textile company official writes of "the attempts of various groups such as spinners and engineers to secure higher wage increases and preferred working conditions over that of common labor or female employees engaged in the production process." In one automobile plant, union officers demanded that Negro workers be accepted in a department from which they had previously been excluded by company policy. When the industrial relations director replied that he might be willing to accede to their request, the union men were dismayed and frankly told him that although an important group within the union was pressing the proposal and they themselves supported it in principle, they had not seriously expected it to be granted. If it were granted, they would be faced with concentrated opposition from a powerful and militant group of members in the department concerned. Would management therefore withdraw its tentative assent to this demand?

At least as difficult of resolution are the conflicting interests of workers in separated plants who are covered by the same agreement. Union leadership, pursuant to a policy of wiping out regional wage differentials, may make a concerted effort to establish a standard rate over a wider area, only to find the groups which had previously enjoyed a higher rate pressing the following year for the restoration of the "traditional" differential. Business firms in one area may be in a position to make a more liberal agreement than those in another area; locals in the more prosperous section of the industry may then become embittered at union leaders who allow themselves to be guided by the financial condition of the "representative firm." Union leaders, whose jobs rest on votes, are necessarily sensitive to such considerations.

In view of the occupational and sectional blocs within unions, one writer has suggested: "An important aspect of the leadership function is reasonably to ensure that every interest group which can exercise effective political pressure is represented in the bargaining process. In a multi-craft union, the important crafts will be represented; in a multi-industrial union, the different branches of the trade; and in regional or national negotiations, the various geographical units of the organization." [6] Methods for achieving an integration of special-interest groups within the union for purposes of collective bargaining are varied. They include allowing their representatives to sit on the policy committee which drafts the union's proposal, as when delegates from all the Chrysler locals come together in conference; provision for representation on the negotiating committee, as when an Amalgamated Clothing Workers' joint board chooses a bargaining committee including someone from each of the four main crafts—cutters, tailors, pressers, and finishers; or opportunity for special-interest representatives to approve the tentative agreement before the negotiating committee can accept it, as when representatives from all the plants of Libbey-Owens-Ford and Pittsburgh Plate Glass (who have been present at negotiations, while leaving the actual bargaining to their national officials) must consent to the drafted agreement before it goes to their membership for final approval. In all these procedures the need for understanding and reconciling divergent interests and points of view is readily apparent. The political process becomes part and parcel of the bargaining process.

There is, then, between the union electorate and its elected officials a relationship which contributes to the making of demands upon the company. A candidate for office or an officeholder must match the promises of his rivals; he must not get too far ahead or fall too far behind in his promises. He may even eliminate rivals through his effectiveness in demanding and getting more and more. His responsibility to the membership is gauged primarily in such terms, and it is on this relationship that his authority largely rests.

Political Threats from outside the Union

In addition to the candidate-electorate bond, there is a second relationship, however, which intensifies this effect—the union-membership relation. To win new members, to hold the interest of members once they have joined, and to stave off the raids of rival unions, it is incumbent upon the union officers—whoever they may be—to persuade employees not only that continuing benefits are to be secured through membership but also that the benefits of this union are relatively greater than could be secured through some other union. It thus becomes an additional responsibility of the

[6] Arthur M. Ross, *Trade Union Wage Policy*, Berkeley, Calif.: University of California Press, 1948, p. 33.

union leader to maintain and if possible to expand the membership—and strength—of the organization which he has inherited. This too is largely a matter of making promises and of seeking to make good on promises once made.

The capacity of union officials to make sweeping promises to employees during organizing drives has been the occasion for wry comment by many members of management. As the National Labor Relations Board once had occasion to observe: "Where groups are to be organized and moved into action it is not unusual for the leaders to promise more than can be secured or to indulge in some exaggeration." [7] But once organized, unions may find that they must work to hold their members by warding off the efforts of rival unions to win them away. Said a vice-president of the United States Steel Corp.: "It has been reported, for instance, that United Mine Workers' organizers have told employees in our iron mines represented by the Steelworkers' Union how much better terms of employment would be wrested from management should those workers vote out the Steelworkers and vote in the Mine Workers." [8]

"No-raiding" provisions within the AFL-CIO have diminished to some extent the political significance of the union-membership relation. Respect by each union for every other union's existing jurisdiction would seem to eliminate much of the pressure to satisfy membership that their union is doing as well as another, since the other is no longer a potential rival. This is true only within limits, however. For one thing, there are rival unions outside the AFL-CIO federation which do not respect its jurisdiction—notably the Teamsters. For another, good performance in one's present bargaining units, compared with the performance of other unions even within the AFL-CIO, is necessary for effective organizing of new units.

The union officers' responsibility to maintain the strength of the union can be enforced at local levels by pressure from national officials; but at the national level, who is there to determine whether officers have been duly responsible to "the organization"? This check is provided, if at all, by the close tie between the leader's responsibility to the present membership and his responsibility to the continuing organization. It is difficult indeed to press for advantages for present constituents if the organization is crumbling away, and conversely an expanding organization finds it easier to win concessions on their behalf. "Trade unions need power in order to materialize their most immediate daily objectives." [9] To some extent, then, the

---

[7] *In the Matter of Rabhor Company, Inc.,* 1 NLRB 470 (1936).

[8] John Stephens, *A Concept of Industrial Relations,* United States Steel Corp., 1948, p. 17.

[9] J. B. S. Hardman, *American Labor Dynamics,* New York: Harcourt, Brace & World, Inc., 1928, p. 104. Hardman has himself been active in the union movement for many years. He continues on this same page: "Generally

membership will itself seek to make officers responsible not only for the achievement of immediate gains but also for the strengthening of the organization, by which future gains can be better assured.

There are thus two major pressures which are focused on union leadership. As candidates for union office they must match the claims of rival candidates, and as representatives of the union organization they must match the performance of other unions. These pressures are felt at all levels of union authority. Both local and national officers must protect their own positions and at the same time ensure that another organization does not wean away present or potential members. But if such pressures exist, what determines their content? Why are some appeals powerful and others weak? What is it in a given situation which causes an electorate to respond, a membership to fall away, or an occupational group or local union to push for special treatment? What influences the members' conclusion as to whether their leader has been responsible to them and their union and so has justified their grant of authority to him?

The answers appear to lie largely in the worker's comparison of his situation with that of others. Discontent leading to membership demands arises because groups are treated differently when they expect to be treated similarly or when they are treated similarly when they expect to be treated differently. Members of the same union working at the same job but in different plants may be paid differential rates, creating a pressure on the union leadership to raise the rates of the "underpaid" group. Skilled workers may become upset because of an insufficient differential between their own wages and the wages of unskilled labor. The skilled auto workers forced the UAW to give special recognition to their claims and to provide special bargaining procedures as well, for example. Dissatisfied with the inadequate wage differential they received in 1955, more than eight hundred skilled men actually left the union to join skilled craft groups. Workers may also compare themselves with members of other unions and become dissatisfied. There is evidence that some of the Communications Workers in North Carolina in 1962 had become discontented with the slow pace of their wage increases. They made an attempt to join the more powerful, aggressive Teamsters. Though the attempt failed, the leaders of the Communications Workers were spurred to new levels of activity by the challenge.

A notorious example of the pressures developed by interunion comparisons is the situation that grew out of the long newspaper strike in New York City in 1962–1963, as ten unions jockeyed for bargaining advantage.

and objectively speaking, trade unionism is a sustained, systematic effort at power accumulation, and this function of trade unionism is also its driving force."

After the largest union, Local 6 of the ITU, had reached an agreement with the publishers' association, the leaders of the smaller unions had difficulty in formulating terms acceptable to their members. A. H. Raskin, of the *New York Times,* described the situation this way:

> For the other unions collective bargaining turned into collective comparison and ultimately into collective confusion. The stereotypers, the mailers, the deliverers and all the other crafts evaluated every offer with slide-rule care to make sure that it added up to exactly the $12.63 in total benefits the printers had received. . . . [Mr. Kheel, a mediator acting for the mayor, remarked], "These union fellows are like Janus. They have eyes in the front of their head and in the back of their head. They see what the other fellow got and what he is going to get, and they want it all." [10]

Invidious comparisons are not wholly responsible for the political pressures upon union officers and the group pressures with which union leaders must contend, but they are important determinants of those pressures and interests. The pressures of invidious comparisons are of course not unique to union members. Senior electronics engineers may be well satisfied with their salaries until they note that junior engineers are being hired at almost as high a salary. The bank vice-president in charge of loans may be exceedingly pleased with a raise until he discovers that the vice-president for foreign accounts received an even larger increase.

The problems of comparative pressures within, and particularly between, unions have probably increased within the last two decades, even as rivalry in organizing new members has been muted. As two union staff men explain:

> Union developments provide news items for the press, radio, and television; and bargaining achievements in one locality produce ideas for future negotiations in far-reaching parts of the country. Improved communications have produced a degree of alertness to bargaining developments among union members and the general public, that were previously absent. Collective bargaining achievements frequently have an influence on the bargaining demands of other unions and on wage determination in nonunion firms. . . . Unions have learned the importance of explaining their demands to the public through booklets, news releases, radio and television programs and paid advertisements. Public relations and education staffs help in various ways to bring collective bargaining information to the union membership and to the public at large.[11]

[10] The *New York Times,* April 1, 1963.
[11] Nathaniel Goldfinger and Everett Kassalow, "Trade Union Behavior in Wage Bargaining," in *New Concepts in Wage Determination,* George W. Taylor and Frank C. Pierson (eds.), McGraw-Hill Book Company, 1957, pp. 71–72.

The wide publicity usually given to labor negotiations undoubtedly stimulates comparisons between groups and helps to generate compulsions which the union leadership cannot resist. They are spurred to action by interest blocs whose members express concern about an "unfair" relationship with others. Ross has termed such pressure "equitable comparison," since it is based on a sense of what is fair or just—what one group is "due" in the light of what has been done for another group or other groups—or "coercive comparison," since it is a contrast of peculiar urgency, often thrusting itself upon the individuals in a group as a stimulus to action, as a relationship which is not simply a datum but one which requires correction, and as an imbalance between groups which calls for adjustment.

It is possible, of course, that comparison may provide cause for complacency or satisfaction—"we are doing as well as the next fellow"—or even for self-congratulation—"we made out better than the others." But the comparison must still be made in order for one to arrive at that conclusion. There is a compulsion in the social environment requiring the comparison—invidious though it may be—before one can determine whether he should be satisfied or not. It is this equitable comparison or coercive comparison, then, which drives union leaders to frame demands on employers in order to satisfy their constituents and retain their votes and their membership.

It is worth repeating that such comparisons have their peculiar importance both to the membership and to the officials. Union members contrast their working positions with those of other workers—in terms of wages, schedules of hours, vacations and holidays, welfare and pension plans, protection against layoffs, and so on. This comparison constitutes one spur to official action. But at the same time, candidates for office in the same union as well as leaders in different unions seek, on their own initiative, to better one another's records. Members compare the drive of union leaders as well as working conditions, and an awareness of this comparison is an independent goal to official action. Even if the union memberships evinced general satisfaction with their terms, the aspiring candidate for office or the union leader reaching out for expanded influence within the labor movement would find the surest route to his objective in pressing for and obtaining some benefit or concession which would set him apart from his fellows. His ambitions might lead him to invite favorable comparison by winning extraordinary conditions for his members.

James R. Hoffa claims that he gets "more and better" for Teamsters members than other union leaders get for their members, and he explains the continued growth of the union he heads as a result of the good wages his tough bargaining provides. In campaigns to win over workers in other unions, the Teamsters compare their strength and gains with the pettier efforts of the other unions and draw the conclusion that the Teamsters' lot is better. The Teamsters does not always win, but its raiding is a potential threat to many unions. Whether drawn by the Teamsters or other unionists, coercive comparisons in collective bargaining are usually in terms of wages and conditions of employment, but the stimulus to the comparisons may arise from the expansionary initiative of union leaders.

Coercive Comparisons among Workers

What is the basis for one group's comparing itself with another? Would an operating engineer be inclined to compare himself with a semiskilled lathe operator? Would a building tradesman compare himself with an automobile mechanic? Is a common laborer concerned with how well he has faired relative to the die cutter? Are there "noncomparison groups" as a modern version of Cairnes's "noncompeting groups"? [12]

Economists would tend to think of labor markets and would suspect that a worker in a given occupation would compare his wages and working conditions with those of other workers in the same occupation in the same community. If a single wage did not prevail or if differential wages between similar workers could not be explained on the grounds that they equalized differential working conditions so that the "packages" of wages and working conditions were equal, then economists would expect coercive comparisons to bring about either a change in terms or a movement of workers. As a matter of fact, however, specialists in labor studies appreciate now that the "labor market" belies its name, in the sense that there is no geographical area within which wages tend toward equality, even for workers of similar skills. Differentials continue over long periods of time.[13]

The absence of an *equality* of occupational wages within a geographic area does not itself support the conclusion that local comparisons are of *no* importance. Research in both the United States and Great Britain indicates that workers accept differences in wage levels of neighboring firms if they

[12] John E. Cairnes, *Some Leading Principles of Political Economy Newly Expounded,* New York: Harper & Brothers, 1874, pp. 70–73. Cairnes, it will be recalled, assumed that there were "industrial layers" within which competition for jobs took place but that workers in one layer did not compete for jobs with workers in other layers. For comment on Cairnes, the reader is referred to H. J. Davenport, "Non-competing Groups," *Quarterly Journal of Economics,* vol. 40 (1926), pp. 52–81.

[13] This matter has been discussed by Lloyd Reynolds in his article "Wage Differences in Local Labor Markets," *American Economic Review,* vol. 36 (1946), pp. 366–375. For a later examination of the persistence of wage differentials where theory suggests they should disappear, see Robert L. Raimon, "The Indeterminateness of Wages of Semi-skilled Workers," *Industrial and Labor Relations Review,* vol. 6 (1956), pp. 180–194.

have existed so long that everyone regards them as customary. Practice and tradition powerfully influence acceptance of differentials which are rooted in little else and may indeed make it difficult to modify existing wage relationships.[14]

Even though comparisons may not drive occupational rates to equality within a community or region, they may serve to keep rates among the companies in that area "in line" with each other, according to traditional relationships. If the hourly rate for maintenance electricians goes up by 15 cents in the dominant firm in the locality, other firms may have to make adjustments of the same amount, even though the rates among companies cover a considerable range. Similarly, if the telephone company or electric utility company raises its typists or secretaries by $5 a week, other employers in the community may have to approximate that adjustment, perhaps with a lag, or face greater difficulty in recruiting replacements when its present secretaries "turn over."

The New Haven survey, of a cross-sectional sample of approximately 450 workers, made this disclosure: "Most workers were able to give the names of two or three other plants in the area, but they knew little about the availability of work at these plants, their wage levels, or their conditions of work. Such information as they had was hearsay, based often on a single remark by a chance acquaintance, and did not necessarily correspond closely with the actual situation." [15] Nevertheless, companies are often ranked by workers on some scale, so that it becomes generally known that company A pays better than B, and B better than C, even though the actual rates are only guessed at. Firms which fail to keep their position on such a local wage ladder or wage escalator invite a loss of morale among their employees which somehow gets communicated to others, including prospective employees. Again we note that wage rates for a given kind of work do not have to attain equality within an area in order to evidence the comparison of rates by workers.

A second likely basis for comparison is some standard wage scale or set of working conditions within the industry to which the worker is attached. Particularly where the bargaining unit includes a number of employers within a metropolitan or regional area, or even the national area, the terms arrived at would seem—from the employee's point of view—to provide the equitable basis for his own terms. Despite the fact that his own company

[14] See Lloyd G. Reynolds, *The Structure of Labor Markets,* New York: Harper & Row, Publishers, Incorporated, 1951, pp. 157–158; and J. W. F. Rowe, *Wages in Practice and Theory,* London: Routledge & Kegan Paul, Ltd., 1928, p. 111.

[15] Lloyd G. Reynolds and Joseph Shister, *Job Horizons: A Study of Job Satisfaction and Labor Mobility,* New York: Harper & Row, Publishers, Incorporated, 1949, pp. 46–47.

may not be included in the larger bargaining unit, he might reasonably entertain an expectation that he should be treated approximately the same as his fellows in the same industry. Moreover, even without the impact of such large-scale bargaining units, many national unions have adhered to the program of a standardized wage scale over an area within which the products of its members are competitive. This is a policy established and pursued by the national union leaders. The local unions are expected to conform in order to prevent one local union from undercutting the wage rates of other locals, thereby permitting price cutting by its employer and leading to a shift of work from the higher-wage shops to the low-wage shop.

The standard wage, as we have previously seen, was designed to prevent the use of wages for such competitive purposes. Some unions, moreover, have given up the attempt to draw any geographical lines bounding the area of competition. They have come to the conclusion that such boundaries cannot be fixed, that they are constantly shifting and subject to breakdown, and that the only feasible method of accomplishing the objectives of the standard wage program is to standardize the wage scale throughout the entire jurisdiction of the union. Thus there have emerged from union headquarters *national* wage policies for the benefit of the entire memberships, deviation from which must be explained by the local union. That numerous deviations from such a national standard customarily have been permitted does not belie the fact that the standard remains the basis for comparison.[16]

Particularly when members receive their union newspapers are they confronted with what their fellows in the industry, on the same kind of job, have won. Week by week, reports continue of settlements in one shop or another. Members begin to develop an expectancy of a certain kind of settlement of the standard union demands. If the standard demands are pared down in their own local negotiations to less than what they have come to expect, union leaders are likely to have a hard time "selling" the agreement to the membership unless their explanations are unusually persuasive. The national union office is also under some pressure to support local unions having difficulty in winning the standard "package." When a national representative is sent in to assist local negotiators, a frequent practice, there is likely to be some compulsion upon him to fight for at least as good a bargain as he has won for other locals in that area.

Industry standards are thus another—and perhaps more significant—de-

[16] The existence of a national standard or pattern does not necessarily mean that all bargains will conform to it or that deviations from it are necessarily a challenge to its validity. The standard is only the basis for comparison, from which deviations must be justified. It is even possible that patterns of *deviation* may develop.

terminant of equitable comparisons within the union, along with the community rate structures, but the question remains of how industry standards become established. Certainly they are not static. What compulsion or what coercive comparison is involved that leads the officials of one national union to determine that last year's goal was an increase of 15 cents an hour, while this year's objective will be profit sharing or sabbatical vacations?

There are in reality two questions here. The first concerns the nature of the union demand—whether a profit-sharing plan, an unemployment benefit, severance pay, or a promotion program. The particular demands are in the long run decided by the social and institutional influences bearing upon the basic objectives of workers. These objectives may be such things as security, a desire for greater participation in determining their own conditions, and the enhancement of self-respect. When the attainment of these objectives is blocked or threatened in the work environment, the workers have an incentive to remedy the situation. On the other hand, no matter how desirable the attainment of these immediate goals, there remains the second question of feasibility: To what extent is it possible to achieve them? For when demands entail costs, the workers may have to sacrifice severance pay for a pension plan or accept a pension plan offering admittedly insufficient payments rather than no plan at all (and hope that increases may be won later).

A union negotiator will frame any current demand, on the one hand, with reference to what the union is *likely* to get from the variety of employers within the industry (though the exaggeration of demands for purely tactical purposes at times makes this a rather unimportant consideration). Now what constitutes an acceptable settlement will be based partly on a consideration of what the variety of employers with whom the union bargains can afford to grant. To the extent that ability to pay is taken into account, it may act as a restraining influence on the negotiators. On the other hand, as we have seen, the political necessity of satisfying the constituency and holding the members' allegiance serves as an upward pressure on demands and acceptable settlements. Will the membership be disaffected if the concessions won are less than those previously received and widely publicized by a rival union? What if a comparable union is able to win greater gains elsewhere after this agreement is signed? Considerations of this nature lead union officials to anticipate what other unions are likely to ask for and win; they are encouraged to seek to match or surpass these anticipated gains in order to make their own positions and that of their union secure.

Interunion comparison is thus a force of some significance—a comparison which may cross community and industry lines. This concern over what other unions have done or are likely to do is not due solely to the fact that other unions may become rivals for members. In some instances relationships become established, inviting comparison even though there is little likelihood of the members' seeking to transfer from one union to the other. Those comparisons must be respected by union leaders if they expect to maintain their authority within their union. For example, in the midst of the 1955 negotiations in the steel industry, David McDonald, president of the United Steelworkers, turned down an industry offer with this statement: "I am almost ashamed to mention the amount the industry is offering. It is an effrontery in this most profitable year in the industry's history. It is less than half of what General Motors gave [to the United Automobile Workers]. What are we—second-class citizens?" [17] Clearly Mr. McDonald felt that his and his union's prestige and status were at stake as he compared the offered gains with those of another large industry and union.

In other instances one union may be the dominant one in the community, perhaps because of the presence of a large manufacturing plant or cluster of plants employing its members. Advances made by it are then likely to constitute something of a standard by which other unions in that area will gauge their own success. "Plants in automotive centers with strong UAW locals faced strong pressure to grant paid holidays in 1947 [a demand won that year by the United Automobile Workers] even though not in the automotive industry, and dealing with a union other than the UAW." [18] These interunion comparisons thus at times involve community standards, and at other times they are unrelated to standards existing in a particular community.

Interunion comparisons become more urgent when unions are competing for the same groups of workers. The greater success of a rival may provide it with a springboard for an organizing campaign in the heart of another's actual or potential membership. Unions seeking to extend their sphere of influence will thus make unusual efforts to do better than other unions working the same territory. If the Teamsters' leadership decides to expand its membership by enlisting workers in a variety of fields totally unrelated to trucking, it must make a dramatic demonstration of the superiority of its bargaining power by winning concessions beyond those achieved by the unions whose jurisdictions it is raiding. The Communications Workers, the Rubber Workers and the United Automobile Workers must answer such inducement by providing similar or equivalent benefits if their members are

[17] Benjamin M. Selekman, Stephen H. Fuller, Thomas Kennedy, and John M. Baitsell, *Problems in Labor Relations,* 3d ed., New York: McGraw-Hill Book Company, 1964, p. 565.
[18] Sylvester Garrett and L. Reed Tripp, *Management Problems Implicit in Multi-employer Bargaining,* Philadelphia: University of Pennsylvania Press, 1949, p. 39.

being lured. If they cannot win any benefits immediately, they must at least present a show of activity—special committees appointed to study the problem and render reports on demands made, even if they are presently without hope of fulfillment, in order to "prepare" management for the eventual concession. Such union rivalries acquire an intensity that truly renders their respective collective bargaining agreements subject to coercive comparison.

The danger of unfavorable comparison in part explains the tenacity with which some strikes are fought. Failure to win a favorable settlement may be a threat to survival only in a degree less real than failure to win an agreement at all. If a rival union has settled its dispute at another plant, nothing less than the terms it won can be accepted—at least without a fight. "Under these circumstances small differences become large, and equal treatment becomes the *sine qua non* of industrial peace. A sixty-day strike over two cents an hour may be irrational in the economic lexicon, but viewed as political behavior it may have all the logic of survival." [19]

From the time of the Wagner Act, and before, until after passage of the Taft-Hartley Act, the breakdown of the traditional concept of jurisdiction intensified rivalry among unions and heightened the political pressures upon them to outdo and out-promise competing unions. Whereas a charter from the AFL once gave some protection to unions from serious raids by other unions within a prescribed trade or industrial area, it came to be almost meaningless. The CIO unions organized when and where they could, and soon the older AFL unions followed in like manner, for a jurisdictional charter claim was not as important as winning representational elections. Not only the work of the CIO but also the election-certification process of the National Labor Relations Board broke down the jurisdictional boundaries of unions. It allowed the workers to decide what union they preferred, making political appeal the basic determinant of jurisdiction.

The double development—the founding of a dual federation and the determination of jurisdiction by election—presented many opportunities for contests between unions to represent the same groups of workers. In such situations, of course, unions found that the competition for members invited comparison. The necessary political basis of unions led rivals to campaign for votes in governmental representation elections. A sure way of winning votes often lay in promise of future gain backed by a record of success in either the same unit or others like it.

The intense rivalry between unions which led to organizing another union's organized members produced bitter strikes in which the employers and the public suffered for little purpose. Public anger at jurisdictional strikes resulted in severe restrictions upon them under the Taft-Hartley Act

[19] Ross, *Trade Union Wage Policy,* p. 74.

in 1947. Unions, too, concluded that "raiding" other unions was a costly and, on the whole, unrewarding tactic. Unions began to work out arrangements and to settle jurisdictional disputes; the building trades unions established a national joint board to resolve their disputes, and many other unions made bilateral agreements to establish the limits of their jurisdiction. After 1955 the merged AFL-CIO used the prestige of its national officers to mediate difficult jurisdictional disputes which arose.

Rivalry continues between unions, particularly the newer industrial and the older craft unions. Industries change with changing technologies, merging old skills and jobs into new or hybrid kinds of work. Firms organized by one union branch out into different areas of manufacturing where another union may dominate, or companies change the method of work, contracting out maintenance and new construction or installation work, for example. Should the shop union be allowed to supply or organize the workers brought in by the contractor, or should they be allowed traditional craft union representation? The question is one of importance to unions when, as at present, membership is declining and each can ill afford any losses.

During the past decade, unions have been defensively maintaining membership and gaining only a little additional protection against further unemployment and job placement. Under such circumstances, coercive comparisons among them have probably been somewhat moderated. Each has had to concentrate on its own affairs and eschew expansionary policies apt to dramatize its standing vis-à-vis other unions. Nevertheless, concern over prestige and status among unions and union leaders and the contests of interest groups within unions will—indeed, inescapably must—continue to create internal union political pressures affecting the course of collective bargaining.

Collective Bargaining and Its Politics: Management

chapter 9

When we examine the political pressures bearing on management, we shall be thinking of management as a particular group of people, those legally empowered to represent the owners of a business. We are thus not regarding management as a function. Our interest centers on the same type of question that has just been raised with respect to unions: Is there something in the nature of the business organization which encourages a kind of action—reflected in the bargaining process—which we might appropriately label "political," involving relationships of authority and responsibility, control and response?

Because of the wide variation in business forms, the problems can be made meaningful only in terms of classifications or categories of businesses. We shall limit discussion to only two of these: the corporation with a widespread public distribution of stock and the trade association. Let us enter upon our decision by asking what considerations guide the management of large corporations. Are its decisions primarily influenced by its legal relationship with, and responsibility to, the stockholder-owners? Does its most coercive comparison run in terms of the company's relative profit position?

Managers as Coordinators of Multiple Interests

That management has been freed from owner control in many corporations is now common knowledge. The fact was well stated by the management of one company, Vick Chemical, in an annual report to its stockholders more than three decades ago:

> In theory under the law, the corporation is owned by its stockholders, who meet annually and elect the best fitted among their number to act as Directors for the ensuing year. The Directors then decide the Policy of the company and elect the best Management to carry out that policy, meeting often enough thereafter throughout the year to change both Policy or Management as needed.
>
> Within the last two decades the public in ever increasing numbers has become shareholders in our large corporations. There are now no large stockholders, or groups of large stockholders, who own a majority of the stock of many of these companies.... Published figures show that a number of our larger corporations have over 100,000 stockholders each. Obviously it is physically impossible for all of these stockholders to attend an Annual Meeting ... there is no hall large enough to accommodate such a meeting.
>
> In other words, annual meetings of stockholders are still held, but few stockholders attend. In four years the high water mark in attendance at any Vick Chemical annual meeting was three stockholders outside of those connected with the company. Stockholders have become "absentee" voters. They vote by proxy, giving the right to cast their vote to nominees, whose names are printed in the proxy form ... printed there by the Management, which necessarily, in the circumstances, must assume the responsibility which formerly was carried by stockholders and directors. "Absentee" voters therefore have forced the Management of many companies in the U.S.A. to assume the responsibility of self-perpetuation ... that is, the Management, for all practical purposes, is elected not annually but for life.[1] [Italics in the original have been omitted.]

There are, of course, exceptions to this pattern. From time to time dissident stockholder groups organize and seek control of proxies sufficient in number to enable them to unseat the incumbent management. It is at such times that headlines reveal the "proxy fight" in such terms as "Group of Stockholders Charges Gross Mismanagement," "Court Bars Antimanagement Faction from Filing 40,000 Proxies," and "Management Wins Stockholder Row." [2]

[1] *Annual Report,* Vick Chemical Co. (1933).

[2] An interesting discussion of the role of the stockholder is contained in J. A. Livingston, *The American Stockholder,* Philadelphia: J. B. Lippincott Company, 1958. Also see Eugene V. Rostow, "To Whom and for What Ends Is

These dramatic political actions within the corporation only emphasize, however, the general validity of the picture drawn by the management of Vick Chemical Co., for the number of proxy fights in any year is but an infinitesimal fraction of the number of corporations whose managements are uncontested in their control, and even where occurring, such contests are seldom settled in favor of the insurgent group.

The fact is that in corporations having widespread stock ownership, management no longer derives its authority from the stockholders in any realistic sense. It is true that its authority receives legal sanction because of a trusteeship relation which it is presumed to occupy with respect to them, but actual freedom from stockholder control has given management great discretion in interpreting its responsibilities. Some managements have used this discretion to *enlarge* their responsibilities. In response to social pressures—and perhaps, too, because of personal inclination—particularly in the large corporations, the philosophy has been growing in recent years that management has obligations not only to the owners, whom it must legally represent, but to other groups as well.

This view was expressed forcefully in a colloquy between a number of top management officials gathered to discuss aspects of their corporate activity. After reviewing the responsibilities of management, and especially of the board of directors, to investors, employees, customers, and community, one added:

> And yet the interest, the self-interest, of these different groups, differs widely. The self-interest of the laboring man might be to get the highest possible wage; the self-interest of the consumer might be to get the product at the lowest possible price. The self-interest of the shareholder might be to get the highest possible return on his investment. Those are not compatible, and the job I think that the board of directors of any corporation has to do is to try to harmonize those things and come out with an average result that will please most people in these various interest groups.

And another commented: "So you have to think of your board of directors not only as keeping an organization together but likewise assuming what seems to me is a set of more or less political responsibilities." [3]

Such a conception of enlarged managerial responsibilities has yet to be given operational significance since it carries no suggestion of how conflicts or responsibilities are to be resolved. Moreover, it fails to encompass the

Corporate Management Responsible?" in *The Corporation in Modern Society*, E. S. Mason (ed.), Cambridge, Mass.: Harvard University Press, 1959, pp. 46–71.

[3] Courtney C. Brown and E. Everett Smith, *The Director Looks at His Job*, New York: Columbia University Press, 1957, pp. 15–16, 13.

prickly fact that managers have their own independent objectives and are not simply passive mediators or coordinators of the interests of others.[4] The conception may nonetheless be accepted as a recognition by modern large-scale business management of the social nature of private enterprise. It is suggestive in its frank admission that stockholder interests are now no longer controlling in the large corporation but must accommodate other interests. There is no denial of stockholder welfare as an objective, but it becomes only one of several. The greater discretion accruing to management when practice frees it from the stockholders' legal leash permits others to claim consideration.

In terms of the corporate political system, the significance of an acceptance of multiple responsibilities lies in the need this creates for accommodating a variety of interests. The pressures upon management are several, and the comparisons by which the interest groups judge the value of their corporate relations are sometimes divergent. Relative profits to stockholders, relative status and prestige to management itself, relative wages and welfare to employees, and relative prices to consumers—these comparisons are *all* coercive with respect to management. They must be reconciled in some manner if the various responsibilities are all to be met.

In law and by tradition we place first among management's obligations the protection of stockholder interests. The profit-making ability of the firms remains a primary objective, even if profit maximization can no longer be assumed to be the sole motivation and despite the lack of effective, independent stockholders' organization. The legal nature of management's trusteeship relationship to the stockholders has been so frequently and fully explored that elaboration here should be unnecessary.

Among all the groups to whom management has admitted its responsibility, the most effectively organized are employees.[5] Though they have no

[4] One such objective appears frequently to be an expansion of operations unrelated to efficiency or earning power. John M. Clark, "Toward a Concept of Workable Competition," *American Economic Review*, vol. 30 (1940), p. 246. Indeed, one economist, Prof. William Baumol, has based a theoretical treatment on the premise that managements seek to maximize sales rather than profits (*Business Behavior, Value and Growth*, New York: The Macmillan Company, 1959).

[5] Indeed, it is this very lack of organization on the part of the other important interest groups which permits management to act as though it were the coordinator and joint representative of the multiple interests. However much management may seek to behave in conformity to its assumed multiple responsibilities, by itself undertaking to accommodate their several interests it seeks an agency relationship to conflicting interests. This anomalous situation is justifiable only in terms of two doctrines which are mutually contradictory: one, that management is in fact the single representative of the stockholders—their legal appointees—and hence is in a position to meet the union in negotiation to

control over the selection of the managers, through their unions they are, in one sense, in a position to grant or withhold authority to those managers who continue in office. Collective bargaining is a method of defining management responsibility to the employees, as one interest group in the business; the signing of a labor agreement constitutes a conferring of authority on management as far as the union and its members are concerned. The strength of the union thus acts to reinforce the obligation to the employees which some managements have voluntarily assumed.

There are those who question whether some managements are acting in good faith when they announce that they are enlarging their responsibilities. These credit the attachment to ownership interests as being stronger than here pictured. No general answer to such skepticism can, of course, be given. Without doubt, however, many managements have a genuine concern for the welfare of their employees. Large-scale organization has not altogether destroyed the bond between worker and manager, even when the manager is no longer the owner and the relationship has become more formalized. Several reasons for such concern may be suggested. First, the very size of the corporation has made managers aware that they have a political relationship with their employees and that the authority which they exercise over the work force must be accompanied by some responsibility to it. Second, public opinion, sometimes expressed through governmental actions, has required managers to respond to the needs of their workers. Third, the pressure of foreign political movements has made some managers aware of the need for satisfying employee aspirations. And fourth, the development of industrial psychology has made managers increasingly conscious of their control over personnel through their ability to *win* a re-

---

accommodate the interests of the two groups represented at the bargaining table; the other, that management, as a representative of all the interest groups, including the employees, bargains with the union as representative of *only* the employees. This second doctrine gives management an independent discretion in determining what are the interests of the several groups, independent even of the *chosen* representatives of those groups. This confused organization is no doubt traceable to a transition phase of industrial organization in this country. To what we are transitioning is much less obvious. One apparent solution would be the more effective organization of the other major interest groups, notably stockholders and consumers, so that agreement could be reached among the exclusive representatives of these groups, establishing a framework within which management—then actually the servant of all—would be free to exercise its discretion. This "solution" of course raises problems of its own. It may be expected that other solutions will be offered, among them nationalization or socialization (which also raises its own heady problems). In the meantime, the analysis here must proceed in line with the actual though unstable fact that management recognizes divergent responsibilities.

sponse. It has stressed that leadership involves eliciting cooperation and that a cooperative response cannot be won if the interests of those whose cooperation is desired are given insufficient consideration. Even in the absence of unionism, therefore, there is reason to believe that managerial decisions would be at least in part guided by considerations of employee welfare. The union serves to stimulate that consideration further.

We do not intend to overstress an aspect of employee-management relations which is sometimes understressed. That some management decisions are made with a regard for employee interests does not imply that conflicts of interest are absent or avoided, of course. For one thing, some managements have insisted on determining unilaterally just where the employees' interests lie. Attitudes of paternalism have not been wholly shaken. There is sometimes a reluctance to give up the belief that responsibility to employees can best be served by *informed* decision as to what conduces to their interest—the idea that management knows best. Thus management sometimes feels obliged to resist the union "for the employees' own welfare." A challenge to this authority may at times be looked upon in the same manner that a father would view his children's questioning of his decisions. This paternalistic attitude may prompt resistance to employees' attempts to form an independent organization. The union's very existence constitutes an unwelcome suggestion that management has "failed" in discharging its responsibilities to its employees, a suggestion which can be rebutted if the union is considered to be not truly representative, but the work of hotbloods, an imposition upon "loyal" employees by self-servers. Such opinions permit managers to assert, in the words of one corporate official: "We are admittedly anti-union, but we like our workers."

Moreover, managements have sometimes disagreed with employees as to what matters are employees' concerns. Working conditions may be considered to be something affecting the employees' welfare, while promotions may be thought of as something which should be the sole concern of owners and their management representatives. Again, managers may not feel the same urgency about certain matters as the employees. Inertia or caution may delay a review of the wage structure, for example, beyond the time when employees feel they are entitled to adjustment. Employees do not subject management to the same pressures that union leaders do; lack of prompt and satisfactory management response to employees does not carry the same danger as failure to meet union officers promptly and satisfactorily. Perhaps as important as any reason is the fact that management realizes that it must satisfy a number of interests of which the employees are only one. Therefore, it sometimes has to say "no" to the employee group because of consideration for the claims of others.

There is no need—nor is it possible—to strike some sort of balance between these influences on management, some leading to acceptance and others to rejection of particular employee requests. Our present interest lies simply in the fact that employee interests do in some degree motivate management.

The nature of management's regard for the interests of its employees is indicated, perhaps, in the attitudes of manufacturing employees in New Haven, Connecticut, as reported by Prof. Lloyd Reynolds. He notes that one of the most important reasons given for seeking to "keep up with the area" in wage levels was the "widespread opinion that management is *morally* obligated to pay prevailing wages." (Italics supplied.)

> The belief that keeping up with the area is the fair thing to do was expressed so frequently in our interviews that it cannot be dismissed as sheer rationalization. One manager, for example, explained that it would not be fair for his company to base its wage rates on the company's current ability to pay. "Your profit margin doesn't influence what you pay for materials. Why should it influence what you pay for labor? We pay what we ought to, and then go ahead and try and stay in business." Another manager said substantially the same thing: "We try to pay what is right; then we go out and stay in business through technical progress and good management."
>
> In several cases, managers explained that they felt responsible for maintaining the real purchasing power of their workers. Since the cost of living was rising during 1946–48, they felt obliged in fairness to raise wages, regardless of union pressures or developments elsewhere in the area. Numerous other companies explained that they felt obliged to raise hourly rates when hours of work were reduced, in order to cushion the decline in workers' weekly incomes.[6]

The ethical considerations that managers bring to wage matters cannot be lightly dismissed as fictitious or deceiving. They reveal that in its relations with its employees, management is guided to an important degree by a concern for their interests *as managers conceive them.* There is thus an

[6] Lloyd G. Reynolds, *The Structure of Labor Markets,* New York: Harper & Row, Publishers, Incorporated, 1951, pp. 159–160. Reynolds also points out:

> These statements were, of course, made during a prosperity period in which most managements had little financial difficulty in paying "fair" wages. Wage increases which managers ascribed to their own sense of fairness may really have been induced by high profit margins. The real test of how firmly management clings to ethical norms in wage setting would perhaps come during a depression, when maintenance of wage levels might involve operating losses.

The ethical consideration of managers in wage setting was also indicated in a Princeton survey of wage policies a few years earlier. See Richard A. Lester, *Company Wage Policies,* Princeton University, Princeton, N.J., 1948, pp. 31–32.

indication that at least a number of corporation leaders are motivated in the area of relevant business decisions by a consideration held in common with the union. Workers, through their union relationship, influence the actions of their union leaders. Through their employee relationship, they influence the actions of their managers. Thus workers are an influential element in the political structures of both organizations. Their political significance in the corporation has perhaps been obscured in the past by the legal tradition of stockholder rights, by managerial opposition to independent forms of employee representation, and by union-management conflict. These factors are all important, of course, but they do not negate the political role which employees play in the corporation. Management, like union leaders, is interested in their support and loyalty. It cannot concentrate its entire interest on them, as the union does, since it must retain the support and loyalty of other groups as well, some of whom have interests conflicting with those of employees.

This conclusion suggests two corollaries. To some extent management's concern for its workers is competitive with the union leader's. Each aspires to win the primary loyalty of the same group of employees. But in some degree, the element of common interest in employee welfare may serve as the very basis for agreement, since the work force is a constituency common to both management and union organizations. In part, it is controlled by both union and management; in part, it controls both.

Interest Groups within Management

So far in this chapter we have treated management as a single interest group pursuing an agreed-upon set of goals. In fact, management is made up of a number of differing and sometimes contending groups who may understand and emphasize corporate objectives in different ways and urge conflicting priorities in the pursuit of company goals. Specialized departments and divisions of a company and specialized staffs are expected to concentrate upon their own responsibilities; by devoting their attention to one area of corporate activities, they give less to other areas and tend to become partisan spokesmen in company councils for their particular interests.

Consider the possible reaction of managers in various company departments to a union demand for extended vacations of three months every five years for senior workers. The finance department may oppose the demand, seeing in it a present costly increase in labor expenses and an indefinite commitment for the future, as the length of service of the labor force increases. The production department may object too, arguing that the agreement will put the company at a competitive disadvantage in labor costs; more than half of the company's workers already have over fifteen years of seniority, while only one-third of the work force of a major compet-itor has as much as fifteen years. The marketing department might argue that acceptance of the demand would be preferable to a strike or any interference with production since sales are rising and a comprehensive advertising campaign has just reached its climax. The engineering depart-ment may favor the union demand for two reasons. First, it hopes to see established in the company a precedence for long leaves with pay so that its people may press such a program for its engineers. With sabbaticals avail-able for its members, the engineering department could keep its expensive talent up to date and also have an extra attraction to offer when bidding for new engineers. Second, the extended vacation demand of the union would raise labor costs sufficiently to justify company investment in a proposed new mechanization process developed by the department. Public relations may point out that acceptance of the union demand could win the company much favorable publicity for having made a responsible and imaginative attack upon the present serious unemployment. The managers of industrial relations may also favor the extended vacation plan, believing that outright rejection of it would bring forth a strike or at least seriously disturb union-management relations, painfully built up after the bitter strike of five years ago. Out of the differing judgments and varied concerns, a single company approach and policy will have to be fashioned.

Union negotiators, aware of the differences of opinion within manage-ment, may make use of their knowledge to strengthen those who incline favorably toward their proposal and weaken those opposed. For example, they may "concede" that only the senior third of the work force should receive the extended vacation, thus answering the objection of those in the production department. Then, with only the finance department still op-posed, the balance within the company may swing toward acceptance of the plan.

At the shop level, the differences among different management groups are easily discernible. Foremen often feel conflicting pressures from two differ-ent groups. Their immediate line superiors may call for increased produc-tion to meet an important schedule. To induce workers to cooperate in meeting the schedule may involve the foreman in concessions forbidden by the industrial relations people. The workers may agree to raise the "work limit" they have customarily imposed and to allow supervisory trainees to perform production work in return for ten more minutes of wash-up time and assignment of a helper to pick up scrap. Both concessions can easily become "past practices," if continued, and precedents for similar conces-sions elsewhere in the company. In time the provisions of the agreement regulating wash-up time and the assigning of helpers can be subverted to the embarrassment of industrial relations. (The union leaders may be upset, too, to discover that their carefully negotiated provisions against supervisors working have been weakened by shop concession to management.)

Many of the pressures on managerial decisions which appear to arise *outside* the business are in reality effective influences only because they coincide with the independent motives of particular management groups. Managers and employers live in the society of other managers and employers, and it is to be expected that they court one another's friendship and regard. This in part explains why "one of the cardinal sins of business conduct is to offer a wage rate or a wage increase, which proves embarrassing to other employers." [7] Managers and employers live in a climate of public opinion which induces them to behave in a manner which is socially acceptable, that is, which encourages *their* social acceptance. We can think of both stockholders and employees desiring managers to make certain decisions without questioning the basis for their respective desires. We can also think of managers desiring to make certain decisions on their own, and without regard to the stimulus, whether the pressure of public opinion or a desire for personal gain, this too becomes translated into a pressure within the corporation.

One significant fact should not be overlooked in this connection. Despite managers' professed responsibility to multiple interest groups, their continued acceptance of profit positions as a reflection of the competency of their performance suggests the strength still remaining in the link to ownership interests. Even where pride in high wages and low prices exists, as evidence of other responsibilities met, these carry less weight than the profit record *within the management fraternity* as an indication of ability, as the source of prestige, and as command over income. To this extent, managerial self-interest remains primarily identified with stockholder interest. At the same time, this conclusion cannot be pushed too far, for managers' interest in expanded profits is in part related to the financial needs and security of the corporation almost as an independent institution, that is, independent of its private owners. Profits, while sought, may be undistributed, retained not only as reserves for hard times, but also as a means of permitting expansion of operations without the need for appealing to the owners for approval in the form of voluntary subscription.

Still with respect to managers, if we think of them as a group of individuals at various levels of authority within the business (not simply as top management), it is clear that some managers have operational authorities over and responsibilities to other members of management. In the corporation there are usually departmental or plant interests that must be accommodated, just as in the case of unions there are occupational and sectional interests requiring recognition. A company-wide policy cannot be set without considering its impact on the component units, and, similarly,

[7] Arthur M. Ross, *Trade Union Wage Policy,* Berkeley, Calif.: University of California Press, 1948, p. 50.

plant or subsidiary policy must take into account the possibility that as a precedent it may affect other plants or subsidiaries. A survey of some years ago of management procedures for establishing policies in industrial relations matters offers the following example, which is still pertinent:

> One of the most complex relationships in policy determination was reported by a company with over 40,000 employees in 100 separate plants. The subsidiaries represent a variety of industries which, for corporate organization purposes, are divided into several operating groups. Top management (that is, the officers and directors of the parent corporation) encourages diversity and decentralization of management functions rather than concentration of decision making at the top level. However, decisions, even in regard to one company, with implications for the corporation as a whole or any large segment of it are made by the top board of directors. Vice presidents and members of the board of the parent company are, in most cases, presidents of the subsidiaries.
>
> The development of a decision on an important personnel or labor policy is somewhat as follows: The first decision or recommendation for action is usually made by the plant manager after discussion with the divisional industrial relations manager. The latter will discuss it with the president of the subsidiary before the decision becomes effective, and it is up to this officer to consider whether the matter has implications for the rest of the corporation, whether the decision is in line with corporate policy, or whether it should be discussed with the top board. Since developments in the various industries represented in the company and the points of view within the board of directors may be many and diverse, "real arguments" are said to occur. It is admittedly difficult for the president of a subsidiary to make a decision that would have the disapproval of a majority of his fellow members of the executive committee of the corporation, even though it is in the best interest of his own company. The vice president of industrial relations is expected to have the broadest point of view on labor matters and is an important influence in gaining general unanimity of decision on matters on which individual company interests may differ fundamentally.[8]

[8] Helen Baker, *Management Procedures in the Determination of Industrial Relations Policies,* Princeton University, Princeton, N.J., 1948, p. 18. Another example is offered in the same, p. 50:

> In one company in which wage changes are subject to collective bargaining on a local basis and with a number of unions, the executive committee had requested the vice president in charge of one division to "hold the line" on wages for the company at the expense of a lengthy strike in one plant. In this case, company-wide interest conflicted with local interest and the broader interest was controlling. It is apparent that wage decisions are made in other multi-plant companies on the same basis.

The last political influence within the corporation which we shall mention defies ready indentification because it constitutes a catchall category. It includes all those business interests which are so intimately involved in decision making that they may be regarded as influences within the corporation—financial groups, banking houses, interlocking commercial interests.[9] Referring to such influences, unions have sometimes complained of being unable to bargain with those who make the actual decisions. Thus the United Mine Workers, in the past, charged that railroad companies and banking houses dominated the decisions of the mine operators, and the railroad brotherhoods complained that financial interests controlled the policies of the carriers.[10] The nature of management's responsibility to such groups and the authority they provide management are matters of controversy. We note here only the existence of these varied business interests.

This must end a rather summary survey of the separate political pressures within the corporation bearing on management: stockholders, employees, interlocking business groups, and management itself, including all its operational subdivisions, as in plants and departments. One further responsibility must be mentioned, however: management's responsibility for the continuing survival of the organization as a whole. As in the case of the union, without this general responsibility, the responsibility to the several interests cannot be satisfied.

It becomes evident that, like the union, the corporation is a political system and that interest groups within that system (as well as the ongoing nature of the system itself) generate compulsions which have their effect upon managerial decisions and the collective bargaining relationship. As in the case of the union, then, we shall have to inquire what it is that determines which pressures arising within the corporation are effective. How does management reconcile the conflicting comparisons which severally may be coercive with respect to the separate interest groups but which are all coercive with respect to it?

This problem, as stated, is too broad for investigation here. We must reduce it to dimensions which permit brief but meaningful exploration.

[9] R. A. Gordon has described some of these in *Business Leadership in the Large Corporation*, Washington, D.C.: The Brookings Institution, 1945, chap. 9. Later discussions of these interests may be found in Wilbert E. Moore, *The Conduct of the Corporation*, New York: Random House, Inc., 1962, chap. 16; and Adolf A. Berle, *The American Economic Republic*, New York: Harcourt, Brace & World, Inc., 1963, chaps. 8–10.

[10] A fuller statement of the charges is given in Neil W. Chamberlain, *Union Challenge to Management Control*, New York: Harper & Row, Publishers, Incorporated, 1948, pp. 68–69.

Within the context of the collective bargaining relationship, the most fruitful approach is to consider how management looks at the issue of wages.

The Coercive Comparison of Wages

The Scylla and Charybdis through which managers must steer in order to accommodate the participating interests are costs and prices. On the one hand, costs will determine the firm's ability to produce at competitive prices, a condition necessary to satisfy any and all of its component interest groups. From this point of view, it would seem desirable to reduce costs wherever possible. But costs arising from "value added by the firm" (which do not include material and supply costs) also represent incomes of participating groups; wages, management salaries, interest, and even dividends are sometimes viewed not as residuals but as charges. Consequently each group is willing to see costs decline only if its own income is not thereby adversely affected, but its own income (a cost or profit item) becomes something not only to defend but, if possible, to enlarge. Expansion of one group's income, however, if productivity remains the same and other participants' incomes are unchanged, may mean not only higher income to the particular group —say, wages to workers—but also higher prices for the product.[11] This may be reflected in reduced sales and output, accompanied by unwanted consequences in the form of reduced employment and incomes. Cost-price-output considerations are thus among the principal orbits of coercive comparison affecting managerial decisions. Profits relative to the profits of other companies; wages relative to other wages; salaries relative to other salaries; and profits, wages, and salaries all relative to one another become the ingredients of managerial policy. It is in this context that managers must consider wages, both as a cost of operation and as income to one of the important interest groups. We have already considered comparisons regarded as coercive by employees and their union leaders. We are interested now in how managers settle upon a wage policy in the light of the multiple interests they represent and the comparisons considered equitable or coercive by each and all of them.

[11] This is not to imply that there is any precise or universal relationship between incomes which are costs (such as wages) and prices. "The only generalization possible is that costs have an obvious influence upon prices, and prices in turn upon costs; the character of the relation in any individual case and at any specific time must be individually appraised on the basis of all the attendant conditions" [*Industrial Wage Rates, Labor Costs and Price Policies,* Temporary National Economic Committee Monograph No. 5 (1940), pp. xxiv–xxv]. This monograph presents a number of case studies illustrating the quoted conclusion. Similarly, all that the text intends to suggest is the existence of some causal relationship between costs and prices.

There is no reason to believe that managers have found any clear-cut formula for resolving the wage problem. As in the case of unions, we shall discover that a variety of comparisons in respect to wages actually are presented to management, one of which may be dominant at a given moment while another takes precedence at some other time, or several of which may be combined. There is some evidence that the basis for management's wage comparison is often the local labor market, that is, "keeping up with the area." This does not mean that firms necessarily seek equality of rates with other firms in the community but that they set their wage structures in relation to other local companies, either higher or lower. Some companies gear their wage policies to the higher wages of "progressive" employers, while other firms choose as benchmarks companies believed to be "similarly situated," which probably really means that they relate wage structures to a *desired* level.

The reasons why management makes community comparisons are more numerous than economic theory generally assumes. It is true that competition for labor in a local market appears to be a consideration. As one business leader phrased his problem, "[the] situation doesn't reflect itself in careful surveys. We get it this way. Are we getting applicants? What do they say about rates? Are we losing workers to other industries? What do they say when they leave us?" [12] This consideration appears to be closely related to stockholder interests. It simply hinges wage rates upon what the market requires in order to secure labor. On the other hand, there seems also to be a consideration of equitable treatment of the employee in such local comparisons.

Finally, the managers find community standards important at times for their own interests; by using these as a gauge, they avoid arousing the animosity of neighboring firms by forcing adjustments at a time when the latter are not yet ready or willing to act. As was previously noted, the respect of fellow managers may be an important objective to management, not to be easily sacrificed by wage actions embarrassing to them, if these can be avoided. "As an executive of company X put it, if one employer voluntarily increased wages in a situation which was not generally accepted as justifying an increase, 'the other manufacturers would be angry, so we must follow the group pretty much.' " [13]

These motivations for making community comparisons can scarcely all be regarded as existing simultaneously; yet accommodation of the divergent interests which they involve may be possible because of the very flexibility

[12] Wladimir S. Woytinsky, *Labor and Management Look at Collective Bargaining: A Canvass of Leaders' Views,* Morris C. Bishop and Thomas C. Fichandler, associates, New York: The Twentieth Century Fund, 1949, p. 92.

[13] *Industrial Wage Rates, Labor Costs and Price Policies,* pp. 7–8.

of the standard. The community offers a *range* of rates, thus permitting a choice of guide. Professor Reynolds has pointed out that the "area wage level" is an ambiguous concept, capable of being defined and used in many ways. Individual managements do not strive to eliminate the differences in their plant wage levels and achieve an equality; rather, "they strive to protect their established position in the [recognized and customary] wage hierarchy of the area." [14]

The coercive nature of this community comparison is at once apparent. It means, moreover, that *by locating the firm appropriately in the "wage hierarchy,"* management may be able to satisfy reasonably well its own objectives of remaining on good terms with brother managers, of satisfying its stockholders' desires for maximum profits by paying labor rates no higher than what the market requires, and of meeting its employees' expectations of being treated as well as some and better than others. In part such a policy is made feasible by differing business preferences as to type and quality of worker wanted.

Some firms which operate a number of plants in scattered communities have adopted a policy of uniform rates throughout the company, regardless of plant location. Motivation for such a policy may sometimes be a belief in the "equity" to the employees of paying equal rates for equal work, particularly when the same price is charged for their products. The interchangeability of employees among plants may also be a factor. In such an arrangement, however, it is likely that the firm's decision as to what the common rate structure ought to be will be largely influenced by industry standards. We thus come to the second of the principal comparisons influencing management's wage policy.

In their encyclopedic study of collective bargaining, Slichter, Livernash, and Healy conclude that intraindustry wage standardization has grown considerably over the past twenty years, reflecting in part the growing significance of industry standards in wage setting.[15] They found that the large firm is particularly influenced by industry wage standards, whether through company-wide multiplant bargaining or through plant-by-plant bargaining. Gearing a company's wage rates to industry standards does not, of course, necessarily imply a policy of equating them with an industry average or dominant rate structure. As with the community standard, some companies may prefer to pay somewhat lower or somewhat higher wages. A few companies, for example, have considered it desirable, from the standpoint of employee morale, relations with the union, or public relations, to pay more than their competitors. The industry standard does appear, how-

[14] The same, p. 158.

[15] Sumner H. Slichter, E. Robert Livernash, and James J. Healy, *The Impact of Collective Bargaining on Management,* Washington, D.C.: The Brookings Institution, 1960, p. 610.

ever, to conduce to greater uniformity within the industry, as would be expected.

Instances of this type of equitable comparison are provided in one study of selected companies in several industries. The investigators reported their findings as follows:

> Particular attention was given to the wage policies of other firms in its own industry by the cotton textile company, company A in the paper industry, and company X in the shoe industry. In fact, the cotton textile company had no other conscious wage policy, according to its officials, than to follow the actions of other cotton textile concerns. Officials of company X in the shoe industry stated that any attempt to adopt a wage policy contrary to that followed by the shoe companies belonging to a trade association in a nearby large city would meet with vigorous protests from officials of these companies, largely because of the effect such action would have on their relations with the union to which both their employees and those of company X belong.[16]

The case of company X, in the shoe industry, suggests, too, what in fact has been the case: that more and more companies have accepted the industry wage comparison as their plants have been unionized. They have responded in some degree to the union's interest in a standard wage. Equally important in some situations has been the desire of employers to escape from the unpleasantness of remaining competitive by competitively reducing wages. This result has been further assured by multiemployer bargaining, which tends to develop an industry orientation of wage policy. Also, trade associations, organized on industry lines, have provided an impetus to uniform behavior, even in the absence of actual conduct of negotiations. Speaking of the American Iron and Steel Institute, one writer has observed:

> Regular interchange of information and views obviously promotes uniformity of behavior. This is further stimulated on some issues by the procedure of taking a vote in the Industrial Relations Committee. This is described as being in the nature of a public opinion poll among the committee members; that is, the companies are not committed to following the views of the majority. Still, when a vote is taken on a question, it would seem to imply that uniformity of action would be desirable in the opinion of some. The companies can guide themselves accordingly, with due consideration to the nature and import of the issue and the views of the other companies.[17]

Only the naïve would ignore the fact that in some instances trade association actions have been used to increase the bargaining power of the indi-

[16] *Industrial Wage Rates, Labor Costs and Price Policies,* p. 16.
[17] Robert Tilove, *Collective Bargaining in the Steel Industry,* Philadelphia: University of Pennsylvania Press, 1948, p. 37.

vidual members as they negotiate with unions. On the surface this would appear to be a denial of responsibility to the employees or a display of relative unconcern for their interests. Such a conclusion does not necessarily follow, however. As we have seen, an employer's conception of his responsibility to employees, where it exists, does not always coincide with the conception of the union officials; there would be no union-management conflict if it did. Even where employers admit such a responsibility, then, they may believe it desirable to strengthen their bargaining power to resist the importunings of the union. What is significant for our present purposes is that uniform action through a trade association augments its members' bargaining power by reducing the possibility of invidious comparison between employees of member firms and their unions; if such comparisons do indeed have a coercive effect, differential company policies are likely to increase the psychological cost to the employees and the union of agreeing on company terms in a company whose wages are lower than those of other companies in the same industry. Uniform wage policies, by reducing this psychological cost of agreement, increase management's bargaining strength.

Trade associations are, of course, not essential to intercompany agreement on a uniform policy:

> Company cooperation in wage changes, fostered largely by collective bargaining, is apparently much more extensive than is generally realized. One industrial relations executive, for example, insisted that most companies, through various consultative arrangements, cooperate on wage policy. He explained that recently his own company had agreed with its chief competitor to restrict all general increases to 10 per cent, so that the competitor had to rescind a notice previously sent out stipulating that any of its plants might grant up to 11 per cent. The executive of another firm stated that the major companies in his industry have rather full knowledge of what competitors plan to do, so that they can all make general wage changes at the same time. He added that the last general increase was instituted by all the large firms on the same day except for his own company, which was held up slightly by a delay on the part of the Board of Directors. A number of other large companies reported consultation and cooperation on wage-level changes. As a wage leader explained, "The other companies in the industry are interested in being in on the determination of the wage increase as it is finally set so that there is a tendency to have industry-wide consultation." [18]

Where the industry standard has become accepted, it often happens that some company or companies assume the position of pacesetter. Just as in a community, there are firms which in an industry provide leadership for other firms. "Companies that have been leaders in their industries in non-

[18] Lester, *Company Wage Policies,* pp. 24–25.

wage matters may consider it only natural that they should lead in wage changes. One company stated: 'We are leaders in the industry and we wish to continue in that position.' Another firm replied: 'The Company has been a leader and the respectable elements in the industry look to it to set wage policy and patterns.' " [19]

One of the best-known examples of industry leadership in collective bargaining matters is provided by United States Steel in the steel industry:

> The almost unvarying practice in the past had been for U.S. Steel to take the leadership in negotiations and settlements. Bargaining committees of other companies ordinarily marked time with their union counterparts until the settlement on a basic contract with U.S. Steel had been achieved. It should be emphasized, however, that the situation has not been quite as stereotyped as the foregoing generalization might suggest. There have been frequent variations from the U.S. Steel settlement on both wages and non-wage items to meet special situations, and there were occasions when a company other than U.S. Steel led in the settlements. [20]

In addition to community and industry comparisons, there is one other comparison of more doubtful standing which may influence managerial wage policy—the comparison of the relative returns to the two major component groups within the company, owners and workers. There is also, perhaps to a lesser degree, the comparison of these two returns with the price charged to the customer. It would be surprising, in view of management's professed responsibility to these three groups, if there were not some sort of comparison of the *relative* advancement of their interests. It seems unlikely that managers would willingly raise wages at a time when dividends payable to stockholders had slumped to a low level, and some sense of obligation to the public might restrain wage and profit increases if these contributed to soaring prices. On this matter there is no conclusive evidence, however. Statements from managers abound that wage setting is not to be confused with a company's rate of profitability; their reliance on community or industry standards, which are general standards and hence not reflective of the profit positions of individual companies, is conceived as ruling out the consideration of wage-profit ratios. There appear to be considerable grounds for believing that price policies have not often been determined consciously in the light of consumer welfare, despite professed responsibilities. Nevertheless, it would be wrong to dismiss such comparisons as altogether uncoercive.

Managers not infrequently find it useful to compare the relative rates of

[19] The same, p. 23.

[20] *Collective Bargaining in the Basic Steel Industry,* U.S. Department of Labor (1961), p. 86.

increases in wages, profits, and prices as a rejoinder to union demands for further pay increases. Of course, this may be viewed as simply an expedient argument rather than an equitable comparison, as when companies advert to their profit showing when it is low but refuse to consider it relevant when high. Yet to dismiss such "internal" comparisons as having no significance would be unwise. Such comparisons may become more important if bargaining units increase in size; negotiators may then be concerned with the equity of *average* benefits—to workers, owners, and consumers. The problem of particular benefits from individual firms would require action only where such benefits might not meet the average. This is an area in which conjecture is all that is now possible, but it would be unwarranted to rule out, for that reason, the relative shares of participants—at least the profit-wage ratios—as a comparison which is coercive in its nature.

There may be other comparisons of an equitable or coercive nature influencing managers' conceptions of a wage policy according with its responsibilities, but these three are probably the most important: the community wage comparison, the industry comparison, and the wage-profit-price comparison. There is no way of predicting which of these will be accepted as controlling at any given time. What is apparent is that managers are confronted with alternative policies from which to choose, and the circumstances of the moment are likely to determine which policy or policies they accept as desirable for a specific occasion. What wage policy is considered desirable will depend on how managers interpret these circumstances to affect their political relationships and lines of responsibility.

There are possibilities, too, for harmonizing seemingly conflicting standards. A community wage standard may be applied to certain employee groups, while others are paid on an industry basis. This differential treatment occurs most often when some workers possess skills peculiar to an industry, so that no comparison with other workers is appropriate, while other workers possess skills in demand in a variety of industries, so that interindustry comparisons, on a labor-market basis, are more feasible.[21]

It is difficult to escape the conclusion that employers, more than unions, have faith in the operation of a local labor market, since they appear to give more weight to community comparisons than the unions do. On the surface it is difficult to reconcile this belief with the evident lack of knowledge of comparative local rates on the part of many workers. It may have its reasonable basis in the notion that even though workers do not know

[21] E. Robert Livernash discusses the way in which different standards affect different wage groups in the same plant in his discussion of job clusters, key job rates, and wage contours. See "The Internal Wage Structure," in *New Concepts in Wage Determination,* George W. Taylor and Frank C. Pierson (eds.), New York: McGraw-Hill Book Company, 1957, pp. 147–160.

specific rates of local companies, they know their comparative *rankings* as wage payers, even in such rough terms as "a good payer," "above the average," or "tight." If this is the case, the very roughness of the community standard is conducive to a simultaneous accommodation of the industry standard, for discrepancies between the two can be tolerated as long as they have no radical effects on a company's placement on the local wage escalator. A company may thus open or close the gap between its rates and those of another local company with which it is being compared without exciting apprehension from either employees or employers as long as the change is not so great as to drop it out of its customary wage "class" and suggest comparison with a company or companies in a different class, thus upsetting established expectations.

To some extent the community and industry standards, as given for a particular company, define a *range* within which wages may be set, not so much on economic considerations as on the political basis of equitable comparisons. The placement of wages somewhere *between* community and industry levels (whichever may be the upper and whichever the lower limit) thus in itself constitutes the conflict. It may not be necessary to accept one or the other as controlling, but recognizing that equity resides in part with each, management may mediate the settlement.

Finally, there may be a movement from the former acceptance of one standard to a more general acceptance of another. There does indeed appear to have been a greater tendency in the past for managers to compare wages on a local basis than is the case today. The increasing agitation by unions for a wage pattern throughout an industry has had its effect on management thinking. Employees, through their unions, have insisted upon the comparison considered more equitable by them, and to some extent managers have been willing to go along; to some extent they have been forced to go along.

Problems in Multiemployer Bargaining

In formulating a wage policy, managers may find it possible to resolve a seeming conflict between the local and the industry wage standards in these and other ways. The reconciliation of conflicting standards would indeed appear to be a prerequisite to the concerted bargaining by numbers of employers in different localities. Even where all accept the same standard, its impact on the companies will differ, requiring a reconciliation of interests. It is appropriate, then, for us to consider at this point the political problems peculiar to employers negotiating through trade associations when divergent interests on their own side of the bargaining table must be harmonized before agreement can be sought with the union.

The reasons leading employers to bargain jointly have previously been suggested. Primarily they involve the effort of the companies to avoid being "whipsawed," a gaming expression meaning to be worsted in two ways at the same time. It is relevant to bargaining insofar as unions try to raise one employer's rates above the others', which, in addition to constituting a victory in itself, permits a second victory by allowing the union to insist that other employers' rates be "brought into line"—an example of the use of comparison to achieve a desired objective. The nature of employers' associations varies markedly, ranging from those whose decisions are automatically binding upon all members to those whose decisions are advisory only. The authority of the association leadership stems from the member companies, and its responsibility is for their collective interests. One equitable comparison which emerges from bargaining between the union and such an association is of the differential effects on members of conditions which are to be accepted by them all.

Resolution of differences between association members may be as difficult as resolution of issues in dispute between the association and the union. Because of variation in the number or efficiency of members of an employers' group, in collective negotiations there are sometimes those who would more willingly make concessions to the union, while others less able to meet union demands will insist upon a united front against such concessions. Differences in personal or business philosophy, geographical location, and traditions and precedents may also lead to divergent views. Conflicts within an association become most apparent when certain members must face the prospect of prolongation of a strike because other members have prevented their granting the union's demands, as they would have preferred to do.

In the 1959 steel dispute, for example, Kaiser Steel pulled out of the industry's joint negotiations and reached an agreement on its own with the union over two months before Presidential intervention secured a settlement for the rest of the industry. The dispute and strike invoked the problem of local work rules, an issue of slight importance to Kaiser, which, as the newest company in the industry, had few restrictive work rules with which to contend. The New York newspaper strike of 1962–1963 was prolonged by the serious differences among the employers. They were united only because of the serious union opposition they faced, and then one employer finally broke with the association. That employer's paper was in a weak financial position and probably was the least able to continue the strike, which seemed likely at the time to go on indefinitely. The remaining six members of the association could hardly agree on anything, or, as one cynical observer put it, they could agree only to "give the union nothing—and do it retroactively." Although the newspapers all sold in New York City, each had its special problem. Some were parts of chains, and some were local papers; some made money, and others did not; and some were morning papers, and some afternoon. Each employer tended to take a different position on almost every issue because each was affected differently.

Where employers' associations have had more experience and have learned to respect and live with the costs of settlement, they have been able to avoid impasses. They engage in the familiar political process of "log rolling" among interest groups within the association, or there is a philosophical acceptance by the weaker or by the minority of the decisions of the stronger members or of the majority. In some cases the divergence of interests among certain groups within the association is frankly recognized, and provision is made for differential treatment by permitting separate group negotiations on certain phases of the agreement, such as wages, though the results must sometimes be approved by the full negotiating committee.

Conclusion

By now it should be evident that in discussing wages it becomes difficult to distinguish which influences are political and which economic. For economists, who in considering the influences on prices have been concerned almost exclusively with the coercive comparisons in the relevant markets, must now admit other (nonmarket) comparisons of a coercive nature which nonetheless affect prices. If economics is concerned only with prices in competitive markets (in which presumably political influences may be disregarded), its sphere of investigation is narrowing to virtual nothingness. If it admits concern with prices (and other economic relationships) in noncompetitive markets, then it must inevitably admit coercive comparisons of the sort discussed in this and the preceding chapter, arising out of nonmarket influences. The political factor becomes an economic phenomenon.

In this and the previous chapter, the emphasis has been upon how standards of wage action reflect, in some degree, the responsibilities of those in authority, those who are in a position to determine policy. Responsibility to particular interest groups which compose the organization (a political relationship) and to the organization as a whole is the basis for selection of the comparisons which are considered equitable, and the comparisons which cannot be escaped—the coercive comparisons—will help to define the meaning of responsibility in the matter of wages. There is here nothing cut and dried, nothing definitive, nothing precise in terms of revealing what standards of comparison will be chosen and how they will affect outcome. There remain to be reconciled the conflicts between the standards deemed equitable by management and those viewed as coercive by union leaders. There is the possibility that standards and comparisons may be manipulated for particular advantage. These problems are inherent in the political systems within which employees, union leaders, and management operate. As concepts of corporate and union responsibility change, we may expect their impact not only on wages but also on the whole collective bargain. In the next chapter we shall examine the manner in which authority and responsibility in union-management relations have been modified over the years by virtue of changes in the law.

The Bargaining Unit

chapter 10

The bargaining unit identifies those employees and employers to whom the negotiated terms of a collective agreement apply. We shall discuss not only the legally determined unit but also those units determined by practice and consent of the parties involved. The legally determined unit is that grouping of workers for whom the NLRB has certified a union as the exclusive representative. It is not necessarily coextensive with the practically determined unit, and often the two bear little resemblance to each other. As workers, union leaders, and managers pursue their coinciding and conflicting interests, they frequently find the dimensions of the legal bargaining unit too confining or too broad to serve their purposes.

The Dimensions of the Bargaining Unit

Since a unit identifies those to whom the terms of an agreement apply, it is clear that its two major dimensions are the grouping of employees and the grouping of employers. The former may conveniently be called the "type" of bargaining unit, and the latter the "area." An examination of the various types and areas reveals the numerous possible configurations that bargaining units may take.

One may distinguish two basic *types* of units: (1) the craft and (2) the comprehensive. The pure craft unit includes only those workers who possess a specialized skill or perform a particularized function. It is usually only a part of the whole body of employees in a plant or company. Examples of such craft units are the technicians employed by an electronics company, pattern makers in an automobile plant, clerical workers in a steel mill, engravers in a textile printing and dyeing establishment, and pilots for an airline. The comprehensive unit enrolls all employees irrespective of skills or functions. It would include, therefore, all the employees of the electronics company, automobile plant, steel mill, textile establishment, or airline, regardless of duty or training.

The groupings with which we are concerned here are within a particular business organization—plant or company. In the one case, members of craft units are united by those common occupational interests which set them apart from workers in other occupations. The members seek to advance their self-interest by gaining special consideration for their skills. Members of comprehensive units, on the other hand, are related to one another by common employment interests which they hold jointly with all other employees on the payroll. They serve their interests by using the organized power of their wider group to press for benefits that all may enjoy. Either grouping may be appropriate, of course, depending upon the particular circumstances.

If we set up polar definitions, we might define a pure craft unit as one that includes only those workers performing a precise function for which they require special skill and training. No other workers in the organization would perform the function or possess the same skill and training. A pure comprehensive unit would include all employees on a particular payroll whether they were involved in professional, clerical, maintenance, or production work, or in subsidiary operations such as cafeteria work or trucking. Throughout industry one can find very few such polar units. In practice, most bargaining units fall into an intermediate category blending elements of both pure craft and pure comprehensive units. Most units resemble one type more than the other, though, so that we commonly label them as either "craft" or "comprehensive." Thus, even though a unit may be more inclusive than the pure craft type, we speak of it as a "craft unit," and although another unit may be more exclusive than the strict definition allows, we call it a "comprehensive unit."

Craft units, then, may be simply groups of employees who work together in a particular department in which there is a substantial nucleus of specially skilled workers; or they may be groups which, "though lacking the hallmark of craft skill," are "identified with traditional trades or occupations distinct from that of other employees . . . which have by tradition and practice acquired craftlike characteristics." [1] In other instances the craft unit has been extended to include all the specially skilled employees, as opposed to the unskilled. Such a unit should probably be considered the outside limit of anything that might be called a "craft unit."

The most frequently encountered comprehensive units are those comprised of all production workers or all production and maintenance workers. Such a unit obviously enrolls less than the total number of employees, for it does not include professional, technical, or clerical workers, groups whose proportion of total employment has steadily increased in recent years. Figure 3*a* may help in visualizing the range of possible employee groupings within any given area of business.

The area of bargaining units, that is, the employer dimension, shows as much variation as the types of units display in their different combinations of craft and comprehensive characteristics. The area of a unit may range from a single department or shop in a plant to an entire nationwide industry. Within the range there are bargaining units of single plants, of several plants operated by a single company (multiplant units), of all plants of a single company (company-wide units), and of several companies (multiemployer units). Each area may include employees of either the craft or the comprehensive type of union. The possible area configurations of bargaining units are readily apparent in Figure 3*b*.

The number of possible different combinations of types and areas of bargaining units is nearly unlimited. When negotiating with a large can company, the United Steelworkers union negotiates a master agreement which covers all its members in all the company plants; the International Association of Machinists, on the other hand, prefers to bargain for its members on a plant-by-plant basis in the same industry. In the case of the General Motors Company, each plant local of the UAW is a bargaining unit for certain subjects, such as relief time; but for most matters, including wages, the whole company is one bargaining unit, and representatives of the international union and the company sign a master agreement.[2] This agreement covers several units but only one employer. On the other hand, an employer or a single company may negotiate with a number of unions in many bargaining units. The General Electric Company, for example, has a

[1] *Twenty-fifth Annual Report of the National Labor Relations Board* (1960), p. 38; see also *American Potash and Chemical Corp.*, 107 NLRB 1418 (1954).

[2] The master agreement is often called a "company-wide" agreement, although it does not cover the plants producing electric refrigerators and other nonautomotive goods.

Figure 3a. Organizational hierarchy agreements.

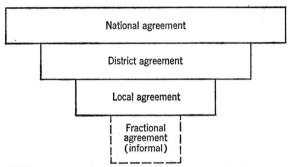

"company-wide" agreement with the International Union of Electrical Workers which covers the production workers in a number of plants, but it also negotiates agreements with about ninety other unions.

A single union or union local may be identified with several employers, as is the practice of locals of the International Typographical Union. A local enrolls members who work for all the papers in a metropolitan area; yet it may negotiate with the different newspaper publishers in separate bargaining units. A single ITU local is thus identified with several units and different employers. Other unions, such as the Amalgamated Clothing Workers, the longshoring unions, the United Mine Workers, and the Teamsters negotiate with employers' associations; their agreements apply to all members of the resulting multiemployer bargaining unit. In other cases, such as in the steel negotiations of 1959, the union may deal with a jointly negotiating group of employers who have not, however, formally banded together into an employers' association. The bargaining unit in steel might be considered multiemployer even though each company signed a separate agreement with the union.

Multiemployer units are often complex associations and display dimensions not found in single employer units. They may be classified by their geographical extent—city (or metropolitan), regional, or national. At the same time, they may be more conveniently classified in other ways. If employers have come together because they produce a similar product or supply a similar service, they may be said to be engaged in "industry-wide bargaining." [3] An example is the Bituminous Coal Operators Association. Or employers may join with one another for the purpose of negotiating because of the similarity of their demand for labor. An example might be construction firms conducting what has been called "labor-market bargaining" with any of the building trades unions.

[3] The term "industry" is subject to confusion in labor relations writings because it is the root word for two different concepts. *Industrial* unionism and *industrial* bargaining units have been so called because they embrace all or most workers in the industry, cutting across craft lines (as distinguished from craft

Figure 3*b*. Horizontal-group agreements.

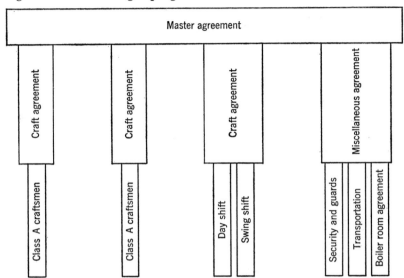

Not all the employers in an industry or labor market who bargain with a union bargain jointly. Some may stay out of the industry employers' association, as small garment makers and coal mine operators often do. Where a formal association does not exist, an employer may refuse to go along with the majority, making a settlement on other terms as the Kaiser Steel Company did in 1959. Thus some multiemployer units are national in scale but not industry-wide in their coverage. We can draw a distinction between the geographical extent of the bargaining unit—metropolitan, regional, or national—and the density of coverage, that is, the proportion of eligible employers in the unit.

The density of the coverage could be a useful dimension to explore. The decline and disappearance of one multiemployer unit may be traced by noting its inability to maintain its density, that is, its coverage of the employees. In 1946–1947, the Full Fashioned Hosiery Manufacturers of America was a bargaining unit which represented about 35 per cent of the full-fashioned hosiery industry. Less than a decade later, it represented no

---

unions, which cut across industry lines). In this discussion the term "comprehensive" has been used instead. "Industry-wide bargaining" has been used to designate the grouping of employers along industry lines. Sometimes this term is used in the sense of the entire industry (nationwide), as when one refers to "the iron and steel industry." But other times it is used simply to designate the association of employers on the basis of the industry attachment in *any* given area, as when one speaks of employers in bargaining for an industry-wide agreement.

more than 20 per cent of the industry, and within a few more years it disbanded as a bargaining unit. The difficulty of ascertaining the facts of coverage by other multiemployer units, however, prevents any adequate measurements. The data generally available are so poor and scattered that they are nearly useless. It is well to remember, nevertheless, that even though a multiemployer unit, such as the Full Fashioned Hosiery Manufacturers of America in its day, covered plants from coast to coast, it was far from being an industry-wide unit in point of density.

Employers' associations conduct most of the multiemployer bargaining. Usually they negotiate the agreements and sign them on behalf of their members. This arrangement is used for approximately 60 per cent of all multiemployer agreements (affecting nearly 90 per cent of the employees under such agreements). About 22 per cent of multiemployer agreements are identical form agreements signed by different employers. This kind of multiemployer unit is most often found in an industry such as metropolitan trucking, where there are many small and competing firms, all organized by a single large union. Although not all the employers participate in the negotiations, the terms of the agreement apply to all.

We have seen how the area of the bargaining unit may be limited to a single department of a single plant or may range up to a multiemployer unit which includes most of the companies in an entire industry on a nationwide scale. We must now take into account the formal and informal bargaining units subsidiary to these primary units. Even within a single department, an individual employee constitutes something of a unit in himself, bargaining for whatever special terms he may find it is possible to secure. More likely is the development of work groups as informal bargaining units. As they are only a fraction of the explicitly recognized unit, their negotiations have been called "fractional bargaining." Informally negotiating through a shop steward with the first-line supervisors and shop time-study men, work groups often arrive at understandings that supplement and at times even contravene the agreement covering the wider unit. More formally, the local union leaders typically negotiate with plant officials supplementary provisions to the company-wide or industry-wide agreement. Occasionally at this level, too, local arrangements will be worked out which run counter to the master agreement negotiated at the company, regional, or industry level.

A whole hierarchy of bargaining units may thus be established, each level having its own field of special competency. The bituminous coal industry provides an example of such a system. Here the union negotiates with the Bituminous Coal Operators Association and the Southern Producers Association, thereby covering a large part of the industry. The agreements set forth the basic rates of pay, hours of work, and other conditions of employment. Under these master agreements, each district of the United Mine Workers negotiates supplementary agreements with district operators' associations. The district agreements are concerned principally with the preparation and cleaning of coal, disciplinary rules and penalties, and other factors involved in the day-to-day operation of the mines.

Such district agreements, however, cannot provide for all the peculiar conditions of the individual mines, and local unions come together with local associations or individual companies to negotiate agreements supplementary to the district agreement. Problems such as the undercutting of coal involve questions of wages and working conditions which can best be settled by reference to actual situations. Then, within the mines themselves, groups of miners may try to resolve problems peculiar to their immediate job situation. They may bargain to change, adjust, or preserve work practices to their benefit, and they may even engage in slowdowns and wildcat strikes to support their demands. Operators and the union refuse to recognize this form of subordinate-unit bargaining and usually frown upon it, but sometimes it receives the support of a provision of the agreement validating local practices so established in the first place.

The hierarchy of bargaining units just described is of a vertical nature; that is, each unit may be identified with a particular *level* of business organization and control. This may be the shop or department of a plant (or mine), the plant unit contained within a multiplant company unit, or the local association of employers subordinate to a district organization. Such a hierarchy follows the organizational lines of both management and the unions. Figure 3*a* diagrams this arrangement.

Another kind of hierarchy is possible which might be said to be horizontal in nature. In this, a single master agreement setting forth general terms is supplemented by a series of separate craft or occupational agreements which provides for the peculiar interests of groups of employees. As in the vertical hierarchy, still narrower work groups at the job level may add supplementary and informal rules and provisions to the craft provisions. The horizontal subsidiary-type unit might be conceived as a number of craft or craftlike units within a comprehensive unit. A number of unions that enroll a comprehensive membership have begun to give special attention to various skilled groups. Both the auto workers and the rubber workers, for example, have established skilled trade departments through which skilled workers may seek more effective craft influence and representation in bargaining.[4] Other unions, such as the American Flint Glass Workers, negotiate only a brief version of a master agreement, leaving the provisions that cover the bulk of working rules to be worked out for each occupational

---

[4] Arnold R. Weber, "Craft Representation in Industrial Unions," *Proceedings of the Industrial Relations Research Association*, 1961, p. 85. A further discussion by Professor Weber is found in "The Craft-Industrial Issue Revisited: A Study of Union Government," *Industrial and Labor Relations Review*, vol. 16 (1963), pp. 381–404.

department of the union. Figure 3*b* illustrates the kind of combination of units that results in these cases.

The Pattern of Bargaining Units

We shall now consider the dimensions of bargaining units from a broader perspective in order to observe any typical patterns that emerge when all units are viewed together. We have no complete or accurate information about all bargaining units because no census of them has ever been made. However, several surveys do provide the basis for an informal judgment.[5] They reveal and emphasize some significant characteristics of collective bargaining in the United States.

First, the distribution of bargaining units roughly parallels the distribution of business firms in size and in number of employees covered. Firms employing less than 500 people make up about 99.8 per cent of the total and include about 48.9 per cent of all industrial employees. At the other end of the scale, the large firms employing over 1,000 are so few that they constitute only 0.1 per cent of the total number, but they have about 33 per cent of the workers in their line.[6] There is a bunching of bargaining units in the small-group sizes, too, and a heavy concentration of employees in a few large units. Bargaining units that cover less than 500 employees account for over four-fifths of all units but for only approximately one-fifth of all the employees. The large bargaining units of over 1,000 employees make up only about 3 per cent of all units, but they include in their coverage nearly two-thirds of the employees.[7]

The parallel distribution of bargaining units and business corporations suggests that bargaining by and large is on a firm-by-firm basis and that unions generally have followed industrial organization in setting up bargaining units. Other data would support this conclusion. Perhaps two-thirds of all agreements cover employees in a single *plant,* and about 80 per cent of all agreements cover workers in a single *company.* Although the proportion of agreements covering several companies (multiemployer units) is

[5] J. C. Nix and L. C. Chase, "Employer Unit in Collective Bargaining," *Monthly Labor Review,* vol. 71 (1950), pp. 695–697; N. M. Bortz and A. Moros, "Characteristics of 12,000 Labor-Management Contracts," *Monthly Labor Review,* vol. 73 (1951), pp. 31–35; *Collective Bargaining Structures: The Employer Bargaining Unit,* Bureau of Labor Statistics Report No. 1 (1953); and N. W. Chamberlain, "The Structure of Bargaining Units in the United States," *Industrial and Labor Relations Review,* vol. 10 (1956), pp. 3–23.

[6] A. D. H. Kaplan, *Big Enterprise in a Competitive System,* Washington, D.C.: The Brookings Institution, 1954, pp. 64–65.

[7] Quite clearly, the two distributions indicate that unions have been more successful in organizing large firms than small firms.

therefore approximately 20 per cent, multiemployer agreements cover at least one-third of all employees under collective agreements. Multiemployer units are numerous and extensive enough to deserve careful attention, but they are not the typical bargaining unit in this country.

In European countries where labor unions are significant organizations, single-employer bargaining has been until recent years more the exception than the rule. The unions typically bargain with industry associations for minimum terms, and in countries such as Germany the government "extends" those terms to cover all workers and employers in an industry, even if they are not represented in the negotiations.[8] European unions most commonly have tended to bargain with a collectivity of employers over the wages and conditions of whole industries. (In times of prosperity, they often find it possible and desirable to negotiate supplementary agreements with individual firms, gaining benefits above the industry-wide minimums.) To the extent that such bargaining is less typical here, American bargaining confronts the union with a different kind of organization of industrial power and business decision making. The less extensive range of bargaining of most American unions tends to obscure the wider responsibilities of union and management negotiators, for they are not directly and explicitly concerned with the impact of resulting agreements—or failures to agree— upon the economy affected by their actions.

The available data on bargaining units also indicate that many unions are dispersed across industry lines. Industrial and union boundaries seldom coincide. In one survey conducted in 1953, the United Automobile Workers had bargaining units in thirty-six industries, the Machinists in fifty-one industries, and the Teamsters, the most widely dispersed of all unions, in fifty-seven industries. Of eighty-five unions, about half had units in more than ten industries. Five unions were represented in forty major industries, and twenty-three had units in eleven to twenty industries. These figures do not indicate the dispersion of membership, of course, which probably would be a good deal more concentrated than these figures suggest.

In many industries several unions bargain for workers performing essentially the same work under similar conditions. In about one-half of fifty-five industries in the same survey, the top two, three, or four unions accounted for 60 to 80 per cent of all units in each industry; the top unions account

---

[8] The American government, through the Secretary of Labor, often makes the same kind of extension with regard to wages, hours, and working conditions for workers employed on government contracts. The Walsh-Healy and Davis-Bacon Acts permit the extension by allowing the Secretary considerable latitude in setting the minimums at those prevailing in the industry. He usually decides that union standards are the minimums prevailing. With the great number of government contracts and the huge government expenditure of recent years, the impact of extending "prevailing standards" may be significant.

for 40 to 60 per cent of all units in about one-quarter of the rest of the industries and for 80 to 100 per cent in the other quarter.

Multiemployer units are most common among the clothing, coal mining, construction, longshoring and maritime, and trucking industries. Whether because these industries predominate in some areas or for other reasons, the geographical distribution of multiemployer units varies markedly. A larger percentage of units are multiemployer in the west than elsewhere in the nation. Considerably more than one-third of all units in the Pacific Coast states are multiemployer, and in the Mountain states from one-fourth to one-third are. In the great industrial states of the East North Central and Middle Atlantic regions, only about one-sixth to one-seventh of all units are multiemployer.

Multiemployer units also appear to be more a big-city than a small-city phenomenon. Sixty per cent of all multiemployer units are found in cities of 100,000 and over, and only about 16 per cent in cities of less than 25,000.

The pattern of bargaining units revealed by the several surveys is reasonably accurate, but the formal distinctions between single-employer and multiemployer units draw a clearer line than exists in practice. Various forces play upon the union and employer firms, leading them to work toward a narrowing or broadening of the bargaining unit at different times. They may experiment with multiemployer bargaining informally for some time before making the arrangement explicit, for example. Perhaps they may become dissatisfied with the experience and return to their former bargaining unit. In other situations, units that started out as multiemployer may dissolve into narrower units, though the process may be gradual, and formal recognition may lag behind actual change. Very likely then, there are more changes and shifts among bargaining units than appear in the record. An examination of the forces that play upon the structure of bargaining units can throw light upon the changing dimensions of the units and make more understandable the existing pattern of collective bargaining in the United States.

The Forces Shaping Bargaining Units

The dominant influence in the shaping of bargaining units appears, at first glance, to be the government acting through the National Labor Relations Board. Until the passage of New Deal legislation, the bargaining unit was not even an explicit concept. It was discussed, but only in terms of the crafts, occupations, or other groupings of workers for whom unions bargained. The Wagner Act necessitated making the bargaining unit formal, for it charged the NLRB with the duty to "decide . . . the unit appropriate for the purposes of collective bargaining. . . [whether] employer unit, craft unit, plant unit, or subdivision thereof." [9] Thus the legal identification of those workers to be exclusively represented by a union in its negotiations of the terms of employment became a matter of public policy and public debate. Thus too did discussion of bargaining units focus upon the formal, legal determinants, almost to the exclusion of other, less formal but nonetheless important determinants.

Board policies primarily reflected a concern for stability in collective bargaining, though public discussion of the "appropriate bargaining unit" showed little interest in, or appreciation of, this concern. The Board rejected any open consideration of bargaining power in deciding what unit would be appropriate. In one case where a union suggested that the power of the union was relevant, the Board replied:

> We do not believe that . . . the inference is warranted that Congress intended that the Board should consider the power factor in unit determination. . . . The application of a power test would bring economic warfare to the forefront of collective bargaining, instead of keeping it in the background where it belongs. . . . The Board would be faced with an impossible administrative problem in trying to decide when equality of bargaining power does not exist. For all these reasons, we reject the proposed power factor as a test in unit determinations.[10]

Lacking clear or helpful guides in the Wagner Act or in the later Taft-Hartley amendments and enjoying no mandates to establish one or another kind of bargaining unit, the Board has determined the appropriate bargaining unit on a case-by-case basis. Generally eschewing a consideration of bargaining power advantages, as such, its decisions have been guided largely by the desires and practices of the unions and managements.

If the two parties agree upon a particular unit, the Board usually confirms it, though there have been instances when it established units contrary to the wishes of both. Where there is a disagreement between the parties over the nature of the unit to be officially established, the Board gives particular weight to any substantial bargaining history of the group. In many cases, of course, the Board is called upon to decide between conflicting viewpoints where there is no history of bargaining. It then relies upon a number of other criteria, using them flexibly. It may consider such factors as the arrangements followed in other plants of the same employer or in plants of other employers in the same industry, the similarities of employment interests among the workers involved, the desire of the employees and

---

[9] Section 9(b).
[10] *Continental Baking Company,* 99 NLRB 123 (1952), p. 777, as reported in *Seventeenth Annual Report of the National Labor Relations Board* (1953).

employers, the nature of the union, and the employer's administrative organization.

This flexible use of the various criteria may have tended to favor the expansion of bargaining units and the growth of wide industrial units over narrow craft units during the thirties and forties.[11] After the passage of the Taft-Hartley amendments in 1947, the Board may have shown a greater willingness than before to allow craft groups to separate from inclusive industrial units.[12] This shift was probably in response to criticisms that through its concern to promote stability in collective bargaining and by avoiding the issue of bargaining power, the Board was encouraging industry-

[11] This result stemmed in large part from the Board's reliance on bargaining history. If a comprehensive type of broad area unit was once established and functioned effectively over a period of years, the Board would be reluctant to disturb the unit upon petition of a craft or smaller area group for separation. Similarly, craft groups with a bargaining history were left undisturbed, but if they wished to amalgamate they were permitted to do so. The effect was to prevent in large measure a contraction of units. Contraction, where it did come, was generally in units which had been operative for too short a time to establish what might properly be called a "history." In these instances, the Board described its dilemma as the need for balancing two considerations: (1) stabilization and certainty in labor relations, which favors adherence to existing bargaining patterns, and (2) the cohesiveness and the special interests of an essentially craft group, which often indicate the appropriateness of separating out a unit limited to members of such a craft group. The Board has partly resolved the dilemma by applying strict tests of what constitutes a "true" craft group before permitting its members to vote on whether they wish to be represented in a separate unit.

On the other hand, where employees expressed willingness—or expressed no unwillingness—or other factors warranted, the Board would sometimes combine smaller area or craft groups to build up larger area and comprehensive units. It could not fail to take account of developments in collective bargaining generally, which—as has already been noted—were expansionary in their trend.

[12] Section 9(b) of the Taft-Hartley Act provides that "no craft unit may be held inappropriate on the ground that a different unit was established by a prior Board decision." Until 1954 the Board consistently disallowed craft severance from comprehensive units in "integrated industries" such as basic steel, basic aluminum, lumbering, and wet milling. Following the American Potash decision [105 NLRB 1418 (1954)], the Board reached the conclusion that separate representation should not be denied merely because of the nature of the industry in which the employees concerned are employed. At the same time, it announced that it would not entertain petitions for craft severances in those industries to which it had applied its earlier doctrine of the "integrated industry." Since then the Board has permitted severance where otherwise deemed appropriate, irrespective of any degree of integration of the employer's operations.

wide bargaining and was thus helping to create serious economic and political problems for the nation.

The public debates over Board policies at that time reflected the traditional concerns with organized labor—the power of unions and the rights of individual workers. The Board's determination of bargaining units was criticized because it did not sufficiently take into account these concerns. Many of the critics assumed—perhaps too readily, but understandably in view of the unions' rapid growth in the decade following 1935—that bargaining units were growing larger and larger. Since enlargement of units might produce inflationary pressures, contribute to the growth of monopoly, intensify the effects of strikes, or deny a chance of full expression to special groups of workers (so the argument ran), the issue was a simple one: Should public policy contribute to, or attempt to stem or reverse, a basic trend?

The dangers of ever-enlarging units were argued in terms of the threat of industry-wide bargaining. Such bargaining can have a variety of meanings and a number of interpretations,[13] but often it is assumed to be a device used by unions to gain standard terms for all workers in a unit, irrespective of the appropriateness of the terms for some of the firms. It follows, therefore, that it would squeeze out marginal firms, discourage the entry of new small firms, and allow, if not encourage, collusion between union and management leaders at the expense of the public.[14] That industry-wide—or, more precisely, multiemployer—bargaining *could* lead to such consequences is well illustrated by the activities of Local 3 of the IBEW, as revealed in the Alan-Bradley case of 1945;[15] however, such a case does not indicate that the feared consequences are *necessary* results of industry-wide bargaining.

Industry-wide bargaining is viewed by some as posing a political as well as an economic threat. There are those who think it welds oligopolistic firms into still tighter groups who could challenge the power of the state since their decisions and activities affect major industries of the nation. Disagreement between union and management in such units could affect the supply of whole industries and inevitably would require the government to intervene, extending its control still further. Such an increase in the concentration of industrial and governmental authority would reduce the oppor-

[13] See footnote 3, p. 237.

[14] For two scholars' analyses of industry-wide bargaining, see David A. McCabe, "Problems of Industry-wide or Regional Trade Agreements," *American Economic Review*, vol. 33, Supplement (1943), pp. 163–173; and John V. Van Sickle, "Industry-wide Collective Bargaining and the Public Interest," in *Unions, Management, and the Public*, E. Wight Bakke and Clark Kerr (eds.), New York: Harcourt, Brace & World, Inc., 1948, pp. 521–525.

[15] 325 U.S. 797 (1945).

tunity for the expression and fulfillment of the aims of individual workers and managers.

The evidence that industry-wide bargaining, however defined, leads to the economic and political monopoly described above is not nearly as convincing as the charge is emphatic. In fact, the emphasis given to the charge by business representatives has declined in recent years. Managers in a number of industries (steel, automobiles, and air transportation, for example) have discovered that industry-wide bargaining is not just a union device. Under certain conditions it has benefits to offer to management and perhaps even to the public.

The *voluntary* expansion of collective bargaining units thus suggests that government determination of bargaining units is not the only or necessarily even the most important influence in determining the size and shape of the unit. NLRB policy does not forbid unions and management to extend the unit for their own practical purposes, nor does it prevent them from informally narrowing the unit if that proves useful to them, and both types of changes have taken place.

The decisions of the Board with regard to bargaining units are not, however, without significance. Once the Board certifies a union in a legal unit, it creates a certain presumption that the unit will be maintained and allows the union to enjoy a kind of legal sovereignty over the unit. A union which exclusively represents the members of a bargaining unit enjoys the right to make laws, to collect revenues, and to exercise disciplinary sanctions. These rights of bargaining unit sovereignty are, of course, valuable as they relate to the success and growth of unions, but valuable as they are, there are practical limits to their enjoyment. Let us continue to examine the forces that play upon bargaining units and explore the complexities unions must face in exercising and maintaining their sovereignty in a world as changeable and varied as that of industry.

In forming unions to negotiate with employers, workers join together in an alliance to increase their bargaining power. The greater the number who ally, the stronger the union, since it can impose a higher cost upon employers who disagree with its terms. Also, the stronger the bargaining position of each member, the stronger the bargaining power of the union. The strength gained from numbers would seem to indicate that unions should enroll as many members as they can; it would seem, too, that the strength gained from enrolling workers who command strategic positions would lead unions to include as many of these workers as possible. The desirability of more bargaining power thus should lead unions to seek to cover all workers who might compete with their members by undermining union wages and working standards.

If the common terms of an agreement are to be effective in reducing competitive pressure, they must operate over the area within which workers are potential threats to one another. They must also cover that area within which employers threaten one another by competitively cutting labor (or, more generally, production) costs. The threat to workers is direct, affecting their wages and working conditions, while the threat to employers' profit margins is indirect. Willingness on the part of any group of workers to accept a lower wage endangers the wages of all workers; pressure by any competitive company to secure a lower wage also potentially endangers the profits of all other companies. Both union and companies have reason, therefore, to expand and maintain the coverage of the agreement to all competitors.

A threat may be initiated in a labor market when a number of competitors are all bidding for the same type of labor. If one or more force down the going wage rates in individual negotiations with the union, there is likely to be an irresistible pressure from other producers to be granted the same favorable terms. A generally lower wage scale will thus have been introduced by individual concessions. Fear of such a result explains why in some instances unions have withstood making special concessions to even a hard-pressed firm. At times unions have countenanced the closing of a company rather than grant special favors which might endanger wage rates in other plants.

On the other hand, the threat to wages may be initiated in the product market, where businesses of lesser degrees of efficiency may be driven to cut costs (including wages) in order to meet the price competition of more efficient competitors. Such cutting could set up a chain reaction as other businesses seek to retain their same competitive positions. Threats from both the labor and product markets are interrelated, of course. Wage cutting in the labor market may lead to price cutting in the product market, and price cutting may stimulate wage cutting.

Economists and labor students have long recognized the importance of competitive pressures in forcing unions and employers to extend the area of their bargaining. Over fifty years ago, Prof. John R. Commons incisively analyzed the way in which an expanding product market intensified competitive pressures on wages and forced unions to extend their organization and to seek national bargaining.[16] He and other observers of the labor scene found convincing evidence that the extension of the product market threatened the financial positions of those firms unable to secure the same wage concessions as their competitors. The Industrial Commission established by President McKinley declared in 1902, for example: "The great advantage

[16] John R. Commons, "American Shoemakers: A Sketch of Industrial Evolution, 1648–1895," *Quarterly Journal of Economics,* vol. 24 (1910), pp. 39–84; reproduced in John R. Commons et al. (eds.), *Documentary History of American Industrial Society,* Glendale, Calif.: The Arthur H. Clark Company, 1910–1911, vol. 3, pp. 18–58.

which is claimed for wide-reaching collective bargaining in trades where there is competition in the general market, is the equalizing of cost of production and of the conditions of labor, in such a way that manufacturers in no one locality can secure an advantage over those elsewhere by cutting wages or otherwise granting less favorable conditions to their employees." [17]

In the face of union weakness in the late nineteenth and early twentieth centuries, employers in a number of industries pushed for national bargaining. In the pottery, bituminous coal, stove, glass, and Great Lakes longshoring industries, employers saw national bargaining not just as a device to establish uniform wages and stabilize costs but also as a means of helping to regulate output and maintain prices. They were as anxious to protect themselves from the intensified competition of the rapidly expanding markets as the workers.[18]

Competitive pressures in labor and product markets are still at work, causing unions and employers to alter their bargaining units. While generally they lead to an expansion of the area of bargaining units, such is not always the case. Other forces such as technological and product changes may intensify or divert the thrust of competitive pressures. Competition may be so directed or redirected that smaller units become more desirable. For example, a manufacturer of flat glassware who has long negotiated with the union on a company-wide basis is now seeking plant-by-plant bargaining. He believes that in order to compete effectively, he cannot allow old work rules and already established wage payment systems to spread to his new plants. Competition from other materials and newer firms requires him to make full and flexible use of the latest equipment and production techniques. Another example is an automobile parts company that recently insisted, at the cost of a long strike, upon plant-by-plant bargaining rather than company-wide bargaining. The broader unit had been satisfactory for many years, but as its different plants had had to compete increasingly with new and different rivals under different conditions, narrower units became more desirable.[19]

A technological change, such as improved transportation, may exert both an expansionary and a narrowing force upon bargaining units, depending upon the industry. In the construction industry of the Pacific Northwest,

[17] *Final Report of the Industrial Commission,* Reports of the Industrial Commission, vol. 19 (1902), pp. 840–841.

[18] For a discussion of these examples, see Lloyd Ulman, *The Rise of the National Trade Union,* Cambridge, Mass.: Harvard University Press, 1955, pp. 519–535.

[19] For a case analysis of the decisive pressures that broke up a multiemployer unit, see Gerald G. Somers, "Pressures on an Employers' Association in Collective Bargaining," *Industrial and Labor Relations Review,* vol. 6 (1953), pp. 557–569.

"improved highways and transportation facilities, mobile construction equipment, and increased numbers of equipment-rental firms permit contractors to take jobs outside the local area of their home offices." [20] The resulting spread of the competitive area of construction work has led both unions and firms to seek regional agreements over broader units. Houses built in Spokane do not compete with houses built in Tacoma, but contractors from either city may and do compete with one another throughout the region because of their potential and actual mobility.

On the other hand, improved transportation has contributed to small plant bargaining units in the chemical industry. Transportation is not the only factor involved, of course, since raw materials are widespread and the products are sold in a number of different markets, but the flexibility and availability of fast motor freight have aided the geographical dispersion of the industry. No single city, state, or region is the dominant site of chemical production, and thus unions are forced to spread out their organizing efforts. Bargaining remains largely on a plant-by-plant basis, even though the four largest firms employ more than one-quarter of all chemical workers. The geographical dispersion is so great and the product markets so divergent that the local labor market becomes the most relevant arena in bargaining.[21] As improved transportation, changing technologies, and diversified product markets allow firms in other industries to move their plants into the suburbs and rural areas, we may expect to see an increased demand by employers for smaller bargaining units, at least in the short run. We may conclude that although the spread of competitive influences usually favors wider bargaining units, there are exceptions well worth noting. As we have seen, competitive pressures may be relieved or redirected by other circumstances.

Technological developments may change not only the area of bargaining units but also the type of units, since skill requirements are often affected. Technological changes may sometimes reduce the skills required of workers. If machine methods of production make less necessary skills that require highly specialized training and experience, a larger number of men with simple mechanical proficiency can enter the labor market. A larger pool of workers is available to the employing companies, and the competitive pressures on the workers are increased. The new technology may create more jobs, but there are also more workers available to fill them. Reduction of skills means greater ease of replacement. This type of development in the twenties and thirties probably helped convince old craft unions to enroll

[20] Kenneth M. McCaffree, "Regional Labor Agreements in the Construction Industry," *Industrial and Labor Relations Review*, vol. 9 (1956), p. 598.

[21] See the analysis of bargaining in the chemical industry by Arnold R. Weber, "The Union-Employer Power Relationship in Chemicals," *Monthly Labor Review*, vol. 81 (1958), pp. 608–609.

semiskilled as well as skilled workers, thus broadening their bargaining unit. An example might be the skilled electricians of a craft local who constructed, wired, and installed complex control panels and other such equipment. Originally they formed an exclusive union, admitting members only after long apprenticeship. With the gradual development of new tools and production processes, however, workers with but a few weeks of training came to perform many of the tasks. As members came to realize what was happening, the union for the first time became interested in the less skilled workers and began to organize workers into comprehensive units.

Technological changes may threaten a narrow grouping of workers more directly and force them to broaden the type of bargaining unit to include other skills. The Printers, for example, became interested in proofreading only after the linotype had displaced some of their members. Also, the Bricklayers sought to widen their coverage to include workers in fireproofing, terra cotta, and cement only when the increased use of steel in construction reduced the demand for bricks and bricklayers.[22]

Technological change may just as often increase skill requirements, of course, as reduce them. In so doing it may bring about the formation of new craft units. Modern technologies require large numbers of technicians and "professional" engineers; where many of these employees have been grouped together, as in aircraft plants and electronics firms, they have organized and sought separate bargaining units for themselves to avoid being included in more comprehensive units.[23] We may well see in the coming years more skilled and technical employees seeking narrow bargaining units and excluding other types of workers.

The form of industrial organization significantly affects the structuring of bargaining units. The growth in the size of the business unit quite naturally led to a growth in the size of bargaining units. The large corporation has its roots in the nineteenth century and before, but its primary growth has been during the twentieth. Its organizational development has been both horizontal and vertical. Firms have spread their control over a greater proportion of a particular production process or product market, and they have also integrated under a centralized authority the supply of raw materials, their conversion into finished products, and their marketing. Large corporations have given birth to subsidiary corporations which themselves might grow to vast sizes. A single plant of one such subsidiary corporation might have more than ten thousand workers on its payroll.

Even though the bargaining unit was confined to a single plant, in terms

[22] Ulman, *The Rise of the National Trade Union*, p. 316.

[23] The Taft-Hartley Act allows professional employees to be excluded from a unit with production workers only with the professionals' approval. Most of the engineering unions began between 1944 and 1946, before enactment of the provision, however, and technicians are not protected by the act.

of numbers of workers and processes covered it meant a tremendous expansion of the scope of the agreement compared with the days of individual enterprise, partnerships, and early corporations. The units need not and have not been confined to single plants, however, and centralized corporate control certainly has stimulated company-wide bargaining units in such industries as steel, automobiles, rubber, and retail trade.

In those industries where individual plants are located in relatively isolated labor markets or produce for markets different from those of the companies' other plants, single-plant bargaining has flourished. Such is the case with companies in the chemical industry mentioned above, with many of the large nationwide food processors (dairies and baking companies, for example), and with retail stores. Nevertheless, centralized financial control works toward widening the coverage of the unit to include not only the plant but also the company and even multicompany groups.

As unions negotiate for, and companies agree to, pension, insurance, and welfare programs, company-wide and multiemployer bargaining becomes more advantageous, if not necessary. Actuarial considerations and also considerations of efficiency in administration make a broad unit of coverage highly desirable. The International Chemical Workers Union and the Oil, Chemical and Atomic Workers International Union secured their first company-wide agreement with Monsanto, American Cyanamid, and Sterling Drug companies when they negotiated company-wide pension and insurance plans.[24] The Retail Clerks International Association has also found that bargaining for pension plans has encouraged multistore and multiemployer units, expanding the coverage of the agreements well beyond the immediate labor market areas, particularly in California.

The location of authority for making agreements on particular subjects is therefore affected by the form of industrial and union organization. Large centralized organizations which encompass many plants may require broad bargaining units for some negotiations such as pensions and life insurance or supplemental unemployment insurance but may need small units for handling other issues such as working rules, piece rate changes, and layoff procedures.

The disadvantage of being unable to get at the source of the other party's authority when negotiating an appropriate issue can be most disturbing to the regular processes of collective bargaining. Either the union or management may face this situation. In the case of a manager, bargaining may be with a national union for changes or provisions over which the national union has no effective control. Such was the situation in the steel negotiations and strike of 1959, when the companies demanded broad and sweeping changes in work rules. Since the rules and practices in question were negotiated in the

[24] Weber, "The Union-Employer Power Relationship in Chemicals," p. 609.

plants by local union leaders and even by committeemen and stewards in the mills and shop departments, the national union officers were hardly in a tenable political position to deal with them. In fact, they refused to agree to any changes. After the strike, a great many changes were made when mill superintendents and foremen sought to negotiate changes in work rules with local and shop union leaders.

Where national unions impose restrictive work rules upon employers, as is the case in some unions, bargaining on work rules may have to be conducted in a nationwide or industry-wide unit. Professor Barnett offered the thesis in 1912 that the only manner in which employers would be able to bargain over such working rules would be by agreeing to negotiate in an expanded unit. The union would then have the chance to bargain for a planned wage scale over a large area as the *quid pro quo* for the employers' chance to negotiate on working rules forced on them by national union policy.[25]

In other cases an employer may run into difficulty when he tries to bargain with a local which is controlled by policy pronouncements of the national union. Some national unions draft form contracts which the local is powerless to alter without approval and which leave to local decision only certain terms which cannot be determined nationally. For example, wage rate deviations from the standard may be permitted, while policies with respect to union security, seniority, hours, and grievance procedures are predetermined for the local. If an agreement is reached at all, then in these particulars it is reached on the terms of the national union. The employer might never meet the national officials, and yet he will have had to submit to their terms.

It will be recalled from an earlier examination of the procedures of collective bargaining that most national unions require local unions to submit local agreements for approval. Here again there is the chance for the national headquarters to determine local policy by refusing to sanction what has been locally agreed to. Thus even without a form contract, an employer may find himself bargaining with a local group which is powerless really to exercise discretion in negotiating some issue.

In the West Coast trucking industry, a desire to negotiate with a responsible—and responsive—group in the union led to a broader unit, not a desire to reach a source of authority. With many small firms, poor man-

---

[25] The International Typographical Union follows a practice of taking some issues out of local bargaining; and employers have complained about it for over sixty years. The union in convention enacts certain rules governing employee-employer relations, making them a part of its national constitution and thereby immune from any bargaining. See George E. Barnett, "National and District Systems of Collective Bargaining in the United States," *Quarterly Journal of Economics,* vol. 12 (1912), pp. 425–443, especially pp. 440–443.

agement, inadequate and inefficient facilities, and autonomous local unions until the late thirties, restrictive work rules flourished. The rules were too inefficient, and practices encouraged by the various locals were too restrictive, for the more aggressive trucking employers. They pressed for wider multiemployer bargaining units, which was also the goal of the leading Teamster officials there. Once the multiemployer units were established, the officials of the centralized regional Teamster organization agreed to wipe out old rules and practices. Employers also found an added benefit in the larger units. The union negotiators now paid relatively less attention to questions involving managerial prerogative than the autonomous locals did.[26]

In 1960, after insisting for many years upon plant-by-plant bargaining, the Boeing Company negotiated its first company-wide agreement with the Machinists. Like the truckers' experience with local bargaining, Boeing's experience with plant bargaining was unsatisfactory, and a more centralized unit with stronger authority and a broader responsibility proved attractive. A company spokesman explained:

> We agreed to a corporate-wide negotiation providing the union would appoint the regional international vice presidents as its negotiating committee, thereby taking the negotiations entirely out of the hands of the local groups. . . . Such a procedure takes the negotiations away from the local union politicians and places the responsibility for negotiations on the union side in the hands of men who tend to be more objective and realistic in their thinking. To a large extent it eliminates the grievance type of negotiation. Further it has the advantage of placing the negotiation responsibility on the part of the union in the hands of men who do not depend on the local group for re-election to their office.

This problem of reaching the source of authority and responsibility may confront the union as well as management. If a bargaining unit consists of only a single plant of a company, the local union may find that local plant management is powerless to override company policy on certain controversial issues. This situation may also arise when a subsidiary of a parent company is involved. Spokesmen for the Communications Workers of America (formerly the National Federation of Telephone Workers) have asserted in the past that the union's negotiations with the individual Bell telephone companies were at times meaningless. The reason was that policies were controlled by the parent American Telephone and Telegraph Company. The union's president stated his case in this way:

---

[26] R. Thayne Robson, "The Trucking Industry," and Van Dusen Kennedy, "Association Bargaining," *Monthly Labor Review*, vol. 82 (1959), pp. 547–551, 539–542.

Collective bargaining between our member unions and individual companies of the Bell System has produced the expected result, namely, that no basic changes in wages, hours, and working conditions are made without the sanction and approval of the parent company. This condition has resulted in the need for bargaining on a Bell System basis between our union and the American Telephone & Telegraph Company with respect to matters designated by the local member unions as items for national bargaining. . . . Each company of the Bell System has its separate plan for employees' pension, disability and death benefits. The provisions and benefits of these several plans are exactly alike and by agreement with the American Telephone & Telegraph Company must conform to the plan established by the American Company. This means that the individual telephone company cannot change its plan for employees' pension, disability and death benefits unless the change first is made in the plan of the American Telephone & Telegraph Company. Local bargaining under such circumstances is futile and productive of industrial unrest.[27]

The effect of such frustration has been an effort by union leaders to expand the bargaining unit to include the principal policy makers. Over the years the CWA has been unsuccessful in its advocacy of company-wide bargaining with AT&T,[28] but it has developed an alternative, pattern-setting bargaining about which we shall say more later. The union now determines a national bargaining policy, and each local company bargaining unit negotiates under the chairmanship of full-time national representatives for the parent company. Whatever the parties agree to in one local negotiation then becomes the pattern to which other local telephone companies con-

[27] U.S. Congress, Senate Committee on Labor and Public Welfare, *Labor Relations Program, Hearings on S. 55 and S.J. Res. 22,* 80th Cong., 1st Sess. (1947), part 3, p. 1210.

[28] The same is true of small unions facing a single company. For example, in 1939 the independent unions that negotiated with the companies of the Bell System found it useful to form a loosely knit federation, the National Federation of Telephone Workers. Increasingly the member unions, or a number of them, felt the need for a stronger federation and in 1946 gave up their autonomy to form a single integrated national union, the Communications Workers of America. In 1950 the CWA approved a more cohesive structure with locals directly chartered by the international, and in 1957 the union centralized still further its bargaining organization, the better to plot strategy and discuss goals to be sought in its negotiations with the Bell companies. The CWA does not yet have a formal company-wide bargaining unit, but the changes it has made over the years have enabled it to secure a pattern-setting arrangement which has moved it in that direction. The union does bargain on a company-wide basis for three groups of employees who are widely dispersed throughout the nation and unattached to any operating telephone company.

form. The union apparently considers pattern bargaining a reasonably good substitute for national or company-wide bargaining.

In the Pacific Coast shipping industry, the longshoremen sought a coast-wide bargaining unit. Unlike the Communications Workers, they succeeded in obtaining a broader unit. The NLRB found that in practice the local employers' associations in the chief ports were extremely responsive to the employers' association for the entire coast, of which they were members:

> Testimony . . . concerning negotiations in May 1946 between the Portland Association [of employers] and the local checkers' union [a branch of the longshoremen's union] shows that (a) the Portland Association submitted to the Coast Association for approval a tentative agreement which it had reached with the local; (b) when the Coast Association did not approve, the Portland Association refused to enter into the proposed agreement; and (c) the Portland Association did not enter into any agreement with the checkers' local unit until certain provisions "recommended" by the Coast Association were incorporated into it, and it has been approved by the Coast Association.[29]

A union or management may prefer a particular kind of bargaining unit at one time and then disapprove of it at another time. Both parties may change positions on the desirability of a particular unit, and not infrequently they use each other's previous arguments. A union which once argued for industry-wide bargaining now borrows management's earlier case for company-by-company bargaining, while management argues in favor of industry-wide bargaining, using the union's former rationalization. As should be clear from the discussion above, there is no generalized union or management position on the particular kind, size, type, or area of bargaining unit.

Much of the public, however, may have the impression that business opposes industry-wide bargaining and that unions favor it; at least in the past, much publicity has been given to the condemnations by business representatives of industry-wide bargaining. Typical of the fervent, uncompromising denunciation was that presented by the then president of the National Association of Manufacturers when Congress was considering the Taft-Hartley amendments:

> Whenever an entire industry is represented by a few spokesmen in matters which affect costs and prices, it is almost inevitable that "understandings" will be reached which will result in price setting. Industry representatives, with their special interests, meeting and bargaining with labor spokesmen, who have their own special interests, may very readily agree on wage rates and prices which will give

[29] *In the Matter of Waterfront Employers Association et al.*, 71 NLRB 121, 132 (1946).

both labor and industry advantages which they could not get under free competition. The public would pay the increased costs because of the monopoly character of such arrangements. Therefore, such arrangements should be outlawed.[30]

If curtailment of a wider bargaining unit lessened a union's bargaining power, a management undoubtedly would approve it. But the effect upon bargaining power, not upon monopoly or free competition, would be uppermost in the minds of the managers. If a bargaining advantage is to be gained from multiemployer units, employers can be persuaded to join them. The San Francisco Employers Council has for some years used exactly this argument with success:

> Operation under a master contract makes it possible for employers to adopt and practice one of Labor's own slogans, which reads—"An Injury To One Is an Injury To All."
>
> It long has been the practice of Labor to gain concessions by striking at the individual employer who was most vulnerable and then proceeding to enforce its demand upon an entire industry through successive strikes. In many industries it is a comparatively simple matter for a strong union to carry the employees who may be involved in a strike at a single plant, by means of strike benefits, but a most serious problem for the individual employer who finds his operations completely paralyzed, to continue in business. It is not a simple matter, however, for a union to carry all of its members when it finds itself confronted with a complete suspension of operations by all employers who are parties to a master contract, until such time as the union is willing to agree upon reasonable terms to render faithful performance of its contracts.[31]

The scope of the bargaining unit will depend upon the pragmatic judgment of the parties as they balance their answers to three questions: (1) Who will gain or lose from changes in the unit? (2) How will relative bargaining power be affected by narrowing or widening the unit? (3) Will the internal authority of the organization support the agreement covering the unit? The balance may be precarious and may change over time; thus it is not surprising that units seemingly well established break up or expand. As the bargaining power of one party increases or decreases, the other party may find it worthwhile to try to change the scope of the unit to improve its position. Such changes may lead to a widening of the unit, but they may also tend to narrow it.

[30] Ira Mosher, *Amendments to the National Labor Relations Act, Hearings on H.R. 8,* 80th Cong., 1st Sess. (1947), vol. 4, pp. 2684–2685.

[31] Almon E. Roth, "Objectives of the San Francisco Employers Council," an address before the Industrial Relations Council of the American Management Association, 1939, pp. 8–9.

Many small companies feel the need of concerted action when they must negotiate with a single large union which has organized a major portion of their industry. No doubt, this is one of the reasons why bargaining associations are common among the many small employers in the garment, coal mining, and trucking industries. The director of industrial relations of a firm engaged in transporting processed foods, for example, explained that over the past ten years his company had joined with similar companies to negotiate with their principal union, the Teamsters:

> Part of this is prompted by union pressure . . . and partially because the companies felt they were in a better bargaining position. This minimizes the problem of one local area using another adjacent local to their advantage and with the companies or the individual company being whiplashed [sic] between the two.

Even large firms may find that association or cooperation with other firms in the industry improves their bargaining position if they negotiate with the same union. Consider the case of the major producers in the automobiles and in steel.

The United Automobile Workers strongly favored industry-wide bargaining in its early years. As it gained membership, strength, and some of its original demands, its officials more forthrightly stated their unalterable opposition to industry-wide bargaining. After the postwar strikes in the industry, there was some talk that the union had been unfair in picking on General Motors and allowing the other companies to operate.[32] Not until 1955, when the union made clear that Ford was its "target," was there obvious evidence that Ford and General Motors had cooperated with each other in their negotiations. Henry Ford II publicly announced his approval of industry-wide bargaining, though he probably did not mean that it should result in a multiemployer agreement. In 1958 and 1961, the Big Three cooperated in determining—or at least accepting—a common goal and strategy in negotiating with the UAW. What has developed in the automobile industry is a system of parallel bargaining, less satisfactory to the union than the older kind of bargaining that produced a pattern for the whole industry from the bargaining with a single company.[33]

In the steel industry from 1937 until the beginning of negotiations in 1955, the companies rejected every union proposal for negotiating on an industry-wide basis. During World War II and immediately after, the union looked to industry-wide bargaining as a means of getting rid of "inequities" in wage rates. Under the 1947 job evaluation program, which was practi-

---

[32] *Amendments to the National Labor Relations Act, Hearings on H.R. 8,* 80th Cong., 1st Sess. (1947), vol. 5, p. 3058.

[33] William H. McPherson, "Bargaining Cooperation among Auto Managements," *Monthly Labor Review,* vol. 83 (1960), pp. 592–594.

cally industry-wide, and with the aid of rapidly rising wages since the war, many wage differentials and inequities were wiped out. Settlements tended to follow a "pattern," but not until 1956 did the twelve major companies turn over bargaining on major issues to a four-man committee. In the 1959 negotiations, a four-man industry committee again represented the Big Twelve, and this time they had authority to negotiate a complete contract. The companies resisted union requests for separate meetings with them to supplement the joint negotiations.

Although the union has not withdrawn its support for industry-wide bargaining, it worked hard in 1959 to get settlements by individual companies. Its success in getting Kaiser to defect from the joint negotiations and then in getting settlements in can, aluminum, and copper certainly did not hurt its bargaining position. The companies and unions have thus moved in the direction of reversing their historical stands on the bargaining unit.[34] However, in steel as in automobiles, although the changes in the procedures of bargaining and in the area of coverage of the agreements are not without significance to the bargaining strength of the parties involved, it is well to remember that there has long been a considerable amount of pattern bargaining. The impact on the industry and the economy of any particular settlement under the more recent conditions of intercompany cooperation therefore will probably not be greatly different from the effects of earlier single-company negotiations, at first anyway. With time, bargaining might take a different turn if cooperation grows and becomes well established.

In recent years a number of formal bargaining associations have dissolved, disintegrated, or ceased to function as their members decided they could do better in negotiations by themselves. In several of the cases the industries have been under severe economic pressure, and the unions involved have seen their bargaining power wane. The situation is illustrated by the Fall River–New Bedford Textile Manufacturers Group (earlier the Fall River–New Bedford Textile Manufacturers Association), which had bargained with the Textile Workers Union since 1942. It simply ceased to function in 1955. In the depressed industry, many member mills had gone out of business, and after two of the largest remaining companies merged, there was little reason for a multiemployer agreement. The settlements since then have been reached through separate, though similar, agreements.

In 1950 the pressed and blown glassware employers' association began to crumble, after more than sixty years of bargaining. By 1952 the association represented only a small group of plants.[35] During the same time, the

[34] Jack Stieber, "Company Cooperation in Basic Steel Bargaining," *Monthly Labor Review,* vol. 83 (1960), pp. 586–588.

[35] Somers, "Pressures on an Employers' Association in Collective Bargaining," pp. 557–569.

Full Fashioned Hosiery Manufacturers Association disintegrated, as each company tried to secure from a declining union the terms that suited it best in a hard-pressed industry.

A declining industry or a weakening union is not necessary to convince either a union or an employer that individual bargaining is desirable. Any time either feels that it is to its advantage to bargain individually, it will press toward doing so. The huge Weyerhauser Timber Company, for example, has withdrawn from membership in the timber employers' associations in order to be free to negotiate and settle as it sees fit. It is big enough so that it can be assured that its settlement will set the wage pattern for the industry in the Pacific Northwest. On the union side is the case mentioned earlier of the Machinists, who prefer to negotiate with the large can companies on a plant-by-plant basis, quite at variance with the United Steelworkers, who have striven for company-wide and even wider agreements. The Machinists feel that the strongest plant local union can move ahead in getting benefits and can also force the company to give the same benefits to the other locals. The Steelworkers union uses its negotiations with the can manufacturers for quite another purpose—for putting pressure upon the steel companies. Thus company-wide bargaining suits it much better.

From our examination of these various cases, it would appear that bargaining units change—expand or contract—as one or both parties try to manipulate the bargaining unit to improve their own bargaining power. We have examined some of the major forces shaping bargaining units, but in doing so we have given the most attention to those formal arrangements recognized in law or written understanding and official titles. There are also informal arrangements that affect the effective operation of the more formal bargaining unit. To these we shall now turn.

The Informal Units: Fractional and Pattern Bargaining

As changeable and varied as the bargaining units are that we have so far discussed, they probably show considerably more stability and less variety than the informal bargaining arrangements made by workers, union leaders, managers, and supervisors as they attempt to take advantage of immediate opportunities and constantly changing situations in the industrial world. In probing the forces that mold bargaining units, we can gain a more complete understanding of them by (1) analyzing the diverse interests of workers and management and the way in which the diversity manifests itself in fractional bargaining units, and (2) examining the influence of settlements in particular units upon other settlements in other units responsive to any resulting coercive comparisons or economic pressure.

Since fractional bargaining is a common, though not always recognized, practice under collective bargaining, it follows that fractional bargaining units are common, though not necessarily recognized, parts of broader bargaining units. The sovereignty that a certified union enjoys over a legally determined bargaining unit is hardly absolute; it is limited by the willingness of its members to dissent and their ability to maintain an independent authority. As noted earlier, most bargaining units are small, but most employees covered by labor agreements are in large units of 1,000 or more members. Almost all unions have become more comprehensive in the past three decades, enrolling workers having a variety of skills, occupations, interests, and concerns. The resulting large unions and large bargaining units have gained strength from the massing together of such workers. More properly, they have gained strength whenever their comprehensive membership has been united, but by incorporating competitive diversity, they have built in cleavages of interests and lines of weakness not present in more homogeneous organizations. The larger the unit, the more difficult it becomes to find issues on which all will agree, and the more likely it is that various members or groups of members will find their own interests served by bargaining independently for certain demands.

Fractional bargaining develops not out of a rejection of collective bargaining but out of a dissatisfaction with the all-inclusiveness of it; the fractional unit does not supplant but rather supplements the larger unit of which it is a part. In the same way that unions and companies often negotiate a company-wide master agreement specifying settlements on matters common to all plants but allow local plant negotiators to settle issues peculiar to their circumstances, fractional bargainers negotiate terms applicable and pertinent to the still more parochial interests of work groups in the plants or of special occupational groups in several plants. In Chapter 6 we saw that fractional bargaining is possible largely because of collective bargaining. For the same reason, the fractional unit is dependent upon the broader bargaining units. Without the organizational strength of the broader unit and the union-secured protection from arbitrary discipline, the members of fractional units could not easily pursue their own interests. In fact, if they had no larger unit protecting rights and securing demands common to them and the other members of the wider unit, they would probably be so engaged in a joint effort with those of differing job interests to secure their common interests that they would pay little attention to their divergent interests. Only after the United Automobile Workers was well established, for example, did the skilled workers demand special consideration of their problems. And only after the United Rubber Workers had effectively organized the tire plants, did fractional bargaining present a problem to the union and plant managements.

The place and role of the unofficial subordinate bargaining units in the wider, formal unit are clearly demonstrated when unions and managements recognize them. In one industry—rubber tires—a number of agreements allow foremen and shop stewards to make departmental arrangements modifying or changing, within limits, some of the agreement's provisions, even as they allow local union officers and plant managers to negotiate supplementary provisions. The foremen and stewards may be free to negotiate such things as changes in the groupings of workers among whom overtime work is equally distributed, substitution of shorter hours for layoffs during times of reduced work, the conditions under which workers may change shifts, and the trial period for a piece work rate. In the automobile industry the recognition of fractional units took a different form with the UAW's acceptance in 1957 of the skilled craftsmen as a subsidiary bargaining unit. The skilled groups were granted separate ratification machinery and "more effective representation in the various levels of the bargaining process." A convention resolution explained the union's action this way:

> We must find new ways to implement the principle of industrial unionism in order to meet today's problems, to meet the problems common to all the workers in our Union and at the same time be able to deal satisfactorily with their special problems. No member of our Union has a right to special privilege, but every member of our Union, who may have a special problem because of the nature of his work, has a right to have this special problem dealt with effectively.

The development of fractional units does not indicate the disintegration of other broader bargaining units; it does indicate a decentralization of bargaining authority for unions and management. It is a manifestation of the complex relationships between workers and between managers as they daily pursue their various divergent and convergent goals. As workers and managers turn their attention to different interests, they organize themselves into different units, in and through which they hope to further these interests. Interests common to many will generate broad units, while specialized, competitive interests will encourage narrow units; however, neither type of interest necessarily excludes the other. If the two conflict, those concerned may have to choose between one or the other, or, more likely, they will work out a compromise which preserves some of the gains possible of attainment in each unit or form some new unit in which the tensions between cooperative and competitive interests can better be accommodated.

The growth of unions and the development of collective bargaining in recent years have brought to public attention the phenomenon of pattern bargaining. The wage settlement reached within a major bargaining unit by a management and union becomes a "key bargain," serving as a guide for settlements in other units. The pattern may be followed in the given industry and also, though perhaps less faithfully, in related industries. Influenced in intricate ways by the "pattern" through effects upon labor markets, wage rates, product prices, and interunion rivalries, other unions and managements may also negotiate more or less conforming settlements. There is not in any strict sense the establishment of a new bargaining unit; yet clearly for those issues set by the pattern, the bargaining unit has been informally extended beyond its official scope.

The patterning of wages occurred before collective bargaining was widespread, of course. Wage leadership in steel existed for at least twenty years before 1933, with the United States Steel Corp. usually acting as leader.[36] Wherever there is a dominant firm or union in an industry or where there is a small group of large producers, wage leadership is apt to appear. Unions and collective bargaining have undoubtedly helped to reinforce (and enforce!) the patterns; they have also helped to spread the patterns further throughout the economy and perhaps faster than before. Union negotiations are not always successful in getting a "wage follower" to agree to the pattern, but the pattern is an understandable, clear-cut basis for beginning the bargaining talks. When the wage pattern is one of decreases, as it has been in textiles at times, management rather than union may take the initiative in demanding the pattern.

The pattern is a goal to aim for; it is not always attained. For internal political reasons, union leaders would like to do as well for one group of members as for another. Unless a follower firm can convince union leaders and workers that economic conditions press too hard to allow the pattern, the union will insist on it. The pattern does not cover all the issues negotiated in collective bargaining by any means. Most generally it is thought of in terms of wage changes, but other major issues such as pensions, health plans, supplemental unemployment insurance, and the length of the workweek have spread in pattern fashion from company to company and from industry to industry. Even these issues have been handled in a variety of ways and adapted to the particular circumstances of different companies and the various industries. Pattern bargaining is more flexible than bargaining in a formal multiemployer unit. The key bargains may not always be made by the same parties, and the application of the pattern may vary considerably from firm to firm in the same industry if different economic conditions impose themselves.[37]

[36] George Seltzer, "Pattern Bargaining and the United Steelworkers," *Journal of Political Economy,* vol. 59 (1951), p. 322.

[37] For studies of patterns and their variations, see Kenneth Alexander, "Market Practice and Collective Bargaining in Automotive Parts," *Journal of Political Economy,* vol. 69 (1961), pp. 15–29; Harold M. Levinson, "Pattern Bargaining: A Case Study of the Automobile Workers," *Quarterly Journal of Economics,* vol. 74 (1960), pp. 296–317; Walter H. Carpenter, Jr., and

The prevalence of the single-employer bargaining units in the United States might suggest at once more isolated determination of labor conditions among firms and less diversity of approach to problems within firms than in practice is the case. The boundary lines of bargaining units are not fixed and unchanging, but variable, the parties in collective bargaining adjusting them to fit their needs. To focus upon the development of multi-employer units or pattern bargaining and thereby conclude that American collective bargaining is imposing a dangerous uniformity upon industrial relations is to overlook the many ways in which diversity is accommodated, if not encouraged. Pattern bargaining of course raises serious problems, as does fractional bargaining, and each deserves careful study and attention; but if both are examined as activities carried on within a complicated, changeable structure, the problems may not seem as insoluble and of the same dimension as they would otherwise.

Edward Handler, *Small Business and Pattern Bargaining*, Babson Park, Mass.: Babson Institute Press, 1961; and Harold M. Levinson, *Collective Bargaining in the Steel Industry: Pattern Setter or Pattern Follower?* University of Michigan, Ann Arbor, Mich., 1962.

The Law of
Collective Bargaining

chapter 11

The key to understanding the law affecting collective bargaining is an appreciation of the problems which unions have posed for a rapidly changing American society. In the nineteenth century, unions had no legally or socially acceptable role in the small-scale commerce and trade of a young, basically agrarian nation. Even as late as 1920, 48 per cent of all Americans lived in rural areas, and more workers were engaged in agricultural work than in any other occupation. The scattered hired farmhands gave little thought to their own organization, and small tradesmen joined independent farmers in viewing the organization of the landless urban workers as a threat to their own values. As long as these groups constituted an effective majority of the citizenry and their political influence was dominant, they approved legal doctrines that hindered, limited, and regulated union organizing.

We shall be less concerned with the doctrines of these formative years— for at best they are ambiguous—than with the problems they were designed to meet. Such an approach helps to strip away the naïve but prevalent notion that for years labor law consisted of little but the prejudiced pronouncements of upper-class judges in the service of business interests, becoming subject, in the 1930s, to more liberal interpretations by men who, with greater objectivity, recognized the pressing needs and demands of industrial workers. Our survey will suggest that throughout the parade of judicial doctrines and legislation the central preoccupation of the courts has been with the legitimate exercise of group power in a democratic society.

Right down to the early 1930s (not precisely coincident with the first New Deal administration, since the Norris–La Guardia Act preceded it by almost a year), the prevailing view of the public as well as of jurists was that American society was rooted in individual freedom, which was threatened as much by powerful private groups as by a powerful government. Court orders and judicial decisions which restrained union power were thus generally well received, particularly if they protected nonunion employees seeking to escape union control.

The interest of the employer, of course, lay with the nonunion worker. He supplied employers with the concept of "outraged individual rights," which could be and was molded by contemporary legal doctrines into a potent weapon against unions. The employers' contest with the unions was thus transformed from a quarrel between private interests into a struggle involving social principle of deep import. That so many cases in American labor law turn on the legality of the closed shops and the propriety of union coercion of *workers* is no accident. In both situations individuals must conform to group demands; that is, they must join a union in order to work in the first instance and must respond to threats and violence in the second.

Individual Freedom, Group Power, and Community Welfare

This legal concern was not simply for the rights of individual workers but also for the community's welfare, since this too may be subject to abuse by private power.[1] Centuries before the emergence of laissez-faire doctrines in economics, English judges had established the common-law principle that private groups were suspect if they were organized for economic purposes. Too easily they could develop restraints of trade and thus unlawfully monopolize a market to exploit the public for private gain. When the late-eighteenth-century enthusiasm for the virtues of free trade was added to

[1] This belief and its application to unions are spelled out with painful explicitness by Henry Simons, *Economic Policy for a Free Society*, Chicago: The University of Chicago Press, 1948, chap. 6. The date of writing indicates the persistence of this notion. Also see Fritz Machlup, *The Political Economy of Monopoly: Business, Labor and Government Policies*, Baltimore: The Johns Hopkins Press, 1952, pp. 339–417; and Donald Dewey, *Monopoly in Economics and Law*, Chicago: Rand McNally & Company, 1959, pp. 265–269.

the long-standing legal condemnation of private restraints of trade, lawyers and judges could hardly be expected to view with anything but deep suspicion the attempts of workers to organize to raise the price of labor.

In curbing the activities of trade unions, judges were thus expressing a legal doctrine which was predominantly concerned with the freedom of individuals and the welfare of the community. Concern for employers as such was merely incidental. Of course, employers profited from the political and legal doctrine of individualism and the economic doctrine of free trade; they supported those doctrines because they were favorable to their interests, and they unhesitatingly employed them to fight unions because they were effective. It would be fallacious, however, to treat early labor law as though it were only the *product* of special interests.

Only an unsophisticated view of lawmaking in a democratic nation would depict businessmen as having the power to create labor law solely for their own benefit and the judiciary as being banefully warped by class considerations. Judges could assert and employers could appeal to such legal doctrines because most of the voting public accepted and approved the underlying sociological presuppositions.[2] Not because judges are less

---

[2] It is worth developing this point more explicitly because of its importance in understanding the development of labor law in this country.

First, on the proposition that the unions were successfully combated in the law for so long only because so many identified their personal interests with business, rather than with worker organization, the comment of Werner Hochwald is pertinent:

> The fundamental question is just this: different social institutions appear to different scholars and groups of the community best designed to realize those intrinsic values of life which constitute ultimate social ends. Whenever some inconsistency of the current instrumental values—some inconsistency between present institutions and community aspirations—is evidenced through social tension and distress, the proper adjustment of, and a new compromise on, instrumental values, therefore, is the real point at issue. For while divergent interests will attach incompatible meanings to their claims for liberty and security, ephemeral human beings can but identify their ideals and hope for a better world with the relative permanence of a self-perpetuating group or institution like the family, the church, the political party, the free market, the trade union, the national state, social institutions to guarantee that maximum amount of individual freedom, security, and opportunity which can be attained only by mutual concession and compromise.
>
> Now there can be little doubt indeed that these groups and institutions will become special pleaders for their members' selfish interests, using verbal camouflage to elevate their particular ambitions to the dignity of final values, just as individuals like to identify their private interests with the public good. But though all this may be conceded, it is only through

class-conscious or employers less concerned with self-interest do we find labor law and legislation now more hospitable to unions than formerly, but rather because our society accords the group a greater role than before. Despite our increased hospitality, though, the focal issue in labor law remains a question to which a democratic nation must continually address itself: What are the appropriate roles of individual, group, and state? The answers which labor law has provided over time indicate that judges and legislators have weighed by changing standards the rights and privileges of individuals against the rights and privileges of the group. As standards have changed, so has the emphasis upon one set of rights over another.

Although this oversimplifies the matter, 1932 may be conveniently taken as the year of demarcation between the legal emphasis upon individual rights in industrial relations and the emphasis upon group rights. Prior to this year, the doctrines of criminal conspiracy and illegal purposes had cast doubt on the legitimacy of union activities, and the use of injuctions and

---

these groups and institutions that man can identify his little self with the larger world of which he is such an ephemeral part; and since the lives of men, if they are to be lived with even a small measure of satisfying conviction, cannot dispense with this emotional attachment to some social group and institution, there is no sharp dividing line in the individual's consciousness between particular and general interest, between instrumental and inherent value.

"Collective Bargaining and Economic Theory," *Southern Economic Journal,* vol. 13 (1947), p. 234.

The reader may thus recall the consumer fear, which persists, that union wage-raising action will work against the public interest by forcing prices upward. (For an early expression of this view, see Chapter 1, footnote 4.) This consumer fear has served powerfully to support business against union interests and is generally offset only if consumers believe that worker exploitation can be remedied without impact on prices.

Second, on the proposition that judges can be presumed—as a general rule—to have been serving community interest (with which it is true they have often identified business interest), there is no intent here to deny a "disposition set" on the part of these officials by reason of their family backgrounds, learning, and social contacts, which means that their opinions often constitute rationalizations of dogma which had their genesis in the preexisting outlook (predisposition) of the judges. Some mind-set, whether of this or another kind, is obviously a part of every man's makeup. What is being argued here is simply that there was probably much less conscious service of special interest than is often charged and that it is a reasonable assumption that most judges approached labor issues with an earnest desire to be fair and impartial, unaware of the subconscious (and for that reason all the more powerful) inclinations which guided, if not governed, their decisions.

the application of antitrust legislation to unions had served as restrictions upon group action through collective bargaining. Beginning with the Norris–La Guardia anti-injunction law of 1932, however, and continuing with the National Industrial Recovery Act and the National Labor Relations Act, Congress accorded signal importance to group action. In the late thirties and early forties, the Supreme Court reinterpreted the laws of picketing and the antitrust laws in such a way that unions were largely exempted from them. Thus it, too, placed the group above the individual worker for the purpose of bargaining with employers. True, the Taft-Hartley Act and perhaps also the Landrum-Griffin Act mark a retreat from the emphasis upon the group, but not a reversal. Both acts demonstrate that the issue of the respective roles in society of the individual and the group continues to be pertinent. Through our laws we do not allow one special-interest group and then another to profit with the turn of public favor.

Unions as Criminal Conspiracies

In surveying the law of collective bargaining, we first encounter the doctrine of criminal conspiracy, a doctrine which is still shrouded in uncertainty and controversy. Such authorities maintain that its substance rendered illegal any concerted action by organized workers, whether or not each worker could have legally undertaken the same action by himself. According to this argument, the combination "tainted" the action. Other authorities assert that the doctrine of criminal conspiracy did not outlaw union action as such but merely condemned certain methods of achieving objectives. Condemnation fell primarily upon efforts to enforce the closed shop and upon violence used to prevent the recruiting of strikebreakers.

One can find cases which support both views, but for our purposes there is no need to reexamine the respective arguments. Quite evidently, the basis for either view lay in the impact of the action upon, first, the economic independence of the individual worker and, second, the economic security of the community. That employer interests were served in defense of these objectives simply marks, as has already been noted, the conceived coincidence of private and public interests, just as at a later date the public interest expressed by Congress and the courts coincided with (private) union interests.[3]

In the economic and political climate of the early nineteenth century,

---

[3] Karl Polanyi has an interesting commentary in this connection:

> Actually, class interests offer only a limited explanation of long-run movements in society. The fate of classes is much more often determined by the needs of society than the fate of society is determined by the needs of classes. . . . The chances of classes in a struggle will depend upon their

employer as well as worker combinations stood condemned before the law.[4] Group action came close to being tinged with treason, a manifesta-

---

ability to win support from outside their own membership, which again will depend upon their fulfillment of tasks set by interests wider than their own. Thus, neither the birth nor the death of classes, neither their aims nor the degree to which they attain them; neither their cooperations nor their antagonisms can be understood apart from the situation of society as a whole. . . .

The "challenge" is to society as a whole; the "response" comes through groups, sections, and classes. . . . There is no magic in class interests which would secure to members of one class the support of members of other classes. . . . An all too narrow conception of interest must in effect lead to a warped vision of social and political history, and no purely monetary definition of interests can leave room for that vital need for social protection, the representation of which commonly falls to the persons in charge of the general interests of the community—under modern conditions, the governments of the day.

From *The Great Transformation,* New York: Rinehart & Company, Inc., 1944, pp. 152–154.

[4] Thus Justice John B. Gibson of the Supreme Court of Pennsylvania held in the case of *Commonwealth ex rel. Chew v. Carlisle,* Brightly's Reports 36 (1821) (see Charles O. Gregory and Harold A. Katz, *Labor Law,* Charlottesville, Va.: Michie Casebook Corp., 1948, pp. 10–11), involving a combination of employers:

I take it, then, a combination is criminal whenever the act to be done has a necessary tendency to prejudice the public or to oppress individuals by unjustly subjecting them to the power of the confederates, and giving effect to the purposes of the latter, whether of extortion or mischief. According to this view of the law, a combination of employers to depress the wages of journeymen below what they would be, if there was no recurrence to artificial means by either side, is criminal. There is between the different parts of the body politic a reciprocity of action on each other, which, like the action of antagonizing muscles in the natural body, not only prescribes to each its appropriate state and condition, but regulates the motion of the whole. The effort of an individual to disturb this equilibrium can never be perceptible, nor carry the operation of his interest on that of any other individual, beyond the limits of fair competition; but the increase of power by combination of means, being in geometrical proportion to the number concerned, an association may be able to give an impulse, not only oppressive to individuals, but mischievous to the public at large; and it is the employment of an engine so powerful and dangerous, that gives criminality to an act that would be perfectly innocent, at least in a legal view, when done by an individual.

It is worth noting that Justice Gibson in this decision appears to view rather

tion of private *authority* that was at least a potential threat to the state.[5] Consider the argument of counsel for the prosecution in the case of the Philadelphia cordwainers in 1806. We quote at some length to establish the flavor of the time:

> Why a combination in such case is criminal, will not be difficult to explain: we live under a government composed of a constitution and laws . . . and every man is obliged to obey the constitution, and the laws made under it. When I say he is bound to obey these, I mean to state the whole extent of his obedience. Do you feel yourselves bound to obey any other laws, enacted by any other legislature, than that of your own choice? Shall these, or any other body of men, associate for the purpose of making new laws, laws not made under the constitu-

---

leniently "the combination of capital" and excuses the combination's conduct on the grounds that it was formed as a defensive move against the union of employees; but the greater sympathy which most members of the bench admittedly felt for employers should not blind us to the fact that class interest was justified—and had to be justified—in terms of public welfare. As Prof. Walter Nelles remarked in his classic article, "The First American Labor Case," *Yale Law Journal*, vol. 41 (1931), pp. 199–200:

> It is not intended to imply that narrowly selfish pressures determined decision unassisted. The cooperative efficacy of honest wills for morality, justice and social expediency was substantial. The coercion of [nonunion workmen] could be abhorred with religious intensity. The dangers of abuse of collective labor power could be felt as outweighing the harms that would result from its emasculation. The manifold prosperities that would be served by stimulation of export manufactures (here narrow selfishness and concern for general welfare tend to become indistinguishably blurred) could be felt as outweighing any imminent hardships to manufacturing labor. . . . Without the cooperation of such pressures more selfish pressures would have been almost completely ineffectual.

[5] Again note the modern expression of this view in Simons, *Economic Policy for a Free Society*, p. 152: "The intricate pluralism of modern democracies is, of course, a commonplace among students of sociology and politics. Equally commonplace, however, is the fact that organized minorities are a continuing threat to democratic order and internal peace." Simons mentions among such organized minorities churches, secret societies, vigilante movements, tariff lobbies, veterans' organizations, farm blocs, and above all unions—"occupational armies, born and reared amidst violence, led by fighters, and capable of becoming peaceful only as their power becomes irresistible." Simons's views were not an expression of any "class interest" but stemmed from an intellectual conviction of the danger of organized groups within society.

See also J. W. Kuhn, "The Combination Acts of 1799 and 1800," *Labor Law Journal*, vol. 7 (1956), pp. 19–23.

tional authority, and compel their fellow citizens to obey them, under the penalty of their existence? This prosecution contravenes no man's right, it is to prevent an infringement of right; it is in favour of the equal liberty of all men, this is the policy of our laws; but if private associations and clubs, can make constitutions and laws for us . . . if they can associate and make bye-laws paramount, or inconsistent with the state laws; What, I ask, becomes of the liberty of the people, about which so much is prated; about which the opening counsel made such a flourish!

There is evidence before you that shews, this secret association, this private club, composed of men who have been only a little time in your country, (not that they are the worse for that,) but they ought to submit to the laws of the country, and not attempt to alter them according to their own whim or caprice.

It is in proof, that they combined together; for what? to say what each man shall have for his labour: no . . . one man may ask more for his labour than any other does. Dubois may do it, or any of the defendants may do it; they may get four dollars for making a pair of boots, if they can get any person to give it, who has more money than wit . . . (as Mr. Young says is the case with some of his customers). It is not intended to take away the right of any man to put his own price upon his own labour; they may ask what they please, individually. But when they associate, combine and conspire, to prevent others from taking what they deem a sufficient compensation for their labour . . . and when they undertake to regulate the trade of the city, they undertake to regulate what interferes with your rights and mine. I now am to speak of the policy of permitting such associations. This is a large, encreasing, manufacturing city. Those best acquainted with our situation, believe that manufactures will, bye and bye, become one of its chief means of support. A vast quantity of manufactured articles are already exported to the West Indies, and the southern states; we rival the supplies from England in many things, and great sums are annually received in returns. It is then proper to support this manufacture. Will you permit men to destroy it, who have no permanent stake in the city; men who can pack up their all in a knapsack, or carry them in their pockets to New-York or Baltimore? These manufactures are not confined to boots and shoes . . . though that is very important, as you learn from Mr. Bedford, that he could export 4000 dollars worth, annually. Other articles, to a great amount, are manufactured here, and exported; such as coaches and other pleasurable carriages; windsor chairs, and particular manufactures of iron. I cannot make a calculation of the importance of manufactures to this city.

If the court and jury shall decide, that journeymen may associate together, and determine that none shall work under certain prices; then, when orders arrive for considerable quantities of any article, the association may determine to raise the wages, and reduce the contractors to diminish their profit; to sustain a loss, or to abandon the execution of the orders, as was done in Bedford's case, who told you he could have afforded to execute the orders he obtained at the southward, had wages remained the same as when he left Philadelphia. When they found he had a contract, they took advantage of his necessity. What was done by the journeymen shoemakers, may be done by those of every other trade, or manufacture in the city. . . . A few more things of this sort, and you will break up the manufactories; the master will be afraid to make a contract, therefore he must relinquish the export trade, and depend altogether upon the profits of the work of Philadelphia, and confine his supplies altogether to the city. The last turn-out had liked to have produced that effect: Mr. Ryan told you he had intended to confine himself to bespoke work.

It must be plain to you, that the master employers have no particular interest in the thing . . . if they pay higher wages, you must pay higher for the articles. They, in truth, are protecting the community. Nor is it merely the advance of wages that encreases the price to the consumer, the master must have some compensation for the advance of his cash, and the credit he frequently gives. They have no interest to serve in the prosecution; they have no vindictive passions to gratify . . . they merely stand as the guardians of the community from imposition and rapacity.[6]

In a similar vein, the prosecution in the 1809 case of the New York cordwainers declared:

This conspiracy, unnaturally to force the price of labour beyond its natural measure, is as dangerous as any kind of monopoly, and if it be tolerated, as well may regrating, forestalling, and every other pernicious combination.

Suppose all the bakers in New-York were to refuse to bake till they received an exorbitant remuneration. Suppose the butchers should enter into a similar combination, and if there be impunity for these,

[6] Reprinted by permission of the publishers from John R. Commons et al. (eds.), *Documentary History of American Industrial Society*, Glendale, Calif.: The Arthur H. Clark Company, 1910–1911, vol. 3, pp. 135–138. Again the correspondence may be noted between this view and that of a modern spokesman of orthodox economic views, Henry Simons, in his *Economic Policy for a Free Society*, p. 122:

What we generally fail to see is the identity of interest between the whole community and enterprises seeking to keep down costs. When enterprise is competitive—and substantial, enduring restraint of competition in product markets is rare—enterprisers represent the community interest effectively; indeed, they are merely intermediaries between consumers of goods and sellers of services. Thus we commonly overlook the conflict of interest between every large organized group of laborers and the community as a whole.

why shall not all other artisans do likewise? What will become of the poor, whose case the counsel so feelingly takes to heart? The rich will, by their money, find supplies; but what will be the sufferings of the poor classes?

Suppose that some rich speculators, acting upon similar principles, should, in a cold winter, combine to purchase up all the wood, and refuse to sell it but at an extravagant advance, should we have no law to protect the poor against such oppression? And would it be argued, that without an express statute the law could furnish no remedy. As such acts would be against the public good, and immoral in a high degree, they would therefore fall under the animadversions of the general law; and as offences against the whole community, be subject to public prosecution.

There are duties which every man owes to the society of which he enjoys the benefits and protection, which never can be detailed, but must be regulated by acknowledged principles of judicature. A baker, therefore, who lives by the supply of the public, shall not abuse that public by a sudden interested and malicious withholding of his ordinary supplies; but though it were otherwise, and that every individual was permitted, as far as in him lay, to distress his fellow-citizens, yet if he combines with others to do so, he is guilty of a distinct and well defined offence, that of an unlawful conspiracy, for which he is indictable and punishable.[7]

The Doctrine of Illegal Purpose

The case of *Commonwealth v. Hunt* [8] in 1842 has often been cited as marking the end of the doctrine of criminal conspiracy. In his decision, Chief Justice Shaw of the Massachusetts Supreme Court, a man of considerable judicial influence, refused to apply it to a bootmakers' union which had been accused of seeking to impose the closed shop. What this case did in fact achieve, however, was simply judicial recognition that group action might have justifiable objectives. In the original trial, Judge Thacher had asserted: "The question is not whether the society [members] have used their power to the extent of mischief of which it is capable but whether they have not assumed a power . . . which in the hands of irresponsible persons is liable to great abuse." Chief Justice Shaw, on appeal, in contrast asserted that abuse—whether actual or intended—must be shown if union action was to be considered unlawful. Important as it was, this single decision did not completely deprive the criminal conspiracy doctrine of vitality, but for the next thirty years there were no significant developments in the law pertaining to collective bargaining.

[7] Reprinted by permission of the publishers from Commons et al., *Documentary History of American Industrial Society,* vol. 3, pp. 313–314.
[8] 4 Metc. 111 (Massachusetts).

Then, beginning in about 1870, opponents of labor began to rely upon civil suits against unions for injunctions and for damages. These almost completely replaced the criminal actions. The old theory of the threat to society by group action was still evident, but in a new format and with Chief Justice Shaw's emendation that the monopoly power of unions does not prima facie indicate abuse. He had declared that it may have justification. The courts now tolerated the activities of organized workers designed to advance their own interests, but with severe qualifications. The activity could not be inimical to public welfare (that is, it had to fit the philosophy of free market competition), and the union could not be involved in the use of force to restrict nonmember workers. Judges quickly enjoined a union or subjected it to claims for damages if its activities did not meet their interpretations of these conditions. Unions dared not damage the employer unless by doing so they furthered their members' immediate advantage; they could not threaten public welfare through what the courts defined as monopoly restraint; and coercing workers to join the union or preventing workers from taking strikers' jobs was forbidden. The new doctrine thus involved little change from the older conspiracy doctrine. It was simply accompanied by different and perhaps more effective judicial remedies.

As is apparent, the legality of a union's bargaining activities turned upon the way in which the courts construed the union's purposes. Some judges were more lenient toward workers' organizations than others. The Massachusetts courts, for example, acquired a reputation for severity, at least when compared with those of New York, but on the whole, court decisions were restrictive of union activities.

In deciding whether a union's purpose was legal or illegal, judges were naturally informed by their own background and training, as any person is in making his judgments. But the union posed problems that were difficult enough for even the most disinterested minds who had to work with legal tools of analysis originally shaped for quite different purposes. It was a relatively novel organization, radical in its challenge to employers and the market. Since the passage of years has not made the solutions to the *same* problems any easier—nor often any more obvious—to disinterested men, we might temper the criticism of our predecessors with charity. Judges, businessmen, and the community at large could hardly be expected to encourage a form of economic and social organization which countered accepted doctrines of individuality and which seemed to threaten society's best interests. From our point of view, their doctrines and social ideas may seem outmoded and mistaken, but for the most part they acted in good faith.

Critics have sometimes charged the courts with preempting the legislators' role, arguing that unions should not have been restricted unless the legislature had so decided. During the nineteenth century, unions posed real social problems and raised novel issues not covered by laws and as yet unexamined by the electorate or their representatives. Until such examination had been made and public policy had been hammered out in free and open debate, the criticism runs, the courts should not have intervened. Since legislatures made virtually no attempt during this period to define the place of unions, except in a few state laws of special application, it is maintained that the courts should have left unions and employers to their own devices. American government is characterized by a separation of powers, with law making and law interpreting assigned to separate and different bodies. The courts were overstepping their limits when they undertook to rule on the legality of unions' purpose and policy. In so doing, they unwisely strayed into the legislative realm of making law.

This criticism of the courts unhappily begs the issue. It emphasizes the laws passed by legislatures and slights the importance of common law, that judge-made law which has been handed down over the years. As Justice Holmes reminded us in a famous phrase, the common law is responsive to the felt needs of the times; it represents, though admittedly imperfectly, the crystallized sentiments of the community about the behavior which may be expected of its citizens in a variety of familiar situations. The common law comes into existence in the form of past court decisions (precedents), but frequently used phrases sometimes take on a vitality of their own. Then, in the form of principles or doctrines, judges and lawyers may apply them to circumstances quite different from those in which they originated. In some instances such application of doctrine serves well, but unless the underlying social relationships are the same, the fitting may be poor indeed. Judges must decide in each case brought before them whether the facts justify application of particular common-law remedies. Only in the event that common-law doctrine is considered *not* pertinent to the facts of a case is the issue a proper one for the legislature rather than the courts.

Deciding whether common law applies or not is seldom an easy matter. Considering the times, judges probably did the best they could. The common law, in line with prevailing political and economic doctrine, clearly condemned restraints by any group less than the state. A person was free to infringe upon the rights and limit the interests of another if he acted in his self-interest through the free, competitive market, but infringements and limitations arising from group action were inadmissible. Thus the courts felt compelled to condemn activities of *organized groups* of workers which infringed the individual rights of *persons*—other workers, employers, and even corporations (which were "persons" by virtue of legal fiction). Moreover, group interference with the workings of the market implicitly threatened the community with higher prices through higher wage costs. Though today we may disavow some particulars of these older beliefs, they once enjoyed (and to some people still enjoy) an apparent reasonableness, and the courts undertook to examine the unions' purposes and procedures in terms of their

conceptions of the proper interests of individuals and society as a whole.
Let us take a single example. From the earliest records of legal actions
against unions, down to our latest labor legislation, the closed shop has
been a thorny issue. Employers have been accused of combating it in order
to reduce the effectiveness of the unions, and without doubt the charge has
considerable justification. But it is also true that the closed shop has been
attacked more generally for its alleged infringement on the "rights" of
individual workers who choose not to be members of the union. Many
citizens of all shades of political and economic faith subscribe to that condemnation today. When nineteenth-century judges held that the closed shop
was illegal and so enjoined strikes to achieve it, one can fairly conclude that
they were seeking to serve more than just class interest and their own
prejudices. There would appear to be reason to believe in the good faith of
such pronouncements as the following:

> We have no desire to put obstacles in the way of employees, who
> are seeking by combination to obtain better conditions for themselves
> and their families. We have no doubt that laboring men have derived
> and may hereafter derive advantages from organization. We only say
> that, under correct rules of law, and with a proper regard for the
> rights of individuals, labor unions cannot be permitted to drive men
> out of employment because they choose to work independently. If
> disagreements between those who furnish the capital and those who
> perform the labor employed in industrial enterprises are to be settled
> only by industrial wars, it would give a great advantage to combina-
> tions of employees, if they could be permitted by force, to obtain a
> monopoly of the labor market. But we are hopeful that this kind of
> warfare soon will give way to industrial peace, and that rational
> methods of settling such controversies will be adopted universally.[9]

Since the closed shop poses the issues of the relationship of individual
and group in a peculiarly striking way, it frequently occupied the attention
of the courts. That they frequently declared it an unlawful objective is not
surprising, for Congress has done the same more recently. In 1947 the Taft-
Hartley Act forbade the closed shop and placed restrictions upon the use of
the union shop, a modified form of the closed shop. The old problem of the
closed shop, now in the form of the union and agency shop, continues to
arise before the courts.[10] Then as now, we seek answers to the perennial
but immediate problem of the rights of individuals and groups in our
society; then as now, we use the courts as a principal instrument for providing us with at least provisional answers.

[9] *Berry v. Donovan*, 188 Mass. 353, 74 N.E. 603 (1905).

[10] For example, *Snavely v. International Harvester*, 39 LRRM 2526 (1957),
and 44 LRRM 2648 (1959); and *Schermerhorn v. Local 1625, Retail Clerks*,
50 LRRM 2055 (1962), and on appeal to the Supreme Court, 53 LRRM 2318
(1963).

As courts came to examine the lawfulness of union purposes, they became the arbiters of what demands a union might make and, to some extent, of what tactics it might employ in collective bargaining. In the words of the Supreme Judicial Court of Massachusetts: "Whether the purpose for which a strike is instituted is or is not a legal justification for it, is a question of law to be decided by the court. To justify interference with the rights of others the strikers must in good faith strike for a purpose which the court decides to be a legal justification for such interference." [11]

For an illustration of the application of this principle, which has sometimes been called the "doctrine of illegal purpose," we may turn to a case in which a theater wished to employ an organist but in which the musicians' union sought through exercise of bargaining power to induce it to employ, instead, a five-man orchestra. The court's opinion reflects the concern of the judges of 100 years earlier, when the conspiracy doctrine had flourished, for the welfare of society in the face of a monopolizing organization:

> If it is legal for a union of musicians to combine for the purpose of forcing a plaintiff (who wants an organist only) to employ an orchestra of several pieces, that is to say, if that indirect purpose of enabling the union musicians to earn more money justifies the adoption of the minimum rule, it is hard to see why it is not legal for a union of carpenters (for example) to refuse to work on a building belonging to the plaintiff unless he uses in the construction of it hand-made doors, window frames and window sashes, in place of doors, window frames and window sashes made by machine. Heretofore it seems to have been assumed that a rule forbidding union members to work on machine-made material in order to get the work of doing it by hand was not a legal combination. . . . There is more money for masons, carpenters and plumbers in building a ten-story store than there is in building a store of two stories. If it is legal for musicians to adopt a minimum rule fixing the number of musicians who shall be employed in all the theaters within its jurisdiction, it is hard to see why a minimum rule may not be adopted by the allied trade unions of masons, carpenters and plumbers fixing the number of stories of which every store to be erected in the business district is to consist. That is to say, masons, carpenters and plumbers may combine to refuse to work on any store less than ten stories in height even though the owner of the land wishes to erect a store of two stories only and even though the owner in his judgment cannot without pecuniary loss erect one having more than two stories. . . . Other illustrations might be put showing the far reaching consequences of a decision upholding the legality of this minimum rule.[12]

[11] *De Minico v. Craig*, 207 Mass. 593, 94 N.E. 317 (1911).
[12] *Haverhill Strand Theatre, Inc., v. Gillen*, 229 Mass. 413, 118 N.E. 671 (1918).

Similarly, when another local of the same union brought pressure upon an operatic society to induce it to substitute "live" music for "canned" music, the court reasoned:

> The self-interest of labor, like the self-interest of any other body, receives immunity only for those objectives which have a legitimate and reasonable relation to lawful benefits which the union is seeking. When the labor objectives are illegal, the courts must control, otherwise there are bodies within our midst which are free from the provisions of the Penal Law. When doubt arises whether the contemplated objective is within the legal sphere, or without and so illegal, it is for the courts to determine. . . .
>
> For a union to insist that machinery be discarded in order that manual labor may take its place and thus secure additional opportunity of employment is not a lawful labor objective. In essence the case at bar is the same as if a labor union should demand of a printing plant that all machinery for typesetting be discarded because it would furnish more employment if the typesetting were done by hand. We have held that the attempt of a union to coerce the owner of a small business, who was running the same without an employee, to make employment for an employee, was an unlawful objective and that this did not involve a labor dispute. (*Thompson v. Boekhout,* 273 N.Y. 390.) So, too, in a case just unanimously decided, we held that it was an unlawful labor objective to attempt to coerce a peddler employing no employees in his business and making approximately thirty-two dollars a week, to hire an employee at nine dollars a day for one day a week. (*Wohl v. Bakery & Pastry Drivers Union,* 284 N.Y. 788.) [13]

This position of the courts involved them in a difficulty. As one court pointed out, in a case where the union was being attacked for its adherence to the closed shop, a single individual has the right "to refuse to work for another on any ground that he may regard as sufficient, and the employer has no right to demand a reason for it." The court then continued:

> The same rule applies to a body of men who, having organized for purposes deemed beneficial to themselves, refuse to work. Their reasons may seem inadequate to others, but if it seems to be in their interest as members of an organization to refuse longer to work, it is their legal right to stop. The reason may no more be demanded, as a right, of the organization than of an individual, but if they elect to state the reason their right to stop work is not cut off because the reason seems inadequate or selfish to the employer or to organized society. And if the conduct of the members of an organization is legal *in itself,* it does not become illegal because the organization directs

[13] *Opera on Tour v. Weber,* 285 N.Y. 348, 34 N.E. 2d 349 (1941).

one of its members to state the reason for its conduct. [Italics supplied.] [14]

According to this view, it is lawful for individuals to cease working for an employer, whether they do so individually or jointly, without explaining why they have done so. No court would find them guilty of any offense for such an action considered by itself. If, while undertaking such (lawful) action, the workers choose to state why they are doing so, that is their affair and adds nothing to their guilt or innocence. That is to say, motive or purpose is immaterial if the action itself is legal. This doctrine did not in earlier years win, nor has it yet won, widespread acceptance, however. It is difficult for courts to ignore the objective behind an action complained of.

The confusion, ambiguities, and inconsistencies surrounding the law of union action throughout this period can perhaps be better understood if we think of the courts as one instrument of society's adjusting to changed social conditions. American industrial society was in the process of rapid and thoroughgoing change.

From the days of conspiracy doctrine in the early 1800s until the end of the century, markets expanded, manufacturers increasingly turned to specialization of production and adopted the use of interchangeable parts, business firms grew enormously in size, technological innovations swept across the nation, the country recklessly exploited its natural resources, and the population increased sixteenfold. All these changes contributed their own special problems, and each required readjustments in social attitudes and patterns of behavior. One of the most evident aspects of the changes was the spread of "combinations" and group actions. Justice Holmes, speaking in dissent from the Massachusetts Supreme Court, had pointed out in 1896 that "the organization of the world, now going on so fast, means an ever increasing might and scope of combination. It seems to me futile to set our faces against this tendency." [15]

The spread of group action, as a response to altered social and economic conditions, did bring changes in the judgments of the courts and legislatures. Technological, managerial, and financial necessities made the combination of business desirable and perhaps even imperative. With some adjustment of view but little change in values, courts were able to stay within the bounds of their legal and economic concepts by pretending that a corporation was not a group of stockholders but a person. For many years, then, a single worker stood in law equal to a corporation, however vast its resources. Since in the contemplation of the law both a worker and a corporation were persons, the courts saw collective bargaining as a process

[14] *National Protective Association v. Cumming,* 170 N.Y. 315, 63 N.E. 369 (1902).
[15] *Vegelahn v. Guntner,* 167 Mass. 92, 44 N.E. 1077 (1896).

by which a *group* of persons (the union) confronted a *single* person (the corporation). Formally, the collectivity of workers' groups was more threatening to trade and individual freedom than the collectivity of the corporate "person." Until the legislators, and later the courts, recognized and took better into account the group nature of corporations as well as of unions, the activities of organized workers were more severely restricted than those of corporations.

Congress attempted to deal with the reality of which Holmes had spoken: the combination movement in the rapidly changing economic environment. It passed the Sherman Anti-Trust Act in 1890 and the Clayton Act in 1914. Although the primary stimulus for these laws arose from a widespread public concern over the monopoly powers of business trusts, the courts applied their restrictions chiefly to unions for some time, partly as a result of the formal legal analysis mentioned above. The Supreme Court decisions interpreting the acts were uniformly unfavorable to unions and restrictive of their activities until 1940.

The history of the law of collective bargaining from the cordwainers case in 1806 to the beginning of the Great Depression may be summarized briefly by saying that the bargaining process had established itself in this country free of any taint of illegality because of its nature. The combination of employees into unions for the purpose of negotiating an agreement with employers and management was not itself unlawful. However, if in the course of negotiations unions employed coercive tactics to strengthen their bargaining position—strikes, boycotts, picketing—and the employer against whom such tactics were directed complained to the court, the court would investigate to determine whether the tactics themselves or the purpose for which they were being employed constituted intimidation of nonunion workmen or otherwise amounted to group infringement of individual rights or raised what the court conceived to be a monopolistic threat to the general interests of society. These concerns, as we have noted, coincided with the special interests of the business community. Until recent years, therefore, the bargaining process was available to unions, but its use for specific purposes and the tactics designed to augment union bargaining power had to be justified before the courts.

The Entrance of the Federal Government

The passage of the Norris–La Guardia Anti-injunction Act in 1932 [16] brought about a fundamental change in the law of union-management rela-

[16] Actually the Railway Labor Act of 1926 might be considered an earliei manifestation of this change, but that act applied to only one segment of the labor movement, while the later legislation was more comprehensive in its coverage.

tions. The act removed the power of federal courts to enjoin virtually the whole range of union coercive activity not involving fraud or violence, except under severely limited conditions. The language of Section 2 of the act warrants notice:

> Whereas under prevailing economic conditions, developed with the aid of governmental authority for owners of property to organize in the corporate and other forms of ownership association, the individual unorganized worker is commonly helpless to exercise actual liberty of contract and to protect his freedom of labor, and thereby to obtain acceptable terms and conditions of employment, wherefore, though he should be free to decline to associate with his fellows, it is necessary that he have full freedom of association, self-organization, and designation of representatives of his own choosing, to negotiate the terms and conditions of his employment, and that he shall be free from the interference, restraint, or coercion of employers of labor, or their agents, in the designation of such representatives or in self-organization or in other concerted activities for the purpose of collective bargaining or other mutual aid or protection; therefore, the following definitions of, and limitations upon, the jurisdiction and authority of the courts of the United States are hereby enacted.[17]

Note that this legislation placed no obligations upon employers. Although it championed the rights of employees to organize and protected the concerted action of unions in striking, picketing, and boycotting, it did so only by clarifying for the federal judiciary formerly disputed common-law propositions about the role of unions in society. This act was followed by similar legislation in a number of the industrialized states. Where such legislation existed, the unions were allowed to employ virtually the full arsenal of their coercive tactics in support of their bargaining demands as long as they avoided fraud and violence.

The National Industrial Recovery Act of 1933 in its Section 7 (a) went a step further. It provided that all the so-called "codes of fair competition" must contain a clause in which employers guaranteed not to interfere with, restrain, or coerce employees who sought to organize for bargaining purposes. The enforcement of the pledge was relatively ineffective, for the intent was to place collective bargaining on a voluntary basis. Unions were to be free to seek concessions from employers, and employers were to be free to reject union demands. Agreement was to be forthcoming, if at all, as a result of negotiation backed by bargaining power.

Of course, under the federal and state anti-injunction acts, unions could use all their coercive weapons. Notably lacking, however, was any compulsion upon the employer to recognize the union or bargain with it. If the

[17] 47 Stat. 70 (1932).

employer was strong enough to resist the pressure of the union, he remained free to pursue his independent path, ignoring as best he could the union's very existence. If he wished, he might encourage and support the formation of a company union in an effort to distract the interest of his employees from a national union. Unions were entitled to an existence unobstructed by law, but their recognition and advancement were to come through their own efforts. Only later did NIRA labor boards administratively decide that Section 7(a) obligated an employer to recognize and bargain with the union. The decisions remained largely unenforceable, though.

Although Section 7(a) was regarded by many as a radical step forward, the National Labor Relations (Wagner) Act marked the complete break with the past. It declared that the policy of the United States was to "[encourage] the practice and procedure of collective bargaining. . . ."

The Wagner Act spelled out what the National Industrial Recovery Act was able to suggest only by administrative construction: the obligation of an employer to bargain with a union designated as exclusive representative of the employees in a given unit. The unit was to be defined by the National Labor Relations Board, and the selection of representative was to be accomplished by majority decision of the interested employees. Moreover, the Wagner Act provided the remedial penalties which the NIRA had lacked. The federal courts were to enforce Board orders, the violation of which subjected employers to punishment for contempt of court.

This was a sweeping change in the law of collective bargaining, and we sometimes overlook its epochal nature. Not more than five years earlier, the attempt by unions to back up bargaining demands by strike, picketing, or boycott was subject to judicial restraint. Judges had had free reign in restraining unions and providing employers with injunction relief if they found union objectives to be inimical to social welfare (as legally construed) or if they regarded union efforts as unduly impinging upon the independence of other workers.

The new legislation made the actions of the majority of workers legally controlling over a minority, specifically sanctioned the closed shop, and placed employers under a legal obligation to recognize and bargain in good faith with certified unions. The earlier Norris–La Guardia Act had weakened, although not removed, the injunctive authority of most courts with respect to the tactics employed by unions. Thus, within the space of five years, there had jelled into law the conviction that unions were a desirable social force, the workers' "alternative to serfdom," [18] as a well-known economist was later to call them. Under law, workers were entitled to an organized, protected voice in the determination of the conditions under

[18] John M. Clark, *Alternative to Serfdom,* New York: Alfred A. Knopf, Inc., 1948, p. 122.

which they were to work. For the first time in American history, collective bargaining was enforced as a matter of public policy.[19]

It is impossible here to review the social, economic, and political setting which gave rise to the Wagner Act, but we may recall the impact of the Great Depression and the popular support of the New Deal reform program as forces that helped bring about a restatement of the law of collective bargaining. The troubling experiences of the thirties led to a redefinition of the roles of groups and individuals in a society in which the organization and the group rather than the individual seemed controlling. The thesis on which the Wagner Act rested was stated in congressional debate by the man whose name the act bears: "Caught in the labyrinth of modern industrialism and dwarfed by the size of corporate enterprise, he [the worker] can attain freedom and dignity only by cooperation with others of his group." [20] However, to conclude that such a conception rose suddenly as a vision would be a mistake. It had been in the making for many years. In the courts it had received explicit expression at least as early as Holmes' Massachusetts dissent in *Vegelahn v. Guntner*. The minority view had been growing, and the economic catastrophe of the thirties transformed it into a majority view. After 1932, the laws defining the rights of individual, group, and government had to be changed, and there was a shift of emphasis from individual initiative to group and state initiative. The effect of this realignment remained open to debate, but its reality could scarcely be questioned.

The significance of the Wagner Act to the role of unionism and collective bargaining in American society is highlighted by contrasting the requirement concerning employers' conduct under the new law with the permissible scope of their actions toward unions prior to 1932. Whereas unions previously not only could be ignored but also could be fought, their recognition was now required when representing a majority of employees, and intimidatory action by employers was made illegal. Whereas previously an employer was under no obligation even to sit down with a union committee, he was now obligated to negotiate in a good-faith attempt to reach an agreement, which had to be put into writing upon request by the union. Whereas previously unions were thrown upon their own resources, union activity was now protected by the federal government. Whereas previously unilateral imposition of disadvantageous terms by one party on the other had been legal and, as we saw in earlier chapters, was commonly practiced, the unilateral conferring of advantage was now considered unlawful, as a denial of good-faith bargaining.

---

[19] The Supreme Court upheld the constitutionality of the Wagner Act in *NLRB v. Jones & Laughlin Steel Corp.*, 301 U.S. 1 (1937).

[20] *Congressional Record*, May 15, 1932, p. 7565.

Problems of Adjustment to the Wagner Act

Employers and union men had difficulty adjusting to the new situation. It is a remarkable testimony to the adjustive powers of American society that so sweeping a change in social relations could have been so successfully accomplished within so short a space of time, despite the resentment of employers and the heady emotions of unionists which it evoked. Continuing violations of the new requirements by specific employers provide little grounds for modifying such a conclusion. In part they represent simply one aspect of the process of adjustment: an immediate unwillingness of some to accept the change at its face value or to believe in its permanence, and in other cases a misunderstanding of new obligations.

However successfully the transition was made, it was in many respects a most painful one. Zealots on both sides were not averse to using violence. The organizing of strikes in automobiles, steel, rubber, and other large-scale industries precipitated mutual resentment and recrimination which died slowly. Many, if not most, managers regarded the National Labor Relations Act as the worst of the New Deal legislation. The background of violence and melodrama was caught by *Fortune* magazine in an article which sought to present an objective portrait of the act and the Board administering it at this time. Illustrative of the conflict between unions and management on which the peaceful processes of the Board had sometimes to be superimposed was this testimony of a witness of a 1937 Michigan labor riot, as reproduced in the *Fortune* article:

> Mr. —— [a member of the general executive board of his union] was attacked by four or five men who kicked him in the general region of his stomach and plugged him from the rear . . . and he was finally forced to the cement over to my left and there a separate individual grabbed him by each foot and by each hand, and his legs were spread apart and his body was twisted over toward the east, and then other men proceeded to kick him in the crotch and groin and left kidneys and around the head and also to gore him with their heels in the abdomen. . . . [And later] . . . the girls were at a loss to know apparently what to do, and then one girl near me was kicked in the stomach and vomited at my feet. . . . I stayed there until practically all the literature had been gathered from the ground and until the girls had been pushed back on the trolley and the trolley had gone and it became very quiet around there and relatively still.[21]

Although violence of this order can scarcely be considered representative, the accompanying bitterness of feeling between the parties was prevalent. It was a period when shifts in social, economic, and political relationships

[21] "The G—— D—— Labor Board," *Fortune,* October, 1938, p. 115.

were occurring swiftly and were deeply, sensitively, and quickly felt. The adjustments called for were profound.

In attempting to describe the magnitude of the changes to which employers had to adjust, Professor Bakke has said:

> It is not an exaggeration to say that when collective bargaining became a part of operations of a company managerial methods underwent a revolution greater than would have been the case if those companies had been nationalized. That revolution, to define it very briefly but adequately, was this. Company managers became virtually *co*-managers with labor leaders in limited but expanding areas where they were formerly *solo* managers, in setting a whole set of high level and general company policies in those areas and in the detailed execution of those policies. And the labor leader "co-manager" was not accountable to the same higher authority who held the company manager responsible for the results of his decisions and acts. Anyone who thinks that the shift from a single line managership to this type of virtual co-managership didn't involve a revolution in the methods of organizational decision making and operations is either blind or uninformed.[22]

Remembering this setting, we may gain some appreciation of the impact of the National Labor Relations Act upon the bargaining process by considering a federal circuit court's review of a Board decision charging an employer with having refused to bargain collectively in good faith. Chief Justice Garrecht, of the Ninth Circuit Court, delivered this opinion, in which he explores the type of relationship which the act calls for between the Montgomery Ward Company and two unions, the Retail Clerks International Protective Association, Local 1257, and the Warehousemen's Union, Local 206, both of Portland, Oregon, and both affiliated with the American Federation of Labor.

> [The] Clerks began organizing Wards' retail employees in February or March, 1940, and by August 6 of that year claimed a majority of Wards' retail clerks, which claim apparently was accepted by Wards, and is not disputed. The Warehousemen was certified by the Board on August 10, 1940, as the proper and exclusive bargaining representative of the unit of Wards' warehouse employees. Wards, through its West coast labor representative, W. B. Powell (assisted at times by the manager of the Portland retail store and the manager of the mail order house), engaged in bargaining conferences with Clerks on September 19, and October 22, 1940; with Warehousemen on November 12, 1940; and in a joint conference with both Clerks and Warehousemen on November 25, 1940. Subsequent to the com-

[22] E. Wight Bakke, "Mutual Survival after Twelve Years," *Proceedings of the Industrial Relations Research Association*, December, 1958, pp. 10–11.

mencement of the strike further conferences were conducted for the avowed purpose of negotiating agreements. Prior to the first conferences each union submitted to Wards a proposed written contract. No stenographic transcript was taken of the discussions at the conferences, due to objection by Wards, but there is no substantial conflict in the testimony respecting what transpired at these meetings. In advancing a reason for his objection thereto Wards' representative suggested that the taking of a stenographic transcript would impair the flexibility of the discussions. At no time did Wards offer in writing any proposed contracts to which it would agree, or offer any written counter proposals. Wards' representative took the position that Wards was seeking nothing from the unions and that the unions were obliged to submit to it contracts with which it would agree.

In general outline, the conferences proceeded with a reading of the unions' proposed contracts, article by article or section by section, to which Wards' representative would reply and state the company's position or objection. On some occasions the union representative would comment respecting the objections, but on others the article or section was simply passed and the next article or section read. The unions did not present or propose new written contracts following the conferences, but at such meeting presented the contracts originally proposed notwithstanding knowledge of the company's objection to certain sections. . . .

There were four major obstacles upon which the conferences reached an impasse: (1) Union or closed shop; (2) increased wages; (3) seniority; and (4) arbitration. In the contract proposed by each union there was a clause which provided, substantially, that the company either would give preference to employment of unemployed union members, or that if non-members were employed they must make application within a specified time for membership in the particular union. Each of the proposed contracts contained a section relative to seniority—that is, that in slack seasons or in the event of lack of work, lay-offs and rehiring should be on the basis of seniority, those with the greater length of service should be laid off later than those with lesser periods of service and that rehiring should be made in the inverse order. Also, each of the proposed contracts made provision for wage increases applicable to the various classifications of employees within the several bargaining units. In addition, the contracts proposed by each of the three unions provided for arbitration of disputes by a "Board of Adjustment," which would have the power to decide questions respecting the meaning or enforcement of the proposed agreement and to settle disputes arising out of discharge of an employee where such employee alleges the discharge to be unjust, and to settle disputes on other questions concerning the contracts. . . .

None of the "bargainers" exhibited any intention to, nor did any of them, recede from the original position taken, until December 13, 14, and 16, 1940, at meetings presided over by one Ashe, a conciliator of the United States Department of Labor, when the unions appeared to waver. At the December 13 conference, counsel for the unions asked Powell, Wards' representative, whether Wards would be willing to arbitrate "the question of what clauses should be included in the contract" if the unions should withdraw their request for a "union shop." The reply was in the negative. The unions then made further proposals for arbitration and concluded with a request to Powell that the company take up the proposed contracts, section by section, and write them out and delete from, and add to, the proposed sections as it desired. Powell replied that it was up to the unions to make proposals which would please the company; that the company had no affirmative duty to do anything. On the following day Wards' representative was asked if the company would be willing to sign an agreement which merely set out its present policies and practices. Powell replied that the question of the form of agreement—verbal or written—was premature at the time; that if an agreement could be reached upon substantial provisions, that question should then be considered. In answer to a question whether Wards would sign an agreement Powell replied that discussion on the question was premature. Obviously, the primary question asked Powell remained unanswered. Neither did Wards change its attitude on the occasion of the last meeting, December 16, 1940; it took the same position as always upon the principal points of dispute. . . .

It appears from the findings of the Board that Wards never, at any time in the course of the negotiations, directly promised to sign a written contract, although its representative was asked on several occasions whether or not he would do so. Always the reply was that the question was "premature," that it had best be answered when agreement was reached. Considering as immaterial the fact that the "parties had not yet reached complete understanding," the Board concluded that this type of answer "was tantamount to a refusal to bargain altogether." Certainly, the answer was evasive and not calculated to reveal whether or not the Company would sign an agreement if any was reached, and may well have had a discouraging influence. . . . We believe the Board was entitled to consider the failure of Wards to state that it would put into writing any contract to which it might agree as a pertinent circumstance on the issue of refusal to bargain. *Hartsell Mills Co. v. N.L.R.B.,* 4 Cir., 111 F. 2d 291, 292.

The Board regarded as an additional factor in a design to refuse to bargain the action of Wards' representative respecting a provision of the proposed contracts. The proposed contracts contained provisions that if the employees were worked in excess of five hours without a meal period, the excess time should be paid for at the overtime rate. Wards' representative insisted that the word "five" be changed to "six" to conform to existing practice. The record reveals, however, that he had been advised by his superior at the home office that "under normal conditions an employee should not be worked more than five consecutive hours without a meal period." Not even Wards doubted the reasonableness of such a demand; nevertheless Powell, its representative, stood firm. No court in the land could hold that the Board was not justified in drawing an inference unfavorable to Wards from its conduct respecting this provision. A reasonable man might conclude that it refused to agree to this provision because it had no intention of entering into a contract, or of binding itself at all. . . .

A further circumstance which supports the Board in drawing the inference that Wards was "stalling," arose out of the conference of November 25, between Wards and Warehousemen. At this meeting Estabrook, secretary for Warehousemen, suggested that he would fly to Chicago for a conference with Barr, Powell's superior, in an effort to induce Wards to change its policy respecting "union shop." Powell's report of this discussion is contained in his letter of November 26, addressed to Barr, and which reads in part as follows: ". . . Mr. Estabrook then suggested he would be glad to fly to Chicago to talk with you, if there were some possibility that our policy could be changed. At first they insisted we give them a reply within twenty-four hours, but later agreed to allow us until noon on Thursday, November 28. *I will wait until Thursday morning at which time I will call Mr. White* [a union representative] in San Francisco and explain that you will be glad to meet with union representatives in Chicago and listen to their argument. . . ." [Italics supplied.]

From this it appears that Powell *knew* on the 25th, or, at the latest, the 26th, what his answer was going to be, and deliberately refrained from informing White until the 28th—and this in face of the union's desire for an immediate answer. Unquestionably the Board was privileged to draw from these delaying tactics an inference unfavorable to Wards' "good faith" in the negotiations. . . .

The incidents just discussed, while, perhaps, not controlling in and of themselves, in cumulative effect give impetus and decisiveness to the Board's conclusions. They are simply manifestations of an attitude—intent, if you will—persisted in by Wards, a negative attitude which amounted to, in its result, a refusal to bargain. In its brief, Wards says, "The duty [to bargain] is to do nothing or say nothing which would make agreement on those terms [mutually acceptable] impossible." This is not a carrying of the burden of the duty to bargain, for, in effect, it means to do nothing or say nothing to make agreement possible. Throughout the conferences there is apparent a studied design of aloofness, of disinterestedness, of unwillingness to go forward, upon the part of Wards, which found its answer in the Board's conclusion of refusal to bargain.

Wards' conduct throughout the conferences was an all too literal adherence to the rule formulated by itself as a fulfillment of the duty to bargain collectively: "to participate in such discussion as is necessary to avoid mutual misunderstanding." To do this and nothing more is to fall far short of the accomplishment of the statutory duty to bargain collectively, because the affirmative efforts of both parties are required—there must be, in a real sense, active cooperation. . . . In *Singer Mfg. Co. v. N.L.R.B.,* 7 Cir., 119 F. 2d 131, 143, the court said: ". . . The greatest of rascals may solemnly affirm his honesty of purpose; that does not foreclose a jury from finding from the evidence submitted that he possesses no trace of such innocent quality. We think the Board had full authority to determine as a fact whether petitioner was acting in good faith or whether its actions amounted to a mere superficial pretense at bargaining,—whether it had actually the intent to bargain, sincerely and earnestly,—whether the negotiations were captious and accompanied by an active purpose and intent to defeat or obstruct real bargaining. [Cases cited.] "

We have, in our discussion, purposely refrained from commenting upon the four major points of the proposed contracts because we believe these questions must be discussed in future negotiations and we desire to leave the parties free to meet them without undue restriction. . . .

The order of the Board will be enforced.[23]

New Laws—Old Concerns

Neither the Taft-Hartley Act of 1947 nor the Landrum-Griffin Act of 1959 reversed the principle of public protection of collective bargaining, on which the above decision was based. In the historical perspective of the government's continuing definition of the rights of individuals, groups, and the public, these two pieces of legislation asserted that although unions are essential in an industrial society, they must not unduly impinge upon the rights of individuals and the public.

Passage of the Taft-Hartley Act (the Labor-Management Relations Act of 1947) was a reaction to the wave of postwar strikes. Between 1945 and the 1947 enactment, the country experienced industry-wide strikes in coal mining, oil refining, lumber, textiles, maritime industries, and rail transportation; multifirm strikes in glass, automobiles, and electrical manufacturing; and general strikes in Rochester, New York, and Oakland, California, along with a statewide walkout by unions in Iowa. The strikes exasperated the general public, which blamed them for delaying the production of consumers' goods then greatly in demand after the wartime shortages. They also alarmed many people because they threatened essential services. These strikes were widely viewed as examples of the concentration of economic power in the hands of a few union leaders. Strong feelings existed and were expressed that such men should not have the power to shut off a city's electricity, to close down the country's coal mines, to force the banking of all blast furnaces, or to stop the vital operations of all railroads across the nation.

[23] *NLRB v. Montgomery Ward & Company; Montgomery Ward & Company v. NLRB,* 133 F. 2d 676 (1943), *affirming* 37 NLRB 100 (1941).

Congress passed the Landrum-Griffin Act (Labor-Management Reporting and Disclosure Act of 1959) in the wake of extended investigations which had revealed a sordid picture of corruption and unethical behavior among some unions and employers and a dismaying lack of democratic procedures within some unions. The AFL–CIO had attempted to deal with the problem by promulgating a code of ethics for all unions and by expelling a number of unions, among them the large and powerful Teamsters union. A few unions had also responded to the disclosures by setting up independent review boards to whom members could appeal for protection of their rights as members, but the unions that most needed to improve made few, if any, changes, choosing to ignore public outcry and congressional denouncements. Again, as had happened twelve years earlier, sentiment emerged for legislation to protect the rights of individual workers and the public and to curb the power of union leaders.

The Taft-Hartley Act allowed the government greater power to curb union "unfair labor practices" and to intervene in strikes threatening national welfare; the Landrum-Griffin Act extended government regulation of the internal affairs of unions, established a "bill of rights" for members, and defined more carefully some unfair labor practices. The sentiment for thus curbing union power and fostering greater individual "freedom" from the union was one on which business groups in conflict with the unions could and did capitalize. However, unless one is willing to consider the congressional majorities—and they were substantial in both cases—to be nothing more than the tool of special interests, one must recognize that the acts manifest the same concern shown earlier by the courts when they first propounded the conspiracy and illegal purposes doctrines.

The desirability of all the provisions of the 1947 and 1959 acts is debatable, of course. The wisdom, indeed necessity, of continuing to redefine the respective rights of individuals, groups, and government is not so open to question. As they have in the past, legislators and judges will review and revise these rights in the future. As a result of the redefining, different interest groups will profit and suffer, and they will support or attack the legal adjustments accordingly. At times the groups will even be influential enough to hold up or hasten the changes, but their special interests are not the only ones influencing legislation and court decisions. To explain our law as nothing but the product of dominant groups is as cynically naïve as to argue that law represents only the general welfare is unsophisticatedly optimistic. To regard changes in labor law as revealing simply whether unions or management has the upper hand at the moment is to miss the central theme of changing conceptions of social relationships, which gives meaning to the law. Even dominant groups must recognize and employ social sentiments if they are to retain their favorable position.

The Encouragement and Regulation of Collective Bargaining

When public policy as expressed in the Wagner Act moved beyond the laissez-faire approach of the Norris–La Guardia Act to the actual encouragement of unions and the enforcement of collective bargaining, some radically new issues faced the federal government: What was it that was to be enforced, and how was enforcement to be achieved? Heretofore, except for a short time at the end of World War I, employers and union leaders had been left free to engage in and define collective bargaining as they saw fit. Neither legislators nor judges had ever tried positively to define the process of collective bargaining, even though the courts had certainly intervened in this process.

In the past, intervention had been in the form of a negative regulation, a decision on whether the demands and purposes for which unions bargained were lawful. Time and again state judges had held the closed shop to be an unlawful demand which unions could not legitimately seek through collective bargaining. The courts had also limited collective bargaining when unions sought such ends as protection from technological change, maintenance of jurisdiction, the removal of foremen who discriminated against union members, and penalties for contracting out work which their members had previously performed. The Wagner Act constituted a radical departure from such repressive concern with collective bargaining.

Government Insistence upon Collective Bargaining

Whereas before, the government had intervened through its judicial organs in a way that favored employers by restricting union demands and activities and protected employers' defense of their property, now (by legislation) it explicitly favored unions and limited the rights and actions of employers. Public policy was now aligned behind collective protection of individual liberty as a matter of public interest, as the preamble to the Wagner Act clearly indicates:

> Section 1. The denial by employers of the right of employees to organize and the refusal by employers to accept the procedure of collective bargaining lead to strikes and other forms of industrial strife and unrest, which have the intent or the necessary effect of burdening or obstructing commerce. . . . The inequality of bargaining power between employees who do not possess full freedom of association or actual liberty of contract, and employers who are organized in the corporate or other forms of ownership association substantially burdens and affects the flow of commerce, and tends to aggravate recurrent business depressions by depressing wage rates and the purchasing power of wage earners in industry and by preventing the stabilization of competitive wage rates and working conditions within and between industries.
>
> Experience has proved that protection by law of the right of employees to organize and bargain collectively safeguards commerce from injury, impairment, or interruption, and promotes the flow of commerce by removing certain recognized sources of industrial strife and unrest, by encouraging practices fundamental to the friendly adjustments of industrial disputes arising out of differences as to wages, hours, or other working conditions, and by restoring equality of bargaining power between employers and employees.
>
> It is hereby declared to be the policy of the United States to eliminate the causes of certain substantial obstructions to the free flow of commerce and to mitigate and eliminate these obstructions when they have occurred by encouraging the practice and procedure of collective bargaining and by protecting the exercise by workers of full freedom of association, self-organization, and designation of representatives of their own choosing, for the purpose of negotiating the terms and conditions of their employment or other mutual aid or protection.[1]

[1] 47 Stat. 449 (1935). Compare the language here with that of the Norris–La Guardia Act, quoted in the preceding chapter. Here the act promises to *encourage* and *protect;* in the earlier act, Congress sought merely to free unions from limitations imposed by courts.

By 1935 Congress was preoccupied not with the power of unions and the limits to collective bargaining but with the weakness of unions and the survival of collective bargaining. The Wagner Act benefited unions, but it was not so much an instrument to further the interests of labor, though it accomplished this, as it was a pragmatic reponse of Congress to the challenge of an urban industrial economy in distress. The conditions of the mid-thirties under which workers might enjoy the rights and the public interest might be served were not those of the late nineteenth and earlier twentieth centuries, and both courts and legislature recognized the changes that had taken place.

That government might intervene to help unions and workers as once it had helped business and employers was a natural development, to be expected in a democracy. As the impact of group power upon individuals and the public changes, the law is changed accordingly. That the government would become involved in defining and regulating collective bargaining (in distinction to simply protecting the unions' right to exist) was probably not, however, an expectation of those who supported the Wagner Act.

At least two serious efforts had already been made to gain business' voluntary acceptance of unions and collective bargaining, but each had failed. Under the leadership of Mark Hanna and Samuel Gompers and with such outstanding public representatives as August Belmont, Grover Cleveland, and Charles W. Eliot, the National Civic Association attempted, at the turn of the century, to develop more peaceful industrial relations by promoting collective bargaining agreements and voluntary machinery for mediating and arbitrating labor disputes. Though the NCA had aroused some interest and gained some influence in twenty-two states by 1905, the NAM's antiunion attack upon the closed shop and vigorous promotion of the "open shop" (really a nonunion closed shop) proved much more congenial to American businessmen generally.

In 1919 President Wilson called a tripartite National Industrial Conference to evaluate collective bargaining and union representation as they had been carried on during the war. The employers would not agree, however, to continue to recognize the right of workers to be represented by national union leaders, and the conference broke up. Even against the urging of outstanding public-minded businessmen, influential employers rejected any voluntary recognition of, or dealings with, unions. In the same year, just before the great steel strike, John D. Rockefeller, Jr., had urged Henry Clay Frick and Judge Elbert Gary, the two most influential men in U.S. Steel, to consider collective bargaining or, at least, employee representation. They refused, Gary objecting that "representation of any kind . . . is only the entering wedge to the closed shop, which . . . is fatal to business." [2] The following year, Herbert Hoover also called upon a number of business

[2] Irving Bernstein, *The Lean Years,* Boston: Houghton Mifflin Company, 1960, p. 147.

leaders in such citadels of capitalism as Standard Oil of New Jersey, United States Rubber, and General Electric to ask them to consider establishing some liaison with unions and their leaders. They gave cool and distant consideration to the suggestion and, along with the managers of most other large companies, elected to fight unions with the open shop "American plan." [3]

A dozen years later, business managers still opposed recognition of unions and the practice of collective bargaining as firmly as ever. With passage of the Norris–La Guardia Act in 1932, unions were freed from most of the restrictive injunctive powers of the courts; their coercive tactics used to promote worker and union interests were given an equality with the tactics of businessmen to limit those same interests. This hands-off approach of the government did not encourage business to accept unions, though. It only fostered increased conflict and more bitter clashes between resisting managers and workers trying to organize. Even Section 7(a) of the National Industrial Recovery Act did not persuade American management that it should voluntarily accept collective bargaining with unions of the workers' choice. It did lead to a widespread development of company unionism, which in time might have led to a voluntary acceptance of independent unions and real collective bargaining, but the pressures of 1935 could not be put off. In the caldron of discontent that was fired by the Great Depression, social change boiled rather than simmered, and the government moved quickly from lifting legal restraints upon union activities, to approval of union organization, and then to the enforcement of collective bargaining.

To enforce the new government policy, Congress established the National Labor Relations Board. Employees were granted the right to organize and bargain collectively through representatives of their own choosing in elections conducted by the Board, and the Board was to prevent employers from engaging in unfair labor practices that would interfere with the exercise of those rights.

One might reasonably assume that much of the work of the Board would become unnecessary as employers came to accept unions and collective bargaining. Such has not yet been the case, after three decades, despite the growth of unions throughout major industries and an elaboration of collective bargaining. Acceptance of unions in one industry has not necessarily induced acceptance in another, and employers who have not bargained with unions show a tendency to view collective bargaining as an alien and threatening ideology rather than a pragmatic, democratic means of resolving industrial problems. Acceptance of collective bargaining may now be so well established in large areas of American industry that government en-

[3] The same.

couragement and protection of it are not needed, but the acceptance is often only in those areas where it has become familiar. Employers who have bargained regularly with production workers, for example, greet the organizing of white-collar workers with something less than graciousness. They frequently are as adamant in bargaining with the newly organized white-collar production workers of the sixties as they were with workers organized in the thirties. Thus the Board still maintains a heavy case load of representation hearings and elections and continues to rule against unfair labor practices by which employers try to discourage and hamper union organization and bargaining.[4]

However much employers may object to collective bargaining or whatever their resistance to the organizing efforts of unions, since the passage of the Wagner Act they have been under a legal obligation to recognize a union certified by the NLRB as the exclusive representative of the work-

[4] Mr. Boyd Leedom, a recent NLRB chairman, expressed his concern over employers' persisting opposition to unions and bargaining in 1959 in "Aspects of Government Regulation and Union Responsibility," a speech before the Industrial Relations Center Labor Conference, University of Minnesota, Minneapolis, February 27, 1959.

> While it is the official position of management to support the concept of collective bargaining by employees, great segments of employers, as evidenced by case after case coming before us involving union elections in the business and industrial plants of the country, take every legal step possible—and many employers overreach legality—to thwart their employees' efforts to organize even when the Union involved is a respectable, decent union. And some employers harbor the thought, I am sure, that there is no such thing as a decent union unless it might be one dominated by their own companies. . . .
>
> Few employers in this enlightened age openly admit that they would, even if they could, completely thwart unionism. Today, however, I want to look behind this façade of general acceptance of our national labor concept and to reach a behind-the-scenes, illusive, undeclared warfare that I believe involves an actual rejection by much of management of these basic principles. Since hostility is likely to beget hostility, I raise the question as to whether this attitude may in turn be at least partly responsible for union conduct that many people regard as quite unreasonable even though lawful. It is quibbling to embrace the abstract principle of collective bargaining and then fight tooth and nail to deny it to one's own employees. When our businesses and industries of common characteristics seem to find it good and necessary to join together to solve their common problems and advance their common purposes, and delegate all sorts of specialized functions to agents of their choice, it seems difficult to find a valid objection to workers' concerted action through agents of their choice.

ers. They have been similarly obligated to bargain in good faith with that union, although they and the unions are to be free to determine autonomously the scope and nature of collective bargaining. Bargaining freedom is a principle which almost all concerned agreed should be preserved unimpaired. Nevertheless, in a number of ways the Board came to influence the approach to, and the tactics and results of, collective bargaining.

The Influence of the NLRB upon Collective Bargaining

During the twelve years of the Wagner Act, the Board's indirect influence upon collective bargaining was probably more important than its direct influence. In carrying out the provisions of Section 9(b), to "decide . . . the unit appropriate for the purposes of collective bargaining . . . [whether] employer unit, craft unit, plant unit, or subdivision thereof," the Board was in a position to affect the structure of collective bargaining.

It is doubtful whether the framers of the act expected the Board to have much difficulty in choosing the appropriate units. The AFL had long been the jealous guardian of union jurisdictional lines and could have been expected in July, 1935, when the act was passed, to have worked out appropriate bargaining units with little intervention by the Board. Five months after passage of the Wagner Act, though, the AFL split over the issue of organizing workers into industrial or craft units. From then on, the Board had to determine the appropriate bargaining unit in the face of conflicting advice from the unions involved. The determination often affected the workers' choice of union and thus of the kind of collective bargaining in the unit.

By including some workers in, and excluding others from, a bargaining unit, the Board could help determine whether there would be any collective bargaining at all. In some plants majority approval of a union as exclusive representative of all the workers might be avoided by *excluding* one group of workers, such as skilled tool and die men, who would have voted heavily for the union. Or in another plant an antiunion group of workers might tip the vote against a union if they were *included* in a unit. With a different determination, a union might gain a majority by a Board decision if the effect of it was to dilute an antiunion vote or one which concentrated prounion votes.

In the early years of the Board, when the big organizing campaigns were sweeping through one industry after another, the inclusion or exclusion of a few workers did not often seriously affect the outcome of representational elections; but later, as unions moved out to organize in marginal areas, Board decisions on the appropriate bargaining unit may have had greater influence. Though judgments here are purely speculative, there have probably been more workers who have found themselves represented by a union against their wishes than there have been workers denied union representation because of the Board's determination of the appropriate bargaining unit. The Board after all was encouraging, not discouraging, collective bargaining.

The Board's determination of membership in a bargaining unit also influenced the kind of demands for which unions bargained. Where the Board included in a single unit all the workers of an automobile company, semiskilled and skilled alike, for example, the greater number of semi-skilled workers might influence union leaders to shape their negotiating demands in a way more satisfying to them than to the skilled workers. Such an influence probably contributed to the popularity of the equalitarian across-the-board wage increases among industrial unions during the late thirties and early forties. All workers received the same cents-per-hour raise, but proportionally the semiskilled workers received more than the skilled, and the wage differential between the two shrank accordingly. Or, to consider another example, in some cases where technicians and near-professionals were allowed to separate from a large body of workers and bargain for themselves in a separate bargaining unit, they sought medical care plans quite different from those they had had to accept when they were in a unit with production workers. These higher-paid employees preferred such plans as major medical care to the comprehensive Blue-Cross type of insurance.

When the Board carved out a multiplant or multiemployer unit rather than a single-plant or individual-employer unit, it encouraged union leaders to concentrate their attention upon solving problems in a way that would satisfy the largest number of workers throughout the unit. Local interests were apt to be ignored or compromised in the wider-unit negotiations. Thus one international union negotiated a system of layoff by seniority for all members of a multiplant unit. The workers in several of the smaller plants, which produced quite a different line of goods from that produced in the two large plants, much preferred the sharing of work during layoffs through a shorter workweek for all. Fewer in number than the workers in the large plants, their preference received less consideration from the top union negotiators.

Although the kind of bargaining unit and type of workers for which a union negotiates no doubt influence bargaining demands, this is not to say that the Board greatly changed the history of bargaining by these determinations. If it favored industrial over craft units before the Taft-Hartley Act, as some of the old-line craft leaders charged, it more likely was reflecting what the workers wanted and what they would have secured even if the Board had not had to determine bargaining units. Whatever indirect effect the National Labor Relations Board might have had upon collective bargaining through determination of the bargaining unit, later experience suggests that it was short run and transitory.

When all workers' wages were low, the skilled were too pleased to get any increase to complain very much that the unskilled received a *proportionally* higher raise. Later, having gained substantial wage increases, they began to grow restive at the narrowing differentials between themselves and the unskilled. By taking political action within the unions and by threatening to break away, skilled workers in many unions have been able to force recognition of their special problems and demands. Quite commonly now skilled workers receive special skill "margins," or unions negotiate percentage increases that maintain or even widen differentials. Unions have also learned to bargain more flexibly than they once did, allowing plant locals and even work groups within the local to negotiate local agreements. As we have seen in Chapter 10 the formal, legal bargaining unit fixed by the Board is not necessarily the actual unit of bargaining in practice. Therefore, after managers recognize a union and they and the union leaders explore the problems and opportunities of collective bargaining, the indirect influence of the Board upon the content of collective agreements through its determination of the bargaining unit probably tends to wane.

After the Board has determined an appropriate unit and the employer has recognized a union as the exclusive representative of the workers, the parties are required to bargain "in respect to rates of pay, wages, hours of employment, or other conditions of employment." Such a statement of legal duty led, soon after the passage of the Wagner Act, to pressures on the Board to define the scope of that duty. The process of definition inevitably required the Board to lay down certain rules for the conduct of negotiations; case by case, the Board progressively set forth the ambits of collective bargaining.

Frequently the issue of whether or not an employer has complied with his obligation to negotiate turns upon the good faith of his conduct during negotiations. Has he bargained with intent to reach an agreement with the union, or has the negotiation been only a smoke screen behind which he seeks to discourage union activity by conceding nothing or undermining the confidence of employees in the ability of the union to accomplish something? Presented in this manner, as it inevitably must be, the question reduces to one of subjective attitudes, the results *intended* by the employer when he adopts a line of conduct. Does an action indicate only a shrewd attempt to secure a good bargain (legitimate), or does it suggest an effort to prevent the conclusion of any agreement at all (illegitimate)?

Yet the Board can scarcely probe the mind of the employer and reach any certain conclusion about his intent. States of mind and intents are difficult to lay bare. Consequently the Board has been forced to adopt the approach of using what it refers to as "objective indicia." This means relying upon circumstantial evidence and deciding whether the established facts—the objective evidence—support a judgment that negotiations were conducted in good or bad faith. The Board examines the subjective factor of intent in the light of what it can reasonably infer from the evidence. The inference that bad faith was present in negotiations may always be rebutted, of course, if the employer presents an equally reasonable alternative explanation of his action.

In upholding the Wagner Act, the Supreme Court made clear that agreement between employer and union is not a necessary result of collective bargaining. Chief Justice Hughes wrote:

> The Act does not compel agreements between employers and employees. It does not compel any agreements whatever. It does not prevent the employer "from refusing to make a collective contract and hiring individuals on whatever terms" the employer "may by unilateral action determine. . . ." The theory of the act is that free opportunity for negotiation with accredited representatives of employees is likely to promote industrial peace and may bring about the adjustments and agreements which the Act in itself does not attempt to compel.[5]

Despite the absence of legal compulsion to force an agreement, the Board's indicia of bad-faith bargaining make it difficult for an employer to avoid some kind of agreement. The Board has ruled that an employer may not refuse to meet or negotiate with the workers' duly chosen representatives. He must make a genuine attempt to achieve an understanding of the proposals and counterproposals advanced, and he must exhaust every avenue and possibility of negotiations before admitting that an impasse exists. An employer may not insist upon meeting with the union at unreasonable times and places. Dilatory tactics indicate bad-faith bargaining, such as in the case of a company that failed to make a single bona fide written proposal to the union over a fifteen-month period of negotiations, despite the union's submission of at least three drafts of proposed agreements. To make an offer directly to employees, going over the heads of the union officers, on a matter that has been considered with a union committee is evidence of bad faith. Refusal to sign a written agreement embodying the terms or understanding reached also indicates bad-faith bargaining, as does the refusal to agree to a clause recognizing the union as the exclusive representative of all workers in a bargaining unit, not just union members.[6]

---

[5] *NLRB v. Jones & Laughlin Steel Corp.*, 301 U.S. 1, 45 (1937).

[6] In 1947 Congress incorporated in the Taft-Hartley Act, Section 9(d), many of the Board's decisions and defined collective bargaining as

> the performance of the mutual obligation of the employer and the representative of the employees to meet at reasonable times and confer in good

An employer may not in good faith take unilateral action on a matter on which the union has a right to be heard. In various decisions the Board has declared that an employer must, if requested, bargain over arbitration bonuses, checkoff, grievance settlement, seniority, and holiday provisions. Further, it has decided that an employer is not bargaining in good faith if he refuses to prove or verify a claim that he cannot meet a wage demand because of his inability to pay.

Governmental Determination of the Content of Agreements

Such decisions as the above, made under the Wagner Act, were intended not so much to shape the content of collective bargaining as to distinguish between real and apparent collective bargaining. Employers and managers often resisted the duty to bargain with considerable ingenuity and stubbornness, requiring the Board to define at least the minimum conditions of collective bargaining. Where both union leaders and employers were still learning to accept and to understand collective bargaining, the Board guided them along lines which had already been tested by those firms and unions that had long practiced it. The Board was primarily seeking to establish the framework within which collective bargaining could take place, not to impinge upon the voluntary determination of its substance.

The burgeoning new unions in the thirties and early forties were usually not concerned with exploring all the possibilities of collective bargaining. They were satisfied to secure recognition, gain a wage increase, and set up a grievance procedure. The first agreements were almost always short and simple. With each negotiation, however, more provisions and more complicated terms were added. By the time of World War II, unions and management were negotiating for such benefits as paid vacations, holidays and sick leaves, group health insurance, and special work bonuses. After the war collective agreements frequently included clauses dealing with pensions, supplemental unemployment benefits, portal-to-portal pay, stock bonuses for employees, and reemployment of displaced employees. More recently the issues of subcontracting, plant location, profit sharing, and job or income security in the face of technological change have become subjects for collective bargaining.

Some employers have refused to bargain on one or more of these issues

---

faith with respect to wages, hours and other terms and conditions of employment, or the negotiation of an agreement, or any question arising thereunder, and the execution of a written contract incorporating any agreement reached if requested by either party, but such obligation does not compel either party to agree to a proposal or require the making of a concession. . . .

on the grounds that they are matters involving managerial authority and responsibility exclusively. In most cases where the Board has had to decide whether management was legally required to bargain, the decisions have been that such issues fall within the legal scope of good-faith bargaining with "respect to rates of pay, wages, hours of employment, or other conditions of employment." [Section 9(a) of the Taft-Hartley Act.]

These decisions pose some knotty problems, however. Is the Board intervening directly in the collective bargaining process and thus interfering with the parties' autonomous shaping of the content and application of collective bargaining? Will the Board's determination tend to set the limits—maximums—that union and management may seek from each other? Interference it undoubtedly is, but how significant and limiting is more difficult to say. With court approval the Board has broadly interpreted "wages, hours, and conditions of work" to include all the varieties of pecuniary emoluments involved in cases which disputing unions and employers have brought before it. Thus there appears to be no limitation imposed by government administrators on this area of bargaining. But in declaring the various pecuniary issues bargainable, the Board and courts have reiterated what Chief Justice Hughes emphasized in that part of his decision quoted above. The parties are under no legal requirement to reach an agreement, no matter what subjects they may have to bargain over. Though a company must bargain at union insistence over a stock-purchase plan, it need not agree to union terms or even to a plan at all.

For example, the finding of the NLRB and federal courts that pension plans are a proper subject for mandatory collective bargaining cannot by itself be said to have resulted in the rapid spread of such plans after 1949, even though it may have been a factor. Strong employee interest in pensions, coupled with union bargaining power, was necessary to secure their widespread adoption. The contrast between the spread of bargained pension plans and the limited acceptance of the negotiated stock-purchase plan, declared a mandatory bargainable issue in 1956, suggests that the NLRB plays a marginal, even though not wholly insignificant, role in pushing bargaining into new areas.

In recent years the Board has excluded from mandatory bargaining some few issues, largely of a nonpecuniary nature. Since under the Taft-Hartley Act the Board must define good-faith bargaining for unions as well as employers, the exclusions have restrained both unions and employers. Under Board decisions an employer may not insist upon bargaining over internal union discipline or require a secret-ballot vote of all employees on the employer's last offer. A union may not insist upon bargaining over illegal provisions such as the closed shop, nor may it insist upon a performance bond which would be forfeited upon any "substantial" but undefined breach of contract. It may not seek to impose requirements such as local residence on employees outside the bargaining unit nor demand a work guarantee from other firms not subject to an employer's control. Neither union nor employer can legally insist that the other negotiate extension of the agreement beyond the designated bargaining unit, nor may either require the other to forgo any of the rights it is entitled to under the Taft-Hartley Act. The Board has therefore protected the party in the weaker bargaining position from having to bargain over, and possibly give up, rights and designations guaranteed by law. Although reasonable men could disagree with the specific decisions of the Board, they could also agree that the Board has moved carefully in defining collective bargaining; it has done little more than protect the framework within which stable, fruitful collective bargaining can function. Under NLRB decisions the parties are free to limit their bargaining or to extend it as they see fit, since the Board seldom intervenes except at the request of one of the parties. Only if one party disagrees and wishes government support in its stand that an issue is not bargainable does the Board intervene at all.

The government has influenced the subject matter of collective bargaining in more direct ways. The Taft-Hartley Act prohibited the closed shop, permitted the union shop only under certain conditions which made it not much more than an agency shop, and limited the form of the checkoff. It forbade, though ineptly and in vain, featherbedding provisions; it required that notification be given sixty days prior to a proposed termination or modification of an agreement; and it limited royalty payments and the applicability, coverage, purpose, and administration of welfare plans. Further, it required that workers be given the right to present grievances without the intervention of the union.[7]

---

[7] The 1959 regulations of internal union affairs, assuring more democratic procedures and less centralized control of union affairs, also had repercussions upon collective bargaining. Locals in such diverse unions as those of the machinists, auto workers, musicians, and teamsters began to act on their own, rejecting national agreements and continuing strikes for local demands long after the officers of the international unions and the chief company officials had reached their understandings. Often company and union officers had to make adjustments and changes in their agreements to satisfy the local union members and leaders. The full effects of the provisions on democratic procedures are yet to be studied, but the first impact of them appears to have been to encourage the negotiation over, and inclusion in agreements of, more parochial worker concerns than formerly. Negotiators may be more responsive to union members, but the result has been more instability in collective bargaining. If we truly believe that government intervention in union affairs to promote more democracy is of value, then we ought to be willing to accept the possible costs to unions, companies, and ourselves as members of the public. Such instabilities may well result in prolongations of labor disputes and "outrageous" demands by local union groups.

The 1947 Congress that passed the Taft-Hartley Act was vehemently and vociferously opposed to government controls and intervention in the economy. Nevertheless a two-thirds majority of its members had no difficulty in approving a considerable degree of direct government intervention in the process of collective bargaining and in opening the legal doors to a good deal of meddling. Having once established and supported the general framework of collective bargaining, the federal government has had to bear the responsibility, not always deservedly, for any adverse consequence of bargaining. If the incidence of strikes was deemed to be too high, government policy was at fault; if certain provisions of some labor agreements were held to be detrimental to private or public values, those adversely affected made government policy the culprit. Since legislation had ultimately encouraged or allowed the abuses to develop, so the argument has run, new and more legislation was the remedy. Thus have critics of government regulation pressed for the government to intervene in the details of industrial relations and collective bargaining.[8]

The basic labor laws have affected collective bargaining and collective agreements in another significant and indirect way. They have opened wide the doors to court review of the content of collective bargaining by allowing either party to bring suit for violation of an agreement in federal courts. Undoubtedly this provision was meant to be used as a method of holding unions accountable for any breach of a "no-strike" committment, but it has proved more useful to unions than to managements. Under the provision, Section 301, unions have sued to require managers to abide by arbitration decisions under the grievance procedure established by the agreement. In passing on such claims, courts may inspect the authority and scope of the arbitrator under the agreement, his definition of the content of the agreement—whether broad or narrow—and the propriety of his award.

In a 1960 suit over an arbitration case, the Supreme Court interpreted the collective agreement broadly indeed. The majority opinion declares that "the collective agreement covers the *whole employment relationship*. It calls into being a new common law—the common law of a particular industry or of a particular plant." The decision goes on to quote approvingly the view of Archibald Cox:

[8] Six months before the passage of the Taft-Hartley Act, the National Association of Manufacturers, while it was campaigning for new labor legislation, widely advertised its view that "the preservation of free collective bargaining demands that government intervention in labor disputes be reduced to an absolute minimum." (Quoted in H. Millis and E. C. Brown, *From the Wagner Act to the Taft-Hartley,* Chicago: The University of Chicago Press, 1950, p. 289.) Apparently the NAM saw government intervention under the Wagner Act as considerably below the "absolute minimum," but intervention which it approved was within its permissible limits.

A collective-bargaining agreement is [not] simply a document by which the union and employees have imposed upon management limited, express restrictions of its otherwise absolute right to manage the enterprise, so that an employee's claim must fail unless he can point to a specific contract provision upon which the claim is founded. . . . One cannot reduce *all the rules governing a community* like an industrial plant to fifteen or even fifty pages.[9]

The implications of this line of reasoning have yet to be established, however.

Problems of Regulating Collective Bargaining

Whether one can judge the explicit and implicit legal restrictions, limitations, and regulations of collective bargaining as good or bad, or wise or foolish, will not be examined here. Rather, we shall consider the problems confronting the government in its attempts to regulate collective bargaining. First is the application of general rules and overall decisions to a highly diversified industrial experience. Collective bargaining in the United States is conducted by a large number of different kinds of unions and firms in a great variety of industries located in disparate sections of the continent. This lack of uniform circumstances can bring about erratic and unforeseen consequences for the varieties of industrial relations subjected to the same laws.

The Taft-Hartley Act, for example, prohibits the closed shop under all circumstances, but in some industries the closed shop has long served a useful purpose for workers, employers, and the unions. Legislators need not forgo restricting the use of the closed shop if they believe that it subjects individual employees to unfair discriminatory treatment, but they would be well-advised to consider the quite different effects the prohibition would have on the unions and firms in industries long used to, and dependent upon it, compared with the effects upon labor organizations which secured it merely for the sake of administrative convenience. Unions in the construction and maritime industries developed the closed shop not only to safeguard their membership and control jobs but also to provide a means of organizing a disorderly labor market in which transient employers might hire seasoned workers whenever they were needed. Construction jobs are scattered geographically, different kinds of workers are employed by different employers, and employers bid on jobs in many different areas and do not usually carry their workers from job to job. They expect to be able to hire qualified workers locally. The individual construction worker finds that his jobs come and go and that he needs a source of information about jobs

[9] *United Steelworkers of America v. Warrior and Gulf Navigation Co.,* 443 (1960), 46 LRRM 2418. (Italics supplied.)

and a means of finding the employers hiring in his locality. To meet the practical problems of the workers and employers, the building trades unions have historically served as the industry's employment agency. Under these conditions, abuses could and did exist. Union officers could discriminate among workers unfairly, they could require kickbacks, and they could refuse membership and thus work to deserving workmen. But the institution of the closed shop did perform quite legitimate functions. Instead of attacking just the abuses of the closed shop, the Taft-Hartley Act prohibited it as a negotiable part of a collective agreement, thereby denying unions and employers its benefits. In some cases where unions had secured the closed shop merely for additional union security, the prohibition probably did cut out a possibility of abuse with little other serious effect, but in the construction industry (and several other industries) it seriously impaired the operation of the labor market as well. The problem was so severe that employers and unions ignored the law for some time. As first the Board and then the courts began to grapple with the problem of enforcement of the general ban on the closed shop, they had to concern themselves with the details of collective agreement provisions in the industry. After ten years of regulatory attempts, the Board finally devised rules that would allow what amounted to a nondiscriminatory union-run employment agency or hiring hall for those industries where such a device was necessary.

Experience has demonstrated the need for differential regulation, and in the Landrum-Griffin Act, Congress recognizes this need by providing special rules for some industries. It treats the building and construction industries separately, largely incorporating the special rules worked out by the Board. Not only does it give exemptions to construction and building, but it also accords the apparel and clothing industry immunity from the restrictions on "hot cargo" agreements. Congress recognized that the maintenance of stable and successful collective bargaining in this industry would be next to impossible if the unions could not police standards by enforcing them against nonunion employers when work was subcontracted to them.

Congress thus has given explicit recognition to the fact that when it enacts laws regulating collective bargaining and asks the Board and courts to apply the same rules to all, the impact of the law can become capricious and harmful to one of the major purposes of that same law—the encouragement of collective bargaining and the development of orderly and peaceful procedures for the settlement of labor disputes. Yet if there are exceptions to the rules, as in fact have been provided, why are there not exceptions made for many other situations similar in fact and circumstances? As the Board is asked to administer a labor law increasingly detailed in its legislative provisions, its application of the law rapidly becomes more complex and difficult. The political pressures of special interest upon it and Congress for more exemptions are stimulated. Further, there is danger that as the Board inescapably wrestles with the practical problem of determining the fine line between exempted collective bargaining activity and nonexempted, it will become bogged down in technicalities.[10]

The ability of Congress, the courts, or the Board to make sound public policy is seriously impaired as the issues of collective bargaining become confused and lost in details. The dangers of regulating minutiae of collective bargaining are not only the loss of unions' and managements' control over their own affairs but also the loss of the government's ability effectively and flexibly to regulate collective bargaining in the interests of the public and individual workers, the historical concern of the government.

The more details a government agency considers in administering and regulating its sector of activity, the heavier its case load is apt to be. Each additional legal provision calls for its own interpretation, multiplies enormously the chances for uncovering new and unforeseen circumstances that require special application of the general provisions, and increases rapidly opportunities for disputes and questions.

It would be unfortunate to see the National Labor Relations Board develop the kind of autonomous, headless colony of "control" that the sixteen-man Interstate Commerce Commission has established. The ICC is so caught up in regulating the details of rail tarriffs, traffic, and practices

---

[10] An independent study group, sponsored by the Committee for Economic Development, strongly urged that as a matter of public policy we would be wise to abandon the effort to legislate bargaining in good faith. In part the statement and recommendation of the group is as follows:

> Parties have been told that they must bargain in good faith, and elaborate tests have been devised in an attempt to determine "objectively" whether the proper subjective attitude prevails. The limitations and artificiality of such tests are apparent, and the possibilities of evasion are almost limitless. In the light of the realities of the bargaining situation, distinctions between matters that are subject to "mandatory bargaining" and those that are not have a hollow ring. Basically, it is unrealistic to expect that, by legislation, "good faith" can be brought to the bargaining table. Indeed, the provisions designed to bring "good faith" have become a tactical weapon used in many situations as a means of harassment. . . . The subjects to be covered by bargaining, the procedures to be followed, the nuances of strategy involving the timing of a "best offer," the question of whether to reopen a contract during its term—such matters as these are best left to the parties themselves. Indeed, the work load of the National Labor Relations Board and of the parties could be substantially reduced by returning these issues to the door of the employer or union. . . .

The Public Interest in National Labor Policy, New York: Committee for Economic Development, 1961, p. 82.

that its ability to respond alertly and flexibly to public needs has atrophied. For the ICC, responsibility has become so diffused and tasks so filled with minutiae that it does not initiate or enforce public policy; it merely responds to pressures and demands. Policy is made, of course, but willy-nilly, at the direction and mercy of the interested parties who appear before the agency. They have the specialized interest and immediate concern which give them reason enough to master the intricate details and seek to use them for their own purposes.

Were the NLRB required increasingly to turn its attention to the details and minutiae of special legislative provisions and exceptions, we might expect a development similar to that of the ICC and other regulatory agencies. The safeguarding of the public interests and of the rights of individuals in labor affairs might well be impaired as effective control of public policy was taken over by union and management experts, knowledgeable in the intricacies of Board procedures and deliberations.

An expectation that disagreements between unions and management would nevertheless protect public interest by requiring one or both parties to appeal to the public for support overlooks the community of interests that exists between them in many cases. For example, the public has shown a good deal more impatience with, and disapproval of, the closed shop than employers in some industries. As long as they have secured an adequate supply of qualified workers, employers in the printing, maritime, and construction industries have not shown too much concern for the abuses that have existed under the closed shop. With good reason we might conclude that since in the past they have not been so much guardians of public interest as protectors of their own, they are not likely to act differently in the future.

Conclusion

We need not decry government regulation of collective bargaining simply because it impinges upon the autonomous determination by unions and management of wages, hours, and conditions of employment. The public and the government have a legitimate concern with collective bargaining and its outcome, and experience has demonstrated that autonomous determination does not always produce felicitous results. On the other hand, government regulation that attempts to remedy too many shortcomings of collective bargaining or abuses that arise under it may become so snarled in its own comprehensiveness that it loses its force in the ever-changing industrial scene.

Since in collective bargaining, as in all other social activities of man, good and bad consequences usually flow from the same activity, we need to be quite sure in our evaluation that we have weighed both. When attempting to remedy the bad, the effect of the remedial action upon the good ought to be considered. Such careful consideration may well persuade us, after reflection, that the price we pay for a number of the benefits of collective bargaining is the sacrifice of some individual and public rights and that the cost of regulating or limiting collective bargaining is the loss of some of the benefits we might have otherwise enjoyed.

Before regulating collective bargaining and labor affairs further, we might look well at the possible gains and losses that would result from such an extension. We need full and open debate upon the probable effects, both good and bad, of any regulation and a clear realization of both the possibilities and limitations of government action. It may be more worthwhile for the government to maintain and alter only the broad framework of collective bargaining and to put up with some abuses than to try to remedy many minor shortcomings by regulating the details of collective bargaining, thereby running the risk of impairing its ability to perform its primary functions.

In first promoting voluntary associations and encouraging collective bargaining and in then restraining the associations and regulating the collective action, Congress was contending with a persisting, ever-reoccurring paradox. Even as it intervened through the Taft-Hartley Act to regulate and to restrain, it reaffirmed its judgment, expressed in 1935, that "full freedom of association" enhances individual liberty and that collective action is beneficial to individuals and to the public. Over fifty years ago, Prof. A. V. Dicey described well the paradoxical problem with which we and our government must wrestle:

> [The right of association which] from one point of view seems to be a necessary extension of individual freedom is, from another point of view, fatal to the individual of which it seems to be a mere extension. . . . This paradox raises a problem which at this moment in all civilized countries perplexes moralists and thinkers no less than legislators and judges: How is the right of association to be reconciled with each man's individual freedom? Curtail the right of association and personal liberty loses half its value. Give the right of association unlimited scope and you destroy, not the mere values, but the existence of personal freedom.[11]

Those who oppose governmental regulation or curtailment of collective bargaining might well remember that more is at stake than the strengthening or weakening of unions, just as those who look with disfavor upon a union organization as curtailing the freedom of its members or of those for

[11] "The Combination Laws as Illustrating the Relations between Law and Opinion in England during the Nineteenth Century," *Harvard Law Review,* vol. 17 (1903–1904), pp. 513–514.

whom it bargains ought to remember that more is involved than simple individualism. Our labor legislation and the administration of labor laws spring in part, of course, from special pleading for unions and business, but only in part. They also spring from deep, continuing, and traditional concerns, at once broader than these organizations (the public interest) and narrower (the individual worker). However much business and unions plead their interest with the arguments of the broader and narrower issues, we will wisely recognize the partial validity of those arguments and not dismiss them out of hand. The result may be less than perfect legislation and court decisions; they may even be as paradoxical as the problems they are designed to solve.

The Economics of
Collective Bargaining:
The Setting of Wages

chapter 13

Economists have often been embarrassed or exasperated by unions and their members' demands for collective bargaining. They have often seen unionists as well-intentioned but seriously misguided men. In early-nineteenth-century England, social reformers such as Joseph Hume, Francis Place, and George White were convinced that workers could accomplish nothing through unions. They argued that since anticombination laws encouraged workers wrongly to believe that unions might offer some help, the laws ought to be repealed. After astute parliamentary maneuvering, they gained their point in 1824. Though workers were then free to join unions, the repealers were confident that the organizations would not last; any benefits that the workers might secure would be temporary. The natural laws of economics would stymie union efforts and prove their futility to the workers. Were higher wages gained, they would not last; they would immediately induce competition for the jobs, which would soon restore the lower natural rates.

To the consternation of the lawmakers, however, workers failed to perceive the futility of their collective efforts and organized unions. They conducted strikes far and wide and made demands for higher wages and better working conditions. The next year Parliament reenacted some of the old restraints upon unions and thenceforth listened to the economists with more skepticism than in 1824.

In the succeeding century, workers in the United States as well as in England persisted in trying to form unions and to raise wages, despite governmental restraints and the warnings by economists of disagreeable and even dire consequences. Though later economists examined union wage policies with more sophisticated tools, such as marginal analysis, their judgments generally continued to be the same—workers could not benefit themselves substantially through collective bargaining, nor could they help others at all. The self-regulating action of the competitive market could not be improved by "artificial" means. At best, any strategically situated group of workers who did succeed in pushing up their wages would reduce the demand for their services and leave some of their number without any jobs at all.

Economists have offered a number of explanations for the persistence of unions and of workers' attachment to them. Some argued that workers must have a myopic view of their own interests; they are encouraged by short-run gains and fail to perceive the disadvantageous long-run results. They might raise their wages, for example, and think themselves better off, failing to realize that they have simultaneously created a problem of unemployment. Other economists assert that unionized workers are motivated by narrow and selfish interests. The well-organized carpenters, for instance, might be pleased with their high wages and unconcerned that they had thereby raised housing costs, to the detriment of other workers.

Some economists admit that in certain situations unions can help workers by offsetting the power of employers who are exploiting them. Such a circumstance might arise if an employer was the only buyer of the services of a group of workers, because of either their geographical isolation or their occupational specialization. In such a case he could offer them less than their true productive value, and they would have to accept, having no alternative employment to which they might turn. In this situation collective bargaining might be beneficial, but only to the extent that it removes such exploitation. It is harmful if it goes further and becomes exploitative itself. Of course, those who see few or no economic benefits from collective bargaining may nevertheless recognize noneconomic merits in such activities as adjudication of grievances.

On the whole, economists are skeptical that unions can or do play any generally beneficial role in the setting of wages. Their most widely accepted wage theories cast unions in parts that range from the misguided reformer to the selfish, calculating monopolist. Based on the values of an individual-istic society or on the assumption that individual action is the norm for market behavior, economic theory tends to cast all collectives in a dubious light. Singularly unable to hide their collectivity behind any legal fiction, as corporations have done, and in name and primary function stressing their united, group nature, unions have presented themselves as obvious and dubious anomalies in the free market system.

The Marginal Productivity Theory of Wages

The most widely taught and commonly held wage theory is that of marginal productivity. By examining it, we can gain an appreciation of the present state of economic thinking about wages and a basis for evaluating wage criteria and the economic consequences of collective bargaining. The marginal productivity theory necessarily rests, as does every theory, on simplifying assumptions. The significant ones are that (1) the economy is composed of a large enough number of small firms so that no single firm is able to exercise a measurable influence on its product or factor markets; (2) each firm strives to maximize profits, and each worker tries to realize the maximum monetary worth from his work; (3) business firms operate under constant or increasing costs of production, so that any expansion of output by a producer does not bring lower unit costs (that is to say, the law of diminishing returns or nonproportional output applies); (4) there is only a "frictional" unemployment; (5) a goodly number of workers possess a high degree of mobility; (6) methods of production are variable over time, so that labor and capital may be combined in different proportions; (7) there is a sufficient homogeneity in segments of the work force so that there are always workers who can substitute for other workers reasonably well; (8) tastes and technologies do not change within the period of time that it takes for economic influences to make themselves felt; and (9) employers and workers possess a good working knowledge of the state of product and factor markets.

The key concept of the theory is the marginal value product—the net value added by employing one more unit of labor. (For the sake of convenience, the marginal value product is often referred to as simply the "marginal product.") The marginal productivity theory of wages, as originally propounded, asserted that labor forces would *tend* to be distributed among firms and industries in such a manner that the value of labor's marginal product would be equal in all enterprises. Since the theory assumes workers of a given skill class to be interchangeable—for most practical purposes one could be substituted for another, given a little time—the wage rate would be the same for all. When all workers were receiving a wage rate equal to the marginal value product in whatever business they were employed and the wage rates for given services were equal in all lines of production, the labor market was in equilibrium. In that situation there were no market pressures operating to force a change in wage rates. Only some extraneous influence, such as a new invention or a change in demand for particular products, could upset the equilibrium. Its reestablishment would take a little time, as workers and wage rates adjusted to the changes, but eventually a new equilibrium would be reached or at least approached.

Under the law of diminishing returns, the larger the work force that is used with a given amount of capital, the smaller is labor's marginal product, and thus the smaller the wage. Even if time is allowed for managers to transform the given amount of capital into equipment more suited to an increased work force (as by reinvestment of depreciation accruals), the output attributable to the "final worker" is smaller than if there were fewer men. Given the capital stock, the more workers, the less the value of their marginal product, and thus the smaller the wage. On the other hand, the greater the amount of capital used with a fixed number of workers, the greater is labor's marginal product, and the higher the wage. Such an analysis overlooks the possibilities that workers might improve their skills and abilities and that capital in the course of being transformed from one kind of technology to another might improve its efficiency through invention and innovation. These possibilities are ignored, not because they are unrealistic (any economist knows they are more likely to be true than not), but in order to simplify the analysis, avoiding complexities which it is believed might obscure underlying tendencies.

The equilibrium wage in this theoretical approach may be considered normal in that it is the wage which the demand for and supply of labor tend to establish and maintain over time. Any rate higher than the marginal product would represent a loss to the firm and would encourage employers to lay off workers until the return from the marginal unit of labor was equal to the wage rate paid. According to the law of diminishing returns, the marginal product would increase as fewer workers used the same amount of capital. Workers who were about to be laid off could avoid that unhappy event only if they offered to work for a lower wage, a wage equal to the value which they were contributing to the company. Their offer would force those still employed to accept the same lower wage, too, since all are substitutable for one another. Thus the wage rate would be brought back to the level of the marginal value product of the original work force. At that rate, and only at that rate, all the workers would be employed.

The same competitive forces would also protect workers from wage levels *below* their marginal product. Should an employer attempt to cut wages, he would find that other employers would bid away his underpaid workers because they could realize additional profit on any wage rates less than labor's marginal product. Competition among employers for the workers would continue until the wage rates were restored to the level of workers' marginal product. The competitive forces that tend to push wages toward an equilibrium level thus safeguard the employment of workers and prevent their exploitation.[1] The attractiveness of such a theory should be readily apparent.

One should note that the theory is stated in terms of *long-run tendencies.* Wages will move *toward* marginal productivity, but only if all the various influences that affect the labor market were free to work themselves out fully would wages actually come to equal the marginal product (strictly, the marginal value product).[2] A great deal of misplaced criticism has arisen from regarding the theory as an explanation of current determination of wages in our dynamic community. The theory's assumption of a static society is admittedly unrealistic, but not invalidating. Although wages might seldom actually equal marginal productivity of workers, they probably do fluctuate around it. The discrepancies between wages and the marginal value product would set up pressures, according to the theory, and in time would "bend" the wages in the appropriate direction. "No one who understands the productivity theory claims that it works with mathematical precision. It is enough if it is a broad and powerful tendency which brings wages into some degree of close conformity to it." [3]

The full significance of the marginal productivity theory cannot be appreciated simply by regarding it as an explanation of long-run wage behavior, however. The tenacity with which economists have supported it is explained by the fact that it is an important link in the theory of the *price system* or, what amounts to the same thing, in a widely held theory of *general* economic equilibrium. From this point of view, wages are actually but one form of price. Price is not only the payments for purchased goods but also the charge for the services of labor or capital and the use of land or raw materials. Some economists—Marshall for example—would add

[1] As a matter of fact, it is only in situations where there is lack of competition among employers for labor (as, for example, in a one-company town) that economists have generally agreed that union action (to raise wages to the marginal productivity level) is warranted, to prevent exploitation.

[2] J. R. Hicks, *The Theory of Wages,* New York: The Macmillan Company, 1932, p. 86. Alfred Marshall, speaking more generally, asserted in *Principles of Economics,* 8th ed., New York: The Macmillan Company, 1938, p. 825:

> And indeed the theory of wages whether in its older or newer form has no direct bearing on the issue of any particular struggle in the labour market: that depends on the relative strength of the competing parties. But it has much bearing on the general policy of the relation of capital to labour; for it indicates what policies do, and what do not, carry in themselves the seeds of their own ultimate defeat; what policies can be maintained, aided by suitable organizations; and what policies will ultimately render either side weak, however well organized.

[3] Paul H. Douglas, *The Theory of Wages,* New York: Kelley & Millman, 1957, p. 77.

the return from the services rendered by entrepreneurs as well. Since all these prices are interrelated, a change in one leads to a change in others. The process by which prices in one sector of the economy, whether for finished goods or factor services, are established and maintained is dependent on the action of all other prices. It is impossible in the brief space which can be allotted to this subject here to portray it adequately, but a telescoped version may serve to recall to the mind of the reader what he has probably encountered in other contexts.

The relationship of competitive factor pricing to general equilibrium theory can be set forth in a series of propositions. First, the demand for the factors of production is a derived demand, arising from the demand for goods and services. Product prices and factor prices are thus directly related, the latter made possible only by the former. Second, the factors of production are reasonably effective substitutes for one another, so that the price for one factor, such as labor, cannot be set independently of another factor, such as capital, which might substitute for it. An example might be employers installing laborsaving machinery because of the high cost of labor. Third, because the factors of production are substitutes for one another, the ratios of all factors' return to their marginal product will be equal in the long run. Fourth, allowing the same assumptions used to support the marginal productivity theory, one may generalize about the long-run tendency of the system: Whatever the factor—land, labor, or capital—each unit will be paid a price equivalent to its marginal product, and that marginal product will be the same in all similar productive uses. Fifth, under the same assumptions, the equilibrating process proceeds more or less automatically. Any deviations from long-run pricing results quickly generate correcting counterpressures. The pressures arise from the competition for factors of production and from their long-range substitutability. Businesses will substitute a lower-priced marginal product of one factor for the higher-priced marginal product of another, until the prices of all factors are proportional to their marginal products and no further gain is possible.

The automatic, impersonal way in which wages and other prices are governed in a competitive price system explains much of the ardent defense of the system's theoretical validity. The price system presumably establishes an allocation of the factors of production among industries according to general consumer preference, given the distribution of income, and thus avoids control by any dominant social group and makes unnecessary any government intervention. The price system, of which the marginal productivity theory of wages is but one facet, thus seems to achieve the organization of the economy along lines which promote economic satisfaction and preserve the Western political ideal of individual liberty.

Because the theory so powerfully argues for, and agrees with, values cherished by most Americans, one needs to guard against confusing the theory as an analysis of empirical events with the theory as a prescriptive doctrine. To maintain that the pricing system represents an ideal, while at the same time holding that it does not represent the forces actually at work in the society, is a logical and consistent approach that quite a few economists take.

If, however, one asserts that the theory is descriptively valid, there is good reason to question whether in fact it is. Although the highly abstract nature of this theory is readily apparent, that in itself is insufficient reason for rejecting it. Theories are admittedly generalizations and as such must concentrate upon central tendencies. To say that the assumptions of a theory do not conform precisely to fact is not to state a defect. Legitimate objection may be raised only if there is reason to think that the assumptions stray far from fact and are unrevealing of central tendencies.

Those economists who find little or nothing to commend in the wage policies of unions make their judgment in the belief that the central tendencies and long-run pressures generated by general equilibrium theory are realities. They conclude that equilibrating forces do "bend" wages in the direction of marginal productivity. Insofar as collective bargaining may distort the wage structure in the short run, they believe that it produces counteracting, corrective influences that secure its ultimate defeat. Or economists may consider the process another way and see collective bargaining interfering with the equilibrium system. They may condemn it for its short-run mischief even if its effects are mitigated in time. These views, of course, stem directly from the wishfully or objectively derived belief that the assumptions of the general equilibrium analysis are tenable characterizations of our society even though they are admittedly imperfect.

Hicks' Restatement of the Theory

The marginal productivity theory received its first systematic exposition shortly before the turn of the century, though its antecedents may be traced back at least another fifty years. In 1932, Prof. J. R. Hicks introduced a recognizable modification of the theory. After observing the growing role of labor unions and the rise of state-supported systems of unemployment compensation, he concluded that unions might raise wages above competitive levels with the consequence of lingering unemployment. As we have noted, the original theoretical formulation allowed for the possibility that excessive wage rates would cause unemployment. It went on to assert, however, that the unemployed would search for work and in competing with their employed fellows would drive the wage rate back to normal levels. To Hicks it was apparent that not only could short-run unemployment emerge, but long-run unemployment was a fact not to be ignored. He pointed out that long-run equilibrating forces might not be sufficient to lower wage rates to normal levels, and thus hard-core unemployment would and did present itself. The unemployment would continue, in his opinion, until new inventions and increased capital accumulations raised the competitive wage rates to the level of the bargained rates. Only then would the unemployed be absorbed.

Hicks' restatement abandoned any notion that marginal productivity by itself determined or regulated wages, but it still suggested, nonetheless, a norm for wage settlement. The level of wages and the level of employment were functionally related to each other through marginal productivity. Whatever the wage, employers would attempt to adjust employment so that the marginal product of labor equaled it. If unions pushed wages above the competitive level, workers would suffer unfortunate consequences. Hicks warned that "[the worker] endeavours to protect himself, through Trade Unionism and the democratic State. But our examination of the effects of [wage] regulation has shown that this protection can rarely be adequate. Carried through to the end, it can only result in a great destruction of economic wealth." [4]

Hicks' restatement provided for the firm a theory of employment.[5] Though wages are fixed by the market, union, or government, employers might vary employment so that the workers' marginal productivity and wages were equated. Under some circumstances adjustment of employment would be slow, while in others it would be fast; in all cases marginal productivity would guide the process, however. The more directly and immediately competitive pressures played upon the employer in his product market, the more quickly he would have to respond to the guidance of marginal productivity. A labor union might use its bargaining power to push the wage rate above the competitive level and even to hold it there more or less indefinitely. But the consequence would be to induce the employer to cut back employment and production. His former marginal return would fall below the new rate, making it unprofitable for him to hire as much labor as he had been. Because of the principle of diminishing returns, a smaller work force in combination with the same fixed capital would produce a higher marginal return—one which could be equated to the new higher wage rate. The union might successfully shield the wage rate from the competition of unorganized workers, but it could not shield all its members from the resulting loss of jobs.

Hicks' restatement makes two assumptions which need to be noted. First, it assumes that any given level of employment is uniquely associated with a particular wage. The relationship of the two variables is thus deter-

[4] Hicks, *The Theory of Wages*, p. 323.
[5] See Alan Cartter, *Theory of Wages and Employment*, Homewood, Ill.: Richard D. Irwin, Inc., 1959, p. 45.

minant. A change in one requires a change in the other. If the assumptions are not true and wages and employment are not uniquely related to each other, wage changes may not set up pressures in the short or long run for changing employment; no single wage may be "normal" for a particular employment. Indeterminateness in the relationship of wages and employment therefore lessens the value of the theory as a norm and as an analytical tool. The greater the indeterminateness, the less the value.

There are good reasons to believe that, in the short run particularly, wages and employment are indeterminately related. For example, on the supply side, employment often appears to be not so much a function of wages as of the number of jobs available. When jobs become scarce, some workers simply leave the labor market and therefore apply no downward pressure upon wages. Younger workers may continue their studies, women may go back to keeping house, and older workers may retire earlier than they would otherwise. When more jobs are open, these same kinds of workers may enter the labor market or stay in it, attracted not so much by higher wages as by the availability of work. Such behavior makes it possible for wages to remain the same even though employment changes quite radically.

Also, employers have shown an increasing tendency to treat more and more of their labor expenses as fixed costs. They are reluctant to lay off white-collar workers as readily as blue-collar workers. The number of the former has increased greatly in recent years and shows every sign of continuing to increase. Employment has been most rapid among the technicians, engineers, and scientists, the group of employees who have experienced the lowest rates of unemployment and layoffs in business recessions.[6] Thus the wages earned by such white-collar workers and the number of them employed may have little relationship to the marginal value product.

Contributing to the indeterminate relationship of wages and employment to marginal productivity is the ambiguity of our concepts of wages and labor. The wage to which workers respond, for example, may be one thing (take-home pay), but the wage to which employers adjust employment may be quite different (labor costs, including a training program and subsidized cafeteria). Changes in the demand and supply of labor are not easily related to any common wage unit in such a situation. Further, the supply of labor in terms of productive units may change with no variations in wage rates. Workers may increase or decrease their productivity by considerable amounts, irrespective of wages, because of changes in morale, interest, or incentives. Whether or not their productivity in a particular firm is fairly stable over time or averages out in time is a poorly explored matter.

[6] See the data presented by Carol A. Barry, "White Collar Employment, I & II," *Monthly Labor Review,* vol. 84 (1961), pp. 11–18, 139–147.

The second assumption upon which Hicks' restatement rests is that firms tend to move toward a competitive equilibrium, adjusting wages or employment to marginal productivity in the long run. The effects of marginal productivity are thus likened to those of the sun upon our weather, as it seasonally moves from latitude to latitude. Surely, but almost imperceptibly, the sun brings the warmth of summer with it as it rises from the spring equinox to the solstice, whatever may be the daily and weekly variations.

Although the concept of the long run may protect the marginal productivity theory from criticism of its usefulness in the short run, it does so by raising further doubts about the theory's relevance. One may point out not only that "in the long run we are all dead," as Keynes did, but more pertinently that in a dynamic, growing economy where war expenditures, antidepression programs, and innovating industries continually introduce new economic forces and alter established institutions, the concept of the long run may be elusive and not particularly helpful. Our situation may require a series of short-term adjustments to continually new or fluctuating situations. Marginal productivity may not produce any sure and predictable effects because its influence in bending wages or employment may be continuously dissipated or transformed over time. It does not necessarily act with the sureness and unalterable purpose of the sun in its annual peregrinations across the equator, to revert to the analogy used earlier. The long-run effects of marginal productivity can be known only as an extrapolation of the present into a future that may never arrive. Always moving off at a tangent from the long-run world, the real world may avoid the consequences predicted by marginal theory—though, of course, it can produce new and unexpected problems.

Machlup's Restatement of the Theory

Economists have given up any attempt to explain short-run wages or unemployment in terms of marginal productivity, and thus they have abandoned a most critical and perhaps most decisive area of wage determination; they may also have given up even a meaningful long-run explanation if they accept the restatement of marginal productivity set forth by Prof. Fritz Machlup.[7] According to him, the marginal product is not an objective value but is something which exists only in the employer's mind. The marginal value product of any factor is whatever the businessman thinks it is. There is no possibility of an error of judgment for theoretical purposes then. One cannot say that a businessman has incorrectly estimated the marginal product because whatever he believes the marginal product to be *is* the marginal product, for purposes of explaining his behavior. In decid-

[7] Fritz Machlup, "Marginal Analysis and Empirical Research," *American Economic Review*, vol. 36 (1946), pp. 519–554.

ing whether to hire or fire, to substitute capital for labor, or to give a wage increase or make a wage cut, the businessman will be concerned with the given wage rate relative to what he thinks the marginal product is. To a particular employer, the marginal product may include not only the actual net addition to revenue resulting from the employment of an extra unit of labor but also those additions he subjectively values. To the marginal value product he may add such things as the effect of a wage rate on the workers' morale, the impact of a wage increase on a union organizing drive, and consumer reaction to his labor policy. The appraisal of marginal product thus varies from employer to employer; only if one can reduce the subjective appraisals to common pecuniary values is a comparison possible between the marginal product in one line of employment and that in another.

This view of the marginal productivity theory robs it of any significant relations to the price system conceived as a self-equilibrating mechanism for the optimum allocation of the factors of production.[8] It is difficult to see in what respects it can be considered a theory of wages. Machlup's restatement boils down to the proposition that any individual businessman will pay a wage rate and hire any given number of men at that rate only if he *believes* that the last man hired, like those who precede him, will add something to total revenue. A once-respected theory is thus covered with the shame that it can no longer be proved descriptively valid, nor is it susceptible even to meaningful application as a norm. It becomes little more than another way of stating the maximizing principle as it applies in a particular aspect of economic life: In hiring workers, employers will strive to maximize their profits. One of the *assumptions* on which the older theory was based now substitutes for the entire theory.

The possibility of testing the validity of the maximizing assumption remains, but not the possibility of predicting or judging the consequence of maximizing behavior in terms of wage rates, employment, or allocation of the labor force. Under competition, wage rates for interchangeable workers would tend to become equal because they represent the same value product. Under Machlup's conditions, the same result cannot be predicted, for wage rates would now be dependent on the employers' evaluation of what they were getting from their wage expenditures. Only by accident might these value judgments be the same. No one could argue, as Hicks has, that if wages are maintained at "artificial" or regulated levels, hard-core unemployment will emerge, since the "artificiality" of wages will depend on producers'

---

[8] Clearly the subjective approach which Machlup brings to marginal productivity is unacceptable in optimum allocation-equilibrium theory generally (of which it is or has been a part). On a subjective basis, an economic stalemate would always be theoretically possible. Producers might *believe* that however low costs or wages were, the returns would not cover them. The assumption of perfect knowledge is obviously unreal, but necessary to the classical system.

subjective appraisals. The Machlup interpretation therefore denies that the marginal productivity theory establishes any standard for general wage policy. It has abstracted the theory of wages from its former equilibrium setting, where the competitive forces no longer operate to allocate labor optimally and determine "normal" wage levels. Machlup rightly insists that one must recognize the subjective appraisals of businessmen as important data, but by admitting subjective evaluations of the marginal product, he defends the principle of marginalism at the cost of its most valuable contribution.

The current state of wage theory is thus one of confusion. The most widely accepted doctrine, that of marginal productivity, if viewed as a description is founded on assumptions which are considerably removed from the realities of modern social organization and wage-determining institutions. Both critics and supporters have misused it. The former have quite commonly regarded it as applicable to the single firm in the short run, while adherents have considered it a sufficient basis for condemnation of virtually all union wage actions in the collective bargaining process.[9] Attempted modifications either have failed to meet basic objections or have robbed the theory of much of its significance for the long run as well as for the short run.

The theory has simplified too much the process by which business decisions are made and has assumed more economic constraint upon those who decide particular wage rates than the world of experience justifies. The

---

[9] Those who have sought to use marginal productivity analysis as a basis for policy have sometimes been as guilty of its misuse as those who have been critical of it. Given a particular situation (say, where a union is asking a wage increase of 10 cents an hour), the argument is sometimes made to run about as follows: If there was a greater marginal value product of labor relative to wages than of capital to interest, the employer would (1) expand production by employing more workers or (2) substitute labor for capital. The fact that he takes neither of these actions indicates the validity of the present wage. On the other hand, to raise wages now will make the marginal value product of labor relative to wages lower than that of capital to interest, leading to unemployment. Thus one is led to the conclusion that normally the current wage is "right." In times of severe unemployment, however, it is argued that wage rates are excessive and that employment will expand only when rates are dropped to the equivalence of the (lesser) marginal product. In periods of boom, the corrective will come through employers' bidding up wages in their efforts to expand their labor forces. One winds up, then, with this approach, with the view that the only justified union action concerning wages is to urge their reduction in time of unemployment! A theory which was designed as a long-run explanation of the level of wages has here been as badly handled, in its short-run application to particularized situations, by some who support it as by some who have rejected it.

neoclassical economic system from which the theory of marginal productivity is derived is founded upon competitive individualism. Society is seen as a collection of individuals, each assiduously and rationally maximizing his own welfare. Since most individuals do not work alone in production, the system needed an organizing force for bringing them together in a productive enterprise. The neoclassicists adopted the entrepreneur, whose coordinating influence brought land, labor, and capital into a working whole. In his search for maximum profits, he initiates decisions on production and marketing; he contracts for needed workers, raw materials, and capital; and he determines the direction and extent of production.

The entrepreneur, thus conceived, was an *individual* responding to opportunities for profit. He fitted well the conceptual apparatus of neoclassical economics, first by preserving the individualism of the system, and second by responding to profit opportunities in a competitive system and directing and using the factors of production to make those goods most desired by consumers (within given incomes).

The personification of the decision-making process in the entrepreneurial function is illustrated by Marshall's chapter on business management in his *Principles of Economics*. The manufacturer, he said, must perform two roles. First, as a merchant and organizer of production he must have a knowledge of all that pertains to his trade, and he must be able to forecast movements of consumer behavior, standing ready to meet new needs or improve upon the methods of satisfying existing wants. Second, as an employer he must be a natural leader of men, possessing good judgment in the selection of subordinates so that he may entrust to them day-to-day administration of the labor force "while he himself exercises a general control over everything, and preserves order and unity in the main plan of the business." [10]

Economic analysis still relies upon this concept of an entrepreneur—an individual with unified personal interests who makes the decisions that determine the activity of his enterprise. He may have subordinates and assistants, who, as specialists, provide him with information, but his de-

[10] Marshall, *Principles of Economics*, p. 297. It is true that Marshall recognizes the existence and character of such organized forms of entrepreneurship as the joint stock company. But he still assumes central direction, though under a management divorced from ownership, and he appears to regard this—like government—as a species susceptible to bureaucratization, a disease which strikes at the economic efficiency of the enterprise, that is, its appropriate responses to economic stimuli. In any event, such collective enterprise is admitted only to be dismissed. The chapter ends in purely personal terms. The organizing factor—"business ability in command of capital"—has its own market and its own supply price.

cision is a personal one.[11] Equilibrium pricing theory is reared on the entrepreneurial form of business organization, as is the traditional marginal productivity theory of wages. In business firms throughout the economy, the entrepreneur—the institutionalized shadow of an individual—balances the wage rate against the judged marginal product; he seeks to equate the marginal product of all factors and their supply prices. If there are impediments to such equating, at least he will not permit marginal product to fall *below* the factor price except under rare temporary circumstances.

Even if one accepts the entrepreneur as a partnership or as a whole management structure, there is the continuance of centralized direction or the presumption of a harmony of interests. Such a conception of the decision-making process is, however, inconsistent with the economic organization of our own society. The fact is that our most interesting and significant problems involve the making of decisions where conflicts of interest must be reconciled in order for any decision to be made at all. Where two groups are interdependent, so that neither is functionally complete without the other, conflicting interests must be accommodated in making business decisions which affect both. Without accommodation, a decision reached by one is meaningless because it will not evoke from the other the cooperation necessary to carry on the business of the enterprise.

Discretion in Wage Determination

In an earlier chapter we suggested that collective bargaining is a political as well as an economic power. It involves two different political systems, unions and management, in a common decision-making process. When two such groups are joined in a single enterprise, it is unlikely that they can accommodate their various interests by equating marginal product and wages even in the long run. If they do equate them, the process will have been a complicated and indirect one. Those manifold noneconomic considerations to which previous attention was devoted demand their expression in the decisions which are ultimately reached; the play of bargaining power is involved in a manner with which we are already familiar. This is not simply contract making in the sense that an agreement may *or may not* be reached, that mutual accommodation may *or may not* be forthcoming. Functional interdependence assures that some decision *must* be jointly reached if the business of production is to go forward at all.

[11] We may note that Marshall looked upon partnerships as allowing coequal authority among a number of men, but apparently he expected the authority of each to be exercised in some specialized field. Moreover, under orthodox assumptions their motives and objectives are identical—there is no conflict of interests involved.

If intergroup processes, such as collective bargaining, are admitted as the media through which business decisions are made at least in part, then it is likely that the personification of the entrepreneurial function and the assignment to it of unified personal interests will have misleading results. In the field of wages, the collective method of wage determination would appear to invalidate or at least modify the conclusions of a theory which rests on the assumption of a small-scale owner-operator entering into a personal contractual relationship with individual workers, with either party free to seek a better contract elsewhere. The principle of marginalism which Machlup has so ably elaborated *may* yet have its impact on one or the other party to the joint decision-making machinery, depending upon the validity of the maximizing principle, but this is something quite removed from a general theory of wages.

Collective bargaining cannot produce decisions different from those achieved through individual bargaining if economic forces allow no discretion. If the economic system is competitive enough to compel unions and management to conform to its requirements on pain of reduced profits, unemployment, or both, collective bargaining and individual bargaining are equally constrained. Insofar as competition is not wholly limiting, however, and the economic environment contains areas of permissiveness, the parties to collective bargaining enjoy some discretion in making their decisions. They are free to abide by standards other than those of the market. They may secure special advantage for themselves, finding that in their situation wages and employment have no unique relationship. As noted already, economists have pointed out that monopolistic competition, with its oligopoly, product differentiation, and price leadership, provides many situations of indeterminateness favorable to collective bargaining.

Despite the support of American unions of antimonopoly programs, unions have benefited from the relaxation of competitive standards. When relieved of inexorable market pressures, businesses are in a position to make concessions in collective negotiations which otherwise they might not be able to make. Unions can enter into a bargaining relationship with management on many matters which otherwise would be beyond the control of either, only because systematic competition does not compel a certain kind of decision. An important result of the relaxation of competitive restraints has been that unions have helped develop monopolistic arrangements among businesses unable to secure them alone. Every metropolitan area has its organizations of building trades contractors, dry cleaners, laundry workers, truckers, barbers, and so on, supported by the labor unions, who realize the damaging effect on wage and working standards of "excessive" competition from those who compose the local industry. Unionists want to avoid any competition which would lead to price cutting and which might, by chain reaction, spread throughout the trade and ultimately threaten to cause a general reduction in union wage standards. When unions have organized employers on a market-area basis, they can then negotiate with associated employers terms that otherwise would have been impossible. Each employer may now accept the terms because all employers accept them. In some instances unions have undertaken to "police the agreement" by refusing to provide workers for those who cut prices as well as wages, insisting on conformity to some general scale of prices which is sufficient to keep the average employer in business and permit his adhering to union standards of wages and working conditions.

Where individual firms are partially freed from the constraint of market pressures, the union can play a greater role in the making of business decisions. Where individual firms are strongly competitive, the union can play its role only by first organizing the industry so that it may bargain as a unit. The possibility of bargaining indicates an area of discretion. Where such discretion enters, the marginal productivity theory loses its significance as a general theory of wages, for that theory, as one aspect of equilibrium theory, rests on an assumed unique compulsion on employers and workers alike to respond to market forces. Stated in other terms, the degree of competition in the product market is inversely related to the elasticity of demand for the product. A high degree of elasticity in the demand for a product indicates the availability of excellent substitutes; perfect elasticity indicates the availability of perfect substitutes—identical products. To the degree that price competition recedes and discretion over price enters, there is an increasing inelasticity of demand for the product. Where such inelasticity exists, higher wages can, if necessary, be accommodated by higher prices. Monopolistic elements such as the differentiation of products, the oligopolizing of competition, and the welding of competitive units into an industry organization all contribute to a reduced availability of substitutes, an increased inelasticity of demand for the product, and a greater degree of control over price.

There is another respect in which it is too much to expect that price and wage changes must conform to certain ineluctable standards. The changing economic environment in which businesses operate appears to rule out any automatic transmission of wage effects to prices. Wage costs and unit labor costs need not vary directly with each other. Changing volumes of operation and changing technologies make a relationship impossible to establish. Further, labor costs as a share of total costs vary from industry to industry and even from firm to firm. In many cases labor costs are overshadowed by overhead or materials costs and vary markedly with the volume of output. Moreover, the relationship between total costs and prices is complex and difficult to identify. As was pointed out some time ago: "The cost structure of a concern and the condition of its markets establish certain limits within which decisions must be made, but within these boundaries there may be a broad field for the exercise of individual [and, it might be added, group] judgment." [12] The complexities of business organization in a dynamic economy rule out the possibility of any straight-line relation between wages and prices; between them intervene a multitude of factors influencing the relationship of wages to labor costs, of labor costs to total costs, and of total costs to price. Along this chain of relationships in an economy where tastes, technologies, and population are changing, lie numerous opportunities for discretionary decision making. Where discretion is possible, the union may enter and claim a hearing for its views. The static theory of marginal productivity is admittedly not applicable in such a dynamic setting.

If it appears that the marginal productivity theory of wages has been subjected to an unduly prolonged flailing here, it is because economists have so frequently resorted to it as an explanation of actual behavior or as a criterion of the desirability of some wage policy. In seeking to discover why it is suitable for neither of these purposes, we have examined particularly its inadequate conception of the decision-making process in a society composed of interdependent economic groups possessing important elements of discretionary control, and particularly in a dynamic society to which it was never expected to apply.

The significance of this conclusion should not be overlooked, however. The principal value of the theory lay in its integration with the doctrine of general price equilibrium. The important consideration is, then, that if the marginal productivity theory cannot be relied upon, there is no present basis for assuming that self-equilibrating forces operate within the economy to allocate the factors of production. If discretionary decision making is admitted, the decision makers and bargainers need some kind of standards or guides. If we cannot rely on automatic market forces to provide those guides and hold the bargainers to them, we must establish other guides and compulsions of a kind compatible with a democratic society. In 1962, for example, the President's Council of Economic Advisors suggested that the nation consider the advisability of setting forth explicit "guidelines" to help evaluate wage movements and bargaining settlements. The council's suggestion of "productivity" as a possible standard aroused much discussion; we shall examine in detail the problem of this and other possible standards in the next chapter.

The elaborate and closely articulated economic theory which nineteenth-century economists built and later economists maintained is beginning to crack. Economic variables do not relate to one another in unambiguous ways. Wages, for example, can no longer be counted upon to serve as the medium for allocating labor in an optimum manner among competing firms

[12] *Industrial Wage Rates, Labor Costs and Price Policies,* Temporary National Economic Committee Monograph No. 5 (1940), p. xxiii.

and industries, even though they are partly effective in that respect. Market research suggests that job availability rather than wage differentials is more effective in distributing labor.[13] Although obviously prices and wages remain as important forces in our society, the price *system* as a comprehensive synthetic means of economic control and economic integration is being recognized as a theoretical abstraction of questionable reliability. We are discovering that in our evolving culture many economic relationships come into existence and are perpetuated or allowed to disintegrate for reasons other than price. The forces operating in our economy are many; they are not all traceable to the market. Which forces are to be encouraged and which sublimated, and how the forces are to be channeled and controlled, are matters confronting us as a society now.

The Need for New Wage Standards

Let us probe a little deeper into the problem of the need for new standards for the allocation of scarce resources, which has traditionally been the chief concern of economists. With respect to the productive factor labor, the problem involves the assignment of workers to a variety of occupations, industries, and locations in a manner which best satisfies some standard generally accepted within the society. In liberal Western society, economists have usually assumed that the standard of allocation should approximate the consuming public's demand. We should allow and induce the labor force to produce that bundle of goods and services which consumers would choose. Goods from automobiles to baby carriages and services from medical treatment to nightclub entertainment would be provided in those proportions which society wishes. As tastes change, the production of goods and services should likewise change, requiring a transfer of workers from one line of production to another. Economists have thus seen the allocating problem as one of making changes or transfers of the factors of production in accordance with the desires of the consuming public.

In the neoclassical theoretical system, change could and should take place largely in accordance with the principle of marginal productivity, which we have just examined. If that principle were followed throughout the economy, workers would be shifted among occupations, industries, and regions in a manner determined by consumer preferences in products. An

---

[13] Thomas Kennedy, *The Significance of Wage Uniformity,* Industry-wide Collective Bargaining Series, University of Pennsylvania, p. 21, giving other citations. Evidence is also to be found in Carter Goodrich et al., *Migration and Economic Opportunity,* Philadelphia: University of Pennsylvania Press, 1936; and Lloyd Reynolds, *The Structure of Labor Markets,* New York: Harper & Row, Publishers, Incorporated, 1951, chap. 30.

increased demand for a particular product would raise the price of that product, permitting the payment of higher wages to attract more workers so that output could be increased. As more workers competed for the favored jobs and as output rose (lowering the marginal value product), both the price of the product and the wages of the men producing it would recede from their temporary high levels. Meanwhile, since demand had shifted away from other products, their prices would decline, lowering the marginal value product and with it wage rates. Lowered wages would cause some workers to leave their employment, and output would consequently drop. With a smaller output, demand would force prices back upward, raising the marginal value product and with it wage rates. The upward revision of wages would first reduce and finally eliminate workers' incentive to seek jobs elsewhere. Movement of workers away from those industries where demand had lessened to that industry where it had increased would cease when the wage rates of roughly comparable workers were equal and reflected similar marginal value products. In this way, consumer choice would have effected a shift in the allocation of resources; changing demand leads to price changes, which affect producers' outputs, and producers' outputs affect their need for labor, leading to wage changes, the effect of which is to drive workers from some occupations and draw them to others.

Allocation according to consumer preference can be assumed, however, only if market forces remain beyond the control of any producer or consumer. The power of any group to control markets spells monopoly, which distorts the price structure, forcing consumers to alter their proportions of goods desired in line with the new price structure. No longer will production conform only to consumer preferences; consumer preferences will in some degree bend to conform to monopoly power. The principle of allocation of resources on the basis of maximum consumer satisfaction is violated.

Monopoly power destroys the optimum distribution of labor when judged by the standard of consumer preference. We know that in varying degrees, producers in almost every industry in the United States enjoy discretion of monopolistic power in the setting of price and output. We are less concerned here with business aspects of the problem, however, than with the activities of unions. Customarily economists have tended to see unions as wielders of monopoly power, pushing up wage rates, disturbing the structure of competitive market prices, and doing violence to the principle that workers, like all factors of production, should be assigned to jobs on the basis of what society in its consumer capacity most wishes.

At the same time, in order to be realistic we must recognize that in the future, businesses will retain an element of market control, and unions will remain an active force in the making of economic and business decisions; monopolistic powers are not likely to disappear. We cannot therefore rely on competitive pricing to secure a precise allocation of resources according to the long-accepted economic standard. A continued acceptance of unions and their use of collective bargaining to participate in the determining of wages implies at least a partial abandonment of our previous standard of allocating economic resources solely by reference to consumer wants.

To repeat, the problem which we must face, then, is this: If the system of free competitive pricing, resting on marginal productivity, cannot be counted on to secure an optimum allocation of resources and specifically of labor, by our former standard of maximum consumer satisfaction, by what new principles or standards shall we distribute our working population among alternative job prospects? Shall we abandon a search for principles and let collective bargaining take whatever course it will, affecting the allocation of workers among productive employments by chance or hazard or according to special rather than common interest within some wider constraints which the market still provides?

If we are to gain anything from an examination of this, we must understand better the reasons why it has emerged as a problem. The rise of monopolistic organizations, capable of distorting competitors' market forces, is the immediate cause, but we can go at least one step further and ask why monopolistic organizations have become commonplace; to what may the weakening of the free market be ascribed? That such a question has a scope beyond the limitations of this book cannot excuse us from considering, if only in the broadest terms, its relationship to the problem we have at hand.

In exploring this matter it is necessary for us to take specific cognizance of two basic assumptions of competitive pricing: (1) In economic affairs, people will be primarily motivated by pecuniary considerations; and (2) the pursuit of monopolistic power is nonsocial, although it is still based on pecuniary motives. In analyzing the labor problem, economists usually assume that workers will be motivated to change jobs and locations if there is a possibility of improving their pecuniary circumstances; differences in wage levels will stimulate worker movement. They also assume that as examples of monopolistic organizations, unions have come into existence to exploit pecuniary advantage. In the words of one economist, previously quoted, "monopoly has no use save abuse." [14] It is because these two assumptions are unsatisfactory *as generalizations* that the problem of optimum allocation is with us.

Economists never imagined, of course, that the pecuniary motivation of individuals operated as an exclusive force. It has been regarded as a concept of relative validity and as an attempt to identify primary motivation in capitalist society. Despite such qualification, it has nevertheless been employed in economic theory *as though* it operated unalloyed. The justification for such an approach is that it permits a more precise and conclusive

[14] Henry Simons, quoted in chapter 7 in connection with the subject of bargaining power.

system of deductive theory and, at the same time, can be supported as a reasonably close approximation to reality. "It is very doubtful that laborers or owners of other productive agents sacrifice money return for other considerations to any large extent on the whole." [15]

[15] Frank H. Knight, as quoted in George Stigler, *Theory of Price,* New York: The Macmillan Company, 1946, p. 109. R. G. Tugwell thus commented: "One great justification . . . for the distributive categories of rent, interest, profit and wages lies in the fact that each furnishes an incentive to distinct individuals to do a distinct thing. . . ." "Human Nature in Economic Theory," *Journal of Political Economy,* vol. 30 (1932), p. 336.

Most economists have followed Adam Smith in spelling out the proposition that competition among (capital or) labor seeking employment will tend to equalize not (profits or) wages, but net advantages. Economists can thus presumably accept all the evidences of nonpecuniary elements of job satisfaction, absorbing it into standard doctrine by arguing that a worker's evaluation of such elements constitutes—along with the wage—the measure of the job's net advantage, to be compared with the net advantages of other jobs, the whole analysis of factor movement proceeding from this point in familiar terms. But if this view is taken, one operates with the unprovable assumption that a wage of given magnitude has the same differential effect (that is, adds up to the same net advantages) for all workers receiving it; however, the other job elements may be differently evaluated by different workers. An alternative assumption —generally accepted since Ricardo—is that all workers (at least all interchangeable workers) regard each nonmonetary job element in the same light (that is, use similar value systems for calculating their worth). Otherwise wages would not have their allocative effect. If all workers, in their calculations, did not attach to the social prestige of a range of jobs the same relative values, for example, or attribute the same relative negative values to the dirtiness of a range of jobs, that is, if there was not some sort of absolute scale of values for all job elements, then a whole range of wage rates would be required to equalize net advantages for workers performing the same jobs, and such differential rates would not be presumed to lead to worker movement.

The job satisfaction studies to be examined now thus cannot be said to make a contribution simply by pointing out the nonpecuniary elements of job satisfaction. However, they mark a different emphasis. Even though economic doctrine has recognized nonpecuniary influences on job satisfaction and labor allocation, it has in fact (by the device of the *ceteris paribus* assumption) stressed the pecuniary influence in such a manner as to make it dominant and controlling. The job satisfaction surveys have reduced the wage to one of a number of elements which must be considered in weighing the attractive qualities of jobs. They suggest that a simple change in the wage rate may not alter calculations of net advantages sufficiently to lead to worker movement. Moreover, some of such studies have emphasized a variant regard by workers for the same job elements. These studies have, in short, tended to restore the doctrine of comparative net advantages (whatever its validity), but with an increased understanding of the factors contributing to a worker's conception of wherein advantage lies.

Perhaps because the possibility of arriving at determinate economic solutions seems dependent on quantitative analysis such as pecuniary measurement allows, there has been a peculiar reluctance to recognize the significance of recent investigations into the related fields of motivation, incentive, and morale in industrial society. We shall not be able to canvass with thoroughness the findings of these studies—to do so would literally require a book in itself—but we may take note of their unanimity in underscoring the importance of nonfinancial incentives. Investigation after investigation in recent years has emphasized that workers' response to money reward is related to only one among a number of worker motives and, moreover, is not necessarily the most powerful of such motives. Let us simply list some of the findings in staccato fashion.

A study undertaken by Hoppock and Spiegler in 1935 in a small worker group revealed that the factors most mentioned for making a job attractive were, in order, (1) work associates; (2) the work itself; (3) the boss; (4) variety; (5) freedom in work; (6) hours; and (7) earnings. On the other side of the coin, the factors most mentioned as causes for disliking a job were the following: (1) the work; (2) low earnings; and (3) long hours. Note that pecuniary considerations enter into these appraisals, but note too that they are not considered dominant.[16]

In a survey the results of which were published in 1938, J. D. Houser sought to determine the relative importance of twenty-eight factors to the nonselling employees of a large merchandising enterprise. Only with the twelfth-ranked factor does one come to something that can be unequivocally labeled as derivative from the pecuniary motive. The first twelve factors are (1) receiving help necessary to get results expected by management; (2) being encouraged to offer suggestions and try out better methods; (3) being able to find out whether work is improving; (4) reasonable certainty of being able to get a fair hearing and square deal in case of grievance; (5) certainty of promotions going to best-qualified employees; (6) encouragement to seek advice in case of real problems; (7) being given information about important plans and results which concern the individual's work; (8) being given reasons for changes which are ordered in work; (9) not being actually hampered in work by superior; (10) not getting contradictory or conflicting orders; (11) being given to understand completely the results which are expected in a job; and (12) pay—assurance of increases when deserved.[17]

S. N. F. Chant, in one of the earliest of such surveys (1932), ranked the stated reasons for job preferences as given in two samples, one of 100

[16] R. Hoppock and S. Spiegler, "Job Satisfaction," *Occupations, The Vocational Guidance Magazine,* vol. 16 (1938), pp. 636–643.

[17] J. D. Houser, *What People Want from Business,* New York: McGraw-Hill Book Company, 1938, p. 29.

department store workers and the other of 150 miscellaneous workers. In both cases the results showed that opportunity for advancement, steady work, opportunity to use one's ideas, opportunity to learn a job, and a good boss were all ranked—in that order—ahead of high pay.[18]

R. B. Hersey sought to discover whether there were differences between union and nonunion employees in the selection of "the most important" among a number of factors relating to their jobs. On the basis of his sample he concluded that both groups placed steady employment above amount of pay, and union workers asserted that the fair adjustment of grievances and safety were likewise more important than pay.[19]

The National Industrial Conference Board sponsored one of the most comprehensive of such surveys. Employees in six plants were asked to select from among seventy-one factors the five they considered most important to them. When the results were tabulated for all employees in all companies, they showed that almost one-third of the employees had placed job security and employment stabilization at the top of the list. Next most frequently chosen (by 8.7 per cent) was compensation (base pay), but the type of work was considered by an almost equal number (7.2 per cent) to be first in importance. Another tabulation listed the number of employees naming specific items as among the five most important to them. On this basis, 44.7 per cent of all employees mentioned job security and employment stabilization; 30.7 per cent mentioned opportunities in the company for advancement; 27.9 per cent mentioned compensation (base pay); and 24.4 per cent mentioned other financial benefits such as group life insurance, sickness insurance, and pensions. One of the instructive results of this study was that it emphasized the variety of worker opinion concerning the factors making for job satisfaction. In one company forty-five different items were selected by one or more employees as first in importance, and seventy-one factors were on the individual lists of the five most important factors.[20]

A study made by Sears, Roebuck and Co. in 1950 of 12,000 responses to a questionnaire showed that workers' relative pay ranked in eighth place

[18] S. N. F. Chant, "Measuring the Factors That Make a Job Interesting," *Personnel Journal,* vol. 11 (1932), pp. 1–4. One of the criticisms made of this study has been that the sample of miscellaneous workers was drawn entirely from persons belonging to the Young Men's Department of a YMCA, which casts some doubt on its representative nature. Thus, in the miscellaneous sample, workers also listed ahead of high pay the opportunity to be of public service.

[19] R. B. Hersey, "Psychology of Workers," *Personnel Journal,* vol. 14 (1936), pp. 291–296.

[20] National Industrial Conference Board, *Factors Affecting Employee Morale,* Studies in Personnel Policy No. 85 (1947).

among the elements related to high morale. Rates of pay, as such, ranked fourteenth, and hours of work ranked twenty-first.[21]

The Survey Research Center of the University of Michigan conducted a study of employee morale in a large Eastern insurance company by intensively interviewing 850 employees.[22] The results of the study suggested that the greater satisfaction of higher-level occupational groups is not merely a function of higher wages and better conditions of work. When length of service and salary were held constant, measurements of intrinsic job satisfaction proved to be significantly related to type of work. Prof. Daniel Katz concluded: "People do derive important satisfaction in the expression of their skills, in interesting and challenging work, and in the sense of accomplishment from successful performance." [23]

Additional studies might be cited,[24] but these should be enough to indicate that to continue to accord to pecuniary motivation dominant importance may be unwarranted. It is true with respect to each of the studies mentioned, and to all of them collectively, criticism may be made. In particular, the "rank" of any factor is a matter so dependent upon conditioning circumstances that it is scarcely worth recording unless related to those circumstances. Nor can it escape attention that factors such as "security" and "advancement" have a pecuniary element in them, even though other considerations, too, are present. The significance of these findings is not that some other factor was alleged to be "more important" to workers than "high pay," however. It is, rather, that a number of factors in addition to pay are of such concern to workers that they cannot be ignored. There is no reason to believe, on the basis of these studies, that workers are likely to change jobs simply because of a difference in wage rates.

A second conclusion has been well stated by two investigators as follows:

> Economic theory usually assumes that workers stand ready at any time to leave their present jobs for better ones, and that all voluntary

[21] James C. Worthy, "Managers, Corporate Structure and Employee Morale: A Case Study," in *Industrial Man,* W. Lloyd Warner and Norman H. Martin (eds.), New York: Harper & Row, Publishers, Incorporated, 1959, p. 253.

[22] Nancy C. Morse, *Employee Satisfaction, Supervision and Morale in an Office Situation,* part II, University of Michigan, Ann Arbor, Mich., 1953.

[23] Daniel Katz, "Satisfactions and Deprivations in Industrial Life," in *Industrial Conflict,* Arthur Kornhauser, Robert Dubin, and Arthur M. Ross (eds.), New York: McGraw-Hill Book Company, 1954, p. 92.

[24] William F. Whyte thoroughly examines the shortcomings of the assumption that pecuniary motivation is dominant among workers in his study *Money and Motivation: An Analysis of Incentive in Industry,* New York: Harper & Row, Publishers, Incorporated, 1955.

movement of labor is of this purposeful character. In actuality, however, a majority of the workers at any time are unwilling to leave their jobs unless forced to do so through lay-off or discharge. Of those who do change jobs of their own accord, the great majority do so because of some unsatisfactory feature of their present job. They are "pushed" into the labor market through discontent rather than "pulled" by any concrete knowledge of better opportunities. Workers who move deliberately from one job to a better job *which they know about in advance* are a minority of a minority—probably not more than 5 per cent of the labor force even in good years. It is doubtful whether this is a large enough group to affect the structure of wages and employment in the way assumed by economic theory.[25]

Unions and Wage Standards

We may thus conclude that the assumption that in economic affairs people are motivated to initiate action primarily by pecuniary considerations, which is one of the foundation stones of the theory of competitive pricing, is subject to challenge. But because this is true with respect to individuals is not sufficient grounds for concluding that it must also be true of organizations such as unions. Even if individuals are motivated by a complex of factors, unions could be predominantly responsive to only one of their needs. The factor of pay remains important in the workers' system of compulsive forces, and it is entirely conceivable that unions, generally speaking, are geared to satisfy primarily that drive. We cannot therefore appraise the validity of the competitive pricing assumption that efforts to acquire monopolistic power rest primarily on the pecuniary motive without examining further the reasons why employees have organized unions and sought to bargain with their employers. We must seek to answer more directly the question of whether union programs show interests broader than the amount which their members take home in their pay envelopes.

First, we may recall the subject matter of collective bargaining, already examined in an earlier chapter. Although many of the matters discussed at the bargaining table are related to wage payments, a number of others appear to be more closely related to nonpecuniary factors. In particular, the unions' high regard for job security is clear, often expressed in the seniority provisions governing layoffs. Opportunity for advancement without arbitrary discrimination is sought through promotional systems based on seniority. The desire for the just disposition of grievances lies behind the

[25] Lloyd G. Reynolds and Joseph Shister, *Job Horizons: A Study of Job Satisfaction and Labor Mobility,* New York: Harper & Row, Publishers, Incorporated, 1949, pp. 87–88. (Italics in original.)

grievance procedure itself. The workers' insistence that employers explicitly recognize their union representatives and that they be treated as equals indicates their interest in dignity.

Even in seeking what appear to be purely pecuniary gains—wage increases and adjustments of pay—workers and unions often are striving for less material benefits. Work groups and union shop leaders frequently set production (and earnings) "limits" to protect their older members from too fast a work pace. In the eyes of the workers, such a "limit" may also contribute to their job security by spreading their work over a longer period of time. Union leaders often seek adjustments in piece rates, not so much because workers want higher earnings as because they seek a "fair" and comparable rate. The slogan "equal pay for equal work" was not merely an expression of a demand for higher pay, but a cry against employers' discriminatory administration of wages and against favoritism. However opportunistically both parties use such nonpecuniary standards as fairness and comparability, each finds them appealing and significant. Management even uses them with some success to resist rate improvements and sometimes to argue for cuts.

For such reasons we may conclude, then, that workers are not stimulated to organize into unions and pursue a collective bargaining policy solely by pecuniary considerations. As with its members individually, a complex of motivating factors appears to lie behind the union's behavior.

A second approach to explaining union organization is to draw on those theories of the labor movement in the United States which have been advanced by students of the subject. Here again we shall have to be satisfied with the briefest of summary statements.

John R. Commons has set forth the thesis that unions arose in this country in response to a widening of product markets which led to a separation of interests between journeyman and employer.[26] In local community markets the interests of the two were nearly parallel. They usually worked side by side; they experienced the same satisfactions in a quality product; immediately felt social pressures served to maintain a reasonable standard for both prices and wages, and journeymen had grounds for entertaining the expectation of graduating to employer status. As markets expanded so that an enterprise sold not only locally but also within a region and then in the national market, however, the financial and employing functions became separated, and competition for sales pressed downward

[26] John R. Commons, "American Shoemakers: A Sketch of Industrial Evolution, 1648–1895," *Quarterly Journal of Economics,* vol. 24 (1910), pp. 39–84; reproduced in John R. Commons et al. (eds.), *Documentary History of American Industrial Society,* Glendale, Calif.: The Arthur H. Clark Company, 1910–1911, vol. 3, pp. 18–58.

on prices, with lower prices made possible through downward pressure on wages. Employees were thus forced to organize as a group with interests opposed to those of their employer, that is, as an anticompetitive force.

Selig Perlman has explained the rise of the labor movement on the grounds that workers were motivated by a scarcity consciousness—an awareness of the scarcity of the economic goods of life and of the scarcity of jobs making possible the purchase of those goods.[27] They banded together in unions to secure a kind of job control, which allowed them a greater sense of security in the midst of scarcity.

Carleton Parker, following a different line of analysis, concluded that worker organization arose as an aggressive reaction to the frustration of deep-rooted instincts brought about by modern industrial methods.[28]

Robert Hoxie denied any single causal explanation of the formation of unions but maintained that the whole complex of environmental and personal influences in a particular setting provided the formative forces. Such influences varied from situation to situation.[29]

The historian Frank Tannenbaum has laid the emphasis on worker reaction to the atomism of society characterizing the nineteenth century. The extreme individualistic philosophy which looked upon every worker as a discrete economic unit, unrelated to his fellows in any significant way, disregarded the fundamental social grouping of men around their work, which trade unions came into existence to protect.[30]

These capsule summaries, although they do an injustice to the careful elaboration of these writers and do not permit an examination of the possibility of the integration of their ideas, serve to suggest that unions have appeared in this country as responses to both pecuniary and nonpecuniary drives on the part of their members. There appears to be little basis for believing that the pay motive has been singled out of the whole range of worker motivation and that unions have operated on that level alone. Moreover, in those theories that stressed the pecuniary motive, as Commons's did, organization is said to have arisen not from an intent to exploit but from a desire to offset exploitation. Simons's opinion that union monopoly power has no use save abuse appears to be nothing more than a restate-

[27] Selig Perlman, *A Theory of the Labor Movement,* New York: The Macmillan Company, 1949.

[28] Carleton Parker, *The Casual Laborer,* New York: Harcourt, Brace & World, Inc., 1920.

[29] Robert F. Hoxie (with Introduction by E. H. Downey), *Trade Unionism in the United States,* New York: D. Appleton & Company, Inc., 1921.

[30] Frank Tannenbaum, *The Labor Movement: Its Conservative Functions and Social Consequences,* New York: G. P. Putnam's Sons, 1921. His thesis is restated in "The Social Function of Trade Unionism," *Political Science Quarterly,* vol. 62 (1947), pp. 161–182.

ment of one of the basic assumptions of competitive pricing theory rather than a conclusion based on obtainable evidence.[31]

We are now prepared to gather together the fruits of this digression on worker and organizational motivation. The evidence strongly suggests that both employees and the unions which they form are significantly responsive to other than pecuniary incentives. Also important is the drive to obtain a greater degree of "job satisfaction"—an improved relationship between workers and their jobs, between workers and other workers, and between workers and management in their industrial societies.

Economists considered the pecuniary motive fundamental because its satisfaction was directly tied to the satisfaction of consumer wants, which was the very reason for the economy's existence. Consumer wants were viewed as unlimited. In an exchange economy, the degree of their satisfaction was dependent on purchasing power, which in turn was dependent upon the payments to the factors—wages, in the case of workers. The desire for wages was therefore presumed to be directly related to the desire for consumer satisfaction. Since the latter was considered to be unlimited, the former was viewed in the same light. The desire for wages—the pecuniary motive—was thus thought to be dominant.

The classical concept of real costs had taught that work was the price which must be paid for the real utilities that came with consumption. Satisfaction was thus derived not from the productive process but from consuming the fruits of that process. Consumption became the end; it was the only good. The system allocated factors according to the principle of obtaining maximum consumer satisfaction. The means by which the labor factor was to be allocated was the money wage, which derived its motivating power from its exchange value. What we are now discovering, however, is that this whole system of reasoning has a faulty foundation in the premise that consumption is the only purpose of the economy. Workers and union leaders are importantly motivated by nonpecuniary considerations. They are not solely interested in satisfying consumer wants; they find satisfactions in the process of production and enjoyment of the job and the worker society. These, as well as consuming, are important parts of living. The workers' interests as producers must therefore be considered along with their interests as consumers.[32]

[31] Indeed, only one of the above-mentioned theories of the American labor movement suggests that an effort to satisfy the pecuniary drive through systematic exploitation has been a motive for union organization. Hoxie, who believed that unions must be explained individually and not as a movement, recognized that from time to time in isolated unions such exploitative efforts might dominate, though by no means did he consider this representative of unions as a whole.

[32] Even classical and neoclassical writers admitted this in employing a con-

Conclusion

When the problem is put in this way, it becomes clearer why it is difficult, if not impossible, to determine whether pecuniary or nonpecuniary considerations are more important. Such a question is tantamount to asking whether workers are more interested in enjoying themselves while they work or enjoying themselves while they consume. The attempt definitely to balance satisfactions in such a manner makes as much sense as an attempt to determine once and for all whether workers prefer leisure or more income. The answer is dependent on circumstances of the moment.

Our knowledge of worker and union motivation should bring us to an important conclusion, however. The notion that unions have interfered with the "optimum" allocation of labor, in the traditional sense, is valid only if one assumes that consumer interests should be paramount. If one is prepared to grant that people may legitimately be concerned with their productive lives and with the kind of society in which they work, even if their views in such respects differ from the views of others, then one can only conclude that the standard of "optimum" allocation is faulty. *Maximum* consumer satisfaction ceases to become the basis for determining what is the best distribution of resources among competing uses. The generalization that unions are exploitative, the judgment that unions disrupt economic organization, and the dictum that unions ignore consumer interests are to some extent based on a criterion which a great many Americans no longer accept as the only one. Failure to recognize this fact sometimes leads people to take a paradoxical position, praising unions for forcing management to pay more attention to workers' needs, while condemning them for upsetting the competitive price mechanism.

What can be said, then, in specific answer to our question of what standards can be used in allocating labor among productive employments? Unions and collective bargaining have made the old standard untenable, and we might justifiably abandon it as an exclusive standard. Workers' interests as producers, as well as their interests as consumers, must be taken into account, and we may expect such interests to vary with the composition of the work group and over time. Moreover, we may conclude

---

cept known as "psychic income," which was sometimes used to explain wage differentials. It was said that the enjoyment which a man derived from his employment might lead him to accept a smaller wage than he could receive elsewhere. So little impact did this concept make on the body of doctrine, however, that it constituted little more than an interesting footnote to the mainstream of thought. There was no appreciation that here they were touching on the phenomenon of producer interest, a matter of such high importance that it was to threaten—in our day—the system which excluded it.

that the basic problem has not been created by unions, but by previous failure on the part of society generally to appreciate the narrowness of a philosophy which placed exclusive emphasis on what a man consumes, without respect to the intrinsic satisfaction that comes from his relationship to a job and to a work group. This is not to say, of course, that unions may not take actions which by both consumer and producer standards are unwarranted. There is evidence that union leaders no less than others in society have misjudged what satisfactions workers are seeking from their jobs.[33] Nevertheless, unions may be putting us on the road to recognizing the validity of the criterion of job satisfaction and the reasonableness of placing it alongside consumer satisfaction in any allocation theory which we may ultimately develop.

Another way of phrasing this general conclusion is to say that "optimum allocation," defined in the old sense of the distribution of the factors of production most conducive to consumer satisfaction, ceases to be the dominant economic problem. No longer can we regard it as the central concern of all economic study. Instead, it takes its place as just one of several major economic problems. The improvement of consumer satisfaction becomes one objective of the economy, alongside other objectives such as the advancement of producer satisfactions, that is, the satisfactions deriving from the work process itself.

Some sort of a compromise may be necessary in reconciling these simultaneously held objectives. Though this is not necessarily the case, satisfaction of producer interests may reduce our capacity to satisfy consumer interests. What becomes abundantly clear, however, is that this conclusion requires some sort of reconciliation between competition and control (or monopoly). Producer satisfaction appears to mean a degree of control by individuals over their own work lives, and this can be achieved only through arrangements which traditionally we regard as monopolistic. Some degree of control (or monopoly) thus appears to be desirable since it is essential to the satisfactions that come from work. Substantial competition is also necessary, however, if we are to gratify our wants as consumers.

But in admitting the desirability of some degree of monopoly, as yet unspecified, are we not opening a Pandora's box of economic troubles? Before we address ourselves to this question, in Chapter 15, let us turn to another aspect of the wage problem.

[33] Evidence to this effect is offered by Clifford E. Jurgensen, *Journal of Applied Psychology,* vol. 31 (1947), p. 562; National Industrial Conference Board, *Factors Affecting Employee Morale,* p. 21; and James W. Kuhn, *Bargaining in Grievance Settlement,* New York: Columbia University Press, 1961, chaps. 6 and 8.

The Economics of Collective Bargaining: Effects on National Income Levels

chapter 14

If the marginal productivity theory cannot be accepted as either descriptive or normative for an economy largely characterized by group rather than individual action, we should emphasize that what we are discarding is a theory of how resources are allocated and its concomitant, a theory of how the national income is distributed. General equilibrium theory in static analysis is not concerned with how the size of the national income itself is *determined*. In the previous chapter, we concluded that group decision making in our society may lead to an allocation of the factors of production and a distribution of income determined at best only within broad limits by market forces, even in the long run. We said that the question of who gets how much is answered by agreement between groups of individuals in various functional roles, the groups possessing a certain latitude of discretion within a loosely competitive framework. The decisions affecting employment of resources and distribution of product may nevertheless have their impact on the size of the national income itself and how it will be distributed.

340

Wage Policies and National Income

By encouraging consumption and investment within the economy, wage policies can contribute to a large national dividend; or by discouraging consumption and investment, they may help produce a smaller dividend. The fact that managers and union leaders have some discretion in determining wage policies does not mean that they will use their discretion wisely. In particular, if we conclude that the marginal productivity theory tells us little about the relationship of wage rates to one another and to interest, rents, and profits, we should be careful not to slip into the error of believing that the distribution of national income has no effect upon output, whether through its impact on employment or on productivity. Recognizing the existence of some relationship between wages, employment, productivity, and output is far from identifying those relationships, however. Changes in output and variations in productivity are parts of economic dynamics, and to examine them we must pass from consideration of the stationary state and the static assumptions with which the marginal productivity theory deals to the analysis of the process of income creation itself.

For a long time economists assumed that the amount of employment would vary inversely with the wage rate *if* the total level of wage income remained the same. Under the assumption of a stable national income, with a fixed proportion going to wage earners, high wage levels (such as might be attributed to union action through collective bargaining) were thus presumed to lead to some unemployment. The result can be traced through the following equation, which represents the "quantity theory of employment": $NW = qY$, where N is the number of workers employed, W is the wage rate, q is the proportion of total money income going to wages, and Y is the total money income.[1] If the proportion of a given total income going to workers (qY) remains fixed, then obviously the number employed (N) varies in the opposite direction from the wage level (W). If wages rise, the number employed must fall; if wages decline, the number employed must rise. But such a relationship could be presumed only if a change in the wage rate did not itself bring about some change in q or Y. Similarly, it could be argued that an increase in Y would add to the number employed provided wage rates remained the same. The classical and neoclassical economists, assuming that Y could be expected to remain the same, tended to argue that the way to expand employment was to lower wages. It was this theoretical view that supported the frequently espoused policy of cutting wages in time of depression to stimulate employment.

[1] Alvin H. Hansen, *Monetary Theory and Fiscal Policy*, New York: McGraw-Hill Book Company, 1949, chap. 8, makes use of this equation, borrowed from Prof. A. C. Pigou, in a lucid statement of wage-income relationships.

"The argument simply is that a reduction in money-wages will [other things remaining equal] stimulate demand by diminishing the price of the finished product, and will therefore increase output and employment" up to the point where the reduction in wages is offset by rising marginal costs.[2]

John Maynard Keynes, in his *General Theory,* in 1936, cast grave doubts upon this classical conclusion. He argued that one could not begin by presuming that income will remain stable. Since total expenditures provide total income, changes in expenditures therefore cause changes in income. A single firm or a number of isolated firms might indeed increase employment if they could cut costs by reducing wages, but it is erroneous, said Keynes, to apply such reasoning to the economy as a whole. If wages are reduced generally throughout the economy, prices will fall too, but not by as much as the extent of the wage decline since other costs enter into production. Workers' expenditures, which constitute a large proportion of national income, will then support a lesser output than formerly. The hope for a *stimulus* to output would have to rest upon non-wage earners, who might conceivably increase their purchases. For this hope to be realized, one must assume that nonwage incomes would be unaffected by the wage-cutting process. If the returns to other factors fell proportionately as much as wages, then everyone would be situated as he was before. If wages, interest, rents, profits, and, therefore, prices are all equally affected, real prices remain the same, and output is unchanged. If nonwage income does not decline proportionately with wages and nonworkers find themselves with the same money income but enjoying lower prices, we must also assume that they would use their extra funds to buy more rather than save more. Or we must assume that even if nonworkers consumed no more than formerly, businessmen would somehow be encouraged to invest more and to expand output and employment in the capital goods industries or that the new lower prices would stimulate greater purchases by foreign countries. Keynes argued that to some extent these assumptions might be borne out in fact but that it is unlikely that the net effect will be to sustain the national income at its previous levels. Under certain circumstances, income may be sustained, but more often than not nonworker consumers and business investors will react bearishly to a falling price level. Income (that is, output) will not be maintained, so that the lowered wage structure could not lead to increased employment. By comparable argument it might likewise be shown that an increase in wage rates does not necessarily or even probably lead to a decline in employment. The results are just not predictable.

With respect to the impact of wage policies on the level of employment and output, we can say little in the absence of more specific data on the

[2] J. M. Keynes, *The General Theory of Employment, Interest and Money,* New York: Harcourt, Brace & World, Inc., 1936, p. 257.

relevant relationships existing at a particular time. "There are few, if indeed any, economists now who will dogmatically assert either that wage cuts will surely increase employment *or* that such wage cuts cannot possibly have any favorable effects. There are too many unknowns that vary with special conditions and special circumstances." [3] The same may be said of the effect of upward wage movements. The effect of bargaining policies upon consumption and investment is dependent on the relevant circumstances of the moment and may be either stimulative or depressive.

Some authorities have been inclined to guess that on the whole, over the years, the unions have raised rather than lowered national income. In fact, we do not know. So many factors affect consumption and investment that to measure the effects of any one separately from the others is impossible. Presumably unions have influenced consumption positively through a redistribution of income in favor of those groups which spend more of their income and negatively through a reduction of employment due to pressured wage increases. But the extent to which unions have actually succeeded in capturing a larger share of income for their members is open to question, as is the degree to which they have been responsible for unemployment due to bargained wage rates.[4]

More important perhaps, by seeking to enforce a policy of no wage cutting in depressions, unions may prevent a decline in national income as great as might otherwise occur. At some point in a declining economy as unemployment mounts, employment will have to be maintained at a level sufficient to produce the goods demanded by those who have the incomes or savings to support their continued spending. When this point is reached, there is no occasion for further decline in employment. Incomes paid out

[3] Hansen, *Monetary Theory and Fiscal Policy,* p. 126.

[4] Concerning the first issue, labor economists are in considerable agreement that statistical evidence is not conclusive but rather suggests that the actual impact of unions upon relative earnings is less than might have been expected from theoretical analysis. Ross concluded that in the organizing stages of union growth, union members may enjoy some slight wage advantage, but in general the studies indicate that unions have an almost unnoticeable effect. See Arthur Ross, "The Influence of Unionism upon Earnings," *Quarterly Journal of Economics,* vol. 62 (1948), pp. 263–286; Arthur Ross and W. Goldner, "Forces Affecting the Inter-industry Wage Structure," *Quarterly Journal of Economics,* vol. 64 (1950), pp. 254–281; J. Garbarino, "A Theory of Inter-industry Wage Structure Variation," *Quarterly Journal of Economics,* vol. 64 (1950), pp. 283–305; Stephen P. Sobotka, "Union Influence on Wages: The Construction Industry," *Journal of Political Economy,* vol. 61 (1953), pp. 127–143; P. E. Sultan, "Unionism and Wage-Income Ratios: 1929–1951," *Review of Economics and Statistics,* vol. 36 (1954), pp. 67–73; and H. M. Levinson, *Unionism, Wage Trends, and Income Distributions, 1914–1947,* University of Michigan, Ann Arbor, Mich., 1951, pp. 80–110.

are just sufficient to purchase current product. If wages were not rigid but flexible, they would be subject to repeated reduction, and an equilibrium point would be reached only at a lower level of income. For only at the lowest possible wage, whatever that might be, could one say that current factor income required current production. Before the lowest level was reached, the still declining labor income would support only a shrinking output. Union resistance reduces the severity of such recurrent wage cuts and by thus "firming" factor incomes at some level gives assurance that output will not be driven lower.

Collective bargaining would presumably influence investment by its impact on wage rates and business expectations. Again the results are problematical. Higher wages may encourage greater investment in laborsaving devices, but they might equally discourage their introduction in low-wage industries or areas by raising the cost of such devices. Also, union intervention into matters that managers have formerly conceived to be subject solely to their own discretion may dampen managerial expectations. The result may be the discouragement of new enterprise or the expansion of existing firms. Yet progress in enlisting the support of the union in improving productivity may lead, as it has in a few cases where successful, to an expansion of output requiring expansion of plant facilities.[5] There thus appears to be nothing inherent in unionism to permit conclusive analysis of its likely effects on the level of income.

One aspect of this problem deserves special attention. We have already observed how Keynes pointed out the potential fallacies involved in generalizing from the particular. A wage policy which may be advantageous to the individual union or firm may lose its benefits if generalized to the economy as a whole. A wage boost in a single local company can aid the immediately affected employees, probably without any detriment to the economy. If the company is not a local concern but rather United States Steel, for example, the results can be different. So large a company can set a pattern for the steel industry, and via coercive comparisons among employees and rivalries among union leaders, it may likewise have an influence on numerous other industries. We can no longer be sure that a policy which benefits employees of United States Steel will result in the same benefits if applied to a large number of other workers.[6] The same caveat

[5] This is a matter to be discussed more fully in succeeding chapters. It should be mentioned—indeed, emphasized—that the effect of collective bargaining on investment expenditures is doubly important. Not only does it influence the size of realized national product, by influencing current expenditures, but it affects potential (future) national product by affecting the kinds and amount of capital equipment to be utilized by the working force.

[6] Otto Eckstein and Gary Fromm, *Steel and the Postwar Inflation,* Joint Economic Committee Study Paper No. 2 (1959).

can be made with respect to wage actions which appear to be advantageous to management in one industry. If followed in other industries on a large scale, the action may prove of no benefit and conceivably of some harm.

Unions and National Wage Policies

We have here touched on a problem that looms as a major one for collective bargaining. In negotiating their agreements with management, unions act independently. True, what one union does or may do influences others, but each makes its decisions in its separate councils. With the present organization of the labor movement in the United States, the Steelworkers union must determine its wage policy *as though* that policy had no bearing upon the actions of other unions, for the Steelworkers union has no control over the wage policies of other unions. Suppose, for example, that the United Steelworkers leaders decided that (1) although the union could probably win a wage increase from the industry this year, wage increases granted throughout the economy would in the existing circumstances largely nullify any gains and perhaps even contribute to unemployment and (2) since other unions would be likely to follow their lead, they would forgo negotiating a wage increase this year. The leaders argue that the union members would lose nothing and that perhaps their forbearance might benefit the economy as a whole. What if, contrary to their expectations, the leaders found that the auto workers did not follow the example of the Steelworkers but struck for a wage increase and won it? For political reasons with which we are already familiar, the steel-union leaders would feel their position weakened. To avoid such an eventuality, union leaders must decide to make demands which come as close as possible to those that rival unions are likely to make. They are in no position to consider the effect of their policy upon the economy as a whole. Because of the phenomenon of wage leadership or pattern setting, national wage movements are thus set afoot by both unions and large corporations. Each is in a position to consider only what would happen to it if others won benefits that it did not. *National* wage policies are thus informally set in motion in the guise of *individual* union or company adjustments.

The fact is, then, that we cannot be sure of the effects a given wage policy will have on employment; the effects will depend upon circumstances peculiar to a given time and place, which must be elucidated before even approximate prediction is feasible. Furthermore, the effects of a wage policy in a particular firm or industry are likely to be quite different from the effects of that same policy applied to the nation at large. Because of the way the collective bargaining process has developed in this country, union and business leaders formulate wage policies *as though* they were intended for only a particular firm or industry; however, because of economic interdependence, the policies of the largest unions and companies become rough precedents. Smaller unions and firms spread their effects to important segments of the economy and then to the whole, presenting a problem of increasing dimensions.

Since union leaders and managers can initiate wage changes which have a significant impact upon general wage levels, the standards they use in their bargaining are matters of public as well as private interest. Insofar as they have discretionary power in fixing wages, they find desirable the establishment of some wage standard which will justify their wage policies. In the heat of negotiations, they may not explicitly recognize or appeal to any easily defined standards, demanding or resisting wage changes opportunistically as fortune and bargaining power favor them. As they have regularized their relationship, though, and have come to understand the possibilities and requirements of collective bargaining, both have learned the value of more sophisticated standards by which wage changes may be justified to their own constituents and to the public.

One or the other party may try to mobilize public sentiment in support of its position, arguing that a living wage requires a high wage or that lack of ability to pay necessitates a wage cut. Union members may be more strongly persuaded of the justice of their leaders' demands if those demands are demonstrably in line with the cost of living; such a demonstration may also weaken management's resolve to avoid a wage increase. Or by favorably comparing its pay scales to those elsewhere in the industry or area, management may help to persuade its workers and the union negotiators that the initial demands were not realistic.

Just because a union or management appeals to a particular standard one time is no guarantee that it will agree to accept that standard another time. Both parties use wage standards expediently, rejecting one formerly used because it now does not support a desired change and pushing another that had been discarded earlier. Despite the expedient use of wage standards and their often devious applications, managers and union leaders appear to recognize something compelling or appealing about certain of them. They use some standards much more than others and limit themselves to a certain few, ignoring many other possible ones. Comparability is the most commonly used, for example, followed by cost-of-living changes and then by ability to pay. Less popular standards are the "living" wage and productivity.[7] Not used in the United States are such possible standards as size of family and unemployment rate.

[7] See a discussion and analysis of the wage criteria most often used in wage arbitration in Irving Bernstein, *The Arbitration of Wages*, Berkeley, Calif.: University of California Press, 1954, chaps. 4–6.

The Standards of Comparability, Ability to Pay, and Cost of Living

Since individual settlements can influence national wage policies, we might well examine why unions and management use the standards they do. The consequences of following different standards may be quite different, and thus national interest may be served better if some are used at one time and others at another time. Confronted with major emergency strikes and major wage disputes during wartime or in an economic crisis, agencies of the federal government have already run into the problem of finding relevant and meaningful wage criteria. They have relied primarily upon those criteria used most commonly by unions and management, and they have discovered that none has been without flaws.

The popularity of "comparability" as a wage criterion is not hard to understand. It can usually provide negotiators with a dollars-and-cents figure, it has an aura of fairness, and often it is in accord with the economic forces pressing upon managers and the political pressures felt by union leaders. That workers performing the same work side by side should be paid the same wage is a standard that was widely used long before unions and collective bargaining were significant. By extension, the standard has been applied to the wages of workers performing the same work in different plants in the same area or even in distant locations. When any important feature of work in one location resembles that of work performed elsewhere, workers or managers are tempted to use the resemblance as the basis for an adjustment in the wage rate. Each may argue that the rates ought to be as comparable (or incomparable) as the work.

The further removed workers are from each other in distance and job content, the more obscure the basis for comparison becomes, and the less useful the standard. It offers no solution to the problem of relative pay for dissimilar workers dissimilarly situated. How should the pay scales for the West Virginia miner compare with those for the New England textile worker, the Pacific Coast lumberman, the Kansas City stockyards handler, or the Detroit assembly-line operator? Even when job duties appear to be much the same for different workers, the conditions under which the duties are carried out may be quite different and the work thus not comparable. A maintenance electrician employed by a university, for example, may bring to his work the same mechanical skills that an electrician hired by construction firms brings to his work. The former will be steadily employed at a single location the year round, in good times and bad, with opportunity to build up vacation and pension benefits; the latter will have to seek work throughout a metropolitan area wherever construction is carried on, moving from employer to employer as each job is completed. He may experience fairly long periods of unemployment when construction slumps, or during booms he may find that overtime pay is an important part of his wage. While apparently each performs the same kind of work, the conditions of employment are quite different, and no doubt a higher *hourly* wage is justified for the irregularly employed construction electrician.

Negotiators may claim that there is a historical dimension to comparability as well as a spatial or job content dimension. A group of workers may seek a wage increase comparable with that of a more highly skilled group, for example, claiming as justification the historic differential between the two. While their work and wage rates are not comparable with those of the skilled workers, they compare the differential pay of the two skill levels in the past with the present differential pay. Of course, should the less skilled group successfully invoke the historical comparison and "restore" the earlier relationship, the skilled group could then argue that it has now lost its hard-won gains of the past. To maintain its "historic" position, it would have to secure a new wage adjustment. Such flexibility in a wage standard commends it to those who wish a tactical argument to justify whatever demand they may have happened upon. With ingenuity and selective use of data, one may make out a case for almost any wage change.

Yet, despite the variability of the standard, it usually measures economic and social pressures to which management, union leaders, and workers are responsive. For all the opportunism with which negotiators use comparability to support their wage demands and offers, they recognize that it often reflects values and facts of their experience. If in the same labor market wages go up for workers in some plants, pressures will soon develop for a comparable rise in the wages of workers in neighboring plants. First, management will not as easily be able to attract a steady flow of adequately skilled workers if its firm's wages lag behind; second, workers will begin to grow restive if their wages do not follow those of workers in other plants whom they know or hear about. Their morale and work performance may be impaired, and a few may even leave for better pay elsewhere. Third, union officers will find their leadership positions endangered if they do not push for benefits at least as great as those secured by workers in "comparable" plants and unions.

These pressures are more apt to develop among the "follower" firms and industries than among those who make the key bargains for industries and the nation. Many smaller firms and nonbasic industries seldom initiate significant wage changes or pioneer in new pay programs; rather, they follow, closely or from afar, the direction of wage changes made by the key bargainers. Although the followers may look to the settlements of others for guidance, the key bargainers cannot. To do so would involve them in fruitless circularity. Thus the key bargainers must look to other wage criteria to guide their demands and wage decisions. They must seek other wage standards.

The difficulty of finding and using other criteria for key bargainers was illustrated in the report of the President's steel fact-finding board of 1949.[8] The board had the duty to investigate the arguments of the Steelworkers for a wage increase and the steel companies' counterarguments. The position of steel as a basic industry in the economy and the size of the nearly one-million-member union assured the board that the settlement would be a key one, influencing many other wage bargains. Further, no other industry or group of workers could be used as a meaningful basis for comparison since steel and the Steelworkers occupy unique positions in the American economy.

The board first pointed out that steelworkers were hardly in want. Their average hourly earnings were over three times larger than the legal minimum wage; therefore, the standard of a living wage was certainly met and provided little guidance as to the desirability of a change in wages. The board suggested that in the absence of other workers with whom the steelworkers might be compared, a comparison might be made "with the ... corporations themselves, the stockholders, and consumers of steel. This involves the subject of ability to pay increased wage rates as related to profits, dividends, and prices." It also involved the criteria of changes in the cost of living and of productivity. After investigating these criteria, the board decided that no wage increase was justified, particularly in light of the nation's need for wage and price stability, but it still recommended fringe benefits amounting to 10 cents an hour. The board rightly pointed out that "there are no mathematical formulae by which to settle the question of whether wage rates or labor costs should be increased at any particular time in a particular industry or particular plant." In this disclaimer the board members also concluded that none of the wage criteria proposed was entirely satisfactory. Since they decided that no wage increase was justified on the basis of the criteria considered and yet recommended a settlement involving an increase, the members apparently found the criteria they used to be only approximate wage indicators at best. Such a characteristic does not prove that they are valueless, of course, only that they are not precise. The value of the criteria lies, no doubt, in their indication and rough measurement of important pressures and forces to which bargainers are responsive.

On its face, ability to pay appears to be a helpful wage standard. Under fully competitive conditions it can indicate the direction wages must take. A declining industry, losing its market because of changing tastes, for

[8] Benjamin M. Selekman, Sylvia K. Selekman, and Stephen H. Fuller, *Problems in Labor Relations,* 2d ed., New York: McGraw-Hill Book Company, 1958, pp. 478–479.

example, might not be in a position to pay average wages, while a new, expanding industry might be able to pay above-average wages. Lower wages in the declining industry would lead to a desired pressure upon workers to leave; higher wages in the expanding industry would attract needed workers. Considering the monopolistic nature of most product markets and the consequent widespread discretionary control over prices enjoyed by management, union leaders are skeptical, though, of any wage conclusions based on competitive assumptions. Further, they are generally committed to "taking wages out of competition." They feel that to agree to lower wages in a declining firm or industry may only increase wage pressures in industries with more successful, growing firms.

If workers are convinced that they have to choose between the same or lower wages and loss of jobs, they may well prefer a settlement that saves their jobs. Only in rare circumstances, however, can both union and management bargainers agree that such a choice must be made; any firm not actually bankrupt and going out of business probably can maintain and even pay higher wages. The cost of doing so may hurt the firm's performance, of course, reducing funds better used for modernization, capital improvements, managerial bonuses, or dividends. Should all bargainers agree that a firm faces bankruptcy or a shutdown unless wages are lowered, union officials may still doubt the wisdom of the union's approving a cut in wages or the forgoing of a wage increase. Not only may wage benefits be more difficult to secure from other firms which seize on the comparability standard and point to lower rates at this company, but there is no assurance that the faltering firm will be saved by the workers' sacrifice.[9]

Although managers usually appeal to ability to pay only when their firms are in a shaky financial condition or when they are regulated by government bodies,[10] unions look to it as a standard wherever management has discretion over price, whether the firm is expanding or declining. If the firm is operating in a monopolistic product market, its management exercises some degree of control over the factors which determine the size of the net revenue available for distribution. Unions find profits a convenient and easily recognized measure of the available revenue and thus of the firm's ability to pay. Of course profits can be interpreted in many ways, and

[9] For an example of such a situation and the differing reactions of the national officers and the union members in the plant, see the comments of Ralph Helstein, president of the Meatpackers union, in *The Structure of Collective Bargaining*, Arnold Weber (ed.), New York: The Free Press of Glencoe, 1961, pp. 144–145.

[10] Public utility companies have used the argument that their ability to pay wage increases is limited by their fixed and regulated rates, passing on wage pressures and bargaining demands to public regulatory commissions or government-controlled agencies.

the wisdom of different distributions of net revenue—whether for new research efforts, new plant and equipment, extra dividends, *or* wages—can be debated at great length with reasonable arguments.

Many managers refuse explicitly to recognize ability to pay as a proper wage standard or even as a matter for discussion in negotiations; they usually refuse to discuss it on the grounds that it involves financial matters that are of legitimate concern only to stockholders and management. They reject the union's involvement in pricing and investment policies as issues outside the scope of union responsibility and competency. Despite rejection by management, union leaders continue to use the standard in a loose, generalized way. Workers, or certainly union leaders, as well as stockholders watch the profit positions of firms.

Although union leaders are seldom willing to forgo any adjustment in wages just because a firm is unprofitable, they realize that wage increases are more easily won and are often larger, the better the profits are. When business is good and profits are high, not only do union members expect wage increases, but managers feel freer to agree to them. Management is less willing to engage in a production-stopping strike when sales are booming and earnings are high. Unionists know as well as managers that at such a time higher labor costs can be passed on through prices or absorbed in an improved productivity.[11] They also know that in times of poor sales and declining profits, wage increases will be difficult to secure. The auto workers in 1958 and the steelworkers in 1959, for example, had to bargain for new labor agreements when unemployment in their respective industries was high, sales sluggish, and industry profits declining. Though their wage demands were substantial, they settled for fairly modest benefits, recognizing that the industries' and firms' ability to pay (or perhaps more aptly their willingness to pay) had diminished from the boom years of 1955 and 1956.

Although ability to pay undoubtedly influences wage decisions under collective bargaining and in extreme cases of financial distress may provide a specific guide for settlement, it is not a particularly helpful standard in most situations. The lack of agreement over the relevance of specific data and their meaning can cause such controversy that ability-to-pay arguments complicate rather than help wage determination. Bargainers ordinarily prefer a standard that is more easily understood, more objective, and more simple to use. The cost-of-living standard as measured by the government's Consumer Price Index achieved great popularity because it apparently provides those characteristics lacking in ability to pay.

The CPI has the merit of providing precise figures, objectively collected and reported; nevertheless, when used as a cost-of-living criterion for wage

[11] The problems raised by these alternative ways of meeting rising labor costs are explored in Chap. 17.

adjustments, it is imprecise and often misleading. The prices of goods in the market basket measured by the CPI are averages which may or may not be representative for any certain group of workers. Members of a union who work in a firm with plants in the four corners of the country may find that the kind of goods they buy and the price movement of the items they purchase display great diversity from one area to another. Steelworkers, for example, live in Chicago; Birmingham; Fontana, California; and near Philadelphia. Living costs are quite different in the different areas, and changes in the prices of even the same consumer products probably affect workers in the various locations differently. A rise in heating-fuel prices, for example, will affect Chicagoans more than those who live in Birmingham, and Southern Californians will be even less affected. If a true cost-of-living adjustment were to be made, it would require a multiplicity of wage changes and levels for comparable jobs.

Further, if changes in cost of living were the only guide for wages determination, they would do no more than assure the maintenance of real wage levels. In a sense the process would hardly be one of determining wages but merely one of adjusting money rates to stabilize the welfare content of workers' paychecks. And the adjustment would be a lagging one, bringing money rates into line with the preceding period's price changes. There would be no opportunity for reallocating labor by changing relative wages among work groups or industries, and workers would have no means of sharing the economy's productivity gains.

To commend it, the cost-of-living standard has, first of all, expediency. It is easy to comprehend, and its apparent precision makes it simple to apply. It is particularly attractive to workers, unions, and union leaders in times of inflation because it provides a sure and reasonable argument for wage increases. When prices remain stable or actually decline, workers find cost of living a considerably less appealing wage standard and usually reject it as a guide to wage cuts. The rise in price level during the postwar period and during the period of the Korean conflict undoubtedly emphasized the relationship of price and wages and contributed in no small way to the popularity of the cost-of-living standard. With the waning of inflation, use of the standard has waned too.

Despite its shortcomings as a wage standard and the fact that it is used primarily in times of rising prices, management and union men find it serviceable, not only for reasons of expediency. A rising price level tends to upset workers' income expectancies, and if wages do not soon follow prices, workers are provoked to make known their dissatisfactions. Union leaders discover political merit in seeking to restore to their members the wage losses inflicted by inflation; they may suffer political defeat if they do nothing to help workers maintain at least a parity between wages and prices. Managers, too, are responsive to the demand for wage increases to offset consumer price rises. Like the workers, they seem to appreciate the unarticulated ethical notion that a man should not suffer a loss of income through price movements beyond his control. Moreover, as already noted, in a time of rising prices managers usually find profit margins improving and costs easy to pass on. Thus, as in the case of ability to pay, at the same time that rising prices generate pressures for wage increases, they weaken the resistance to them. Under such circumstances we can hardly be surprised that managers as well as unionists use cost of living as a guide for wage determination. In fact management has been a more eager promoter of the cost of living guide than union leaders have been.[12]

However useful bargainers find the cost-of-living standard, at times they have recognized its inadequacies. If applied strictly, it would be much too rigid a standard, not allowing wages the flexibility needed to adjust to the many changing economic conditions other than price movements. The cost-of-living standard as used has also been widely criticized for encouraging too much upward flexibility in prices. When used to justify continually increasing wages, which in turn push prices higher, it may contribute to inflation or at least offer little resistance to inflationary pressures.

Productivity as a Wage Standard

Public fear that unions and management will reach inflationary wage settlements, to the detriment of the economy, has prompted economists and government officials to offer productivity as a standard for wage determination. In time of full or near-full employment, wage increases greater than productivity gains must either squeeze nonwage income or push prices upward. Since non-wage earners make every effort to escape any squeeze on their incomes and usually succeed,[13] most of the impact of wage rises greater than productivity is transmitted to prices. Insofar as such wage gains push up prices generally, workers gain in real wages only the amount of their increased productivity. Thus the only *effective* means by which workers as a group may improve their real income is through increasing productivity. If wage settlements in periods of full employment are to benefit workers generally and are not to contribute to inflation, they need to be in line with increasing productivity.

As a criterion for wage determination, productivity appears to have

[12] See the analysis of J. W. Garbarino, "The Economic Significance of Automatic Wage Adjustments," in *New Dimensions in Collective Bargaining*, H. W. Davey, H. S. Kaltenbonn, and S. H. Ruttenberg (eds.), New York: Harper & Row, Publishers, Incorporated, 1959, p. 161.

[13] See Clark Kerr, "Labor's Income Share and the Labor Movement," in *New Concepts in Wage Determination*, George W. Taylor and Frank C. Pierson (eds.), New York: McGraw-Hill Book Company, 1957, pp. 269–279.

considerable merit; it would tend to guard the public against inflationary settlements and at the same time emphasize to workers and managers the best source of further and continued improvements in real wages. Surprisingly, then, we find that productivity is not a popular wage standard. Though the management of General Motors in 1948 persuaded a skeptical UAW to accept an annual improvement factor related to a productivity increase, few other managers elsewhere have sought to tie general wage levels to productivity. Of all the common wage criteria, productivity has been probably the least used in collective bargaining negotiations. Nor has it been much used in arbitration.[14]

Its lack of favor among management and union negotiators and arbitrators may be due to the difficulty it presents in application. Some of the technical difficulties of devising and applying a productivity standard for wages were carefully and succinctly explored by the President's Economic Council in its 1962 report:

> If the rate of growth of productivity over time is to serve as a useful benchmark for wage and price behavior, there must be some meeting of minds about the appropriate methods of measuring the trend rate of increase in productivity, both for industry as a whole and for individual industries. This is a large and complex subject and there is much still to be learned. The most that can be done at present is to give some indication of orders of magnitude, and of the range within which most plausible measures are likely to fall [for example, in recent years a high of 3.0 per cent and a low of 1.9 per cent].
>
> There are a number of conceptual problems in connection with productivity measurement which can give rise to differences in estimates of its rate of growth. Three important conceptual problems are the following:
>
> (1) Over what time interval should productivity trends be measured? Very short intervals may give excessive weight to business-cycle movements in productivity, which are not the relevant standards for wage behavior. [Productivity shows] . . . erratic . . . year-to-year changes. . . . Very long intervals may hide significant breaks in trends; indeed in the United States—and in other countries as well —productivity appears to have risen more rapidly since the end of the second World War than before. It would be wholly inappropriate for wage behavior in the 1960's to be governed by events long in the past. On the other hand, productivity in the total private economy appears to have advanced less rapidly in the second half of the postwar period than in the first.
>
> (2) Even for periods of intermediate length, it is desirable to segregate the trend movements in productivity from those that reflect

[14] Bernstein, *The Arbitration of Wages,* p. 98.

business-cycle forces. Where the basic statistical materials are available, this problem can be handled by an analytical separation of trend effects and the effects of changes in the rate of capacity utilization.

(3) Even apart from such difficulties, there often exist alternative statistical measures of output and labor input. The alternatives may differ conceptually or may simply be derived from different statistical sources. A difficult problem of choice may emerge, unless the alternative measures happen to give similar results. . . .

The proportions in which labor and non-labor incomes share the product of industry have not been immutable throughout American history, nor can they be expected to stand forever where they are today. It is desirable that labor and management should bargain explicitly about the distribution of the income of particular firms or industries. It is, however, undesirable that they should bargain implicitly about the general price level. Excessive wage settlements which are paid for through price increases in major industries put direct pressure on the general price level and produce spillover and imitative effects throughout the economy. Such settlements may fail to redistribute income within the industry involved; rather they redistribute income between that industry and other segments of the economy through the mechanism of inflation. . . .

What are the guideposts which may be used in judging whether a particular price or wage decision may be inflationary? The desired objective is a stable price level, within which particular prices rise, fall, or remain stable in response to economic pressures. Hence, price stability within any particular industry is not necessarily a correct guide to price and wage decisions in that industry. It is possible, however, to describe in broad outline a set of guides which, if followed, would preserve over-all price stability while still allowing sufficient flexibility to accommodate objectives of efficiency and equity. These are not arbitrary guides. They describe—briefly and no doubt incompletely—how prices and wage rates would behave in a *smoothly functioning competitive economy operating near full employment.*[15] Nor do they constitute a mechanical formula for determining whether a particular price or wage decision is inflationary. They will serve their purpose if they suggest to the interested public a useful way of approaching the appraisal of such a decision.

If, as a point of departure, we assume no change in the relative shares of labor and nonlabor incomes in a particular industry, then a general guide may be advanced for noninflationary wage behavior, and another for noninflationary price behavior. Both guides, as will be seen, are only first approximations.

The general guide for noninflationary wage behavior is that the rate of increase in wage rates (including fringe benefits) in each

[15] Italics supplied.

industry be equal to the trend rate of over-all productivity increase. General acceptance of this guide would maintain stability of labor cost per unit of output for the economy as a whole—though not of course for individual industries.

The general guide for noninflationary price behavior calls for price reduction if the industry's rate of productivity increase exceeds the over-all rate—for this would mean declining unit labor costs; it calls for an appropriate increase in price if the opposite relationship prevails; and it calls for stable prices if the two rates of productivity increase are equal.

These are advanced as general guideposts. To reconcile them with objectives of equity and efficiency, specific modifications must be made to adapt them to the circumstances of particular industries. If all of these modifications are made, each in the specific circumstances to which it applies, they are consistent with stability of the general price level. Public judgments about the effects on the price level of particular wage or price decisions should take into account the modifications as well as the general guides. The most important modifications are the following:

(1) Wage rate increases would exceed the general guide rate in an industry which would otherwise be unable to attract sufficient labor; or in which wage rates are exceptionally low compared with the range of wages earned elsewhere by similar labor, because the bargaining position of workers has been weak in particular local labor markets.

(2) Wage rate increases would fall short of the general guide rate in an industry which could not provide jobs for its entire labor force even in times of generally full employment; or in which wage rates are exceptionally high compared with the range of wages earned elsewhere by similar labor, because the bargaining position of workers has been especially strong.

(3) Prices would rise more rapidly, or fall more slowly, than indicated by the general guide rate in an industry in which the level of profits was insufficient to attract the capital required to finance a needed expansion in capacity; or in which costs other than labor costs had risen.

(4) Prices would rise more slowly, or fall more rapidly, than indicated by the general guide in an industry in which the relation of productive capacity to full employment demand shows the desirability of an outflow of capital from the industry; or in which costs other than labor costs have fallen; or in which excessive market power has resulted in rates of profit substantially higher than those earned elsewhere on investments of comparable risk.

It is a measure of the difficulty of the problem that even these complex guideposts leave out of account several important considerations. Although output per man-hour rises mainly in response to improvements in the quantity and quality of capital goods with which employees are equipped, employees are often able to improve their performance by means within their own control. It is obviously in the public interest that incentives be preserved which would reward employees for such efforts.

Also, in connection with the use of measures of over-all productivity gain as benchmarks for wage increases, it must be borne in mind that average hourly labor costs often change through the process of up- or down-grading, shifts between wage and salaried employment, and other forces. Such changes may either add to or subtract from the increment which is available for wage increases under the over-all productivity guide.

Finally, it must be reiterated that collective bargaining within an industry over the division of the proceeds between labor and nonlabor income is not necessarily disruptive of over-all price stability. The relative shares can change within the bounds of noninflationary price behavior. But when a disagreement between management and labor is resolved by passing the bill to the rest of the economy, the bill is paid in depreciated currency to the ultimate advantage of no one.

With such limitations and qualifications as those described by the Economic Council, a productivity standard would appear to provide little help to union leaders and managers concerned with determining wages in specific situations. A number of officials in both unions and business organizations rejected the council's suggestion that productivity be a guide for appraising wage behavior; the rejection appears to have stemmed as much from the fear that government would interfere in collective bargaining by suggesting "guideposts" as from doubts about the usefulness of the guideposts themselves. The shortcomings of productivity as a wage criterion are no greater than those of the other criteria, and it would not require more careful use. None of the criteria provides clear, unambiguous guidance in wage determination, and they are all subject to opportunistic use and manipulation. Productivity's lack of popularity among negotiators may not stem from its limitations as a wage standard but rather from its abstract nature.

Productivity changes, as such, do not produce any direct effects which managers, workers, and union leaders recognize as social and economic pressures. Productivity does affect profitability and costs and eventually prices and wages, of course, but the relationship is not direct or easily known or defined. Its changes are almost unnoticeable to even the businessman, being revealed only through sophisticated analysis. In contrast, a comparison of wages can develop direct and immediately perceived coercive pressures upon employers and workers; observation of profit levels can also excite both employers and workers to demand changes in wages. All can directly and easily understand the meaning of price change in consumer goods. Whereas comparability, ability-to-pay, and cost-of-living (and living-wage) standards are based upon data and knowledge that are a part of the common daily experience of those concerned with labor agreements, productivity is a figure devised by economists from unfamiliar, if not arcane, sources.

If managers and union leaders are to be persuaded to consider productivity regularly and seriously in their wage negotiations, they must see the relevance of it to their deliberations and feel the force of some necessity to measure their settlements by it. Since productivity changes do not manifest themselves directly and clearly through the usual mechanisms of the market and the political procedures of unions and companies, we need other means of impressing the parties with the importance of productivity.

The President's Economic Council has made a start in developing an awareness among labor and management bargainers of the significance of, and need for, productivity guides in wage determination. It has suggested the use of productivity as a guide for appraising wages as a matter of public policy and has stimulated public discussion of the merits of productivity as a wage standard. Government spokesmen in recent years have also stressed the desirability of noninflationary wage increases, urging public condemnation of settlements larger than those justified by productivity gains. Government agencies and bureaus increasingly have been making available more and better productivity studies, data, and information, bringing productivity more and more to public attention. As the public becomes more informed about productivity and as government concern is expressed more forcefully, wage negotiators may more and more discover the prudence of measuring wage demands and offers against productivity gains.

Use of a productivity standard in wage determination will hardly end disputes over the kind and size of wage adjustments, nor will productivity supplant other wage standards. It can help protect the economy against inflationary wage settlements, and more importantly it may emphasize for those engaged in the productive process the value of increasing productivity. Serious consideration of productivity and an understanding of its implications suggest that wage determination need not be merely a matter of distributing income but can also be an effort to increase income. In its emphasis upon productivity, the marginal productivity theory thus contained a valuable lesson. Even though we may not accept the theory as an explanation of how productivity gains will be shared, it provides some insight into the relationship between productivity and the creation of income.

Improved productivity is likely to result in increased income to the firm where it occurs. The imperfections of competition which allow an individual firm some discretionary control over price and production policy make possible the appropriation of a good share, though usually not all, of the productivity gains. Through lower prices or better service, a firm may pass along to its customers some of the gains. The source of the gains may be the more efficient use of materials by avoiding waste and scrap, so that costs are cut without reducing the need for labor in the firm, or it may be the more efficient handling of new business with the same work force, thus increasing revenues but keeping costs stable. The use of new and more efficient machines, technologies, or work methods *may* reduce the number of workers, but not necessarily. Depending upon the elasticity of demand, an improvement in the product or service, a lowering of price, or both may increase sales. Any increases in production to meet sales will tend to increase employment and will thus offset the reduction in the number of workers.

Insofar as revenues increase because of lower costs or higher sales, productivity can provide added benefits for workers and management. The particular distribution of the benefits and the effects upon employment will be subject in some degree to the bargaining process. Workers may prefer to take some of their benefits in the form of higher wages, fringe benefits, a reduced workweek, more holidays, or longer vacations.

Not only is productivity the decisive influence in improving workers' incomes in the long run, but it also provides them with the opportunity to increase their incomes in the short run if their representatives and their managers can agree upon ways to promote productivity and to share in its bounty. Workers and their union have an interest in productivity in other firms as well as in their own. Higher productivity elsewhere is likely to lead to price declines, to act as a drag on prices, or to provide improved products; either higher wages from productivity gains in their own firm or lower-priced products from other firms raise real incomes. Increased productivity would seem to be an attractive goal for union leaders and managers to pursue through collective bargaining, but despite the benefits that productivity increases promise, unions and managements have joined together only occasionally, under rare circumstances, to raise productivity.

Problems in Using the Productivity Standard

During World War II, when full production and high productivity were clearly matters of national interest, the government encouraged unions and management to form joint committees for the purpose of raising productivity. Of the thousands formed, however, many did not function, only a few hundred were able to operate well enough to have produced noticeable results, and only a handful were able to maintain themselves after the war.[16] Both before and after the war a number of firms experimented with plans requiring joint effort to increase productivity. The best known is

[16] Dorothea de Schweinitz, *Labor and Management in a Common Enterprise,* Cambridge, Mass.: Harvard University Press, 1949.

probably the Scanlon plan.[17] Usually neither managers nor unionists have been willing to consider, let alone participate in, such a plan unless the firm was in poor financial condition and was threatened with failure. Why workers, union leaders, and managers have shown so little inclination to join together to increase productivity—to their mutual benefit—is a problem of major importance.

As already suggested, the abstractness of productivity is a major difficulty for workers. However important it may be to the level of their wages, productivity does not directly impinge upon their experiences. Unlike changes in prices, wages in comparable occupations, and corporate profits, productivity changes produce no effects easily identifiable with them. In fact, a significant change in productivity may not be noticed at all. The change may show up as a rise in profits, a decline in prices, or an alteration in customary wage differentials between two industries, but in the absence of an index of productivity itself, productivity changes can easily go unnoticed.

If the Department of Labor continues its present studies of productivity, increasing the number of its reports on productivity trends in various industries and making them more comprehensive and of a better quality, we shall have a measurement, similar to consumer price indices, which may make productivity more meaningful to workers. At the same time, a productivity index, or several industry indices, would encourage negotiating discussions of productivity and focus increased attention upon it. The widespread debate over our lagging rate of productivity growth during the past decade has helped to make productivity figures more meaningful economic expressions and better understood, relevant data than in the thirties and forties.

Another difficulty in linking productivity to wages is the popular confusion between *production* and *productivity*. Even economics majors in college sometimes assume that higher production means higher productivity. It does not necessarily do so. During World War II, when the nation strained every resource to increase output and production totals rose to new heights, productivity sagged. We were using our less efficient resources to turn out the extra flow of goods; aging and obsolete machines, tools, and plants were pressed into service, and inexperienced youths and women as well as slower-working oldsters were employed. All contributed to an increased production, but their input of labor and capital did not result in as great an output as trained workers and up-to-date equipment would have produced. Productivity rises only when output increases with the same or smaller input of resources. If the larger output is merely the result of a greater input of labor or capital, productivity will not have changed.

Workers have not infrequently been promised higher pay for greater

[17] Frederick G. Lesieur (ed.), *The Scanlon Plan: A Frontier in Labor Management Cooperation,* New York: John Wiley & Sons, Inc., 1958.

productivity through their participation in an incentive wage system. To the workers, the higher pay may seem to come only from harder work; the more units they produce, the higher their wage, but also the more they produce, the more effort they must expend. Such "productivity" does not particularly commend itself to the worker (of course, he may also discover that he can produce more by being more efficient in the use of his effort and thereby truly increase his productivity). He is much more apt to notice an increase in effort, however, and therefore be skeptical of all productivity plans and ideas.

Workers' difficulties in appreciating the role of productivity in improving wages and their misunderstanding of the term may well explain the reluctance of union leaders to join management in productivity plans. Why managers have not made a greater effort than they have to convince workers and unionists of productivity's importance to wage betterment is not so easily explained. Insofar as managers are interested in increased efficiency, lower costs, and increased output, productivity is a term of real meaning and of persistent concern to them. One might have expected them to have sought union and worker cooperation more than they have and to have tried harder to impress workers with the value of improving productivity. Management has often sought increased productivity from workers, but seldom through genuinely cooperative methods. It has traditionally been considered a matter solely for management direction and administration. Workers have generally been assumed to respond to the rewards and penalties meted out by management, contributing to productivity gains only as management learns to harness their interests and to exploit their motives.

With respect to business practices, one may safely generalize that on the one hand, managers have placed heavy reliance upon incentive wage systems—piecework, bonuses, and rating plans—to elicit greater worker response. For many years, as scientific management methods gained wide acceptance, industrial managers adopted incentive wage plans as the indispensable means to volume production at low cost. On the other hand, management has maintained a widespread belief in the efficacy of contingent punishment—the loss of a job for poor work performance, insubordination, or personality characteristics inimical to maintaining order or morale in the workplace. Management has thus relied primarily upon pecuniary incentives to motivate employees: extra pay for improved performance and loss of pay or job through discipline for a poor worker.

Industrial incentives have almost always been defined and instituted by American managements very much as they might specify and install a more efficient, more effective machine. That workers might respond to motives and pursue interests unrecognized by the usual incentive systems has been largely ignored in practice. The systems rest on the assumption that workers simply seek more income. Management assumes too easily perhaps that consumer wants are unlimited and that they dominate other possible motives. To the extent that workers are interested in satisfying wants of a different nature—an increased enjoyment in work and a greater control over work environment, for example—and to the degree that workers' consumer wants may be something less than infinite, a range of workers' aspirations remains unrelated to the job, and the potential satisfaction of those aspirations is not made the driving force for improved, more productive performance. A close examination of the assumptions of the usual incentive systems might have revealed to management that workers were not merely passive participants in the production process, interested in jobs only for the pay which would allow them to buy enjoyment in the consumers' market. In fact, through their support of unions and collective bargaining, they have demonstrated that they are not instruments to be manipulated in the interests of management-imposed goals; they are active participants in the production process who, as cooperative partners, can benefit themselves and management or who, as antagonistic subordinates, can restrict and hamper the achievement of industrial goals.

Workers and unions have weakened both the positive and the negative incentives heretofore relied upon by management to increase productivity. In general, unions have registered opposition to incentive pay plans. Examples of union support for such plans are easy to find, but generally unions have expressed preference for wages geared to time worked rather than to specific performance.[18] The United Automobile Workers, for example, has gone on record as being against the use of piece rates and other forms of incentive payments, arguing that extra energies should not be extracted from workers over and above a fair day's work.[19] It secured the elimination of incentives in the major automobile companies. Also, many managements have become disillusioned with incentive systems, discovering that workers have either "captured" the system bit by bit through restrictions introduced in grievance settlements and arbitration or subverted the system through informal agreements to limit production.[20]

Unions have thus been cutting away at the pecuniary incentives which management has long considered appropriate, but they have been even more effective in undermining management's reliance on the negative in-

[18] For the early attitudes of unions toward piece rates, see Robert Hoxie, *Scientific Management and Labor,* New York: D. Appleton & Company, Inc., 1916; and for more recent union approaches, see Sumner H. Slichter, E. Robert Livernash, and James J. Healy, *The Impact of Collective Bargaining on Management,* Washington, D.C.: The Brookings Institution, 1960, pp. 492–519.

[19] In part this opposition centers less on the system itself than on flaws in administering it.

[20] Slichter, Livernash, and Healy, *The Impact of Collective Bargaining on Management,* pp. 492–519.

centive discipline. The increase in union strength, coupled with the greater use of grievance procedures to protest disciplinary penalties, has led some members of management to avow that they are no longer in control of their plants.

> Corporate officials in several of the major [automobile] companies agree that it is at best difficult for a foreman to maintain discipline within the shop. This situation, they maintain, results from two fears on the part of the foreman: (1) that the organized workers will strike against the imposition of a penalty on one of their number; and (2) that any penalty imposed may be reversed by an impartial chairman or umpire, lessening the foreman's status in the eyes of his men. On the strength of these fears, say these company officials, foremen are more inclined today to overlook actions that merit discipline on the argument that it is better policy to keep the shop operating and to forego a contest over authority which may only serve in the end to lessen that authority. Another management representative makes the statement that "most companies in this industry wouldn't dare to fire a union steward no matter what he did." [21]

The formal seniority system, too, has reduced one of the risks of punishment that formerly attended the nonunion worker. Good performance on the job was considered one of the chief determinants of which workers would be retained when a layoff was necessary. At times of unemployment, delayed retribution would be visited on the heads of those workers who had not measured up to supervisory expectations. This risk of layoff therefore constituted one inducement to do a good job. With the advent of a system under which layoff is determined chiefly, if not solely, by length of service, however, this risk of layoff due to poor performance was removed for most of the work force. The risk of layoff remains, but it is nothing which can be lessened by personal effort. There is, moreover, a union movement to reduce if not eliminate the risk of layoff from any source. Guarantees of employment and wages for short periods of time, up to a week, have been written into some collective bargaining agreements, and agitation for annual guarantees continues. In periods of full employment, the risk of unemployment is further lessened even without specific guarantees in labor agreements.

If one thus observes the cumulative effect which unions have had upon the industrial incentives on which management has relied, the conclusion

---

[21] N. W. Chamberlain, *Union Challenge to Management Control,* New York: Harper & Row, Publishers, Incorporated, 1948, pp. 270–271. For a discussion of the ways in which union representatives may restrict the disciplinary authority of foremen through the grievance process, see James W. Kuhn, *Bargaining in Grievance Settlement,* New York: Columbia University Press, 1961, pp. 116–119.

appears inescapable that the result has been to weaken them. One student of discipline in the unionized firm reached the following conclusion:

> In the unionized section of the economy, at least, employers no longer have the plenary right to punish misconduct. In 19 cases out of 20 they share their authority with the union by the specific terms of the agreement. These agreements cover approximately half of the employees in private business—between 18 and 20 million employees directly and another 3 to 5 million indirectly (nonunion employees in unionized firms)—and their influence does not end there. . . . On the whole, [industrial discipline] has a well-established structure and is rapidly acquiring a pattern of substantive content which defines the rights of employees both as to tenure and to the wide variety of privileges and exceptions which mark their protected status under the agreement.[22]

Yet in fairness to the unions it must be added that to some extent the weakening was justified. Discipline in industry is obviously necessary, but there is no necessity for arbitrary discipline. Punishment may be imposed to secure compliance with recognized requirements of production, but the punishment may itself proceed according to generally acceptable rules, such as are now in force in many companies. In part, the emphasis on seniority for layoffs is likewise an expression of the desire for greater certainty of justice. To rely on managerial designation of those to be laid off leaves open the possibility—by no means a remote one, as preunion evidence testifies—of favoritism based on simple friendship, bribery, antiunion activity, or that vague quality "company loyalty." [23]

---

[22] Orme W. Phelps, *Discipline and Discharge in the Unionized Firm*, Berkeley, Calif.: University of California Press, 1959, pp. 9–10.

[23] The union's program of rationalizing personnel policies, providing rules which are relatively objective in application and known to those to whom they are applicable, has been resisted by managers sometimes for good reason, as noted by Phelps in *Discipline and Discharge in the Unionized Firm*, p. 4:

> One process may be and is abused. It is cumbersome, time consuming, inefficient, and annoying. Rules grow, rule interpretations multiply, precedents accumulate. Rapid shifts of policy to conform to changing conditions become more and more difficult. There are more people to consult, more precedents to consider, more vested interests opposed to change. For these and other reasons, some of them much less objective, persons in authority have tended steadily to oppose the extension of due process in disciplinary actions, on the whole with considerable success.

Alvin Goldner explained management's dislike of rationalized rules in "Industrial Sociology: Status and Prospects," *American Sociological Review*, vol. 13 (1948), p. 398:

Moreover, unions may credit themselves with this favorable influence on morale: To some extent they have provided a reinforcement to worker societies and engendered a greater feeling of security in, and attachment to, a particular company. If, as some evidence suggests, there is a relationship between morale and productivity, this contribution, which is inherent in the very nature of the union, has probably constituted something of an offset to its adverse effects upon output. Yet even this is not to argue that the union's morale effect has brought a net improvement in productivity. On balance it appears a reasonable guess that the total effect of unionism thus far has tended toward a net decrease in the effectiveness of management-devised and management-applied incentives to improve productivity. The pecuniary incentive, both positive and negative, has been weakened— whether justifiably or not—and nonpecuniary incentives have been strengthened only incidentally, scarcely enough to have provided much of a counterweight. If workers' interest in productivity and union leaders' concern for productive efficiency were secured only by management's customary pecuniary incentives, then, the prospect for improving productivity with worker and union help appears bleak. Many businessmen undoubtedly would agree that the view is an accurate one, as they note the frequent strife and bitterness in labor relations over technological change. Accustomed to thinking of incentives in terms of a carrot in front of, or a stick behind, the "human donkey," they dismayingly conclude that neither is as effective as they once thought it to be. Unions may have whittled away both carrot and stick until they are hardly effective.

More importantly, unions have destroyed the basis for the donkey metaphor. Workers no longer can be treated as creatures to be manipulated by managers; they cannot be driven or enticed to travel a road, to take a direction, or to maintain a pace determined by "supervisors." They are people as rational and as concerned with their self-interest and as responsive to a wider interest as managers, employers, and businessmen. As we shall see in Chapter 17, The Future of Collective Bargaining, there is sufficient experience to suggest that they will join with employers to increase productivity if employers meet them as men whose interests and

---

Bureaucratic rules fulfill typically different functions for different ranks in the industrial bureaucracy. It would seem, in fact, that under certain conditions, it is necessary and normal for the rules to be such as to make prediction difficult or impossible for lower strata personnel. For given the implicit but common assumption that anxiety and insecurity are effective motivation, then employers will tend to leave undeveloped those rules which would structure the aspirational horizon of workers. It is, perhaps, in part for this reason that employers are loathe to grant trade unions contractual arrangements providing for conditions of promotion and, in particular, establish seniority rules.

values are to be taken seriously and given due respect. Workers will not willingly give up present benefits, guarantees, preferences, and protections for possible but problematic gains from work and technological improvements unless they can help determine the incidence of the resulting losses and gains. Through their union representatives, they will cooperate with management to increase productivity for the benefit of themselves, the business, and the public if they are assured that they will not be required to bear the brunt of the change and suffer all or most of the burden of the costs involved. The same unions that have been responsible for weakening existing incentives can be the means of generating a kind of work performance, under new and mutual incentives, never before possible.

The writers believe that unions can be made positive forces for improving productivity at the same time that they advance the genuine interests of their members and that by this approach there is more likelihood of curbing unwarranted absolution of the individual from a personal responsibility that must be accepted by every member of society. This approach does not waive the desirability of certain positive (legislative) restrictions upon the exercise of union power, but it treats as equally important making the unions an integral and responsible part of society.

Conclusion

The matter of incentives and their relationship to productivity has been dwelt on here at considerable length because of its importance. Often treated as primarily a psychological problem, it is no less an economic one. It constitutes one of the greatest present challenges to our intellectual and moral capacities as individuals and as a society. Incentives selected to reinforce socially approved motivations can be enlisted in the solution of our gravest problems of human organization, whatever one's shade of political or philosophical belief.

It should not pass without specific notice, too, that to the extent that unions and their worker-members can be enlisted in the cause of increasing productivity—not by being driven or coerced, but by appealing to a fuller range of interests through an appropriate system of incentives—such problems as the encouragement of investment in support of full employment will be eased. Under such circumstances, union activity can be an asset. The kind of union for which an enterprise is known will be as important in attracting capital funds and inducing investment as, for example, the reputation of the product itself. The relationship between union and management will be a favorable expansion factor in some situations, just as now it is regarded in some industries as a restraint on expansion. The problem of increasing productivity within the limits of our abilities is thus in essence a problem of securing the effective cooperation of the human factors.

If the potentialities of this approach are to be realized, the unions them-selves must obviously respond to the challenge. It is not solely a matter of society's recognizing the legitimate aspirations and needs of workers, but of the unions', as agents for workers, recognizing the aspirations and needs of the broader society of which they are only a part. Motivational problems which still remain to be solved thus include not only how individuals can be stimulated to advance their own welfare, but how they can be stimulated to respond to the very necessary notion of "social responsibility" as long as that concept remains as nebulous as it is.

We shall develop this theme more fully in later chapters.

The Economics of Collective Bargaining: Aspects of the Monopoly Problem

chapter 15

We are now in a position to return to the question which we asked at the end of Chapter 13. There we concluded that if producer interests are to be accommodated along with consumer interests, some degree of control over market forces is necessary. Such control is what economists call "monopoly power." Monopolists are not subject to the full pressures of the competitive market, and they enjoy a power that may permit exploitation of groups with lesser power. In Chapter 14 we observed that the efforts of general wage changes are uncertain, depending on the conditions under which they are made; for that reason we would be unwarranted in assuming that *upward* wage movements are *always* desirable. But does not monopoly power in the hands of unions permit them to push wages ever higher and higher, without necessary regard for the adverse effects on others? And does not the political necessity resting on every union to keep up with rival unions drive them in this direction?

We also observed in the preceding chapter that for the economy at large and even for workers as a whole, an increase in productivity is the only effective means of adding to income. Yet this essential truth is often of little significance as a determinant of policy in the individual company or

368

union. In moving from the general to the particular, from society at large to the single enterprise, we find this interesting fact: The same benefits which come from an improvement in productivity (that is, from *larger output* with the same cost structure) may come from *higher prices* with the same cost structure. In either case, the unions' interest would appear to be the same. Both provide a larger kitty out of which to bargain wage increases for its members. Thus, although unions *as a whole* can gain benefits for their members substantially only through increased productivity, *individual* unions can equally well obtain increases through exercising whatever monopoly power they have to raise prices. Since using monopoly power appears to be easier than raising productivity, will not unions be tempted to resort to it for their gains?

This question is not easy to answer. Probably we do not yet have all the information necessary to provide a satisfactory solution, but this cannot excuse us from attempting tentative appraisals, since time cannot wait. Even should our first approximations be shot full of holes, simply the making of them will clarify our thinking and make it easier to discern our errors. To refuse to tackle problems which are now pressing because they are "too big" or because we do not have "all" the data is escapism of the worst sort. Let us see, then, what we can say about these issues within the brief space of a chapter.

First, let us restate the questions we have posed, reducing them to two: (1) By admitting that monopolistic power (control over market forces) is in some degree desirable, are we not giving a license to the strong groups to exploit the weaker ones and allowing the stronger to distort the structure of relative wage rates to its own advantage? (2) Although we cannot say that upward wage changes are *always* advisable, under *any* given conditions, does not union monopoly power coupled with union political pressures perpetually push union wages upward, with detrimental effects upon productivity, employment, and output?

Monopoly and Ability to Pay

Our approach to these problems can perhaps best be made by referring again to the principle of ability to pay. In one sense, it can be regarded as the productivity principle modified for application to situations of imperfect competition. In this sense, a firm's ability to pay—its capacity to sustain a particular cost structure—is measured partly by productivity changes and partly by the effects of discretionary or monopolistic control over price. Higher wages may be supported not only by greater output from a given input (lower labor cost per unit) but also by the exploitation of the firm's advantages in the product markets. The union may thus improve its wage bargaining position not only by cooperation in respect to productivity but also by cooperation in respect to monopolistic advantages. The union label has long constituted one form of product differentiation which seeks to take the products of favored companies out of competition with other companies. The boycott, both primary and secondary, has been used in support of market restrictions against would-be competitors. Multiemployer bargaining may lead to interfirm price agreements to which the union may or may not be party but with respect to which it may play a motivating role.

The ability-to-pay principle has another, less sinister connotation, though. It can be regarded simply as the union's recognition that net *value* productivity—a firm's ability to earn income—is the source of its members' wage receipts and that, moreover, within limits most firms can affect their relative earning capacity. They may expand it by careful, efficient management or contract it through neglect. The economic limits to a union's interest in managerial efficiency were once thought to be imposed by market forces which determined wage rates independently of the individual manager. But now the belief is widespread that market forces are not always dominant. Thus the view is that a union may press for wage increases to the limit of the ability of the business to provide them and that ability is directly dependent upon the total operation of the business, in which a large element of discretion exists. All the aspects of a business operation obviously relate to a company's success as a revenue-receiving (and consequently a revenue-paying) institution. A union may therefore improve its chances for a better wage bargain not only by increasing worker efficiency but also by insisting upon improved performance in any and all aspects of a firm's operations, both of which measures enhance the firm's ability to pay.

The possibility of wage gains from management efficiencies provides unions with a reason to become interested in aspects of business operation which have traditionally been conceived as being of sole concern to management. Does accounting procedure understate the amount of revenue available for distribution? Is the marketing policy weak, so that the plant constantly operates at a disadvantageous level of output and sales are spotty, reducing revenue available for distribution? Does an inept financial management impose an unwarranted charge against the firm's finances? Does lack of interest in research and development jeopardize the company's future profitability? Depending upon the quality of its leadership, a union might easily conclude that factors like these affect its ability to bargain wage increases for its members, and it might seek assurance of improvement in managerial efficiency.[1] The approach to the wage ques-

[1] A recent arbitration case involved an auto union member, also a company stockholder, who was fired because he wrote to the head office pointing out the inefficiencies and wastes of the local management. The union argued that such

tion thus becomes entangled with the question of the appropriate subject matter of collective bargaining.

The ability-to-pay principle, then, looks upon the wage-paying capacity of the business as not limited by market forces which lie beyond its control, but as expandable within limits. Such expansion of wage-paying capacity may be effected by (1) exploiting a firm's monopolistic advantages or (2) improving business performance, increasing not only labor productivity but managerial productivity in all aspects of business operations.

Unions sometimes appear to deny the principle of ability to pay by their adoption of a policy of standard wages. In pursuit of such a policy, unions seek to raise the rates of competitive producers simultaneously and equally, without respect for individual profitability. They seem to establish some standard *external* to the firm as a substitute for the ability-to-pay principle, which is concerned with only the individual firm itself. This conclusion is more apparent than real. First, in the very setting of their standard wage demands, unions concern themselves with the relative abilities to pay of all the firms with which they deal. They cannot ask for a wage which only the most efficient producer can afford to pay, for then they would prove unable to enforce their demands on the majority, nor can they set the standard where it will be satisfactory to the least efficient producer, for then they would deny possible wage increases to the majority of their members. The standard must be set somewhere between the most and the least efficient.

Unions cannot afford to ignore the problems of struggling firms without inflicting penalties on their members who work for them. Sometimes, as in coal mining, union officials make the hard decision to demand a standard rate above the level that marginal firms can afford, expecting to force them out of business, to the long-run benefit of the industry and the employed miners. Many of the small, unmechanized mines have closed, and others have gone nonunion. With high unemployment in the mining districts, the latter were able to hire miners to work below union rates in sufficient numbers to supply over one-quarter of all bituminous coal in 1962, to the detriment of organized firms and union membership. More frequently, however, unions are more careful to modify the ability-to-pay principle by not insisting on higher wage payments from the weaker firms.[2] The more efficient firms may simply continue to earn Marshallian "rents."[3]

interest and action were legitimate and should not be penalized. *Whitney Chain Company,* 35 LA 668 (1960).

[2] See Sumner H. Slichter, E. Robert Livernash, and James J. Healy, *The Impact of Collective Bargaining on Management,* Washington, D.C.: The Brookings Institution, 1960, pp. 824–826, for a report of differing union reactions to marginal firms' inability to meet high wage rates.

[3] In some instances, unions may secure the same result, however, by seeking a more liberal incentive system from the more prosperous businesses; by accept-

There is a second reason why the unions' common rate is not necessarily a departure from the principle of ability to pay. Multiemployer bargaining units allow unions to make demands upon an entire market and make possible a consideration of the ability to pay of a whole industry. A union might try to increase productivity, for example, by securing the general modernization of machinery and plant or the undertaking of market and industrial research; but it may also try to exploit monopolistic practices, such as keeping out competitors or refusing to supply labor or needed materials of firms not adhering to a price policy which permits the demanded wages. Both productivity and ability-to-pay wage standards thus may become entangled with the question of the comprehensiveness of the bargaining unit since multiemployer and especially industry-wide units may permit wage benefits not feasible in a smaller unit.

In examining wage bargaining, the fundamental distinction that we have already made between the productivity and ability-to-pay standards should be kept in mind: Productivity necessarily involves a larger revenue-paying capacity, not only for the individual business, but for the nation as a whole. The workers in the particular firm or industry in which productivity increases benefit, but, as consumers, other workers also benefit to the extent that prices decline. Even should the product price remain stable, with the whole benefit accruing to the particular workers involved, other workers are at least not adversely affected. The wage rates set in accordance with the ability-to-pay principle do not necessarily give the same result. They may reflect the rewards of monopoly as well as of productivity. Insofar as the wage increases come from monopoly power, the nation as a whole gains no return, and other workers may suffer through higher prices of the products they purchase. Only members of the particular union gain, and at the expense of everyone else. This may not be a result consciously pursued by the union, it is true, but simply the consequence of demands for higher wages made without respect for productivity increases in firms possessing discretionary monopolistic pricing powers.

To the extent that businesses operate in imperfectly competitive product and factor markets,[4] then, wages are set on the basis of relative bargaining

---

ing stricter production requirements from the poorer companies, even though base rates are the same for all; or by seeking (or forgoing) nonwage benefits, such as perhaps a pension or sickness plan, which are not urged upon all companies under contract but only upon those which can afford them.

[4] If the product market is perfectly competitive, short-run prices will be set without respect to wages; if the labor market is perfectly competitive, short-run wages will be set without respect to product prices. When both markets are imperfect, the result is unpredictable, but it does appear that there is a more direct relationship between wages and prices: Price discretion permits wage discretion.

powers, in which ability to pay enters as an important consideration from either the union or the management point of view, or both. Whether consideration of ability to pay is helpful or harmful to the consuming public as a whole will depend upon the relative stress placed on its components of productivity and price control.

The issue implicit in the ability-to-pay approach may be phrased in various ways, some of which have already been mentioned. How can we accommodate producer interests through organizations possessing monopoly power without at the same time permitting their excessive use of that power to exploit others? Can we render compatible the need for organizations which by their very nature possess monopoly power and the need for restraining the use of that power? To some it is a question of the extent to which monopoly shall be allowed to restrict competitive forces. To others it is a question of the extent to which security aims achieved through exploitation of monopoly power are warranted. It might also be regarded as a question of the extent to which unions shall be allowed to improve their conditions by joining with employers to exploit the consumer rather than by joining with employers to improve methods of production.

The fact appears to be that the satisfaction of workers' interests on their jobs, including a degree of job security, requires something less than the rigorous price competition of economic theory. At the same time, there is a need for continuing competition if we are to avoid stagnation and group exploitation. Where can and should we try to strike the balance? How much competition is too much, and how much is not enough?

Let us first put the question with specific reference to relative wage rates. Consider the situation in the steel industry, where, in the years after World War II, steelworkers, under the leadership of Philip Murray and then David MacDonald, were able materially to improve their wage rates, securing uniform rates for uniform jobs throughout the country. Between 1949 and 1959, gross average hourly earnings of production workers in steel rose by over 87 per cent, while for auto workers they went up 57 per cent, and for all manufacturing workers 58 per cent. Steelworkers were also able to improve their fringe benefits, such as vacations, holiday and severance pay, supplemental unemployment benefits, and insurance and pension contributions, until they were equal to one-quarter of straight-time hourly earnings. These gains could be achieved only because the United Steelworkers bargained with substantially all steel employers and secured uniform terms. With no significant amount of steel production from unorganized mills, the danger of competition from steel produced at lower labor costs was virtually eliminated. The cost of employer concessions to the union could thus be passed along to the consumer through price increases.[5]

[5] For statistics of the steel industry during the 1940s and 1950s, see *Background Statistics Bearing on the Steel Dispute: Supplementary Tables,* U.S.

On what grounds can we judge whether the steelworkers were entitled to their benefits when these were made possible only by the steel consumers' paying higher prices? Steelworkers' jobs are demanding and often require heavy physical labor, and these workers may well have deserved their benefits and amelioration of their lot. The question remains, however, of what balance of interest should be struck between the steelworkers and other workers who, as consumers, purchase goods made of steel? Were some of the consumers as deserving of benefits, and their conditions of work as much in need of improvement?

More generally, shall each group of workers in collaboration with its management be entitled to extract from consumers whatever its strategic position permits? Shall grocers, automobile companies, furniture companies, and construction workers, in turn, charge the steelworkers whatever they can get away with? Shall our distributive standard be nothing more than bare economic power—the exploitation of whatever monopoly advantage one possesses and can defend from dilution?

Shall each group of workers be permitted or encouraged to determine its own rates, depending upon its bargaining power vis-à-vis its employer and the particular industry's bargaining power vis-à-vis the public, based largely on the elasticity of demand for its product? If our answer is "yes," for want of any alternative, are we not simply acceding to the exploitation of the weaker, less strategically situated groups, allowing the makers of products with a low elasticity of demand to gain at the expense of those whose products have available substitutes? The former raise their wages by raising the prices of their products; the latter must pay the higher prices but cannot themselves take similar action for fear of an adverse effect on the demand for their products. Is the only restraint they can impose on unions, then, that provided by whatever elasticity there is in the demand curve facing their company or industry?

Those favorably disposed toward the unions have generally met such arguments with the contention that as unions "mature" they will develop a sense of "social responsibility" which will lead them to moderate their actions. Yet such reassurances as these are not fully satisfying. They rely, in the final analysis, upon self-restraint on the unions' part, and the history of reliance upon self-restraint to moderate private interests suggests that firmer assurances are needed to prevent the undue use of market control. If the power of a union to satisfy the income wants of its members rests upon the ability to pay of the firms with which it deals, and if that ability to pay can be augmented not only through the increasing of physical

---

Department of Labor, August 25, 1959. For a discussion of inflation and steel's contribution to it in the postwar period, see Otto Eckstein and Gary Fromm, *Steel and the Postwar Inflation,* Joint Economic Committee Study Paper No. 2 (1959).

productivity but equally through the more effective exploitation of monopolistic advantages, will not human nature take the union along the latter
course of action? With such an easy alternative, what reason do we have
for assuming that notions of social responsibility will deflect the union
along the harder paths of increasing technological efficiency?

Is there no restraint other than that which the unions may themselves
impose? It seems clear that there is; few unions, however strong, can
immunize themselves indefinitely from the forces of a rugged kind of competition. Monopolistic exploitation, whether by unions or management,
cannot be so firmly entrenched as to be forever free from competitive
threat. The problems appear at first so insoluble because we are accustomed to view their *immediate* effects. By widening our time horizons
somewhat, the problem falls into a proper perspective.

Competition through Innovations

Prof. Joseph A. Schumpeter pointed out that the problem of monopoly
business power is one with which economists have stubbornly wrestled for
years, without satisfactory result.[6] Their classic economic models assumed
business units so small that they were incapable of exerting any influence on
the market. Their competition led to an optimum allocation of resources in
accordance with consumer wants and a distribution of income that accorded with each individual's contribution to the economic system. Although their normative judgments seemed conclusive, their assumptions
were not. Business units grew ever larger, and with the growth of the large
corporation came widening control over the market—monopolistic powers
over prices and production. But, *mirabile dictu,* despite the increase of
monopoly powers, the consumer's position improved. Prices of goods declined over the years, the quality of products improved, and the standard of
living advanced. Monopoly powers did not seem to bring with them the
evils which economists had foreseen.

The reason for this seeming paradox, declared Professor Schumpeter,
was that economists had been worrying about the wrong kind of competition. They had been concerned about price competition among small units,
while the more significant price movements were long-run declines caused
by mass-production techniques. Small units could not avail themselves of
such technical developments since these were feasible only with large ag-
gregations of capital equipment. Businessmen would not undertake the
huge investments of capital, though, unless they could reasonably expect some measure of financial protection derived from that monopolistic
power which economists had condemned. The corporate leaders who sank

---

[6] The argument is set forth in his brilliant *Capitalism, Socialism and Democracy,* 3d ed., New York: Harper & Row, Publishers, Incorporated, 1950.

large sums of money into fixed capital did not do so unless they were reasonably sure that competitive price cutting would not deprive them of an adequate return on their investments and that patent protection would give them some security from immediate imitation. The prerequisite condition for the investment of large sums in mass-production techniques was thus some degree of monopolistic control over the market. Economic theory was turned on its head; monopoly was the instrument through which the prices of goods were reduced to the consuming public. Paradoxically, monopoly power carried with it *benefits* to the public. It provided that degree of security which was necessary to foster business actions that in the long run favored consumers.

Schumpeter did not concede, however, that the large investing monopolists were immune to all forms of competition. If they had been, there would have been nothing to *force* a lowering of product prices even though costs of production declined through improved techniques. There was a competition at work different from the simple price competition of orthodox economic theory, said Schumpeter. It was a dynamic kind of competition. No business, however large or strategically situated and however great its monopoly powers, could preserve itself forever from the competition that came with innovations—new products and new technologies. Innovations might come from other firms within an industry; they might equally well come from other industries. Their introduction could be tentatively delayed by collusion, agreement, or suppression, but such practices were not likely to be effective indefinitely. Inventiveness, ingenuity, and initiative in one quarter or another almost certainly assures us that although monopolistic power may provide a necessary short-run protection to large capital investments, it cannot give permanent protection against competitive products or technologies.

Large firms maintain extensive research departments, Schumpeter said, because these are a necessary condition of business survival. If firms were not constantly looking for new techniques and products, they would lose sales to some new and better product or to a similar product sold at a lower price because of improved methods of production. Competition forces businessmen to anticipate such eventualities, and this innovative competition, argued Schumpeter, is infinitely more effective than the simple price competition of theory.

We may seem to have digressed from a discussion of the monopoly powers of unions. Yet Schumpeter's argument should suggest one possible answer to our question of whether unions, whose wage objectives are limited by the ability to pay of the firms with which they bargain, will seek to expand that ability to pay by the route of monopolistic exploitation or through improved productivity. We may concede that unions may exploit monopoly and that in the short run they may in some degree succeed in making undue gains. We may also conclude that monopoly exploitation by the unions cannot have much more chance of indefinite prolongation than is true of businesses. A noted group of labor experts reported in 1961 that they were

> ... impressed with the restraints imposed on powerful unions or employers by open product markets, in which new products compete with old, in which trade among nations challenges the position of entrenched producers in the home country, in which the ingenuity of men in declining industries may recapture business long since lost. The large firm is forced to produce the small car; plastics are substituted for steel as steel prices rise. The development of "piggybacking" by the railroads challenges the trucking industry and the Teamsters union. Thus, truly open product markets are a check of great significance on the power of unions and employers in the labor market.[7]

The union which pushes up wages, unmindful of the impact on prices, will in time be brought up short by the development of a new product replacing the one on which its members are dependent or by the introduction of new production methods which drastically affect employment. Unions' monopoly powers can be exerted only *through business units,* and the persistence of those powers is dependent on the monopoly advantage *of the business units.* To the extent that these business units are subject to the dynamic competition pictured by Schumpeter, so too are the unions subject to the same restraint.[8]

It is true that this may not be so strong a protection for consumers as we would wish. That it nevertheless constitutes an important bulwark seems undeniable. If the power of the steelworkers is used to exploit their earlier strategic advantage, raising prices through raising wages, then substitute materials (some of them new), new uses for aluminum, new kinds of plastics, and new and more automated technologies will make that victory a temporary one. In this way, the once proud position of the coal miners has been seriously weakened by coal substitutes for both heat and power. The rising threat of the use of atomic energy for electric power generation has further reduced the once seemingly invincible monopoly of coal. Neither the Steelworkers nor the Mine Workers union has thus been immune to the

[7] *The Public Interest in National Labor Policy,* Committee for Economic Development (1961), p. 138.

[8] E. S. Mason argues this same point of view in "Monopoly and All That," in *Labor and Trade Unionism: An Interdisciplinary Reader,* Walter Galenson and Seymour M. Lipset (eds.), New York: John Wiley & Sons, Inc., 1960, p. 120.

effects of its own policies, any more than steel producers and mine operators have been. The exploitation of the advantage probably has hastened the arrival of products and processes competitive with both steel and coal, for the competition was a kind not wholly within the power of the union to control.

It appears, then, that there are two chief limitations upon the power of an organized group of workers to raise their rates relative to the rates of other workers: (1) in the short run, the elasticity of demand for their product [9] and (2) in the long run, the competitive restraint of new products and new techniques of production. Let us now turn to the question of whether these two checks operate with equal effectiveness when unions bargain with single companies and when they bargain on an industry basis.

The first of these limitations, the elasticity of demand for the product, is more effective if bargaining proceeds on a firm-by-firm basis. If the union at Ford raises its rates higher than the union at General Motors, adversely affecting costs of production and prices of Ford cars, a shift in demand from Fords to Chevrolets will act as a brake on its action. Our earlier investigation of the bargaining unit question should suggest, however, that the likelihood is slim that bargaining will necessarily continue indefinitely to follow a company-by-company basis. Some units have grown over the years to cover virtually an entire industry. Even where large-scale units have not been established, frequently key bargains set a pattern which other negotiators are constrained to follow. In these situations, will not any restraint normally supplied by interfirm competition, with differential labor costs an important competitive factor, be substantially reduced? Since all firms similarly situated are granting roughly equivalent increases, will not managements more willingly grant wage demands, with the consequence that rates in that industry in the short run will rise without much limitation? There is less of a check on union pressure since the elasticity of demand for an industry product is considerably less than that for any particular output of a firm in the industry.[10]

There is a measure of truth in this argument, but it is overstated. The fact that the wage rates of all competitors in an industry rise simultaneously does not mean that all will be affected to the same degree. The more efficient firms may be able to accommodate such an increase without any impact on prices whatsoever. Other firms may be able to meet the increases by improving the efficiency of their organizations. But some firms are likely

[9] This involves both simple price elasticity and also cross elasticity of demand, that is, the effect of a change in price on the quantities demanded of that product and also of other products (the substitution effect).

[10] This and additional arguments underscoring the problems of monopoly unionism are perhaps most clearly and starkly elaborated in Charles E. Lindbloom, *Unions and Capitalism,* New Haven, Conn.: Yale University Press, 1949.

to face the prospect of accepting losses in operation or forcing an increase in prices in order to pay the higher labor rates, and an increase in prices may reduce the demand for the products of the less efficient firms. The union may well concern itself with the problems of these struggling firms and seek to improve their efficiency, as we observed in discussing the relationship between the standard rate and the industry-wide bargain earlier in this chapter. This is not always welcomed by managements, however, nor is it so simply done.

The reader will recall from Chapter 9 the kind of problem introduced on the management side of the bargaining table in resolving conflicting interests among management representatives when bargaining is conducted on a multiemployer basis. The differential impact of wage increases on the business positions of the various firms will act as something of a restraint on the unions, solidifying management opposition to rates which work undue hardships on certain of their number. The bargaining power of those for whom the cost of agreeing to the union's terms is greatest rises relative to that of both other members of the employers' association and the union. Industry-wide bargaining may relax somewhat the restraint provided by the elasticity of demand for the product, but it certainly does not lift the lid and permit "easy pickings" for the union.[11]

Moreover, industry-wide bargaining does not affect the Schumpeterian kind of competition insofar as firms within an industry remain competitive among themselves on all except wage rates, so that each is striving to improve its product offerings and to better its methods of production. Research into new products and technologies will still serve to limit the power of unions to push rates upward. Wages in the innovating firms may be raised, but in other firms that feel the competitive pressure of the innovation, wage and price ceilings will exist. Such "dynamic" competition occurs between industries no less than within a particular industry, it must be remembered, as the cases of steel and coal remind us.

With respect to the effect of union monopoly power on relative wage rates, then, we can say that our major restraints are the elasticity of demand for the product and the differential impact of wage changes on profits, in the short run, and the competition of new goods and new productive methods, in the long run. These restraints operate not only between whole industries but also between individual companies within an industry, as long as effective product competition remains. This latter proviso is one which we shall have occasion to explore more fully in Chapter 17.

[11] This is not to say that under industry-wide bargaining in an industry characterized by oligopoly or price leadership a wage increase may not lead to *uniform* price action but only that the differential impact of the wage increase on the firms in that industry will act as a limitation on the size of the increase.

The Impact of Monopoly on Productivity, Employment, and Output

Let us turn now to the second aspect of the union monopoly question which we shall consider here: its impact on productivity, employment, and output. Economists have argued that employment is adversely affected by unions' monopoly power because they can bargain rates up to "excessive" levels, at which fewer employees will be hired. Unemployed men would like to work and would be willing to work at the rates being paid, but to hire them at existing union rates would be unprofitable to employers. Some of the unemployed would be willing to work even for *lower* rates, but the union through its monopoly hold on the employer will not permit their effective competition with its members on the job. The presence of pools of unemployed workers is thus blamed directly on the unions.[12]

Moreover, it is said, the strength of unions and the pressures of coercive comparison, based on union rivalries, provide an almost irresistible and persistent upward pressure on wages. It may be that the effects of any given wage increase can be predicted only in the light of circumstances existing at the moment, but it seems a fairly safe prediction that continuous wage increases must certainly lead to recurring unemployment. If union bargaining—that is, monopoly—power establishes ever-higher wage levels, surely from time to time under a particular combination of circumstances the level of rates will serve as a bar to the employment of idle but willing workers. Union power will adversely affect not only employment but also productivity and output whenever it is used merely exploitatively rather than to help increase productive efficiency and share in it. Over the years, as wage rates rise without relation to increases in productivity, we are likely to encounter the double phenomenon of pockets of unemployment and pockets of inflation.

The validity of this argument rests on the assumption that union power is not likely to meet effective resistance, allowing organized workers to push rates up to "excessive" levels. We have already seen, however, that union power is not irresistible and that effective restraints on its exercise do exist. There is no need to repeat here anything but our previous conclusion that the elasticities of demand for particular products and the development of new substitute products and techniques are, in general, important checks to union pressures which are often ignored or underrated. In particular instances where these general restraints prove ineffective, they require strengthening or supplementing.

There is no reason to assume that management's bargaining strength is

[12] For an analysis of this kind, see Harry Henig, "A Functional Criterion for Wage Appraisal," *Journal of Political Economy,* vol. 60 (1952), pp. 44–59.

likely to wither away over time. Managers have powers of resistance of which the unionists are acutely aware, even if the public is not.[13] Their motive in resisting union demands is to preserve their competitive status vis-à-vis not only other firms in their own industry but also other industries. If the price of their industry's product rises, they are likely to find that consumers will begin to divert their incomes to other uses. The wage policies of particular unions with a strong bargaining position may cause unemployment here or there and may exert some inflationary pressure in one area or another, but the union strength that can produce these consequences is not apt to persist without the appearance of an effective check.

Employment and wages manifest a reverse relationship which should not escape our examination. Are there conditions under which these checks on union power may be undependable? If there is a continuous high demand for all labor throughout the economy, will not unions be placed in the position where they can boost their rates without employer resistance, since the scarcity of labor will cause employer to compete against employer and industry against industry? Will not union leaders and members discount any adverse effects on employment due to rising costs and prices if those workers who lose their jobs can count on quickly finding others? A period of high prosperity brings with it a competitive bidding for labor and a strong demand for products, which make possible the easy payment of higher wages. Managers try to avoid strikes which interrupt profitable production and threaten the loss of hard-to-get workers. The union's strategic position is improved therefore at the very time that the employer's will to resist is weakest. Wage increases can be compensated by price increases with little injury to demand. The cost to the employer of agreeing on the union's terms declines, and the cost of disagreement on those terms increases. The situation that existed following the removal of wage and price controls at the end of World War II was an example of the likely result. In the words of one of the principal exponents of full-employment measures, "the fact remains that there is no inherent mechanism in our present system, which can with certainty prevent competitive sectional bargaining for wages from setting up a vicious spiral of rising prices under full employment." [14] Here is one relationship between collective bargaining and levels

---

[13] Even so strong a critic of unions as Jules Backman has written: "But the use of monopoly power by labor unions requires the assent of the employer in the form of a contract. The power of the union may enable it to wrest somewhat larger gains from the employer than would be obtained by the weaker union, but the process of negotiation can and does act as a restraining force." "Are Union Practices Monopolistic?" *Proceedings of the Eighth Annual Meeting of Industrial Relations Research Association,* 1955, p. 217.

[14] William H. Beveridge, *Full Employment in a Free Society,* New York: W. W. Norton & Company, Inc., 1945, p. 199.

of national income that has come to be regarded as crucial for the economy.

Since full employment has been accepted as a legitimate aim of the federal government, as evidenced in the Employment Act of 1946,[15] the danger of a wage-pushed inflation could appear if the government vigorously pursued the national objective of full employment instead of merely talking about it. We can create the conditions under which unions can push for wage increases without fear of the consequences. Unions could then readily substitute price increases for productivity increases to achieve their several wage objectives, generating a "creeping inflation" with all its economic inequities and dangers.

Some economists, it is true, have been less concerned than others about this problem. Professor Hansen has argued that a continuing assurance of full employment will provide less occasion for unions to exploit individual advantages. Unions will develop a sense of responsibility founded upon an intelligent appreciation of the changed economic environment since "under full employment, arbitrary advances in wages, out of line with productivity and a balanced wage structure, will clearly be at the expense of consumers—in other words at the expense of labor as a whole." It is pointed out that "during the war, in all the democracies, labor has demonstrated a sense of social responsibility. When society as a whole, through the government, undertakes responsibility for full employment and social welfare, labor may be expected, on past experience, to respond by living up to its social responsibilities." [16]

There are some who believe that the issue can be resolved by making a central labor federation, uniting all the major national unions and party to a national wage policy. "The position of the labor movement as a whole is very different from that of the constituent unions. The labor movement as a whole is large enough to be concerned with the interests of all groups of workers. . . . It presumably has the responsibility of protecting the interests of all workers against the excessive claims of any particular group." [17] It is

---

[15] Although this act does not in any sense "guarantee" employment, it states the responsibility of the United States government to encourage and initiate measures designed to assure a full-employment economy. Creation of the Council of Economic Advisors—one of the provisions of this act—was intended to provide a continuous survey of the economic health of the nation, which would be a basis for the President's recommendations to Congress of actions which in his judgment are required to meet the policy goals set forth in the act.

[16] Alvin H. Hansen, *Economic Policy and Full Employment,* New York: McGraw-Hill Book Company, 1947, p. 246.

[17] Sumner H. Slichter, "The Responsibility of Organized Labor for Employment," *American Economic Review,* vol. 35 (1945), p. 206. Along the same lines, Professor Slichter has suggested elsewhere that the greatest possibilities of

thus suggested that in time unions will learn to bargain jointly rather than singly, developing a common policy rather than seeking to "top" one another in effectiveness. Representatives of labor and of business will meet to frame a national wage policy to which the actual wage bargains in firms or industries must conform. With a certain optimism, Professor Slichter suggested: "Once the day is reached, as it eventually will be, when the broad outlines of a national wage policy are fixed for the purpose of producing the largest possible pay-rolls and profits, relations between employers and workers will undergo a revolutionary change and the basis will be laid for cooperation between them in promoting expansion and technological progress—a cooperation which will give the economy far greater power to raise production than it has ever possessed." [18]

Here again it is to be noted that such suggestions as these rely upon the unions' voluntarily limiting their powers, and we may reasonably question whether some more reliable control might not also be needed. The danger

---

collective bargaining are not likely to be realized "until representatives of labor as a whole and of business as a whole are able to fix the broad outlines of a national wage policy." "Labor after the War," in *Postwar Economic Problems,* Seymour E. Harris (ed.), New York: McGraw-Hill Book Company, 1943, p. 254. Prof. Arthur M. Ross finds himself "driven ineluctably to agree": *Trade Union Wage Policy,* Berkeley, Calif.: University of California Press, 1948, p. 97.

[18] Slichter, "Labor after the War," pp. 254–255. The proponents of such a course of action admit the remoteness of such an event, it is true.

> The tradition of the labor movement in this country is one of autonomy. Indeed, the American Federation of Labor was founded, not to dominate its constituent unions, but to help them preserve their independence. Each national union in the United States makes its own policies quite independently of the American Federation of Labor or the Congress of Industrial Organizations. Neither federation would venture to oppose or criticize the wage policy of a national union, no matter how that policy might affect the rest of labor.

Slichter, "The Responsibility of Organized Labor for Employment," pp. 206–207. Nevertheless, it is believed that in time unions will be driven to modify their emphasis on autonomy in order to avoid governmental intervention.

One might expect such a development to have occurred to a greater extent in Europe than in the United States. French unions, for example, participate—even though not very effectively as yet—in their country's planification efforts. A sense of responsibility on the part of French unions to preserve wage-price stability has not, however, been notable. On the other hand, the labor movements in Sweden and Holland after World War II and during the fifties and early sixties have conformed more nearly to Slichter's expectation.

arises from the full-employment program, and the elimination of the danger must be achieved by careful framing of that program. A full-employment economy sets the stage for inflation, *not solely because of union action,* but also because of the possibilities it affords for *all* groups in society—business and farmers no less than labor—to push up prices with little fear of consequences. The possibility that bargaining power, otherwise restrained by the forces of both short- and long-run competition, will under a full-employment policy lead directly to a creeping inflation is therefore not a problem unique to the unions, nor can it be met simply by limiting their power. Full employment under nonunion conditions will still permit inflation from pressures generated by the business sector of the economy. "Full-employment inflation" is thus not a problem of union monopoly power at all. It is one which runs throughout the economy, touching all sectors and originating in *all* economic transactions.

Inflationary dangers from a full-employment program inhere in the nature of the program itself. Inflation can be met only by care in framing and administering whatever employment measures are undertaken. In particular, it will be important not to eliminate, through employment guarantees which are either implicit or explicit, the *necessity* for personal and group responsibility.[19] We must, of course, avoid a policy equally destructive of private responsibility, that of using fear of unemployment and failure to compel extra exertion and of using them as "big sticks" to provide an unremitting incentive.

Summary and Conclusion

In summary, it would appear that the monopoly power of unions is considerably overstated. With respect to the possibility of strong groups

[19] In this connection it may be noted that specialized unemployment, while occasioning relief measures, should be cautiously examined before being made the basis for public assistance to the industry directly in continuing operations on a business-as-usual basis. For unemployment is a price which should be paid if it is a consequence of excessive use of monopoly advantage. In this connection we may recall the plea of the coal industry in the spring of 1950 for tariff protection against foreign oil, the competitive effect of which was said to lead to unemployment, or the pleas of unions and management in the garment and textile industries in 1962 for tariffs or import restrictions on Japanese goods. Without judging the merits of the argument, since more data would be necessary for judgment than are available to the newspaper reader, one might nevertheless have urged a most cautious consideration of the plea (joined in by both management and union) on the grounds that the industry as a whole and employers and unions severally have shown what appears to be an excessive regard for private interest, unmindful of the potential effect on their consumer-supporters.

exploiting the weak (the question of appropriate relative wage rates), the power to exploit does exist and is likely to be used, but there are effective limits to its use from price, product, and technological competition. These restraints are the more effective where business firms are actively competitive among themselves. With respect to the effect of monopoly wage practices upon productivity, employment, and output, it is true that union-supported wage rates in particular firms or industries can lead to unemployment. In these cases we must rely upon the previously enumerated competitive restraints to bring the consequences of such action home to the parties responsible for it. The fear that full-employment programs will divert the attention of unions from improved productivity as a basis for wage increases to simple price-boosting practices is not just a union problem but one involving the behavior of all economic groups. The control of inflation obviously depends on the kind of full-employment policies undertaken.

Thus there are greater restraints lying upon the unions' monopoly power than we are often inclined to believe, and their monopoly threat is much less potent than we are often wont to assume. This is not to say that it may not also be advisable to proscribe excessive practices, devices to limit product competition, or activity meant to hinder the introduction of new techniques. That innovation constitutes a powerful restraint on the aggrandizement of power seems scarcely open to question. What remains to be questioned is the methods by which the path of innovation is kept open for all. It is in this area, perhaps more than in any other, that effective "antitrust" action is needed. There is no reason why public policy should not be directed to breaking down unwarranted monopoly powers of either unions or businesses, as these appear and are identified.

The conclusion that unions are subject to substantial restraints is important as a guide to public policy. We can accept the unions for the desirable role which they play in giving security to their members and in allowing workers to participate in the business process, without forever subjecting ourselves to the exploitation of the monopolistic powers which union organization brings. Specific union policies, like specific business practices, may be examined for their effects; if they are found to be peculiarly immune to competitive restraint or particularly adverse in their impact on important sectors of the public, special provision can be made. But to the extent that we can rely on the effectiveness of competition—price, product, and technological—within the economy, we can secure the social advantages which come from unionism and escape the bleak alternatives of giving in to union domination, striving to crush the unions, or accepting a "strong" government which decides authoritatively what price and wage relationships shall be.

We have thus found that both competition and private control (monopoly) are necessary and tolerable in our social economy. The question inevitably, then, is: How much competition and how much private control (monopoly)? What shall be the blend or mix of these two? This is a question which, it is submitted here, cannot be answered once and for all time. The answer will change with society, over the years. It will probably involve more of an *ad hoc* approach than the price economics of the past, which has sometimes been presumed to be timeless in its teachings. We may begin, for example, simply by drawing up lists of control or monopolistic practices which appear at the moment to pass beyond a "reasonable" regard for private group interests and to move into the realm of exploitation of others. We may think of these as unfair labor practices of labor or management which adversely affect the consumer.[20] The banning of such gross practices will presumably leave unions and managements a sufficient degree of control to permit them to protect their interests as creative producers and yet leave them subject to competitive forces sufficient to protect the public which looks to them for the satisfaction of consumer needs. We shall encounter the same problem of achieving a workable balance again, in other contexts. So pragmatic an approach may fail to please those who insist upon rigorous solutions, but it appears capable of meeting present issues. The neat, systematic solution has not yet disclosed itself, and when it does arrive, as it undoubtedly will, in time, events will probably have already begun to outmode it. In the meantime, we can at least read the signs and discover the general directions in which we should move to reach the desired objective.

Monopoly powers of unions exist and cannot be denied; they are necessary to the very existence and functions of unions. That their exercise will not be intolerable seems likely as long as they are balanced by competitive restraints. The large union, like the large corporation, has become an integral part of our society. We need to seek a more effective integration of worker organizations into our society, understanding their strengths and limitations and their powers and weaknesses, rather than make them objects of uncritical acceptance or unreasoned fear. We accept their monopoly power (or control) just as we have that of the large corporation. We broadly approve of the purposes which both serve. And just as in the case of the large corporation, we must be assured that such control is not used in ways and for purposes which show themselves to be inconsistent over time with other broad social objectives.

We may now pause to survey the territory over which we have passed in this and the preceding two chapters. We set out to examine some of the

[20] The reader will find it a rewarding exercise to draw up a tentative list for himself, articulating the reasons for including certain practices but excluding others, being careful to base his judgments on the importance of a particular practice to the producers and consumers who are involved.

major economic problems which collective bargaining has introduced. In doing so, it was found advisable to inspect the most widely held theory of wages, the marginal productivity theory, as a possible basis for evaluating union wage actions. That theory, however, was found deficient in important particulars; especially does it ignore the nature of actual business decision making in our society. Market forces have been weakened, discretion in the decision-making area is possible, and unions share in the exercise of that discretion. The unions, through collective bargaining, are in fact participating in decision making, long considered a managerial function.

Moreover, the marginal productivity theory proceeds from the premise that the appropriate standard of resource allocation must be one of maximizing consumer satisfaction, whereas we have learned that producer satisfaction or job satisfaction is likewise important and entitled to more specific consideration.

The result is that not only does the marginal productivity theory fail to provide us with a description of reality, but it also fails to offer us a normative guide to what wage actions may be approved or disapproved. Its terms are applicable to another kind of society, more individualistic than twentieth-century Western society, in which autonomous groups negotiate with one another to effect important economic relationships. We find that collective bargaining, as one of those intergroup relationships, has brought with it this problem: If our old standards for determining whether wage rates are acceptable or unacceptable cannot be applied, what new standards can we adopt?

Unionism, with its collective bargaining program, inescapably confronts us with the fact that the wage standards suitable to an individualistic society are inapplicable where autonomous groups negotiate economic agreements. They are inapplicable where competing groups must accommodate one another's interests in a common discretionary decision-making process in order for production to take place at all. This conclusion can hardly be surprising. Economic *standards* in a democracy must largely be couched in terms of procedures. Where action and decision are left to private individuals and groups, we normally judge by the methods they employ rather than by the decisions they reach. However much we may disagree with the price policy of a firm or the wage policy of a union, we are inclined to grant the firm or the union the privilege of its own decision, *provided* we believe it is operating within the "rules of the game" as they may be defined at a particular time. Only in emergencies or distress situations or in cases that do not lend themselves to prevailing procedures do we impose standards in the form of substantive decisions—wartime price control, minimum wage laws, or public utility regulations, for example.

The competitive system did not base the justice of its arrangements on the particular price or wage which emerged from it. There was no substantive standard by which actual prices and wages could be judged. There was no "fair wage" of so many cents per hour for Grade A labor and no "fair price" of so many cents for a particular product of a given quality. Such standards had been used in earlier days, it will be recalled, when the state regulated prices and wages and, through guilds, guarded quality and performance. The competitive process was adopted, however, and used as a procedural standard: *Whatever* wages and prices emerged from a market which was beyond the influence of any group and in which buyers and sellers had knowledge of the alternatives offered and were free to take advantage of any such offers were fair and just because the *process* guaranteed that result.

Having departed irrevocably from such competitive arrangements, we live now in a society where large corporations can devise their wage and production policies, large unions can frame their own policies on the same matters, and decisions come by negotiated agreement between the two. We tend to turn to substantive standards for help in determining the acceptability of wages. None has proven to be entirely satisfactory; none can be expected to be satisfactory in the way the competitive standard was, for substantive standards are not apt to provide the same service that the procedural one did. The most-used standards are those of comparability and cost of living; they reflect the market influences intimately known by workers and managers. Their use suggests that we can expect acceptance of other standards only if they, too, are meaningful and relevant to workers, union leaders, and managers. Productivity, a standard that is to be commended if for no other reason than because it emphasizes the source of improvement for the general income level, seldom makes itself felt directly or meaningfully. We suggested in the last chapter that the meaning and implications of it could be made clearer and that workers could contribute more to it than they are now encouraged to do. Employees are not persuaded to step up production by any psychological sleight of hand. They respond as managers do—or as anyone else does—when they receive meaningful recognition of their interests in the total productive effort and of their ability to contribute creatively to production.

There has been a considerable exortation to the unions to use their efforts to improve efficiency. But the problems of productivity and monopoly are joined in the principle of ability to pay. A union's wage objectives can be met, in a *particular* firm or industry, by *both* increased productivity and exploitation of monopoly advantage. The monopoly route to wage increases is generally so much easier than the productivity method that we might reasonably expect most unions to follow it.

By following the suggestion which Schumpeter has made with respect to the monopolistic practices of business, we concluded that the competition which comes, over time, from the introduction of new products and new technologies is likely to prevent any long-run exploitation of consumers as a whole by special producer interests (both union and business). Over time, short-run exploitations may emerge—first on the part of one group, then on the part of another—but even in the short run these will be somewhat checked by the effect of differing price elasticities of demand for products and the differential effects of wages on the profit positions of individual firms. As for harmful effects on employment, these can indeed emerge. Our protection against such effects lies in the same price, product, and technological competition to prevent any group from perpetuating an undue short-run advantage. The related problem of whether full-employment conditions give an unacceptable support to union power we found to rest largely on a misconception. The threat of inflation under such circumstances is not a union phenomenon.

Our conclusion was that we need some kind of a workable compromise between the power of private groups to control their own affairs (which we have generally labeled "monopoly") and the competitive process (which limits the extent of such control). For producer satisfactions, we require a measure of monopoly; for consumer interests, we require a measure of competition. It is a blend of these which is needed.[21] In general and as a first approximation, the blend which has resulted from union practices does not appear to place excessive power in the unions' hands. By taking action to curtail *specific* practices which appear to be more destructive of consumer interests than their benefit to producer interests warrants, we can proceed on a tentative basis to assure the needed balance. This is admittedly a pragmatic rather than a systematic approach.

[21] This is the conclusion which Prof. John M. Clark presents in his *Alternative to Serfdom,* New York: Alfred A. Knopf, Inc., 1948.

Strikes and Collective Bargaining

chapter **16**

Those whose knowledge of collective bargaining is based only upon news reports very likely believe that strikes and collective bargaining inevitably go together, assuming that, like love and marriage (and a horse and carriage) in the popular song, "you can't have one without the other." In fact most collective bargaining proceeds without strikes. Reliable estimates indicate that the number of bargaining negotiations for new agreements or changes in old agreements, each year, is approximately 125,000; unions and management negotiate peacefully and reach agreements without any strike in at least 96 to 97 per cent of these situations. Some unions and managements have conducted collective bargaining for years and even decades without strikes. The ILGWU, for example, bargained with the major New York City employers' association for twenty-five years, between 1933 and 1958, without resort to a major walkout, and Actors' Equity experienced no strike during the many years from 1919 to 1960. The coal industry and the United Mine Workers have not engaged in an industry-wide strike since 1952, and many of the railroads and rail brotherhoods have bargained together since 1951 with no strike.

Although the strike quite clearly does not inevitably accompany bargaining, its availability as an instrument of pressure is an important condition of collective bargaining as we know it. Management and union negotiators reach agreement when the terms proposed by one party are judged to be more advantageous by the other party than disagreement on those terms. Since a strike hurts management by stopping production and workers by cutting off their wages, neither party is apt to reject terms proposed by the other without serious consideration. Acceding to the proposals or demands of the other party usually involves a cost, but so does a strike, which may be brought on by refusing to accede. The two costs must be balanced.

As long as a strike threatens greater loss to at least one of the parties if it disagrees than if it agrees with the other's demands, there is reason for them to settle. Without such a threat they may continue to disagree indefinitely and never bargain seriously, each simply refusing to give ground in an effort to reach a settlement acceptable to both. The right of management to disagree to union terms in the face of strikes or strike threats is quite as important as the right of unions to use strikes and the threat of them to gain concessions. Thus, though collective bargaining need not and does not always result in strikes, the possibility or ultimate threat of strikes is a necessary condition for collective bargaining.

For many years, however, the public—and even trade unionists—had good reason to believe that strikes themselves were an intimate, inevitable part of bargaining. In the early days of unions, both parties imposed terms unilaterally, as described in Chapters 1 and 2, and the strike quite overshadowed any other aspect of collective bargaining. Even after more stable bargaining relationships had been established in some industries, such as that in the stove industry following 1881, the strike continued to dominate the collective bargaining area. Employers generally opposed unions and bargained with such fierceness that they contributed to, and provoked a good deal of, violence in strikes. Since strikes disrupted the orderly industrial process that delivered goods and services to the public, they caused popular concern in the first place; when violence, accompanied by damage to property and injury to persons, was added, a large part of the articulate public expressed outright hostility to strikes, and many people rejected strikes as a suitable activity under any conditions.

Even after 1842, when state courts began to recognize unions as legitimate organizations in themselves, not restraints of trades per se, these courts insisted that unions could use the strike only within limits. A common means of limiting strikes was for courts to decide that a strike was for an "illegal purpose" and thus unlawful. The judge, of course, decided for what purposes the workers could strike. All too often they failed to perceive any legitimate worker purpose but easily recognized—and condemned—the injury caused by a strike. Justice Holmes, on the Massachusetts court, argued in 1896 that strikes were but a manifestation of competition and should be no more limited than competition among businessmen:

> [A new tradesman may drive established rivals to ruin, but the courts do not call this unlawful.] The reason, of course, is that the doctrine generally has been accepted that free competition is worth more to society than it costs, and that on this ground the infliction of the damage is privileged [as long as] . . . the damage is done not for its own sake, but as an instrumentality in reaching the end of victory in the battle of trade. . . . [If] the conflict between employers and employed is not [seen as] competition . . . if the policy on which our law is founded is too narrowly expressed in the term free competition, we may substitute free struggle for life. Certainly the policy is not limited to struggles between persons of the same class competing for the same end. It applies to all conflicts of temporal interests.[1]

Holmes's "less popular view," as he called it, was not accepted as a basis for public policy until the enactment of the Norris–La Guardia Act in 1932. The delay in acceptance is understandable, as is the steady movement away from his view since. Although one may properly understand union-represented workers and their employers as being competitors, the analogy of their competition with that of business rivals is imperfect. A strike injures not only the parties but also consumers who depend upon the stopped production; normal market competition may destroy a man's business, but the public is not thereby injured. The successful competitor justifies the injury to his business rival not merely by his own interest and gain but also by his presumed better service to the consumers.

Now, certainly the public generally may benefit from strikes if workers secure better wages and working conditions. Consumer expenditures may be thereby stimulated, and the health and welfare of the workers and their families may be improved. But if these benefits do accrue, they are indirect and diffused; judges—and the public—have found it difficult to evaluate and compare them with the direct, sharply concentrated losses suffered as a result of strikes. Whatever the benefits, they have usually been obscured by the immediacy and dramatic quality of strikes.

As they contemplated the losses and the possibility of immediate and irrevocable damage from disputes such as the great railroad strikes of 1877, 1885, and 1894, courts increasingly turned to the injunction as a means of curbing strikes. It was a less cumbersome procedure and seemed to promise protection for the public as well as employers against injury. Used and abused as it was in labor disputes, the injunction no doubt hindered union activities, but it was not just an antiunion, proemployer device, even though it was also that frequently enough. It was meant to serve the wider purpose of protecting the public against the impact of strikes and the violence that often accompanied them.

[1] *Vegelahn v. Guntner*, 167 Mass. 92, 106–107 (1896).

How effectively the injunction served this purpose is questionable. The record of strikes that did occur sheds little light upon what the record might have been had the injunction not been used, but neither the number of strikes nor the number of strikers shows any noticeable change between 1890 and 1905 that might be attributable to use of injunctions. The relative number of strikes and strikers did decline significantly from the highs of World War I to new lows around 1930, but economic conditions were as likely a cause as legal action. (See Table 3.) Even as they declined during the twenties, strikes continued to plague industry and the public, however.

The most bitterly fought strikes prior to World War II were usually the result of worker attempts to organize and to secure recognition. Once the union was recognized and in a position to negotiate collective agreements, the business-minded leaders of the AFL unions made clear their desire to avoid strikes and to reach peaceful settlements. They turned to the strike with reluctance and as a last resort. An obvious way to control strikes, so it appeared then, was to encourage unionization and collective bargaining. Assured of the opportunity to bargain, unions would use the strike sparingly, and organizing strikes could be virtually eliminated. Proponents of the Wagner Act had other and broader aims than lessening the incidence of strikes, but clearly this was an important one. In the act is this declaration of policy, which is repeated in the Labor-Management Relations Act of 1947:

> Industrial strife which interferes with the normal flow of commerce and with the full production of articles and commodities for commerce, can be avoided or substantially minimized if employers, employees, and labor organizations each recognize under law one another's legitimate rights in their relations with each other, and above all recognize under law that neither party has any right in its relations with any other to engage in acts or practices which jeopardize the public health, safety or interest.

The period of the Wagner Act, 1935 to 1947, was exceptional in the history of government control and regulation of strikes. Both legislatures and courts allowed nearly free rein to unions to engage in strikes. As long as strikers avoided violence, almost any concerted activity was permissible. The Wagner Act imposed no restriction upon jurisdictional strikes, secondary boycotts, or strikes of any kind. By 1940 the Supreme Court had gone so far as virtually to enshrine picketing as a form of free speech in the Fifth Amendment,[2] and in the following year it interpreted the Norris–La Guardia Act in such a way as to exempt most union activities from antitrust proceedings.[3] The government did not allow such freedom simply because strikes had become more acceptable instruments; rather, it did so to effect a better "balance of power" between unions and management and

---

[2] *Thornhill v. Alabama,* 310 U.S. 88 (1940).
[3] *United States v. Hutcheson,* 312 U.S. 219 (1941).

thus ultimately to lessen the incidence of strikes. Such an expectation assumed a great deal. The reluctance with which management accepted collective bargaining, the irresponsibility of some union leaders, and the inexperience of many union members were certainly not conducive to a restrained use of the strike.

Already angered by the coal strikes during World War II and the many wildcat strikes that increased as the end of the war came nearer, many citizens and an overwhelming majority of Congress lost all patience with the wave of strikes which occurred in the year immediately following the end of the war. One great industry after another was shut down. Workers walked out of coal mines, steel mills, and automobile and meat-packing plants; they closed most of the electrical manufacturing firms, the ports, and the textile mills. Even the railroads were stopped for nearly two days. In the following year the Taft-Hartley Act imposed explicit strike restrictions, the most dramatic of which were the provisions for handling national emergency strikes.

The act recognizes that the right to strike is essential to free collective bargaining, but it seeks to curtail strikes whose benefits to the parties are judged too small to justify their costs and injury to the public. Dissatisfaction with our strike experience and the legal restrictions that our legislators have imposed upon strikes to do not indicate a lack of confidence in collective bargaining or a desire to ban strikes. They do reflect, however, a belief that this weapon must be used with full regard for its impact on others and only after all other reasonable efforts to achieve agreement have been exhausted. As a distinguished group of labor students pointed out in the report *The Public Interest in National Labor Policy*,[4] "the importance of the right to strike (or to take a strike) does not mean . . . that a strike is always the right course of action for parties in disagreement to follow."

Public policy has encouraged collective bargaining for over a quarter of a century, partly in the hope that the burden of strikes and their accompanying losses might be lessened. The public has shown a willingness to bear the costs of strikes insofar as these may be part of the *necessary* price of decentralized decision making in economic matters. The articulate public, at least, expresses its impatience with strikes that affect whole industries or those that disrupt indispensable local services such as transportation, food delivery, garbage collection, and hospital care. It also wants assurances that the price paid in *any* strike is not merely a cost of inefficient negotiations or willful actions by stubborn or emotional men.

The Trend of Strikes

An examination of the statistical record of strikes indicates that unions (in contrast to unorganized workers) have successfully asserted their con-

[4] Committee for Economic Development (1961), p. 86.

trol over major strikes. Nevertheless, the hopes expressed in the Wagner Act have not yet been realized; the growth of unions and the spread of collective bargaining apparently have not minimized strikes' interference in commerce and production. In the past, before collective bargaining was as widespread as it is now, unorganized workers conducted a large share of all strikes without union sponsorship or direction. Only since the mid-thirties has it become uncommon and unusual for nonunion strikes to take place. Between one-third and one-half of the strikes between 1890 and 1900, for example, were not ordered by unions.[5] As late as 1916, over one-sixth of all strikes were conducted by nonunion workers. The proportion of nonunion strikes declined as union membership rose (though the ratio rose briefly between 1925 and 1933, as union membership dropped off), until today nonunion strikes are insignificant.

Since worker efforts to organize and to gain recognition for collective bargaining seemed to provoke so many strikes at an earlier time, legislators and the public might reasonably have expected strikes to decline after government protection of unionization had had its effect. If this has happened, it is difficult to detect. Strikes have several dimensions by which we may measure them, and they have not all changed in the same way. One may safely conclude, though, that we have averaged more lost time in the late fifties through strikes than was lost twenty years earlier. Mandays idle as a percentage of total working time averaged nearly 40 per cent larger in 1955 to 1960 than from 1935 to 1940. And if because of increasing productivity a man-hour lost recently is in fact a greater loss than one lost earlier, the absolute strike losses of the late fifties were even larger than these figures indicate. Even the number of workers involved in strikes over the six years from 1955 to 1960 as a percentage of the total employed averaged a bit larger (2.4 per cent) than during the period from 1935 to 1940, and about one-eighth larger than during the period from 1895 to 1900, sixty years ago! The only statistic that shows improvement is the frequency of strikes (i. e., the number of strikes relative to nonagricultural employment). Between 1955 and 1960, this number decreased by almost one-fourth over the period between 1935 and 1940, and it has declined even more measured against the turn of the century (by 35 per cent since the period between 1895 and 1900) and the period during and immediately following World War I (by 48 per cent since the period between 1916 and 1920) (Table 3).

[5] Arthur M. Ross, "The Natural History of the Strike," in *Industrial Conflict,* Arthur Kornhauser, Robert Dubin, and Arthur M. Ross (eds.), New York: McGraw-Hill Book Company, 1954, p. 24. For a discussion of union attempts to gain control of strikes before World War I, see Lloyd Ulman, *The Rise of the National Trade Union,* Cambridge, Mass.: Harvard University Press, 1955, chaps. 6, 12, and 14.

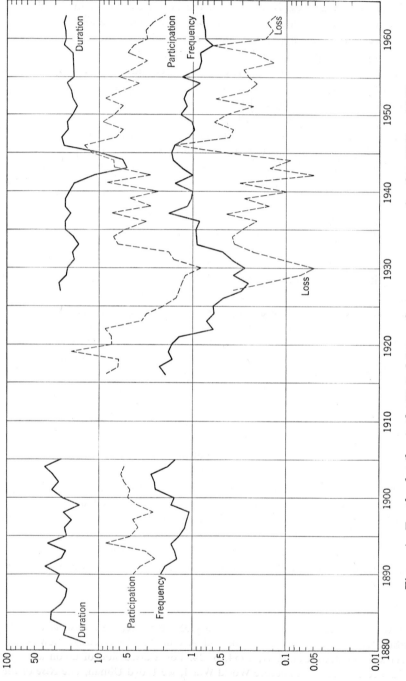

Figure 4   Trends of strikes in the United States; four measurements of strikes, 1881 to 1963

Table 3 ***Trends of Strikes in the United States; Four***
Measurements of Strikes, 1881 to 1963

Year	Duration [a]	Frequency [b]	Participation [c,e]	Loss [d,f]
1881	14.0			
1882	24.0			
1883	22.7			
1884	33.4			
1885	33.0			
1886	25.6			
1887	22.9			
1888	22.3			
1889	28.8			
1890	26.6	2.136	4.2	
1891	38.4	1.948	3.6	
1892	25.7	1.484	2.5	
1893	22.6	1.528	3.2	
1894	35.6	1.689	8.3	
1895	22.5	1.357	4.4	
1896	24.0	1.199	2.8	
1897	20.1	1.147	4.3	
1898	24.7	1.085	2.6	
1899	16.7	1.659	3.9	
1900	25.4	1.586	4.9	
1901	32.1	2.457	4.6	
1902	27.9	2.528	5.4	
1903	32.0	2.731	5.9	
1904	39.1	1.812	4.3	
1905	25.4	1.520	2.1	
1906–1915	n.a.	n.a.	n.a.	
1916	n.a.	1.989	8.4	
1917	n.a.	2.247	6.3	
1918	n.a.	1.676	6.2	
1919	n.a.	1.815	20.8	
1920	n.a.	1.682	7.2	
1921	n.a.	1.388	6.4	
1922	n.a.	0.601	8.7	
1923	n.a.	0.718	3.5	
1924	n.a.	0.591	3.1	
1925	n.a.	0.608	2.0	

See page 399 for footnotes.

Table 3   Trends of Strikes in the United States; Four Measurements of Strikes, 1881 to 1963 (Continued)

Year	Duration [a]	Frequency [b]	Participation [c,e]	Loss [d,f]
1926	n.a.	0.470	1.5	
1927	26.5	0.300	1.4	0.37
1928	27.6	0.256	1.3	0.17
1929	22.6	0.368	1.2	0.07
1930	22.3	0.278	0.8	0.05
1931	18.8	0.379	1.6	0.11
1932	19.6	0.467	1.8	0.23
1933	16.9	0.912	6.3	0.36
1934	19.5	0.909	7.2	0.38
1935	23.8	0.935	5.2	0.29
1936	23.3	0.853	3.1	0.21
1937	20.3	1.835	7.2	0.43
1938	23.6	1.128	2.8	0.15
1939	23.4	1.049	4.7	0.28
1940	20.9	1.000	2.3	0.10
1941	18.3	1.526	8.4	0.32
1942	11.2	0.989	2.8	0.05
1943	5.0	1.308	6.9	0.15
1944	5.6	1.636	7.0	0.09
1945	9.9	1.670	12.2	0.47
1946	24.2	1.571	14.5	1.43
1947	25.6	1.106	6.5	0.41
1948	21.8	0.959	5.5	0.37
1949	22.5	1.071	9.0	0.59
1950	19.2	1.387	6.9	0.44
1951	17.4	1.174	5.5	0.23
1952	19.6	1.272	8.8	0.57
1953	20.3	1.188	5.6	0.26
1954	22.5	0.839	3.7	0.21
1955	18.5	1.313	6.2	0.26
1956	18.9	0.866	4.3	0.29
1957	19.2	0.819	3.1	0.14
1958	19.7	0.861	4.8	0.22
1959	24.6	0.619	4.3	0.61
1960	23.4	0.757	3.0	0.17

Table 3 Trends of Strikes in the United States; Four
Measurements of Strikes, 1881 to 1963 (Continued)

Year	Duration [a]	Frequency [b]	Participation [c,e]	Loss [d,f]
1961	23.7	0.751	3.2	0.14
1962	24.6	0.793	2.7	0.16
1963	23.0	0.715	2.0	0.13
1895–1900	22.2	1.340	3.8	
1935–1940	22.6	1.133	4.2	0.24
1955–1960	20.7	0.872	4.3	0.28
1961–1963	23.8	0.720	2.6	0.14

Data on duration of strikes from 1880 to 1905 from John I. Griffin, *Strikes: A Study in Quantitative Economics,* New York: Columbia University Press, 1939, p. 87. Rest of data from *Handbook of Labor Statistics,* Bureau of Labor Statistics (1950), table E-2; and *Analysis of Work Stoppages,* Bureau of Labor Statistics Bulletin 1302 (1960), table 1, and later, yearly bulletins.

[a] Duration: average duration, calendar days. Figures are simple averages; each stoppage is given equal weight regardless of size, thus overemphasizing short strikes. Since reporting of short strikes has improved in recent years, the decline in duration may be only apparent, not real. The real duration may have increased.

[b] Frequency: number of strikes per 10,000 employed (total employed workers explained below).

[c] Participation: workers involved in work stoppages as a percentage of total employed.

[d] Loss: man-days idle during year as a percentage of estimated total working time.

[e] Total employed workers: based on nonagricultural employment reported by the Bureau. As used here, this refers to all workers except those in occupations and professions in which there is little, if any, union organization or in which strikes rarely, if ever, occur. In most industries, it includes all wage and salary workers except those in executive, managerial, or high supervisory positions or those performing professional work, the nature of which makes union organization or group action impracticable. It excludes all self-employed workers, domestic workers, agricultural wage workers on farms employing fewer than six persons, all federal and state government employees, and officials (both elected and appointed) in local governments.

[f] Estimated working time was computed for purposes of this table by multiplying the average number of employed workers by the number of days worked by most employees. This number excludes Saturdays when customarily not worked, Sundays, and established holidays.

The thirties and the fifties were, of course, quite different periods. During one we enjoyed general prosperity with short intermittent recessions; the other was marked by our greatest depression as well as by the rapid growth of unions and extension of collective bargaining. A time of high unemployment and low production is hardly conducive to strikes, and thus perhaps the lower incidence of strikes in the thirties is not surprising. Yet that was a time of great travail for labor and management, as unions pushed organization into new industries and confronted many workers and managers for the first time with the powers and responsibilities of collective bargaining, and one might reasonably expect strike activity in these more "settled" times to be less than in those more hectic days.

Though strike losses measured in man-days lost have only in very recent years begun to decline, as proponents of labor legislation hoped a generation ago, collective bargaining may receive credit for having lessened the violence of strikes. Seldom do labor unions and management engage in strikes with the bitterness and vehemence that often characterized strikes of the thirties and before. Once collective bargaining is established, it entails a continued working relationship from which neither party is able to escape. No matter how long a strike lasts or how deep a disagreement may temporarily separate union and management, they must eventually come together, reach some conclusion, and continue the day-to-day administration of their agreement. Unless one or both parties reject collective bargaining, they realize that the injection of bitterness and the rancor of violence inflicts not only a present wound but also a lasting injury. Thus past experience in bargaining with each other and the expectation of doing so in the future usually persuade labor leaders and managers of the wisdom of avoiding violence.

Commonly now when union and management negotiators face the reality of a strike, they proceed to call out the workers and then close the plants with businesslike regard for plant, equipment, and future production. In steel, the blast and open-hearth furnaces are carefully banked to minimize damage; in automobiles, passes are issued to nonstrikers and supervisors, allowing them to enter and leave the plants and to take care of essential maintenance; in electrical equipment, a company allows striking employees to draw vacation and other special pay, and it even grants pay advances to strikers returning to work as soon as the strike ends. Most strikes are kept under sufficient control, so that however unpleasant their consequences or inconvenient their effects, they can hardly be called primitive. At least they are no more primitive than the campaign charges, angry countercharges, half-truths, parades, emotional rallies, and general folderol of political rivals for public office. The simplified, obscurant arguments advertised in the news media, the frantic appeals to the public, and the grandstanding requests for government investigation are no worse than what is used in a "stockholders' " fight. Striking pickets seldom march with more furor than that displayed by Catholic War Veterans picketing a banned movie, nor are they apt to intimidate passersby with epithets and catcalls as effectively as a picket line of Hungarian Freedom Fighters, Mothers for Peace, or parents belonging to Save Our Neighborhood Schools.

Here and there, violent strikes flare up—in Kohler in Wisconsin, in Perfect Circle in Indiana, or in the textile mill towns of the South. In such disputes pickets have marched in massed rank, disgruntled workers have overturned cars, shotguns have been fired, plants have been bombed, and machinery has been sabotaged. Also, long-established union-management relationships have been destroyed, local unions have been weakened beyond repair, and union organizers have been run out of town—or worse. These are, however, occasional incidents, as untypical of today's industrial relations as bloody battles between strikers and strikebreakers were common at an earlier time, when employers could refuse even to contemplate union recognition, let alone a continuing process of bargaining. The violence and damage that once accompanied dealings between union and employer raised questions about the desirability and feasibility of collective bargaining; that bargaining still has recourse to strikes as often as it does now raises questions only about its efficiency and methods.

If careful calculation of strike strategy and businesslike direction of strike activity are hopeful advances, we may be further encouraged by a closer reading of the strike statistics. First, the data suggest that the nation may have reached a turning point in its incidence of strike losses. Perhaps strike activity has reached its peak and is now declining. Since the great strike upheaval of 1946, strike losses have declined irregularly, more or less paralleling their decline from a 1937 peak to a nadir in the midst of World War II. If the postwar trend should continue, avoiding blocks like the long, costly steel strike of 1959, strikes in the United States may reach a new low; as yet, however, the record is hardly one about which the nation can boast. The duration of strikes is increasing, indicating that once a strike occurs the parties are dealing with more intractable issues or are better able today to endure the costs involved in work stoppages.

Second, we may find encouragement in the fact that strikes do not plague all sections of the economy or raise serious problems in all manufacturing industries. Overall figures are often misleading, and those of strikes certainly are. Strikes have been particularly concentrated in a few key industries, thus limiting the scope of the problem with which public policy must deal. Six of them—coal mining, contract construction, basic steel, machinery, electrical equipment, and automobiles—have accounted for about 54 per cent of all man-days of idleness due to strikes in the years from 1927 to 1960, though they employed in 1960 not quite 14 per cent of all nonagricultural workers. If textiles and apparel are added, the eight industries have accounted for almost 61 per cent of strike idleness and for a little less than 18 per cent of all nonagricultural workers. The incidence of strikes has not been uniform among these industries, nor has it been uniform over time for any one of them. For example, in the apparel industry strikes were much more of a problem in the early thirties than in recent years; major strikes in coal mining have declined remarkably since the stormy, strife-ridden years up to and during World War II, while strike losses in the machinery and electrical equipment industries have increased since then.[6]

The concentration of strikes in a few industries at any one time suggests why the public expresses its concern, even though the total losses of mandays of work are small. The losses are indeed small when compared with the total man-days worked—0.17 per cent in 1960, or about four hours for each man-year worked. And they are small when compared with other losses. On-the-job accidents cause nearly 2½ times more lost working days, and the common cold no doubt imposes losses still greater. But a strike usually brings production to a complete stop or seriously threatens it in the affected plants or industry. It has a far more noticeable impact than slow losses to production throughout industry generally due to worker accidents or illness. Furthermore, the public can be more or less continually annoyed and alarmed by strikes if, as seems to be the case, they disappear from one industry only to develop a little later in another.

As noticeable and inconvenient as strikes may be in their impact, the economic losses due to strikes are usually more apparent than real, according to industrial relations experts. Stockpiling, postponable demand, and substitute supplies lessen the effects of strikes upon consumers and producers; prestrike anticipation, poststrike makeup, and cyclical or seasonal variations in production and employment can also whittle away strike losses for the workers and companies involved. A group of experts, headed by Prof. E. R. Livernash, who conducted an extensive study of the steel strikes between 1952 and 1959, found that economic data do not indicate any serious general losses for the economy as a result of those strikes. They conclude:

> It is our opinion that the economic impact of strikes on the economy are [sic] usually seriously exaggerated. Too often the losses of production, unemployment, and wages are evaluated in a context which assumes that there would have been continuous high-level operation had there been no strike.[7]

[6] Arthur M. Ross, "Prospects for Industrial Conflict," *Industrial Relations,* vol. 1 (1961), p. 66.

[7] *Collective Bargaining in the Basic Steel Industry,* U.S. Department of Labor (1961), p. 48. See also Irving Bernstein, "The Economic Impact of Strikes in Key Industries," in *Emergency Disputes and National Policy,* I. Bernstein, H. L. Enarson, and R. W. Fleming (eds.), New York: Harper & Row, Publishers, Incorporated, 1955.

Why Is the Public Concerned about Strikes?

If the experts are right, is the public then wrong in its concern over strikes? It would appear that the situation is well expressed in the limerick:

> There once was a faith healer from Deal
> Who said, "I know pain isn't real
> But when I puncture my skin
> With the point of a pin
> I dislike what I fancy I feel.

Though the experts assure us that the pain of strikes is not real, the public continues to object to it. Perhaps, then, the economic pain of strikes that the experts assure us is greatly exaggerated may not be what most concerns the public.

First, the public becomes exercised over the potential losses of strikes as well as over their actual losses. There may be enough coal "on the grass" to meet demand for a three-month strike, and there may be sufficient inventories of steel to carry production through a 116-day strike, and a bit longer. But if the strikes were to continue after the stockpiles were gone, real and rapidly spreading injury to the economy could be expected. Should the public remain calm and unworried until the potential injury materialized, the pressures for settlement would not be exerted upon the parties until the time when real losses could mount rapidly and disastrously. For the public to await the full force of an emergency before showing much concern for the strike that caused it would be like not consulting a doctor until one was sure an illness was indeed serious, if not fatal. If the parties are not subjected to the fierce thrust of popular criticism and the rough-and-ready judgment of the public, will they display much regard for the public interests? Granted that the daily headlines of strike losses and the cumulative effect of constant reporting magnify the real effects of strikes, do they not also serve the purpose of alerting the public to the potential dangers of the strike and of warning union and management that more is at stake than just their own interests?

We need not and should not, of course, disregard the analyses of strike losses made by the experts. They give us reason to believe that even in emergency strikes *immediate* settlement seldom need take precedence over the *kind* of settlement. There is time to make the most of all the techniques for reaching an understanding among the parties. The knowledge that measurable economic losses of past strikes have seldom been judged to be excessive may warn us to avoid a hysterical evaluation of a future strike. It would be unfortunate, though, if it persuaded people to display any less determination to impress the parties with the public's concern and willingness to help both resolve their disputes peacefully.

The second public concern provoked by strikes and not measured by mere economic loss is the overt, dramatic exercise of power by men who are not responsible or necessarily responsive to all those affected. When union members empower their leaders to call a strike, they grant them the authority to close down a plant and the power to stop a flow of goods and services to consumers, to shut down suppliers and retailers, and to affect the business and income of those who depend upon the purchases and expenditures of the strikers. A strike may have only limited adverse effects if it closes down only a small portion of an industry or only one plant out of many. In such a case those not directly involved can probably turn to other sources for the production now stopped or find other outlets for the goods they would otherwise sell to the struck firm. Small strikes, though annoying and costly to some in the community, are usually too limited to arouse much concern or to have a significant impact upon public welfare. In such a case the power wielded either by union leaders in calling the strike or by managers in taking the strike is not overweening.

Strikes and the Public Interest

The strikes which most clearly demonstrate the power to affect the public interest by men not responsible to the public are those which close down whole industries, stop vital services, or touch the economic life and welfare of a wide community. A strike which closes down 92 per cent of American steel capacity, the world's largest, undoubtedly is a demonstration of great power. Only the federal government or a foreign enemy with force of arms might be able to force so drastic an action. A strike by the electrical workers against General Electric which closes the largest source of employment and income in Pittsfield, Massachusetts, and Schenectady, New York, imposes a heavy burden upon those communities as well as upon the workers and the company; the same is true in South Bend, Indiana, of a strike by the UAW against Studebaker. A strike by maintenance-of-way and other nonoperating workers on the Pennsylvania Railroad can tie up the traffic of the whole Philadelphia metropolitan area and interfere with the work and activities of over four million people. A strike of East Coast maritime workers or West Coast truckers can disrupt the distribution of goods and materials vital to hundreds, if not thousands, of firms and millions of consumers. To no public official and to no government body does our nation entrust such power without regular, formal accountability to those affected by the decisions made. Even the governor and the legislature of the least populated of the states, Alaska, whose total number of inhabitants (226,000) is no greater than the number of workers employed by a single large automobile company, may not tax or otherwise penalize those doing business within the state without answering to those on whom the burden is laid. There is no formal, regular procedure for calling union leaders and managers to public account for their actions, which can inflict penalties upon great numbers of people and communities. Any public responsibility shown by either party is self-assumed, not imposed, and thus subject to neglect when contradicted by private organizational responsibilities.

Whatever the ramified effects of a strike may be and however many people may be affected, a union leader may well deny that in leading his striking members he is exercising power. He can explain that he is acting simply as he has to act, responding to the force of circumstances largely beyond his control. The rise in the cost of living, increased wage benefits received by workers in other industries, and the threat of technological unemployment excite among his members and their local leaders demands for improvements. Should he not respond to these demands and bargain with all the skill and force available to the union to secure the best possible terms, he could find his position threatened and perhaps even lose his office. Moreover, he neither calls nor conducts a strike on his own authority. The union members must agree to it, and unless they support it, it will not be maintained. As he contemplates the restrictions and necessities within which he must act, a union leader can conclude that he has little choice and thus little real power; he sees himself as merely responding to demands and pressures. He does not consider himself the initiator. He feels caught between the demands of an electorate to whom he is accountable and a management deaf to his negotiating arguments; a strike is forced upon him. Whatever the effects of the strike, he can reason that they are not consequences of his particular actions but rather of a whole set of conditions.

Before questioning this possible view of power manifested in strikes, we should remember that the power to stop production and thereby affect the well-being of many people and whole communities is not uniquely displayed in strikes. Plants, firms, and industries may run far below their capacity. While the impact of the resulting unemployment and lowered incomes in the immediate community is less drastic and spreads its detrimental effects in other communities less dramatically than that of the strike, the final losses and effects may be as great or greater. The steel industry, for example, produced 8,000,000 more tons of steel in 1959, despite a four-month strike, than in 1958, when it suffered a curtailment of 40 per cent of its capacity production. With an average unemployment of about 100,000, 30 to 35 million man-hours in steel were lost in the single year 1958, compared with the nearly 42 million man-days lost as a result of the strike.[8] The recession-induced declines in incomes and expenditures ad-

[8] For data from which computations were made, see *Background Statistics Bearing on the Steel Dispute: Supplementary Tables,* U.S. Department of La-

versely affected businesses of many kinds in steel towns and spread the pall of recession and depression over more than just the steel industry. When managers close down factories in one town and build new plants in another, many people are affected for good or ill and yet may have no say in the decisions made.[9]

Both union leaders and business managers are involved in decisions and activities whose spreading consequences affect people far removed from the immediate concern of company or union. The larger the organizations through which they transmit their decisions, the greater and more significant the effect will be. Business and labor leaders who can influence the performance of a few huge corporations in a key industry, such as steel, may impinge upon the welfare and well-being of a sizable portion of our nation. Yet neither the leaders of unions nor the leaders of corporations have any legal responsibility to the people they influence, nor is there any direct or regular process by which those affected might hold the leaders accountable for their decisions.

Like the labor leader, the business manager may well deny that he is exercising power when he cuts back production and orders the layoff of workers. He argues that he is not acting out of choice but rather is conforming to the implacable demands of the economic system. When orders for steel slack off, he would be foolish indeed to maintain production. He must respond to the market, setting production at the most profitable level; to produce more steel than can be sold would bring losses or a decline in profits. He would endanger the firm's reputation and jeopardize his own position. If the losses continued, he would undoubtedly be replaced. Thus the labor leader can argue that whatever the unpleasant consequences of his particular actions, they stem from a set of circumstances over which he has little, if any, control.

Anyone who understands the working of the market system and the nature of economic requirements appreciates the coercive influences to which businessmen respond. Were business units as small as those postulated by the theory of perfect competition (where the activity of any one

---

bor, August 25, 1959, tables 2a and 3a; and *The Dimensions of Major Work Stoppages, 1947–1959,* Bureau of Labor Statistics Bulletin 1298 (1961), p. 3.

[9] The action of a single company may even have the kind of sharp impact upon the economy and people that strikes do. For example, in 1961 the Ford Motor Company bought out the minority stockholders of British Ford for $300 million. The payment, which added to an already serious drain upon our gold holdings, came at a critical time when government monetary authorities had become worried about the United States balance of payments. Partly as a consequence of the Ford action, the government found it necessary to make emergency cutbacks in military expenditure, requiring families of military personnel in Europe to come home.

firm has no significant effect upon the market and all prices are given to the firm), the businessman could correctly plead that he was only a responder to, not an exerciser of, power. When business units are large, as many are today, and share oligopolistic markets, however, managers enjoy some opportunity to affect, and perhaps even to change, the conditions of the market. They can influence the demand for their product by adjusting prices and differentiating the product; they need not necessarily take supply prices as given where, because of ownership or dominant size, they may be able to secure price modifications. One can reasonably conclude that managers are not as passive and as lacking in control over their market circumstances as they may like to assume when discussing public responsibility. On the other hand, neither are they as free of coercive market pressures as their critics may like to think.

Since the large labor union is a much newer institution than the large firm and is less easily fitted into the market system (a union's successes and failures cannot be summed up meaningfully in a statement of profit or loss), it may be more difficult to appreciate the coercive influences to which union leaders respond. Though the external market as well as internal politics subject both firms and unions to pressures, the generally more democratic form of government among unions emphasizes the political. Since political affairs appear to be more amenable to personal direction than the market, people tend to believe that unions are more influenced by arbitrary, personal decisions than firms. Further, in America there is a tendency to personify unions in their chief officers and to depersonalize large firms. Walter Reuther more clearly personifies the United Automobile Workers than "Tex" Cobert ever personified Chrysler; Philip Murray seemed to be the embodiment of the United Steelworkers more than was true of Ben Fairless and United States Steel; Al Hayes could be more readily identified with the Machinists than Robert Gross with Lockheed or William Allen with Boeing.

Popularly we explain union stands and demands as if they were those of only a single man, and thus we oversimplify the forces that influence unions; the actual position of union leaders in making policy is not unlike that of businessmen. They are both subject to coercive political realities which limit their ability to gain benefits for their organizations. Union leaders have opportunities to affect and perhaps even to change the political situation within which they operate, of course. They can help mold their members' demands and seek techniques that mitigate contention within the union and between the union and management.[10] Yet, although they have

[10] If a union has effective control of employment in an industry or locality and the means to prevent entry of products from other areas, the union officers may be able to influence the economic conditions as well as the political. The high wage rates of electricians belonging to the IBEW, Local 3, in New York

some freedom to maneuver and can play an active role in their organizations, they are not as free to determine union policy or to order strikes or make or break agreements as union critics may like to assume.

Both union and business leaders often act as they do in given circumstances because the penalties are too great if they act otherwise. Assigned certain responsibilities by law to members of their own organizations and through various procedures held accountable to individuals or groups who seek their own private interests, the leaders are not always in a position to display a lively concern for public interest, even should they recognize it. Since the great organizations of which they are a part can and do seriously affect the public interest, a question of responsible use of power arises. How can the agents of mighty corporations and strategically located unions best be *made* to consider the public interest in their decisions as well as private, parochial interests?

The question arises in specific form when we consider the pricing policy of industries such as steel and electrical equipment, but it arises more dramatically, insistently, and unforgettably when we feel the effects of a strike or contemplate the potential damage of a continuing work stoppage.[11] Thus the public concern over strikes—and the results of collective bargaining—does not grow just out of a prejudice against unions, though they may be involved. Public anger and anxiety over strikes arise from a wider concern with the private exercise of great organizational power in a highly interdependent, urbanized, industrial society. The public has good reason to feel that the leaders of such large and powerful parts of the national polity as corporations and unions should increasingly display a growing sense of responsibility to an ever-wider community.

Our brief consideration of the influences that play upon union and business leaders warns us that the ways will not be easy or simple by which we may encourage or require a wider responsibility on the part of these organizations in the use of the strike. Unions and management meet in an encounter where vital interests, rights, and prerogatives are at stake. Incessant demands of stockholders, customers, and suppliers press upon corporate managers, and the constant necessities of democratic politics limit union officers. These men can afford to respond to a public interest as they bargain with one another only if the cost of not doing so is great enough to

---

City, are made possible in part by the ability of the union to prohibit the use of much electrical equipment assembled or wired outside of New York.

[11] The public displays the same kind of sensitivity to the dramatic in accidents. More pronounced concern is expressed by public spokesmen at the news of the death of ninety-five airline passengers in a single plane crash than is expressed over the news that 38,000 people were killed in automobile accidents in 1959. Such a response does not indicate that the public is not as concerned over automobile safety as over air safety.

impress them. And the public can safeguard its interests only if it is willing to bear the cost of impressing its will. Admonishment by newspaper editors and exhortation by Secretaries of Labor are not apt to accomplish much unless they have behind them the threat of unwelcome penalties. Unions and management must have reason to withstand the private coercive pressures that play upon them if such a stand is in the public interest; they need to be at least allowed, if not required, to consider the public's as well as their own private interests in collective bargaining.

In spite of the difficulties of grappling with so basic and thorny an issue as the social responsibility of "private" organizations, public concern over strikes and the power they display makes necessary a search for new, and a reappraisal of old, approaches to collective bargaining. A chairman of the National Labor Relations Board in late 1959 expressed the judgment that

> ... collective bargaining ... has failed to achieve that stability essential both to the growth of the country and for national defense. The American concept of collective bargaining must be supplemented to avoid work stoppages. There must evolve, in the public interest, an adequate substitute for the strike and the lockout.[12]

A few months later, then Secretary of Labor James Mitchell declared, "that the bargaining table was 'an antiquated institution' for meeting the impact of technological change upon traditional work rules and practices." [13] And Arthur J. Goldberg, Mitchell's successor, has said: "Traditional practices, which have served us so well, and which could continue to do so if we were really at peace, must be adapted to a period when our whole way of life is being challenged." [14] The opinion presented by these distinguished public officials suggests that unions and managements should be wary of confusing private advantages with democratic liberties; indeed both may need to contemplate the implication of Justice Brandeis's words that in industrial relations "all rights are derived from the purposes of the society in which they exist." [15]

Despite the risk of complicating the process of private collective bargaining by further public involvement, the offer or requirement of more outside aid to union and management negotiators can be defended for a reason

[12] Boyd Leedom, chairman, National Labor Relations Board, speech at the Commerce Alumni Association Dean's Day Ceremony, New York University, New York, December 5, 1959.

[13] Quoted in G. H. Hildebrand, *The Use of Informed Neutrals in Difficult Bargaining Situations,* Cornell University, Ithaca, N.Y., 1961, p. 1.

[14] Bureau of National Affairs, *Daily Labor Report,* August 17, 1960, E:1–4.

[15] Quoted by David L. Cole, "Government in the Bargaining Process: The Role of Mediation," *The Annals of the American Academy of Political and Social Science,* vol. 333 (1961), p. 52.

other than public concern. In the United States, state and federal legislatures have shown an inability or reluctance to act boldly in establishing labor standards, developing social welfare, and helping industry and labor adjust to technological change. The result has been to thrust upon collective bargaining many abrasive issues only lightly touched on in the political process. Nonurban legislators wield a veto power in most state governments as well as in Congress, and unionists have often felt that they have received too little recognition of their needs and problems. Urban labor has had to gain its benefits and protection by relying chiefly on its economic power. There should be little surprise that the conflict can become sharp indeed and that public interests do not dominate in the resolutions of issues.

In the late forties, pensions to supplement minimal social security benefits became a bargaining issue over which a number of serious strikes occurred. Later supplemental unemployment insurance arose as an issue as workers sought more protection from recurring depressions than state and federal governments would provide. Pensions and social insurance benefits were the major issues in disputes that contributed almost one-fourth of the losses resulting from strikes that involved 10,000 or more workers from 1947 to 1959.[16] More recently the states and Congress have shown but slight interest in comprehensive major programs to help workers meet the problem of technological change. Convinced that they must look to their own restrictive devices and protection of the *status quo* to defend themselves against change, workers in steel, glass, automobiles, transportation, and meat-packing have resorted to strikes. Some of these strikes have been long and bitter, indicating in part the depth of feeling of workers in an unstable, insecure work world; they also indicate the poverty of aid extended by the community to them and to management. As long as the nation does not see fit to provide adequate protection against economic insecurity, there is a reason, and perhaps a duty, to offer more aid to the collective bargaining process, helping the parties to use that process as efficiently and effectively as possible.

Procedures to Aid Peaceful Settlement

No single procedure is applicable or useful in all bargaining situations. The issues in dispute and the importance to the community of services jeopardized by a possible strike may vary greatly from dispute to dispute. A procedure that might successfully contribute to a settlement of a dispute involving a public utility and a union might be most inappropriate in a steel dispute, and still a third procedure might be necessary to produce a settle-

[16] *The Dimensions of Major Work Stoppages, 1947–1959,* Bureau of Labor Statistics Bulletin 1298 (1961), p. 9.

ment of a strike involving tugboatmen in the major Atlantic ports. Effective aid to peaceful settlement is apt to be forthcoming only if a number of procedures are available. Reliance upon any one method has obvious shortcomings. If it is sufficiently innocuous to be used frequently, the government may overuse it and the parties learn to calculate its possible effects. Once the procedure becomes a part of their calculations, each will maneuver its negotiations and plot its bargaining strategy to minimize the impact of the procedure upon its goals. In such a case the procedure may not aid settlement but discourage it. Apparently, the fixed process for dealing with emergency strikes under the Taft-Hartley Law has had this effect.[17] One side or the other may resist settlement, feeling sure that no economic pressures will develop during the eighty-day injunction period or that the situation may turn more in its favor in the meantime.

There is a variety of possible substitutes for the strike or for means of averting strikes. Some have had extensive use, and labor students have had time to examine thoroughly their strengths and shortcomings; others have seen little use; and some are but speculative suggestions. Nevertheless, whether they have been used or only suggested, even a brief examination of the procedures reveals that there is available a range of approaches to peaceful settlement. To seek to avoid strikes by using only one technique is to deny industrial relations the full range of possibilities for peaceful resolution of conflict.

In a democracy that wishes to preserve free collective bargaining, simple prohibition of strikes is hardly feasible or desirable. However, through a number of different procedures the government and the parties themselves can encourage or induce peaceful settlements. Some methods avoid any explicit sanctions on the parties for failing to reach agreement. Others are harsher, threatening or applying sanctions if a strike occurs, and some even provide for the terms of a temporary settlement. The first kind of procedure preserves the system of private decision making, and the second seeks to continue union-management relations and to maintain public service with little or no interference.

"Soft" Approaches

The softest approach of all is found in the procedure of admonition. It has long been used by Presidents, Secretaries of Labor, and their spokesmen to express governmental and public dissatisfaction with the threat or occurrence of strikes. Sometimes Presidents have admonished union and management privately, but more often they speak out publicly, deploring

---

[17] W. Willard Wirtz, "The 'Choice-of-procedure' Approach to National Emergency Disputes," in *Emergency Disputes and National Policy*, Bernstein, Enarson, and Fleming (eds.), p. 147.

the intransigence of either side or both, expressing public concern over the consequences of particular settlements, or warning the parties that the government will act to resolve the source of trouble and to protect the public. Secretary of Labor Arthur J. Goldberg has suggested that admonition may be worth developing as a formal, regularly used procedure. He has said that the government has a proper role in helping to bring about a socially responsible agreement without strikes. In a speech at Chicago in March, 1962, he maintained: "Government has the obligation to define the national interest and assert it when it reaches important proportions in an area of economy. I think the Government has got to give more help to the collective bargaining process."

Governmental definition and verbal assertion of the national interest are not in themselves strong pressures for peaceful settlement, but they do encourage union and business leaders to define publicly their own interests in terms that at least appear consonant with the national interest. Also, insofar as government pronouncements help to create a climate of opinion unfavorable to strikes and to strengthen public conviction that peaceful settlement should be possible, the risk of government intervention or sanctions is increased if negotiations break down. Admonitions exert the greatest influence if they are not used excessively and if they carry with them an implied threat of stronger action by the government.

Encouragement of peaceful settlement of labor disputes by exhortation is probably the easiest method to use but the most difficult with which to succeed. Its ease of use recommends it, but its limited effectiveness cautions against placing much reliance on it. If labor and management discover that they can safely ignore presidential admonitions because they are merely high-placed opinions supported by no threat of forceful action, these will have slight effect upon bargaining. Should they be followed by stronger governmental action, though, government spokesmen must consider carefully the consequences of becoming directly involved in particular disputes and bargaining issues. Involvement in disputes can be politically embarrassing if it is not successful. It can also complicate settlement. As the federal government increasingly finds itself concerned with the problems of economic growth, productive efficiency, inflation, avoidance of depression, the country's competitive position in world markets, and full production of war materials, its officials will no doubt increasingly feel a responsibility to "define the national interest and assert it." To assert it successfully, however, they may have to do more than admonish. They may have to provide some explicit, understandable guidelines for nationally powerful unions and management and standards by which the public can judge the reasonableness of their actions.

A second procedure for encouraging peaceful settlement without the use of sanctions is mediation. It is one of the simplest and most frequently exercised methods of strike prevention; paradoxically, it is also the most successful, yet the least effective, of all the procedures. Mediation is successful because it has helped unions and management resolve their differences and conclude agreements in hundreds, if not thousands, of negotiations year after year. It contributes to settlements between large, powerful protagonists who have had to resolve difficult issues and it also helps small, relatively inexperienced bargainers negotiate routine agreements. There is nothing in mediation that compels agreement, however, and its voluntary nature makes it ineffective when the parties in collective bargaining prove intransigent and the issues intractable. When a strike is very likely, then mediation—at least routine mediation—fails or is at its weakest.

Just because mediation sometimes fails, it does not follow, then, that it must be viewed as a weak instrument. The Federal Conciliation and Mediation Service, along with state and local mediation bodies, has developed a cadre of experts skilled in exposing the areas of basic disagreement and in discovering opportunities for agreement. These experts know how best to encourage the parties to display that additional bit of flexibility which fits demands and concessions together into an acceptable agreement. They are usually knowledgeable about the economics and technologies of industries and able to understand the peculiar problems and to speak the special language of the men with whom they deal. Men from outside the mediation services sometimes serve as mediators. Public officials, community leaders, and university teachers may be called to assist in some local disputes, but increasingly mediation has become a job for professionals. In graver national situations, however, there has more recently developed a practice of calling in a special *ad hoc* mediation panel consisting of prominent individuals whose judgments cannot lightly be ignored.

Mediation may take place before negotiations reach an impasse or a strike occurs. In such a case of preventive mediation, the mediator may join the bargainers in their early sessions. He will then be familiar with the background of the negotiation and have an inside knowledge of the issues and their implications for the parties, should his active services be needed later. Also, his presence may be useful in reminding the parties that public interests are involved which should not be disregarded. Since negotiations often move from one critical stage to another, rather than progress toward one overall crisis, a mediator may be able to offer suggestions or perform services during the course of negotiating which help reach a final agreement. Perhaps more often the parties themselves request a mediator when their negotiations have become deadlocked. In some situations, such as those involving rail or air transportation and some local public utilities, legislation prescribes mediation before a strike can be carried out. The parties are usually compelled only to accept the mediator's services, not his decisions or suggestions.

Even where mediation is compulsory, any agreement which may result is still voluntary. In fact, it is the noncompulsory nature of mediation that encourages unions and management to use it. It may help the parties reach an agreement, but it cannot endanger any essential principle or interest of either. Thus it does not threaten to interfere with free collective bargaining, nor does it threaten any penalties or control if that bargaining results in strikes harmful to the public.

Within recent years collective bargaining has shown its vitality by beginning to develop a new procedure to aid peaceful settlement. It is so new that it has no recognized name, being referred to as a "voluntary tripartite study device" or the "informed neutral approach." [18] An appropriate name might be "consultation," which suggests an important part, though not all, of the functions performed by the informed neutrals called upon to help union and management meet and solve difficult problems involving them both. It resembles mediation, but unlike that procedure it can be applied to problems before they reach a bargaining stalemate or crisis. Preferably consultation is used before an issue has come to the bargaining table. The informed consultants deal with anticipated problems and with those which have existed for a long time but which may best be handled apart from current negotiations. Contributing his services as a guide, adviser, and conscience to both parties, in anticipation of identifiable, incipient problems, the informed consultant may be able to help union and management approach each other as problem solvers and not merely as negotiators. Since the consultation proceedings are divorced from immediate pressures to reach an agreement, they can most effectively be applied to problems involving long-term relationships between the parties. By shifting emphasis from the present agreement and pending issues to longer-term, lasting problems, the parties can, perhaps, exercise a greater degree of foresight, imagination, and constructive administrative talent, thus raising the process of collective bargaining to a higher level.

Several companies and unions have used consultation when confronted with long-range, difficult problems. Kaiser Steel and the United Steelworkers in 1959 empowered a special joint committee to explore the long-range problems of automation, equitable sharing of corporate revenues, improvement in grievance procedures, and more effective work rules. The Armour Company and the meat-packers set up a tripartite study committee in 1959 to handle the problems of automation. In the same year, the Pacific Maritime Association and the Longshoremen used a neutral consultant to help them deal with the problem of mechanization. There have been other situa-

[18] George H. Hildebrand, "The Use of Tripartite Bodies to Supplement Collective Bargaining," *Proceedings of the Industrial Relations Research Association,* 1961, p. 657; also Hildebrand, *The Use of Informed Neutrals in Difficult Bargaining Situations.*

tions where consultation has been used with some success, but there have also been times when the results have been less than spectacular. Even where consultation brings forth a report after careful study, as in the case of the Presidential Study Commission for the railroad industry, bitter disputes and perhaps even strikes can follow.

Consultation can be an effective means of avoiding or settling disputes only if both union and management can and will contemplate long-term planning of their relationships. Both must be sophisticated in their approach to business planning and control; management must be willing to admit to its confidence both the union and the neutral consultant, while the union must be responsible to that trust. Further, this three-way confidence is difficult to achieve because both union and management are usually fearful that a consultant's recommendations may be unacceptable to one of them, while handing to the other a bargaining weapon of considerable value. This procedure is thus no guarantee of peaceful settlement of disputes and control of strikes.

A third technique that can help to avert strikes is "fact-finding." The term is an anomalous one, since the finding of facts is its least important aspect. Labor experts mean by fact-finding a device for securing proposed terms of settlement which will secure wide public backing and require the parties to give careful, serious attention to them. The terms may be formulated by a tripartite board, which usually has such prestige, by virtue of the authorities appointing it and the members themselves, that its advisory proposals command respect.

Fact-finding can be effective, but its misuse under the Railway Labor and the Taft-Hartley Acts has tended to discredit it. If it is the only procedure made available to the government, it may not be appropriate in the given circumstance and may fail to accomplish anything. It has the greatest chance of success when used as a kind of voluntary arbitration. In such a case, the government is assured beforehand that the parties will abide by the recommendations of the board, barring an unexpectedly outrageous decision. The assurance protects the government's prestige and keeps the procedure from being merely a delaying tactic before more forceful action has to be taken.

The Railway Labor Act makes fact-finding virtually the only means of handling a dispute before a strike can be invoked. Knowing that it will be used and hoping to take advantage of it, the parties are apt to conduct their voluntary bargaining with an eye only toward the presentation they will later make before the fact-finders. Negotiations between the two parties often fail as a result. Under the Taft-Hartley Act, once a President declares a dispute an emergency, he must appoint a fact-finding board that has no power to make recommendations. Without that power, a Taft-Hartley board can accomplish nothing. Moreover, once the President moves under the act, the parties know what the sequence of procedures will be, since they are fixed. When the parties know what kind of intervention to expect, even mediation, as well as regular bargaining, is disrupted.

The Advisory Committee on Labor-Management Relations in Atomic Energy Installations reported in 1957:

> If, in a difficult dispute, the mediator knows along with the parties that if the dispute is not settled at a given point of time the panel will step in and take over, neither the mediator nor the parties will be able to accord the mediation efforts the importance and vitality they must have to be effective.[19]

Such judgments suggest that fact-finding, like the other soft-approach procedures, can contribute to peaceful settlement of disputes only if used more wisely than present legislation allows. The fixed reliance upon it required by our basic labor laws does not allow its most promising benefits to be realized. But even a full realization of these in fact-finding or in mediation, consultation, or admonition would not solve all the problems of strike control, though more effective use of these devices should go a long way toward meeting legitimate public interests. If labor, management, and the government used them more efficiently, fewer negotiations would probably stalemate and then break down into strikes, but some encounters that involve interests and rights which the parties viewed as vital would no doubt be too sharp to be resolved by reason or moral suasion. In these cases sanctions may have to be applied and penalties levied before the parties will forgo a strike which threatens to injure the public. A "hard approach" may then be necessary.

"Hard" Approaches

In taking a hard approach, the government may either provide a settlement which the parties reject on pain of penalties or penalize one or both sides until an agreement is worked out. The oldest procedure for limiting strikes is that of the injunction. As a short-run means of preventing a strike, it is without equal, though as an instrument for settling the dispute which gives rise to the strike, it is nearly useless. Historically the injunction was not used or intended as a means of settling disputes. Legally it is an order of the courts by which an action is forestalled. It is granted upon petition and proof of an appellant that otherwise he will suffer irreparable injury. Under the Taft-Hartley Law, a finding that a strike threatens national health or safety substitutes for a finding of irreparable injury. Its effectiveness depends upon the severe penalties a court may impose if an

[19] Advisory Committee on Labor-Management Relations in Atomic Energy Installations, *Report,* U.S. Department of Labor (1957), p. 26.

injunctive order is not obeyed. Disobedience of an order puts one in contempt of court, for which a judge may inflict whatever fines or jail sentences he finds appropriate. For example, in 1946 in a famous case involving John L. Lewis and the United Mine Workers, Judge Goldsborough fined Lewis $10,000 and the union $3,500,000.

Though it may solve the immediate problem of a strike, the injunction is hardly suitable for long-run control of strikes. It is basically inequitable, favoring whichever party has the most to gain from preservation of the *status quo* and injuring the party seeking change. Since unions usually have been the initiators of change in industrial relations, they have felt that they had the most to lose from injunctions. For this reason and also because of their atavistic remembrance of the easy use (and misuse) of the injunction before 1932, unions have heartily condemned the Taft-Hartley injunction procedure. Management could, however, find the injunction working against them if they desire to change existing conditions. Such was the case, for example, with a railroad that wanted to eliminate a number of freight crews when it switched from steam to diesel engines.[20] The dispute was not classified as an "emergency," and it arose under the Railway Labor Act rather than the Taft-Hartley Act, but it demonstrated that conditions may not always allow the injunction to favor the same party.

The favoritism inherent in the use of the injunction tends to block rather than speed settlement of disputes. Whichever party is favored will probably relax its efforts to reach an agreement as long as the injunction is in force. Under the Taft-Hartley procedures, an injunction must be lifted after a maximum of eighty days, and experience has shown that seldom have the parties used that time seriously to reach a settlement.[21] Even if a later settlement is retroactive to the beginning of an injunction, there may still be gains to be secured by waiting. Production cycles may change to the advantage of one or the other party, and workers' enthusiasms and hopes may fluctuate, so that whatever settlement is ultimately worked out reflects a shift in relative bargaining strengths from those existing at the time the injunction was imposed.

Despite its limitations, the injunction clearly has a useful role to play in dispute settlement, not as a prime lever to achieve the settlement, but rather as a powerful means of protecting the public from the detrimental effects of a strike. Used wisely and with caution, it is a valuable tool.

A second forceful procedure, more powerful than the injunction, is governmental seizure and operation of a plant, firm, or industry involved in, or threatened by, a strike. With few exceptions, the government has used

[20] *Locomotive Engineers v. M-K-T Railroad,* 46 LRRM 2429 (1960).

[21] Frank Pierson, "An Evaluation of the Emergency Provisions," in *Emergency Disputes and National Policy,* Bernstein, Enarson, and Fleming (eds.), p. 138.

seizure only in wartime because of the constitutional protection of private property. A few states have provided for seizure in strike-control legislation, however.

Seizure can have the same result as the injunction, that is, maintenance of the *status quo,* unless the government is authorized to make "reasonable" changes in the terms and conditions of work. Furthermore, the government may be compensated for its managerial contribution, receiving at least its costs or perhaps a percentage of the profits. Under seizure, the government's purpose is to make both parties less than satisfied with its performance, the union receiving less than it hoped for from management, and management losing more than it would have under an agreement with the union. The hoped-for result would be to drive the parties to settle their dispute and allow the government to remove itself from the scene.

There are obvious dangers in the government's use of seizure. It could degenerate into a cumbersome and awkward form of compulsory arbitration. Since special boards would be needed to determine just compensation for the owners and workers during the period of government operations, their proceedings and court appeals therefrom could snarl the whole procedure into an unworkable political and legal tangle. Another danger is that the government inadvertently (or out of political favoritism) might establish terms or conditions quite satisfactory to one party or the other. If that were to happen, there would be little pressure upon that party to compromise its stand, and settlement of the dispute would be frustrated. Finally, if seizure were made the only instrument available to the government for dealing with strikes, it would not help in most strike situations. Seizure is so drastic a step that it is a "last resort" means of handling a strike and in any case would be used but rarely. Until Congress passes legislation authorizing presidential use of it, however, it remains only a possible, though in appropriate circumstances a promising, procedure. One state, Virginia, provides for it under special circumstances.

A third procedure which relies upon "the persuasion of power rather than the power of persuasion" is compulsory arbitration. It is a much simpler process than seizure, and unlike the injunction it provides a settlement. If the parties are unable to reach an agreement, an outside authority examines the claims and arguments of each and then fixes the terms of a settlement which must be accepted.

Unions and management strenuously oppose any compulsory arbitration in this country, seeing it as a threat to voluntary collective bargaining. Their opposition to it enhances its value as a possible means of settling disputes or stopping strikes. Even the possibility of its use should exert pressure upon the parties to reach an agreement on their own. If the government were empowered to intervene in true "emergency" disputes with compulsory arbitration, even though it seldom chose to exercise that power, the parties might be encouraged to submit their differences to voluntary arbitration. It thus would be an instrument of last resort, serving mainly as a prod to bestir the parties to approach voluntary dispute settlement more creatively than they had up to that time.

The main criticism of compulsory arbitration is that it undermines voluntary collective bargaining; it allows the parties to avoid the often unpleasant confrontation of their own difficulties, creating a dependency upon public authority. The criticism is valid if we judge the experience of a country such as Australia, where compulsory arbitration has long been used to handle all disputes. But if the government were to use compulsory arbitration infrequently, as only one of several means of handling large, disruptive strikes, the criticism loses much of its force. In fact, the frequent and regular use of arbitration does not appear to be a very good means of reducing strike losses. In Australia, strike losses are proportionally nearly as large as those in the United States, though our losses result primarily from strikes of several weeks' duration, and theirs from short strikes lasting only a few days.[22]

A fourth procedure for dealing with strikes and aiding peaceful dispute settlement is referral to Congress. Most labor experts agree that except in the most unusual circumstances Congress is a completely inappropriate body for adjudicating specific labor disputes. Yet the Taft-Hartley emergency strike procedures end with the unresolved dispute presented to Congress for its action. The fear of complicating an already difficult dispute with uninformed partisan politics may have contributed to the settlement of some emergency disputes. In 1959, for example, neither the steel union nor the steel companies cared to contemplate the consequences of their dispute being taken to Congress, and they settled shortly before that action would have had to be taken. Though the occasion would doubtless be rare, referral of a dispute to Congress might be helpful if a single important and easily grasped issue involving principle were in dispute. The effectiveness of the mere possibility or threat of referral to Congress is, however, the better argument for the procedure. In either case, we might expect its use to be extremely limited.

One further suggested procedure for protecting the public from the injuries of a strike and inducing the parties to reach an agreement is the statutory strike.[23] During such a strike the employees would continue their work at the direction of the government unless, as individuals, they chose

[22] Arthur M. Ross and Paul T. Hartman, *Changing Patterns of Industrial Conflict,* New York: John Wiley & Sons, Inc., 1960, p. 207.

[23] Neil W. Chamberlain, *Social Responsibility and Strikes,* New York: Harper & Row, Publishers, Incorporated, 1953, pp. 279–286; and David B. McCalmont, "The Semi-strike," *Industrial and Labor Relations Review,* vol. 15 (1962), pp. 191–208.

to resign. The government would also direct management to continue production. The interest of the public would thus be preserved insofar as it would continue to enjoy the goods and services usually supplied by the parties in dispute. To encourage the parties to reach an agreement and to permit them to impose upon each other the same kind of penalties levied by a strike, the government would limit the earnings of each to less than would normally be received. Since by threatening or calling a strike each party indicates a willingness to take a loss itself in order to impose a loss upon the other, they should, at least in logic, have no objection to the statutory strike. It could even be made a desirable alternative by penalizing the parties only a portion of the loss that would result from a regular strike. The workers would forfeit some fixed proportion of their usual wages, and the company would give up a proportionate share of earnings. Both would thus sustain losses and be under pressure to reach an agreement, but the public would not be affected by the dispute. The contest of economic endurance would continue until the parties worked out concessions or arrived at some compromise acceptable to both. Once they reached a settlement, the government would end the statutory strike, and the parties would again receive their full earnings.

An obvious difficulty with this procedure is in adjusting the penalties so that the relative bargaining power of the parties is not greatly changed. If the penalties under a statutory strike hit one party harder than those of a regular strike would, the government is influencing the outcome of the dispute and the kind of settlement. Nevertheless, as one of a number of possible procedures which might be invoked in a critical situation, the statutory strike would appear to have enough merit to warrant serious consideration. To date, though, it has received little attention and almost no use.[24]

There is thus available such an array of procedures for promoting and

---

[24] The Miami Transit Company and its striking drivers agreed to a statutory strike in 1960. The company paid for fuel and maintenance during the strike but collected no fares. The drivers agreed to work without pay. The strike lasted forty-two days, and an agreement was finally reached when, in the words of the general manager,

> The American public, being what it is, felt obligated to offer a tip to the driver. Since the bus companies were bearing the expense of operating the buses and were not benefiting by these gratuities, which in most cases equalled the amount of the fares, they withdrew their buses from the streets. The drivers then got permission to operate their private cars as courtesy cars provided they did not charge fares. Here again the passengers felt the obligation to tip. The final settlement came on November 11, 1960, when the buses were returned to the streets and the employees received an 8¢ per hour increase.

inducing peaceful settlement of disputes and for avoiding strikes that the high incidence of strikes in the United States compared with other free countries seems unnecessary.[25] The potential threat of strikes and their display of great power wielded privately for private interests suggest that the public, through its representatives, might wisely urge the government to encourage, if not demand, that labor and management resolve their difficulties with a greater sense of responsibility to those outside their own organizations. To repeat a thought expressed earlier in the chapter, some strikes are a necessary price we pay for private decision making in a pluralistic, open society, and for that reason we should not be misled into too ready a condemnation of all strikes. However, some of today's strikes may be simply a price exacted from the public for less efficient and less responsible negotiations than we have a right to expect. Suitable governmental action may prod unions and managements to give more attention to improving their social as well as their technological machinery.

[25] Ross and Hartman, *Changing Patterns of Industrial Conflict.*

The Future of
Collective Bargaining

chapter 17

Collective bargaining has changed considerably over the past century and a half, and we may expect it to continue to change as workers and managers adapt it to meet new needs and circumstances. In the early nineteenth century, unions existed in the shadow of illegality; the public was suspicious of their activities, and employers made clear their hostility. Organized workers responded with tactics and strategies that they believed to be appropriate. Consulting only among themselves, they formulated their final terms, and when the economic or political tides pulled in their direction, they sought to impose the unilaterally determined terms upon employers. When the tides turned, the initiative might pass back to the employers, who would retaliate by unilaterally imposing *their* terms of employment. They imposed their terms without discussing them with the workers affected, just as the unions sought to impose theirs without consulting with the employers.

The unilateral process of setting wages and determining terms of employment emphasized conflicting interests, not those which the parties had in common, such as the continuity of the business or sales to customers. As the century wore on, a small but significant number of union leaders and employers began to appreciate the fact that although they had conflicts, the continued presence of the union and the members' dependence upon the employer required them to deal with each other. They discovered that in such a situation, they could achieve better results for both if they jointly discussed the terms of employment than if the temporarily stronger party imposed them unilaterally. By the end of the century, collective bargaining as we know it today began to assume importance.

Meeting jointly to discuss and explore their demands was no small advance. The two parties threshed out issues among themselves, contributing in some degree to each one's knowledge of those things of chief concern to the other. They gained some sense of participation in the resulting decisions, which gave an enhanced standing to the agreed-upon policies. Each had a greater sense of security, being assured that the terms of the agreement would remain fixed for a specified period.

The need for the joint bargaining was great. As the nation grew, the range of people's activities multiplied; organizations grew apace in size and complexity, and they became increasingly important in the conduct of private and public affairs. Increasingly, individuals had to deal with groups and found themselves members of still other groups. Where joint efforts were necessary, as they were in more and more of economic, social and political life, joint group decisions had to be reached; the alternatives were authoritative compulsion by the state or a dominant group, both of which went against the vague but strong democratic impulses of the American people. Collective bargaining thus filled a pressing and immediate need of the society and accorded with the values and traditions of American history.

Although collective bargaining represents an important advance for workers and employers in a democratic industrial society, we should not credit it unduly. We have no reason to believe that as it has evolved to date, collective bargaining is, in itself, the most desirable process of adjusting interests among different industrial groups or of making decisions that affect the operations of an industrial society. Just as unilateral procedures of determining the terms of employment have given way to joint negotiations, we might well expect collective bargaining to be modified and adjusted to meet the needs of new institutions and changed economic conditions. The continuing process of adjustment to cultural change is not likely to bypass collective bargaining. We need not refrain from giving conscious shape to changes that our convictions and observations suggest are desirable. Wholesale remaking of union-management relations is neither possible nor desirable, but we can encourage advances in new directions which promise better results than now accrue to the parties or to society.

Mutual Dependence versus Contract

In examining collective bargaining, we should be careful not to perpetuate the confusion that comes from regarding it as analogous to the negotiation of a contract between two individuals. In some few (very small) bargaining units, such an analogy may still be applicable, but in most units the size of the business enterprise or bargaining group has served to render the comparison obsolete. The most characteristic aspect of contract in Western society—its voluntary nature, which we subsume in the phrase "freedom of contract"—requires the possibility of alternatives. Freedom to contract is dependent upon freedom *not* to contract, and the latter in turn depends upon the opportunity to make another choice. On an individualistic basis, such freedom not to contract is frequently available. On a collective basis, it seldom exists. There is little chance for a *body* of employees, refusing the terms offered by their employer, to find alternative employment collectively, as a body.[1] Only somewhat less forcefully, the same result is encountered by management. There is little chance for an employer of hundreds or thousands of workers to replace them with another complete working force if he cannot reach an agreement with his workers' representatives. As long as the system of *collective* bargaining is preserved, there is no alternative for most employers and groups of employees other than coming to terms with their immediate bargaining opponent.

Collective bargaining in most instances today thus *requires* that some agreement be reached between the parties. However prolonged the strike to settle disputes over divergent interests, some agreement must ultimately be forthcoming if collective bargaining continues. Thus neither party is independent under collective bargaining. Neither can perform its function without the other. Only by ridding itself of collective bargaining, which allows workers to participate in negotiations and to resist managerial demands, can a company be said to gain an independence of operation. When collec-

[1] In the case of many large enterprises, it would not even be feasible for a body of employees to find alternative employment individually. For all employees of any company employing, let us say, arbitrarily, 5,000 workers, there is only one job prospect—the company where they are employed. If a few of that number were laid off, they might be absorbed by other companies; but if all 5,000 were dismissed, only the relief rolls would ensure sustenance for many of their numbers. Such a situation was well illustrated in late 1963, when the Studebaker Corporation closed its automotive plant in South Bend, Indiana; a few workers found employment elsewhere, and some retired early on their social security pensions, but many were still looking for work months later.

tive bargaining is accepted, however, the great change which takes place is the creation of two organizations, in one sense independent of each other but in another sense mutually dependent. For each, the achievement of its own function is dependent upon a working relationship with the other. Where collective bargaining is the prescribed system of industrial relations, neither company alone nor union alone has any functional significance; rather, they acquire significance only in relation to each other.

This fact of mutual dependence cannot be overstressed, for it is perhaps the most fundamental aspect of modern industrial society.[2] Its newness is indicated by the lack of an adequate terminology with which to discuss it. The term "collective bargaining" is most frequently used to mean any form of agreed-upon association between union and management, but such blanket use necessitates resort to other terms if we wish to differentiate among kinds of association. To describe simply the relationship where union and management come to agreement through sheer functional necessity, let us use the term "conjunctive bargaining."

Conjunctive Bargaining

Conjunctive bargaining, in the sense used here, does not arise because of one party's sympathetic regard for the other or because of its voluntary choice of the other as partner; it arises from the absolute requirement that some agreement—*any* agreement—be reached so that the operations on which both are dependent may continue. Conjunctive bargaining represents the striking of a working relationship in which each party agrees, explicitly or implicitly, to provide certain requisite services, to recognize certain seats of authority, and to accept certain responsibilities in respect to the other. Without such an agreement, there could be no operation. Such bargaining may therefore be thought of as the minimum basis for organization of the company and union into a going concern.

Neither party can secure its objectives without a joint working relationship. Reciprocally, the terms of that relationship define the extent to which each attains its objectives. The terms of the relationship, that is to say, deal with matters of divergent interests, and each party secures its interest to the extent of its relative bargaining power. Coercion is the principal ingredient of conjunctive bargaining power. The resolution of divergent interests through conjunctive bargaining provides a basis for operation of the enterprise—and nothing more. With whatever coercive powers are at its disposal, each party has wrested the maximum advantage possible, without much

[2] Mutual dependence does not hinge on a system of private property. It would exist also under public ownership or control if some form of employee representation were maintained.

regard for the effect of this on the other.[3] The bargaining relationship comes into being because it is inescapable, and neither party grants more than is necessary. It is probable that conjunctive bargaining is the most common form of bargaining relationship in the United States.

Conjunctive bargaining has produced benefits for both employers and managers, despite its limitations. It has challenged company officials and employers to manage rationally and to examine policies carefully and objectively. Several outstanding students of labor concluded a detailed examination of collective bargaining with this comment: "The challenge that unions presented to management has, if viewed broadly, created superior and better balanced management, even though some exceptions must be recognized. . . . If one single statement were sought to describe the effects of unions on policy-making, it would be: 'they have encouraged investigation and reflection.' " [4]

There is also a real possibility that conjunctive bargaining has benefited the public. As unions pushed managements for costly benefits, the latter had to seek increased efficiencies, which helped to lower prices (or maintain them) and improve quality. Managers often admit as much; one railroad executive, for example, has said: "If it wasn't for those damn unions, we'd be using as many man-hours to do every job as we did twenty years ago. Every time they get an increase, we have to get off our duffs and find a cheaper way to do things." [5]

Conjunctive bargaining has also benefited workers by providing protection against arbitrary demands made upon them at their place of work. A major achievement has been the system of industrial jurisprudence, whereby employer and employee settle disputes under the agreement rationally and peacefully. The present form of bargaining has also enabled workers to present their interests to managers, and it gives them a voice in some of the decisions that vitally affect their work lives. As Louis D. Brandeis pointed out when unionism was still in its infancy: "Men are not free if dependent industrially upon the arbitrary will of another. Industrial liberty on the part of the worker cannot, therefore, exist if there be overweening industrial power. Some curb must be placed upon capitalistic combination. Nor will even this curb be effective unless the workers cooperate

---

[3] This may still be compatible with not pressing a maximum *short-run* bargaining advantage because of a belief that certain restraint will prove beneficial in the long run. The tactical possibilities are varied. In conjunctive bargaining, however, the emphasis is on a coercive and competitive relationship.

[4] Sumner H. Slichter, E. Robert Livernash, and James J. Healy, *The Impact of Collective Bargaining on Management*, Washington, D.C.: The Brookings Institution, 1960, pp. 951–952.

[5] Quoted in Max Ways, "Labor Unions Are Worth the Price," *Fortune*, May, 1963, p. 245.

benefits - better mgmt
worker protection

as in trade unions. Control and cooperation are both essential to industrial liberty." [6]

Because unions and managements all too often have not been able to move beyond conjunctive bargaining and mix cooperation with control, they have inflicted costs upon themselves and the public that might well have been avoided. The rigidities of conjunctive bargaining lead unions and managements to cling to established work arrangements simply because they have the power to do so; and such bargaining can encourage strikes whose impact and effects spread beyond the parties. Both the rigidities and strikes tend to reduce the benefits of conjunctive bargaining. More importantly, if unions and management do not progress beyond conjunctive bargaining, they forgo opportunities from which both might benefit.

In a joint relationship which is based on necessity, the *extent* to which either party or both parties can attain their objectives is dependent on the business performance. This performance is measured by the total rewards of the enterprise minus its total costs. Both rewards and costs should include more than pecuniary considerations, of course. The leadership position of the company in its field, the prestige of a quality product, a reputation for public service functions, for example, might be included in business performance, along with actual profit. Similarly, monotonous and routinized operations, disadvantageous location, or health hazards might be viewed as costs, along with the outlay for materials and services obtained outside the enterprise.

The business performance which attaches to the company as a whole defines what the parties will divide between them. The division is of costs as well as of rewards. Management and unions have thus fought not only over the distribution of pecuniary gain but also over who shall take the credit for good performance in other respects, such as the quality of the product, the welfare of the employees, and increased productivity, and who shall take the blame for poor performance in such matters as unsafe conditions, restrictionist policies, and strike responsibility. No matter how strong the bargaining power of one relative to the other, the advantages which each can derive or the costs which each seeks to shrug off are dependent on total performance of the enterprise. At the extreme, business failure means its complete incapacity to satisfy the objectives of both owner-managers and union member-employees.

Numerous factors determine business performance, among them all the forces impinging on the demand for the product and the supply costs of production. There is one factor of peculiar interest to us in the present

[6] From his address, "True Americanism," quoted by William Feldesman, solicitor, National Labor Relations Board, in a speech before the Graduate School of Business Administration, University of Virginia, Charlottesville, Va., October 18, 1963, p. 3. (Mimeographed.)

context. We have just noted that under a system of collective bargaining, some joint action of the parties is essential to the very operation of the enterprise. It may now also be added that *how well* the parties act jointly will determine, in an important measure, how well the enterprise operates. Business performance is in part dependent on the nature of the relationship between the parties. Business performance fixes the boundaries within which each party can achieve its objectives, but it is itself limited by the relationship existing between those parties.

Conjunctive bargaining, through which the parties agree to terms as a result of mutual coercion and arrive at a truce only because they are indispensable to each other, is but one kind of relationship between them. It provides no incentive to the parties to do more than carry out the minimum terms of the agreement which has temporarily resolved their divergent interests. The obligations which each has assumed to the other in the conduct of the business and the advantages from business performance which each has wrested from the other are fixed. For one party to give a superior performance by cooperating more effectively with the other is not likely to win it any further concession because concessions are predetermined. Conjunctive bargaining allows the minimum required cooperation of each with the other, which tends to become the maximum actual cooperation as well.

Indeed, there sometimes arises a fixed determination on the part of owner-managers or union member–employees not to meet their obligations in any greater degree than what the other party can exact. The result sometimes takes the form of "getting away" with as much as possible. Unions have charged managements with denying members the full rights of the collective agreement. In the words of one labor official who was speaking of a supervisory training program: "So far as we can see all the company is trying to teach its foremen through the program is how to be diplomatic in chiseling the worker." Managers have indicted unions for encouraging relaxed effort on the job. One industrial relations manager reported that he was convinced that in his plant employees were literally subjecting themselves to greater fatigue through their efforts to delay work and slow down operations.

Because of its emphasis on minimum obligation, conjunctive bargaining limits and restricts business performance. It imposes limits on the ability of each to secure its objectives, regardless of its relative bargaining power. If a better working relationship can be established between the parties, so that they recognize something more than a minimum of mutual obligations, business performance can be improved. The potentialities of the enterprise for satisfying the objectives of the parties will thus be more effectively realized.

Cooperative Bargaining

Neither a union nor a management feels free to establish a more fruitful bargaining relationship unless it believes that it will gain something from the added benefits which the improved business performance will make possible. This amounts to saying that neither will gain additional advantages unless the other gains too. Neither party will expect the other to give up something for nothing. Realistically, we may expect that the effort of one party to best the other will never be abandoned, but this does not rule out the possibility that intelligent union and management officials will observe that the mutual relationship can be improved, to the advantage of each, by holding out the promise of benefit to the other party too. This appears to be a prima-facie case for cooperation based on personal benefit rather than altruism or adherence to the golden rule, however valuable those approaches may be.[7]

The basis for cooperative bargaining is the fact that each party is dependent on the other and, as a matter of fact, can achieve its objectives more effectively if it wins the support of the other. This means that when one party is seeking a change the better to secure some objective, it is more likely to succeed in its design if it anticipates what objections may be raised by the other party, *on whose cooperation in the matter the degree of its own success depends*. For such objections raise issues of divergent interests, and unless these are resolved, it will prove impossible to define an area of common interest in which cooperation can be established. In order to win the necessary cooperation, the initiating party may have to make concessions—greater perhaps than it considers "fair" or "just" and despite the fact that such concessions may be unnecessary as a matter of traditional authority. They are made because, on their granting, a joint effort is forthcoming which produces a greater advantage to the initiating party than would have been possible without them.

The distinction between the divergent interests and the common interests of unions and management may appear to be a simple one, but it is actually quite subtle. Where interests are *accepted* as common rather than divergent, the notion that the agreement sums up what had to be given up or all that could be gained fades; the parties approach bargaining with the realization that the better the performance of each, the better the joint

---

[7] Cooperation with the other party because motivated by moral principle is not to be slighted. The argument here is simply that cooperation is not dependent on a spiritual conversion or religious or ethical belief but can be supported on the basis of personal advantage (with advantage defined in broader terms than pecuniary return).

performance. Further, each understands that the better the joint performance, the greater the advantage for both.

Cooperation is not an unheard-of activity of unions and management in the United States, but it has usually come in the form of a joint protection of industry interest from competitors or a joint demand for special concessions from government. Thus it has not been unusual for unions and industry spokesmen to join together to lobby for public subsidies and special legislation. The United Mine Workers coal employers' association has argued against federal government support for fuels that compete with coal; and Textile Workers of America have campaigned for restrictions on textile imports; the Teamsters and trucking associations have fought relief legislation for railroads; and the rail brotherhoods have joined rail managers in pushing for restrictive regulation of motor transportation. The maritime unions have backed industry representatives as they sought to preserve the legal barriers against foreign flagship operations in domestic trade, and the American Federation of Musicians was as vocal and as active as the employers and managements in the entertainment industry in working to halve the cabaret tax in 1960.

Not at all uncommon has been the joint cooperative effort of union and management to persuade consumers to buy the products or services with which they are chiefly concerned. The cigar makers' and hat makers' unions have conducted advertising campaigns to persuade the public to buy more; and unions, such as the United Rubber Workers, have from time to time urged consumers to buy goods produced by companies with whom they negotiate, publishing the names of the companies and their products. The whole effort of the AFL–CIO's union label department has been directed toward improving sales of goods produced by organized companies. The garment unions particularly have supported the union label program.

A few unions have cooperatively dealt with employers to help them cut costs and improve efficiencies by supplying technical experts and engineering advice. This kind of special help is usually needed immediately after a shop is organized so that it can produce efficiently enough to pay the new, higher wage rates and yet survive. Unions have from time to time cooperated with management to implement programs of cost cutting, explaining the program and persuading the workers to accept it. Such cooperation is usually of a limited nature, restricted in both time and comprehensiveness.

As the fifties drew to a close, unions and management found themselves confronted with the large and difficult problems of adjusting to rapid economic change in a lagging economy, automation, and a quickening shift of the work force from blue-collar to white-collar workers. A number of unions and managements began to experiment with new forms of cooperative bargaining. There developed a new willingness to try to resolve their divergent interests through continuous attention to problems in order to evoke a cooperative effort to improve their joint performance in specified areas. Although the results of the experimentation now going on cannot yet be finally judged, there are hopeful signs that American labor and business may slowly be changing the dominant pattern of collective bargaining in this country.

One of the most dramatic developments of cooperative collective bargaining is that involving the Pacific Maritime Association and the International Longshoremen's and Warehousemen's Union. After four years of careful exploration of their common problems and five months of hard negotiation, the PMA and the ILWU reached an agreement in late 1960 to begin the process of orderly mechanization of work and changes in restrictive work rules. After a year during which both parties addressed themselves to the difficult task of measuring the real but elusive benefits of mechanization and the probable effects upon maritime traffic, the union agreed to allow changes in work rules that interfere with efficient utilization of new techniques in return for management's agreement to establish a multimillion-dollar fund to maintain the earnings of displaced workers. Both parties hope that the increased efficiencies will lead to an increase in traffic and actually increased work for the union members and revenues for the companies. The program requires, of course, continuing joint study, careful attention to new and unforeseen difficulties, and swift adjustments to solve problems as they arise. Meeting together to increase benefits for both parties and recognizing that each legitimately expects something of value for whatever concessions it makes, the PMA and the ILWU have taken an important step toward cooperative collective bargaining.[8]

As an aftermath of the great steel strike of 1959, the United Steelworkers and a number of the steel managements began to move away from mere conjunctive bargaining toward a more rewarding form of bargaining. In one experiment at the Kaiser Steel Company, union and management created a joint, tripartite committee to devise a long-run plan for *equitably* sharing the company's progress. The committee met over a period of two years, carefully studying the problems of both parties before it made its recommendation. It recognized that

> . . . in order to attain and maintain mature labor relations, constructive attitudes must be engendered: constructive employee attitudes toward their jobs, toward the importance of the success of the business enterprise, and toward management, reflected individually and collectively through their union. An integral requirement for achieving such attitudes on the part of employees and of the unions is the development on the part of management of appropriate attitudes con-

[8] Charles C. Killingsworth, "The Modernization of West Coast Longshore Work Rules," *Industrial and Labor Relations Review*, vol. 15 (1962), pp. 295–306.

cerning all of the human factors involved. Not the least of these human factors is the need for security, recognition, equitable treatment and appropriate sharing of progress.[9]

Recognizing the interests of both workers and management, the resulting agreement provides that they share the savings in costs due to better work, changed work rules, and improved equipment and also protects workers against loss of job due to improved efficiencies.[10]

At United States Steel, union and management officials joined together in a human relations committee to discuss common problems away from the pressures and tensions of the bargaining table, hopefully paving the way for peaceful negotiations of future agreements and resolution of sticky problems as they arise. The wide-ranging exploration of issues and careful examination of problems that the committee makes possible during the long stretches between biannual or triannual negotiating sessions appear to have helped the parties to resolve a number of contentious issues. Work-rule changes have been allowed to proceed in the mills bit by bit, protecting workers but also allowing greater flexibility to managers. David J. McDonald, president of the union, reported early in 1964 that from discussions in the committee, union representatives had gotten a better grasp of the problems of internal and external competition for steel's markets and the internal problems of financing mill modernization to keep pace in the competitive battle.

Other attempts to develop more cooperative bargaining also show some promise. In 1962 U.S. Industries and the Machinists established a foundation to study automation and employment. The joint work could lead to a fruitful partnership between labor and business in dealing with a troublesome problem. Most heartening perhaps is the fact that the foundation grew out of the harmonious relationship that developed between the company and union as they jointly organized and financed an earlier effort in 1956 to remedy problems of health, medical care, and welfare.

Other joint programs begun by unions and managements in other industries have been disappointing in their results. The attempts of the Packinghouse Workers and the Meatworkers and the Armour Company, for example, to deal jointly and constructively with the problems of automation and displaced workers, from 1959 to 1963, have not produced results as effective as the union leaders hoped. The bitter words exchanged by union and

[9] *The Long Range Sharing Plan of Kaiser Steel Corporation and the United Steelworkers of America,* Fontana, Calif., December, 1962, pp. 2–3.

[10] Workers on especially favorable incentive rates were not asked to give these up without compensation. The company offered a "lump-sum" settlement to these men as an inducement for them to abandon the old individual incentive system and join in the new long-run profit-sharing plan.

management officials injured the possibility of cooperative bargaining and made likely a reversion to conjunctive bargaining. We cannot be sure that the other experiments in cooperative bargaining will survive, let alone succeed.

Barriers to Cooperative Bargaining

Reaching and maintaining cooperative agreements is no easy task, for neither party is apt to want to concede more than is necessary to win the required cooperation. Negotiations have to continue; each must "feel out" the other party and measure the relative bargaining powers. The possibility of a breakdown in negotiations is always present, of course. But in striving for cooperation, they now negotiate and bargain within a different context, since the objective has changed. Recognition of the benefits of cooperation increases the chances of resolving divergent interests and modifies the measure of bargaining power, even if it does not eliminate the possibility of impasse.

The "divergent interest" over which an impasse in negotiations is most likely to develop between parties seeking to cooperate is not wages or any other money item. Even though money is often a thorny issue, parties that can appreciate the benefits of a cooperative relationship can reasonably make the appropriate estimates of the advantage of an agreement. Even if an agreement does not bring everything each party has wished for, it may still be attractive enough to conclude. If a money advantage is sought to the point of disrupting a cooperative association, there is much more lost than simply the cost of the strike or lockout. The cost also may include the restoration of conjunctive rather than cooperative bargaining, a cost that falls upon both parties.

A real barrier to an agreement on divergent interests which would make cooperation possible is, paradoxically, a fear of cooperation itself. Although one may be able to establish a prima-facie case for the preferability of cooperative to conjunctive bargaining, there is a prevalent fear on the part of management, union, and employees that its potential benefits are outweighed by its potential dangers. The parties, for the most part, have been willing to accept the limitations on business performance imposed by conjunctive bargaining rather than subject themselves to the dangers which they foresee in a more advanced relationship.

What are the dangers which union leaders and managers envisage in a union-management program of cooperation? For managers, it is a loss of their prerogatives; for union leaders, it is a loss of function, rendering their role and office unnecessary; for employees, it is a fear of the possibility of increased insecurity caused by improved efficiency and reduction of jobs. Let us examine these fears more carefully.

In an earlier chapter we considered the issue of the appropriate subject matter of collective bargaining, and we encountered the opinion generally expressed by members of management that there are certain matters concerning which the union's right to seek agreement should be confined. All other matters are subject to the sole discretion of those who are legally appointed to exercise authority in business operation. Corporate law recognizes the right of owners (stockholders) to designate through elected boards of directors certain officials (management) to act in their interests. To permit unions to have a voice in business decisions, according to this opinion, would dilute the powers of owners and the rights of property. To recognize a union's interest in production problems would simply widen its area of control within the company, leaving management without its highly prized right to make the decisions necessary for the long-run welfare of the company as a whole. Cooperation thus carries an implicit threat to the structure of authority within the enterprise.

This is an issue which cannot be lightly disregarded. There is no doubt that a union run by officials who are ideologically opposed to private property interests may pursue a disruptive course whose damaging effects will be enlarged as their influence is extended.[11] This is only to say, however, that cooperation is not possible with a union which does not accept cooperation in good faith. If good faith is present on both sides, the basis for managers' fear is most likely to be a failure to distinguish between matters of divergent and common interest. If divergent interests are involved in production, for example, in the form of speed of operation or work loads they will in time find their way to the bargaining table for resolution in any event. We have already observed the increasing scope of union interest in business decisions, which over the years has caused management to negotiate with unions on issues which earlier it had refused to discuss. By refusing cooperation for fear that it will widen the union's area of participation in business decisions, management may be gaining no greater long-run protection from the dilution of its authority, and at the same time it may be losing the fruits of cooperation.

To the extent that cooperative bargaining is successful, unionists may fear the possibility of a "withering away" of union functions. This threat is premised on a widely circulated belief that if management understood the worker and satisfied his needs, there would be no place for a union. If cooperative bargaining can be made to work, creating a spirit of common interest between worker and company in important areas, will this not rob union members of their militancy and even their desire to maintain a

[11] The success of the agreement between the PMA and the ILWU, led by Harry Bridges, a man of left-wing political persuasion, suggests that we should not be led astray by union rhetoric. The words of labor leaders, particularly the older ones, are often not at all consistent with their actions.

separate organization responsive to their peculiar interests? To some extent this is a persistence of the fear aroused by the company unions of the 1920s. If harmony of interest between employee and employer is stressed and if the employer is careful to give the employee some "cut" in the benefits of harmony, what need is there for a union?

Once again, it is evident that this is an issue which cannot be brushed aside. There is one school of managerial thought which regards independent unions as unnecessary and undesirable and which would welcome their passing from the scene. Where there is such lack of good faith, cooperation is not feasible. Where good faith exists and continues, however, the union's fears, like management's, appear excessive. Divergent interests between employees and employer will always remain. Indeed, cooperative bargaining in any meaningful sense cannot succeed until employees have become convinced that their special interests have been fully considered. This conviction cannot be sustained unless workers are represented by organizations which, because they are independent, can present the workers' case adequately and press for its recognition by agreement. The element of bargaining power is not ruled out by cooperation, even though its coercive expression may be reduced, and organization is essential to such power.

Finally, employees sometimes fear that a union which accepts cooperative bargaining may become little more than an adjunct of management, stressing efficiency to the detriment of employee welfare. Joseph Scanlon, who pioneered in the introduction of cooperation programs, pointed out that cost reduction, methods of improvement, and the installation of new equipment are associated in the minds of workers with layoff and wage reduction. Their drive for job security develops a resistance to this kind of program.[12] If their union becomes a partner in such activities, on what can the workers depend for protection?

The union's protective role will be lost only if the union becomes responsible primarily to an authority other than its membership. To the extent that the membership retains control over its organization, there is a reasonable safeguard against its perversion for other interests. Moreover, as Scanlon suggested, cost reduction programs with their attendant threat to worker security will be sought by management whether unions cooperate or not, and the workers' greatest protection will come through participation in their introduction.

Thus there appear to be solid grounds for believing that where good

[12] Joseph N. Scanlon, *Labor's Philosophy Concerning Cost Reduction Programs,* American Management Association, Production Series, no. 160 (1945), pp. 33–39. See also Douglas McGregor's evaluation, "The Scanlon Plan through a Psychologist's Eyes," in *The Scanlon Plan: A Frontier in Labor-Management Cooperation,* F. G. Lesieur (ed.), New York: John Wiley & Sons, Inc., 1958.

faith exists between the parties, the dangers to each of cooperative bargaining have been overstated. Where good faith is present, the benefits of a well-planned program would appear to overbalance the disadvantages. But even if this conclusion is valid, the development of cooperation raises other problems and dangers which should not be ignored. First, a cooperative effort has usually been sustained most readily on the basis of face-to-face relationships and intimate, personal involvement and participation. Providing such a basis for cooperative bargaining is not easy in an economy of large-scale organizations and sprawling bargaining units.

Cooperative Bargaining and Small Groups

The importance of face-to-face relationships in establishing the morale on which cooperative effort must build does not make cooperation impossible among employees of large corporations, but it may require a reorganization of the production process for maximum effectiveness. To the extent that collective bargaining is carried on in larger units—market-wide or industry-wide—cooperation would seem to be less feasible. Can one expect bargaining for a nationwide firm or industry, however cooperatively conducted, to establish successfully the local conditions necessary for a truly effective program of cooperation? Will the settlement of issues of divergent interests by a method which requires consideration of the needs of many differently situated plants or firms permit agreement on matters of common interest in the single plant or firm?

The answer can be "yes" if unions and management continue to develop a "federal" system of bargaining units by a process which links plant and company and even industry. Some problems are so comprehensive that small groups cannot exert any meaningful control over them; they involve relationships and interests that transcend the parochial concerns of local groups. But other problems affect only the smaller group or have but slight "spillover" influence upon other groups. The officers of the larger, more comprehensive group are appropriately involved in the first kind of decision but are unneeded in the latter. Similarly, local competencies are more apt to be satisfactory, or at least satisfying, for local problems than the expertise of the larger group, but they are out of their depth on more general issues. Cooperation is more effective when decisions are reached in the units which are most appropriate to the subject involved. No less than in other social organizations, however, there is a need in industrial relations for decision-making units of varying sizes.

In fact, if the technique of cooperation, which appears to offer such promise, is to be promoted, there is important reason for retaining in the local jurisdiction as much of the bargain as can be left there. Local resolution of divergent interests permits a better framework for the identification of areas of common interest; excessive control from above can frustrate local initiative. Instances are not wanting where local unions have quietly disregarded the instructions of national officers and where local plant managements have violated the limits of their discretion because they recognized that their successful relationships depended on terms differing from those which had been prescribed for them by higher authorities within their respective organizations.

This operation by unions and management within a *system* of bargaining units parallels the frame-within-frame approach by which management proceeds in the individual business.[13] Each operational level or frame of management prescribes the limits within which management at the next lower level must operate. But the limits allow an area of discretion—as wide an area as can be permitted and still ensure the accomplishment of the objective of those in the superior frame. Similarly, in a system of bargaining units, the decisions in the larger unit prescribe only so much as is needful to ensure the objectives sought, objectives which are themselves limited to those which cannot adequately be secured in a jurisdiction of lesser scope. Directive authority—embodied in the agreement—does not attempt to eliminate discretion in the administrative ranks below it but is concerned only with stating standards for the guidance of administrative authority within a framework conducive to the primary objectives sought.

Thus a bargaining agreement on an industry- or company-wide basis does not rule out the possibility of differential terms or conditions between firms or plants. The wider agreement prescribes the standards which must be observed by all component units and the programs which are operated on a pooled basis, such as pensions. Supplementary agreements at the level of the individual firm or plant cover other matters of local interest not in conflict with the general terms. Cooperative bargaining may thus be established in both types of units with respect to the relevant issues. Local members and officials become involved in a responsible way.

American labor and management have already gone far toward establishing the basis for a federal system conducive to cooperative bargaining through the grievance process, which involves those in the shop as well as at the head offices in continuous, daily collective bargaining. On the job in the shop or office, workers, managers, and union officials have plenty of opportunity to learn the wisdom of respecting one another's interests and to learn to appreciate the mutual benefits to be gained by bargaining cooperatively. Here, where foremen, workers, and shop stewards must confront each other daily and join together to produce effectively and efficiently, an appreciation of *quid pro quo* bargaining is strong. From long experience they

[13] This approach is described at some length in Neil W. Chamberlain, *The Union Challenge to Management Control*, New York: Harper & Row, Publishers, Incorporated, 1948, chap. 2.

have learned to base their cooperation on a realistic appreciation of each man's desire to protect his interest. And there is available to them the device of the grievance process, through which they may openly discuss their demands, protect their interests, and arrange mutually satisfactory settlements.

The strength of American unions in the shop and the prevalence of the grievance process have already helped to produce a good deal of lower-level cooperative bargaining that has helped in the introduction of technological change. Grievance bargaining is not always cooperative, but the common practice of discussing work rules and writing them down makes them explicit and easier to deal with than if they were merely tacit arrangements protected by tradition. They are on view and can be bargained about and often traded off. If managers are willing to offer value for value and not merely insist upon a sacrifice of valuable rules by workers, changes can be secured without stubborn resistance. The cooperative approach to technological change in this country has impressed foreigners. The many teams of British managers and of trade unionists who visited this country after World War II to investigate American production methods were nearly unanimous in their finding that American workers were responsive and adaptable to change, readily accepting and expecting it. "Team after team noted the interdependence in American industry of the 'sense of camaraderie and freedom of expression based on mutual respect,' the readiness to change working assignments and consitions, the willingness of unions to conform to new methods or apply new machinery (with hard bargaining for due reward!), and the all pervading belief in the need to raise productivity." [14]

Competition and Cooperation

Cooperation alone does not necessarily foster increased productivity, though, and it may not bring benefits to the community. If unions and employers can evade the strictures of competition, they may well cooperate to protect themselves from change, or they may even cooperate to restrict competition by lobbying for legal aid to protect their position, as we have noted above. Too much competition between the parties, though, may undermine any cooperative effort they undertake. The balance between cooperation and competition is a second condition important to the future of constructive collective bargaining. The evils of excessive reliance on cooperation and association appear no less great than those of excessive reliance on competition. The conclusion seems inescapable that for a healthy economy, we require a proper admixture of the two.

[14] G. Hutton, *We Too Can Prosper,* New York: The Macmillan Company, 1953, pp. 145–146.

Competition between groups with divergent interests, whether between two companies or between union and management, has the advantage of avoiding collusion at public expense. Each keeps the other "on its toes," as it were. But carried to excess, competition can break down a system of *social order*—just as "cutthroat competition" occasionally does in product markets, or industrial strikes in labor-management relations.

Cooperation between groups with common interests has the advantage of encouraging fuller exploitation of the special contribution which each can make to an improved joint performance. They pull "in harness," as it were. But carried to excess, cooperation can be a means of massing economic power to exploit third parties, as when unions sometimes cooperate to impose a secondary boycott on a neutral employer or when companies form a cartel.

It is in society's interests for its economic agents to promote cooperation, as long as they face competition from others, and to compete, as long as they do not engage in economic warfare.

Conjunctive bargaining fails to extract the full advantage which cooperation between unions and managements can bring to society. It cannot make as great contributions as cooperative bargaining is capable of making. Cooperative bargining appears to be at least a stage higher in the industrial relations evolutionary hierarchy. But for cooperative bargaining to avoid the evils of union-management collusion at the expense of the public, it must function within an economy which subjects the union and management partners to effective competition from others.

If the requirements of effective cooperation and effective competition are not met, the result is rather predictable. First will come public exhortation for the parties to behave like good citizens and refrain from injuring the public by competing against each other with "crippling" strikes or by too readily increasing wages and profits through higher prices. If such admonitions are ineffective, as they are likely to be, the next step will certainly be regulation and strike controls on the one hand and wage-price controls on the other.

If unions and managements wish to retain private discretionary decision-making authority, they must improve the processes of collective bargaining by experimenting with devices which induce cooperation and at the same time provide some mechanism, perhaps a form of arbitration, for resolving competitive differences between them. If they are to retain freedom of action, they cannot deny the need for institutionalizing both the cooperative and the competitive aspects of the system of economic relationships of which they are a part, and institutionalizing them in such ways as to render unnecessary—or at least *less* necessary—governmental intervention to preserve the reasonable interests of third parties and the public.

Index